UKRAINIAN:
A COMPREHENSIVE GRAMMAR

Ukrainian: A Comprehensive Grammar is a complete reference guide to modern Ukrainian grammar.

It presents an accessible description of the standard language, concentrating on the patterns of use today. The authors have consulted a great number of sources, in addition to a wide range of native speakers. The result is the first reference grammar of Ukrainian published outside the Ukraine, which will be a useful work of reference for many years.

The volume is organized to enable students of the language to find the information they seek quickly and easily, and to promote a thorough understanding of Ukrainian grammar. It presents the complexities of the language in a systematic and user-friendly form.

Features include:

- detailed tables in each chapter for easy reference
- numerous examples throughout
- thorough descriptions of all parts of speech
- list of grammatical terms in English and Ukrainian
- complete descriptions of the word-formational processes of Ukrainian
- an overview of past and present changes in the language
- bibliography of works relating to Ukrainian
- full index

Ukrainian: A Comprehensive Grammar reflects the richness of the language and is an essential purchase for all students of Ukrainian.

Stefan M. Pugh is Reader in Russian and **Ian Press** is Established Professor in Russian, both at the University of St Andrews. They are the authors of *Colloquial Ukrainian: A Complete Language Course*.

UKRAINIAN: A COMPREHENSIVE GRAMMAR

Stefan M. Pugh and Ian Press

London and New York

First published 1999 by Routledge
2 Park Square, Milton Park, Abingdon, Oxon, OX14 4RN

Simultaneously published in the USA and Canada
by Routledge
270 Madison Ave, New York NY 10016

Routledge is an imprint of the Taylor & Francis Group

Transferred to Digital Printing 2005

© 1999 Stefan M. Pugh and Ian Press

Typeset in Times by RefineCatch Limited, Bungay, Suffolk

British Library Cataloguing in Publication Data
A catalogue record for this book is available from the British Library

Library of Congress Cataloguing in Publication Data
Pugh, Stefan.
    Ukrainian: a comprehensive grammar/Stefan M. Pugh and Ian
Press.
      p.   cm. – (Routledge grammars)
    Includes bibliographical references and indexes.
    1. Ukrainian language – Grammar.   I. Press, J. I. (J. Ian)
II. Title.   III. Title: Ukrainian, a comprehensive grammar.
IV. Series.
PG3819.P84   1999
491.7′982421 – dc21   98–32358
                             CIP

ISBN 0–415–15029–9
ISBN 0–415–15030–2 (pbk)

CONTENTS

3   The adjective   145

PREFACE

Ukraine is – by European standards – a large country with a large population, and its international visibility has grown rapidly since the achievement of independence in 1991. Russian was the overall *lingua franca* in the Soviet Union, including, of course, Ukraine; since 1991, however, the Ukrainian language has gradually been displacing Russian in official functions and is now in the process of assuming the role of a true national language. Outside of Ukraine, the growing awareness of Ukrainian as an independent language (read: 'not Russian') has been leading people – whether students, tourists, businesspeople, or diplomats – to study the language. This phenomenon is also reflected in the recent publication of new grammars and handbooks of Ukrainian outside Ukraine, for example *Colloquial Ukrainian* (Routledge, 1994). This book, as a 'Comprehensive Grammar', can also be described as a 'reference' grammar: a book to be consulted on a wide variety of questions concerning the Ukrainian language. To our knowledge, no comprehensive grammar of Ukrainian has appeared outside of Ukraine; grammars produced in Ukraine – with the exception of some textbooks to be used in a classroom setting – are naturally written in Ukrainian, and are therefore of limited use to those who do not yet read Ukrainian.

For a language such as Ukrainian, in which there is great regional and stylistic variation, probably no one speaker will agree with every point made in the book: the authors therefore must take full responsibility for making the choices that had to be made. Even in the process of writing a grammar of a 'standard' language, it soon becomes apparent that some rules are fluid, as language itself is fluid; we recognize and indeed welcome that a book of this kind will inevitably be open to suggestions of every kind, as there will always be much more to be said about this – as every other – language.

Ukrainian is a very rich language, as are all the elements of Ukrainian culture, including literature, music, and film. Ukraine has a long literary tradition that is all but unknown to the vast majority of non-Ukrainians. To put this statement in perspective: some – if not many – of the great works of Russian literature could be named by the average citizen in London, Paris, and Washington, but it would be a rare person indeed who could name a single Ukrainian novel or poem. Of course, not a few Russian writers were born in Ukraine, such as Gogol and Akhmatova, who are counted as part of the Russian literary tradition. The richness of the literature is fed by the richness of the language: the lexicon is enormous, the grammatical and word-formational processes flexible and productive. Part of the problem with learning or teaching the Ukrainian language is the very richness that we are describing. In terms of the lexicon, for example, the traveller will note strong differences between East and West Ukraine: this is a function not only of the great distances involved (approximately 900 kilometres from East to West), but also of the perceived 'Russianness' of the East, and 'Polishness' of the West. While Soviet rule was indeed responsible for a certain Russianization of the language, care must be taken not to identify word 'X' or 'Y' as 'Russian', and therefore as 'not Ukrainian'. In practice, bilingualism in Ukrainian and Russian has led to the common use of a number of (originally Russian) words in everyday Ukrainian: one speaker might say **телефонува́ти** 'to phone', while another might prefer **дзвони́ти**; the first speaker might avoid **дзвони́ти** because it looks and sounds like Russian **звони́ть**. We have made every effort to describe Ukrainian from a neutral standpoint, *viz.* by including some words or constructions that may be of Russian origin – if they are currently used by a reasonable number of people.

Ukrainian: A Comprehensive Grammar is not primarily meant to teach Ukrainian (other books are available for that), but presents the standard language in a systematic and user-friendly fashion. We use the word 'standard' with caution here, as there is a great deal of variation in the language: for example, often there can be more than one acceptable case ending in a given set of nouns (Chapter 2); in the dialects one finds even greater variation, but that must remain the subject of another study. Variation can extend to pronunciation as well, as in all languages: the city name **Льві́в** L'viv (Russian *Львов* L'vov), for instance, is described in 'standard' works (for example, ULVN) as [lʲvʲiw]; this is certainly how it is pronounced in western Ukraine, and in L'viv itself, but in other parts of the country – and even on national radio – it can be heard to be pronounced [lʲvʲif] as well as [lʲvʲiw]. Some might argue that the former is a result of Russian influence (and therefore incorrect), while others might consider this variant to be a native phenomenon.

The structure of the book is as follows: a general table of contents lists major subdivisions of the chapters (for example, the noun, declensions, and such), together with lists of subheadings, so that the reader can immediately find the particular subject they are looking for. Each chapter first presents the material (the Ukrainian verb, for example), then describes how it is used, with examples throughout; the word-formational processes characteristic of the major grammatical categories (verb, noun, adjective) are also described in some detail. For individual items – such as key grammatical words or topics – the index will be of additional help. Lists of grammatical terms (in both English and Ukrainian) and of abbreviations used are provided at the beginning of the book; abbreviations referring to sources consulted can be found at the end of the Bibliography. Readers who are interested in furthering their study of the language or literature are encouraged to refer to the bibliography at the end of the book; this lists grammars, dictionaries, and other sources, many of which were extensively consulted during the writing of this grammar.

Finally, the authors are indebted to many individuals who helped make this book possible, including Marina Kharitonova, Olena Bekh, John Sullivan, Serhij Moroz, Craig Rollo, Jennifer Pickurel, and an anonymous reader; finally, we owe many thanks to Routledge for their patience.

INTRODUCTION

0.0 HISTORICAL BACKGROUND

Ukrainian (formerly known as Little Russian) is an East Slavonic language closely related to Belarusian (formerly known as Byelorussian, and earlier as White Russian) and Russian; all three use the Cyrillic alphabet. At the time of the Christianization of Rus' – the East Slavonic territory that stretched from Kyiv (the Ukrainian form of Kiev) in the south to Novgorod in the north – in 988, the East Slavonic group of dialects as a whole was relatively uniform, differing only slightly from region to region. The differences that today separate the three languages from one another were not brought about by internal linguistic change alone; just as important in this regard were events in the realm of political change, mostly in the form of invasions by non-Slavs and annexations by other Slavs.

THE TATARS   The first cataclysmic event of this kind was the protracted invasion and ultimate destruction of Kyiv by the Tatars in 1240. Immediate consequences of this event were the dissolution of the state, the establishment of smaller principalities on the periphery of the territory, and therefore a break in the continuity of linguistic evolution – heretofore centred on Kyiv. Tatar rule had no lasting affect on the development of local dialects, barring the adoption of a few words that were specific to Tatar material culture.

THE POLES   The eventual collapse of Tatar control over Kievan Rus' left a power vacuum, into which the Polish-Lithuanian (but primarily Polish) state entered in the course of the fifteenth century. This historical development differed markedly from the Tatar period, as Polish became a true *lingua franca* in the Ukrainian-Belarusian lands: Polish rule penetrated deeply into daily life in these regions, with the result that Polish was widely spoken. The consequences for later Ukrainian (and Belarusian) remain evident today, as a substantial proportion of the Ukrainian lexicon consists of borrowings from the Polish language. The lexicon is therefore the one component of the modern language which differentiates Ukrainian from Russian the most. Of course, there are significant differences in the phonology and morphology as well, but these are the result of gradual linguistic developments that are not as immediately obvious as is the sheer weight of thousands of Polish lexical items. It was this period more than any other that resulted in the formation of a Ukrainian language essentially as we now know it; and, as the lexical developments took place across the entire Ukrainian-Belarusian territory, modern Ukrainian is closer to Belarusian than it is to Russian.

THE RUSSIANS   Polish hegemony lasted until the middle of the seventeenth century, after which much of what is Ukraine today was brought into the Russian Empire; after a short period of independence following the Bolshevik revolution of 1917, Ukraine was made part of the Soviet Union. This entire period – which ended in 1991 – had the same linguistic effect as the Polish period (on Belarusian as well as on Ukrainian): Russian-Ukrainian bilingualism and Russo-centric political life and education throughout the twentieth century resulted in the widespread daily use of Russian lexemes in everyday Ukrainian. The proportion of Russianisms was naturally greatest in the press (as organs of the State) and the language of government and politics.

These issues, the interaction of Polish and Russian lexicon with the native Ukrainian lexicon, as well as changes now taking place in the language, will be addressed in more detail in **0.1** below.

0.1   UKRAINIAN TODAY, THE LEXICON

The development of the linguistic component that we speak of as the 'lexicon' has been outlined above, if only very briefly, but what of the language today? Although the Polish and Russian periods can be equated, given the massive use/importation of lexemes from both languages, there is one critical difference. In the seventeenth century there was no such thing as a 'standard' language, no grammars, no prescriptive rules, no mass media; consequently, much of what had entered the language from Polish remained there, as 'Polish' words had become 'Ukrainian' words. Speakers used them in speech, later in writing; speakers today will not consciously think, as they say **Дякую** '(I) thank you', that this was a borrowing from Polish (Pol. *dziękuję:* ultimately from German *dank*). There was no move to purge Ukrainian of words adopted from Polish, as there was no language planning. Now, however, Ukrainian is a national language; it is the language of a large country finding its identity after centuries of being part of another, even larger, one. Thus, in the process of Ukrainianizing the nation, introducing Ukrainian as a language of instruction at all levels, as the language of State and commerce, the unasked question may be 'What *is* Ukrainian?' Some native speakers, in describing to us their active use of Ukrainian, tell us that they occasionally make conscious decisions about what particular lexeme to use: if a word (presumably) borrowed from Russian has been in use in Ukrainian (such as **спір** 'argument', compare Rus. *спор*), but a more Ukrainian variant exists (in this case **суперечка**), he/she will now tend to use the latter. Of course, a Russianized Ukrainian, or a Ukrainian whose first language is Russian, might still use the former.

Questions of this kind will take many years to sort out; individual lexemes of Russian origin may or may not survive, although a great many will do so simply because (i) there have been so many, used for so many years, and (ii) because it is sometimes difficult to decide whether a particular word is actually a Russian word or one that is of common East Slavonic origin. In the case of **спір**, one can argue that the latter is the case: (i) it is attested already in the fifteenth century (as **споръ**), albeit semantically somewhat different from its modern counterpart; and (ii) it reflects the vocalic evolution of o – i in a closed syllable; if this word were a recent borrowing, it would be unlikely to reflect this feature. A 1997 dictionary of Ukrainian, under the English headword 'argument', gives both **суперéчка** and **спір**, with the former evidently as the first choice; in the 1997 orthographic dictionary, however the latter is absent. Future grammars and dictionaries, then, will present us with the officially 'accepted' words that make up the Ukrainian lexicon; but, as ever, what is actually used in speech or writing by an individual is a function of his/her choice.

0.1.1 SHARED EAST SLAVONIC LEXICON

A discussion of the Ukrainian lexicon begins with the historical developments outlined in **0.0**. The development of this component of the language began with a pool of lexemes shared by all of the modern East Slavonic languages. Thus, lexemes basic to all three will be more or less identical (allowing for historical phonological changes specific to each individual language); this will include kinship terms such as 'brother', 'mother', 'son', 'sister', personal and possessive pronouns 'I', 'you', and so on, 'my', 'your', 'his', and so on, lexemes denoting basic realia of life 'house', 'table', and so on. Compare (note that stresses are not marked in this Introduction):

Ukrainian	Belarusian	Russian	Meaning
брат	брат	брат	brother
мати	маці	мать	mother
сестра	сястра	сестра	sister
син	сын	сын	son
я	я	я	I
ти	ты	ты	you (sg.)
він	ён	он	he
ми	мы	мы	we
дім	дом	дом	house
стіл	стол	стол	table

Verbs:

читати	чытаць	читать	to read
писати	пісаць	писать	to write
ходити	хадзіць	ходить	to go

Adjectives:

зелений	зялёны	зелёный	green
молодий	малады	молодой	small
старий	стары	старый	old

One of the lexical developments that further distanced Russian from the other two languages was the widespread adoption by codifiers of Russian of words, forms of words, and word-formational processes from Church Slavonic, the liturgical language of the East Slavonic (Russian) Orthodox Church. This can be explained as a result of the transfer of the seat of the Church to northern Rus' (ultimately Muscovy) during the Tatar period, as well as of Polish rule over the Ukrainian-Belarusian lands. The influence of the Orthodox Church was therefore minimal in Ukraine, while it grew in stature and societal importance in Muscovy. Although it is true that, during the end of the sixteenth and beginning of the seventeenth centuries, a number of Church Slavonic grammars and dictionaries appeared in Ukraine-Belarus', they were written in order to counteract the use of the Polish literary language and the influence of the Catholic Church. But the effect was to create a kind of diglossic relationship between the language of the Church and the spoken local language: one was limited to the Church and learned writing, the other was used in everyday life. In the end, the latter took little from Church Slavonic, and Church Slavonic was not used as a source during the process of codification in later centuries.

0.1.2   POLISH LEXICON

The Polish period was, therefore, crucial for the current shape of Ukrainian, because of the role of Polish itself and because of the reduced role of Church Slavonic for a prolonged length of time. The development of the Ukrainian vocabulary can be described as two-pronged: (i) the straight borrowing of Polish lexemes that would not be perceived as specifically East Slavonic (i.e. that are somehow different), and (ii) the semantic shift of a number of lexemes that were ultimately from the same Slavonic source under the influence of the meaning of corresponding Polish forms. The following examples are but a very few that could be listed (thousands belong in the first group):

(i)	дякую, дякувати	'thank you', 'to thank', but Rus. *спасибо, благодарю, благодарить*. But: Ukr. **спасибі**, 'thanks' most likely shared East Slavonic, cf. Pol. *dziękuję*.
	вдячний	'thankful', cf. Pol. *wdzięczny*, but Rus. *благодарный*.
	ганок	'steps', 'porch', cf. Pol. *ganek* < Ger. *Gang*, but Rus. *крыльцо*.
	навіть	'even' (adv.), Pol. *nawet*; but Rus. *даже*.
	місце	'place', Pol. *miejsce*, Rus. *место* (cf. **місто** under (ii)).

умова		'condition', 'accord', 'agreement', Pol. *umowa*, but Rus. *условие, договор*.
дбати		'to care for, about', Pol. *dbać*, but Rus. *заботиться*.
будинок		'building', Pol. *budynek*, but Rus. *здание*.
жартувати		'to joke', Pol. *żartować*, but Rus. *шутить*.
допомагати		'to help', Pol. *dopomagać*, but Rus. *помогать*.
задоволений		'content', 'satisfied', Pol. *zadowolony*; but Rus. *довольный*.
година		'hour', Pol. *godzina*, but Rus. *час*.
треба		'It is necessary', 'One must', Pol. *trzeba*, but Rus. *надо, нужно* (cf. Rus. *требовать* 'to demand').
(ii)	місто	'town', 'city', Pol. *miasto*, cf. Rus. *город* 'city', 'town', but *место* 'place'.
	кордон	'border', Pol. *kordon* (*graniczny*), cf. Rus. *кордон* 'cordon', *граница* 'border'.
	час	'time', Pol. *czas*, cf. Rus. *час* 'hour', *время* 'time'.
	захід	'west', Pol. *zachód*; but Rus. *заход* 'sunset', *запад* 'west'.
	схід	'east', Pol. *wschód* (with simplification of the initial cluster ws- > s-), cf. Rus. *сход* 'alighting', 'gathering', or 'assembly', *восход* 'rising' (*в. солнца* 'sunrise', 'east': obsolete), *восток* 'east'.

All such lexemes have long been used in Ukrainian without evoking a sense of 'Polishness' in the speaker's or listener's ear. Of course, occasionally there are lexical forms which will be more common in one area of Ukraine than another; thus, a western Ukrainian lexeme can be perceived by an easterner as a Polonism, for example, **пан** 'mister' (Mr.: compare Polish *pan*), a form that has been described in some grammars as one that is used primarily by émigrés and occasionally by western Ukrainians; it is, however, present in the latest Ukrainian dictionaries. Even a basic word like 'please' can differ from East to West: **прошу** can be used anywhere in Ukraine, but is more common in the West (compare Pol. *proszę*), vs. **будь ласка** in the East. Sometimes the reverse occurs: in the West a 'letter' (of the alphabet) is more often **буква** - which is the same as in Russian – than **літера**, the word encountered elsewhere in Ukrainian and in Polish. Although this might be surprising – given the geo-linguistic realities of Ukraine – the history of all languages is full of such twists and turns. Other regional differences may be more subtle (suffixation, for example), as in the word for 'snapshot', 'photo': compare West **знимка** (not based on a Polish form), East **знімок** or **знимок**; the latter may have this form under the influence of Russian **снимок**, but phonetically the Ukrainian version is different enough from the Russian that it is not markedly heard as Russian. The Russianness of a given word is only clearly felt in lexical items that either have no Ukrainian related counterpart or belong to an obviously

Soviet lexical inventory (political, (Soviet Russian) economic, and the like); this phenomenon is examined in **0.1.3**.

0.1.3 RUSSIAN LEXICON

The growth of the Russian contribution to the Ukrainian lexicon during the eighteenth and nineteenth centuries can be attributed in part to the gradual industrialization of some of the regions of the Russian Empire: new industries, new products, new words. Of course, many of these new lexemes were internationalisms in any event, and represent borrowings in Russian as well; the source languages were primarily French and German, and ultimately often Latin-based. It is easy to see how this component of the Ukrainian lexicon developed, as specialist terminology in a variety of disciplines (socio-economic, political, educational, scientific) developed very quickly during the eighteenth century in Russia. Ukraine was part of the empire, ruled by Russians. Russian and Ukrainian used practically identical alphabets, and the languages were closely related: the adoption of ready-made lexemes could not have been easier. Naturally the same is true of the twentieth century, but the nature of the borrowings was different for political reasons; the following might be termed neutral borrowings, if only because they were adopted without overtly political meanings:

документ, матеріал, психологія, серйозний, період, делікатність, сфера, національний, максимум, проблема, інтерес, оригінальність, трагічний, *et al.*

It is naturally difficult to determine when exactly words of this type entered the language; it is also possible that some (or even many) were used before the annexation of Ukraine by Russia, but that their semantic coloration could have changed under the influence of Russian. It is much easier to identify Russian words adopted, given, or simply used during the Soviet period (but note again that these are international in nature):

партійний, соціалізм, революція, пленум, культ (as in **культ особи** 'personality cult'), **класовий, колектив, фашизм**, *et al.*

It bears repeating, however, that the influx of Russian words during the Soviet period was not entirely political, as Ukrainian-Russian bilingualism also led to the common use of neutral Russian lexemes. But the role of Russian throughout Soviet society was openly declared to be that of (i) the language of all Soviet peoples and (ii) the source language for the enrichment of the other languages of the Soviet Union. It is now no longer the language of all former Soviet citizens, but *a* language; a language that is commonly being avoided in some of the former republics with established, old literary traditions of their own (such as the Baltic states, Georgia, Armenia). It is also no longer the source language for neologisms in languages outside of the

Russian Federation – with the possible exception of Belarus'; for Ukrainian in particular, the question will be 'What will happen to Russian lexemes that once enriched the language?' A very good discussion of current debates among linguists and codifiers in Ukraine (regarding the standardization of Ukrainian with reference to all major components of the language) can be found in Pickurel (1998).

As a final note on the role of Russian, there exists a mixed Russian-Ukrainian form of speech known as *suržyk*. Although it is thought that it originally arose as a mixed form of language among peasants, in the recent past it has been used – mainly by the young – in certain well-defined contexts, for example, in popular music, as a way of expressing irony, protest, or simply of making a statement. As a non-standard form of speech, it is not generally found in print and has no effect on Ukrainian in general; indeed, the use of *suržyk* now tends to be decreasing (Pickurel 1998: 242).

0.1.4   UKRAINIAN TODAY

In the passages above, as in the Preface to this book, we have noted that there can be great variation in Ukrainian. In the grammatical sphere, this primarily consists of the existence of variant case endings in the noun. The pronunciation of Ukrainian can also vary, according to region and individual speaker; although this can be a function of one's dialect, we also note occasional variation under the influence of Russian (as noted in the Preface regarding the realization of the city name Львів as [lʲvʲiw] or [lʲvʲif], where the second variant reflects Russian influence: compare the Russian variant [lʲvof]). The lexicon is that component of the language which can undergo the fastest transformation: before 1991, it was Russian which served as the source language; today, given the rapid attempts to transform the Ukrainian economy into a market economy, English business and advertising terminology is widely encountered in the media. Whether or not the new lexemes are retained in the language of the future remains to be seen, and may depend on the success of the market economy in the long run; English-based computer terminology is likely to remain, however, as the use of computers grows.

Perhaps more importantly for the living spoken language is the language of the young: since Ukraine has opened up to the West, western (and especially English-language) popular culture is adopted and widely imitated. English-language teaching programmes, many of them private enterprises, are to be found in appreciable numbers in all of the large cities of the country; those who are learning the language are primarily – but not exclusively – the young. The effect that all of these factors will have on Ukrainian of the future can only be surmised, but here we may take German, which has been under the strong influence of English-language culture since the 1950s, as a point of comparison. An English speaker who peruses German popular magazines, watches German television (especially advertisements), and speaks to young

Germans cannot help but be struck by the immense number of English lexemes in constant use. Very often such words are no longer consciously used as
cultural markers or as an indication of 'coolness': this is a clear indication of
their transformation from English words into German words (in other words,
into true borrowings). English is 'rapidly replacing Russian as the language
of international communication' in Ukraine (Pickurel 1999: 242); this development, alongside the use of Anglicisms/Americanisms as markers of popular culture, will in time affect at least the lexicon of Ukrainian in a significant
way. In years to come, new dictionaries of Ukrainian will attest to this aspect
of change in Ukrainian, much as new dictionaries of Russian reflect the same
phenomenon in that language.

0.2 ABBREVIATIONS USED

Abbreviations relating to sources consulted are to be found at the end of the
Bibliography.

A., acc.	accusative
act.	active
adj.	adjective
adv.	adverb
arch.	archaic
coll.	colloquial
comp.	comparative
cond.	conditional
conj.	conjugation
deadj.	deadjectival
D., dat.	dative
decl.	declension
dem.	demonstrative
dePP.	de-Prepositional Phrase
desubst.	desubstantival
det.	determinate
dial.	dialect
dim.	diminutive
f., fem.	feminine
fut.	future
G., gen.	genitive
imp., imper.	imperative
imperf.	imperfective
indecl.	indeclinable
indef.	indefinite
indet.	indeterminate

inf.	infinitive
I., inst.	instrumental
intrans.	intransitive
lit.	literally
L., loc.	locative
m., masc.	masculine
neg.	negative
n., neut.	neuter
N., nom.	nominative
num.	numeral
part.	participle
pass.	passive
PAP.	past active participle
perf.	perfective
pl.	plural
poss.	possessive
PPP.	past passive participle
PrAP.	present active participle
prep.	preposition
pres.	present
pron.	pronoun
PrPP.	present passive participle
recip.	reciprocal
refl.	reflexive
rel.	relative
sg.	singular
subst.	substantive
sup.	superlative
trans.	transitive
V., voc.	vocative

0.3 GLOSSARY OF GRAMMATICAL TERMS USED IN THIS BOOK

accusative	case of the direct object (see p. 10): **Він читáє книѝжку** 'He reads *the book*'.
adjective	modifies a noun, answers the question 'What is X like?', 'the *long* book', 'an *interesting* story'.
adjectival participle	an *-ing* form of a verb which means the same as 'who/which . . .', e.g., 'He phoned the man *selling* a canoe' (= 'who was selling'), a synonymous term in Slavonic grammars is 'participle'.

adverb	modifies action, answers the question 'how': 'He reads *slowly*', 'John does this *well*'
adverbial participle	see 'gerund'.
article	'*the* book' (definite); '*a* library' (indefinite).
aspiration	the puff of air which accompanies the pronunciation of sounds to varying extents, e.g. in standard English 'p' at the beginning of a word is accompanied by quite noticeable aspiration; this is *not* a feature of Ukrainian in such sounds as *p, t, k,* when they are hard, but is present to some extent in palatalized consonants.
cardinal	numeral indicating how many (one, two . . .).
case	form of a word (noun, adjective, pronoun) showing the function of that word in a sentence, expressed by an ending.
collective	a form referring to a group, e.g. of people.
conjugation	inflection of the verb by means of endings to indicate who or what is carrying out the action: 'John read*s*' (*vs.* 'I read'), **Микола читає**.
dative	case of the indirect object.
declension	set of case endings (see 'case' above).
definite	see 'article' above.
direct object	thing/person at which a verbal action is directed: 'She bought *the book*', 'We saw *John*'.
ending	element(s) added to the stem of a word: book + s, **книжк + а, пол + е**; an ending in Ukrainian can be 'zero': **брат** (+ *zero*).
gender	'natural' gender: distinction of sex (male-female), 'grammatical' gender: distinction of declensional types according to the ending in the nominative singular.
genitive	case of possession, often English 'of': 'the capital *of England*', '*England's* capital'.
gerund	an -*ing* form of a verb which means the same as 'when, if, because . . .', e.g., '*Looking* through the window, Joan saw just what she had been looking for' (= 'When she was looking . . .'), 'They were so tired they went to bed *without undressing*' (= a negative adverbial participle); a synonymous term is 'adverbial participle', or 'verbal adverb'.
hard	in reference to consonants: not soft/palatalized.
imperative	the verb form used to convey commands: '*Write* this down immediately!'
indefinite	see 'article'.

indirect object	recipient of the direct object (see above): 'The teacher gave the book *to the student*'.
instrumental	case expressing 'by means of', 'together with'.
interjection	a word or phrase expressing emotion: 'Oh!'
lexicon	the set of words ('lexical items') that make up the vocabulary of a language; sometimes = 'vocabulary'.
locative	case of location (*in* the city): in Ukrainian this case is used only with a preposition; in other grammars it may be referred to as the 'prepositional'.
mood	a verb form conveying the attitude of the speaker to what is being said, e.g. the 'indicative' mood conveys plain statements, as in 'I am reading a book', and the 'conditional' mood hints at an underlying condition or 'if': 'I would like to go to Kyiv'.
nominative	case of the subject (see below).
noun	object (pencil), person (John, woman), or concept (freedom).
ordinal	numeral indicating relative order ('how-manieth': 'first', 'second' . . .).
palatalization	the modification of the pronunciation of a consonant when it is almost simultaneously accompanied by a 'y'-sound, thus the variations of the *ss*, *t*, *d*, and *n* in English *issue*, *tune*, *dew*, *new*. Such 'palatalized', or 'soft', consonants are a feature of Ukrainian pronunciation.
paradigm	a set of declined or conjugated forms (e.g. the present paradigm of **ітй** 'go', is **ідý, ідéш, ідé, ідемó, ідетé, ідýть**).
participle	see 'adjectival participle' and compare 'adverbial participle'.
plural	when reference is to more than one item or person ('pencil*s*').
prefix	element added to the beginning of a word to denote an action or state different from that of the unprefixed form: 'Jack *pre*paid the bill', 'I *under*estimated him'.
preposition	grammatical word relating two things/people: a book *in* a library, the letter *from* mother; use of a preposition in Ukrainian requires that the following word occurs with a particular case ending.
pronoun	*personal* 'I', 'you', *possessive* 'my', 'your', *interrogative* 'who?', 'what?' and so on.
root	the core of a word, to which can be added prefixes, derivational suffixes, stem-marking suffixes, endings.

singular	when reference is to a single person or item, e.g. 'a pencil' (*vs.* 'pencil*s*'), or something collective or uncountable, e.g. 'foliage', 'honey'.
soft	= palatalized, see 'palatalization'.
stem	the form of a word minus the ending, e.g. кни́жк-, добр-, прочита́й-, гово́р-и-, переда́й-.
stress	greater emphasis on one vowel/syllable within a word: compare the two different places of stress in English *cóntent vs. contént*.
subject	actor, thing/person carrying out the main action of a sentence: '*John* read the article'.
suffix	a word-formational element: e.g. English *-tion, -ment, -ness, -er* (the speak*er*); Ukrainian **-ик**.
tense	time as expressed by the verb (past, present, future).
verb	word expressing action: 'Louise *writes* letters'.
vocative	case of address: 'John!' Nouns in Ukrainian have a distinct form in the singular: **Іва́н*е*!** (*vs.* **Іва́н**, in reference to Ivan).
voice	in pronunciation, a sound articulated with accompanying vibration in the throat (the vocal cords or folds), e.g. 'voiced' *z* as against 'voiceless' *s*; in the verb, the contrast between, for example, the 'active' voice in 'John sees Mary', and the 'passive' voice in 'John is seen by Mary'.
word formation	the process of building words from a given word or base form: *transform > transformation*.

0.4   UKRAINIAN GRAMMATICAL TERMS

(Note that forms are cited first of all in the nominative case, with genitive forms supplied.)

accusative	**знахі́дний відмі́нок, -ого -нка**
active voice	**акти́вний стан, -ого -у**
adjectival participle	**дієприкме́тник, -а**
adjective	**прикме́тник, -а**
adverb	**прислі́вник, -а**
adverbial participle	**дієприслі́вник, -а**
alphabet	**абе́тка, -и, алфа́віт, -у or алфаві́т, -у**
animates	**на́зви істо́т** (from **на́зва, -и** 'name', and **істо́та, -и** 'being')
aspect	**вид, -у**

assimilation	**уподíбнення, -я** (also **асимілáція, -ї**); the opposite, referring to when neighbouring sounds become less like each other, is **розподíбнення, -я** (also **дисиміля́ція, -ї** 'dissimilation')
cardinal numeral	**кíлькісний числíвник, -ого -а**
case	**імéнник, -а**
combination	**сполýчення, -я**
comparative (degree)	**вúщий стýпінь, -ого -пеня**
conditional	**умóвний спóсіб, -ого спóсобу**
conjugation	**дієвідмíна, -и** (in the sense of a group or class)
conjugation	**відмíнювання, -я** (in the sense of the changing of endings; also 'declension' in the same sense)
conjunction	**сполýчник, -а**
consonant	**прúголосний, -ого** (adjective functioning as a noun; **звук** is understood)
dative	**давáльний відмíнок, -ого -нка**
declension	**відмíна, -и** (in the sense of a group or class)
declension	**відмíнювання, -я** (in the sense of the changing of endings; also 'conjugation' in the same sense – for a verb **дієвідмíнювання** may be preferred)
demonstrative pronoun	**вказівнúй займéнник, -ого -а**
ending	**закíнчення, -я**
future tense	**майбýтній час, -ього чáсý**
gender	**рід, рóду**
genitive	**родовúй відмíнок, -óго -нка**
gerund	**дієприслíвник, -а**
hard	**твердúй** (the related noun is **твéрдість, -ості**)
imperative	**наказóвий спóсіб, -ого спóсобу**
imperfective aspect	**недокóнаний вид, -ого -у**
impersonal form	**безособóва фóрма, -ої -и**
inanimates	**нáзви неістóт,** (from **нáзва, -а** 'name', and **істóта, -и** 'being')
instrumental	**орýдний відмíнок, -ого -нка**
interjection	**вúгук, -у**
interrogative pronoun	**питáльний займéнник** (substitute **прикмéтник** as required), **-ого -а**
language	**мóва, -и**
lengthening	**подóвження, -я**
letter	**лíтера, -и, бýква, -и**
locative	**місцéвий відмíнок, -ого -нка**
mixed	**мíшаний, -ого**
mood	**спóсіб, спóсобу**
negative pronoun	**заперéчний займéнник** (substitute **прикмéтник** as required), **-ого -а**
nominative	**називнúй відмíнок, -óго -нка**

non-syllabic	**нескладови́й, -о́го**
noun	**іме́нник, -а**
number	**число́, -а́**
numeral	**числі́вник, -а**
ordinal numeral	**порядко́вий числі́вник, -ого -а**
part of speech	**части́на мо́ви, -и мо́ви**
particle	**ча́стка, -и**
passive voice	**паси́вний стан, -ого -у**
past tense	**мину́лий час, -ого ча́су́**
perfective aspect	**доко́наний вид, -ого -у**
person	**осо́ба, -и**
personal pronoun	**особо́вий займе́нник, -ого -а**
plural	**множина́, -и́**
possessive adjective	**присві́йний прикме́тник, -ого -а** (substitute **займе́нник** as required)
preposition	**прийме́нник, -а**
present tense	**тепе́рішній час, -ього ча́су́**
pronoun	**займе́нник, -а**
pronunciation	**вимо́ва, -и**
qualitative adjective	**я́кісний прикме́тник, -ого -а**
reflexive pronoun	**зворо́тний займе́нник** (substitute **прикме́тник** as required)
relative adjective	**відно́сний прикме́тник, -ого -а** (substitute **займе́нник** as required)
sentence	**ре́чення, -я**
singular	**однина́, -и́**
soft	**м'яки́й** (the related noun is **м'я́кість, -ості**), **-о́го**
sound	**звук, -а/-у**
speech	**мо́влення, -я**
stress	**на́голос, -у**
stressed (sound)	**наголо́шений (звук), -ого (-а/-у)**
superlative (degree)	**найви́щий сту́пінь, -ого -пеня**
syllable	**склад, -у**
tense	**час, ча́су́**
unstressed (sound)	**ненаголо́шений (звук), -ого (-а/-у)**
verb	**дієсло́во, -а**
verbal adverb	see 'gerund'
vocative	**кли́чний відмі́нок, -ого -нка**
voice	**стан, -у**
voiced	**дзвінки́й** (the related noun is **дзві́нкість, -ості**)
voiceless (unvoiced)	**глухи́й** (the related noun is **глу́хість, -ості**)
vowel	**голосни́й, -о́го** (adjective functioning as a noun; **звук** is understood)
word formation	**словотві́р, -тво́ру**

0.5   BASIC GREETINGS

It is difficult to place sections on greetings and interjections thematically within the chapters of a reference or comprehensive grammar; although greetings will be found in basic textbooks or in books on the colloquial language, interjections will not always be included. Both of these elements are included here, as not all forms, phrases, and especially variants will be easily found in dictionaries, and they are rarely found together in one place in any book.

HELLO'

Formal:	добрий день	lit. good day
	добридень	same as above, but slightly less formal
	доброго ранку	good morning
	добрий вечір	good evening
	добривечір	same as above (cf. добридень)
	доброго здоров'я	lit. '[I wish you] good health', often in response to one of the preceding greetings
	вибачте!	Excuse me (when addressing someone whose attention you would like to get; also in the sense 'sorry!' (see below), or to introduce an objection 'excuse me, but . . .')
Informal:	вітаю!	lit. I greet, I welcome.
	привіт!	hi
	здоров!	hi (quite familiar, often between men only)
On the phone:	алло, гàлло, галлó	hello
	слухаю	lit. 'I'm listening' (not rude), also used by staff in shops waiting to serve a customer

'GOODBYE'

до побачення	until (we) see (each other again) = (au revoir, auf Wiedersehen: this is the most common and neutral form used)
усього найкращого!	all the best
на все добре!	all the best (more informal than above)
будь здоров!	lit. 'be healthy!', masculine
будь здорова	feminine
будьте здорові	plural (Note that будь, будьте may be replaced by бувай (sg., more familiar), бувайте (pl., or more polite sg.))

бувáй! бувáйте!	bye! (even more familiar without the element здорóв)
бувáйте па!	bye! (plural, informal)
щаслúво!	cheerio!
до зýстрічі!	until we meet again, see you next time
прощавáй(те)!	farewell! (*sg.* and *pl.*)
добрáніч!	good night!

'THANK YOU', 'PLEASE', 'YOU'RE WELCOME', 'EXCUSE ME'

прóшу	please, You're welcome, here you are ((when handing someone something); also: Don't mention it, more Western Ukraine)
будь лáска	(same as above, more Eastern Ukraine)
дя́кую	thank you
дýже дя́кую	thank you very much
не вáрто подя́ки	don't mention it (lit. 'It's not worth thanking')
немá зá що!	(same as above (lit. 'nothing to (thank me) for'))
вúбачте (менí)	excuse me
пробáчте (менí)	excuse me, I'm sorry
перепрóшую	I'm very sorry

0.6   INTERJECTIONS

о	oh (in expressions of pleasure or consternation, depending on context)
ох	oh! ah! (cf. óхати 'to groan', óхання 'groans', 'groaning')
ах	ah (with expression of delight, enthusiasm)
ой	depends entirely on context: surprise, delight, impatience, and so on
ех	negative, introducing a critical/negative statement
ну, ну й	imparts an ironic or jesting coloration to a following word or phrase (accompanied by an appropriate intonation)
гей	hey!
гóсподи!	heavens!
жах!	horrors!
ґвалт!	help!
урá!	hurrah! hurray!
чорт!	damn (it)! hell!
геть!	(get) out! (get) away!
стоп!	stop!
брáво!	bravo!

In practice, any vowel alone and almost any vowel in combination with certain consonants, especially й, х, г, н, ф, can constitute an interjection whose expressive nature is tied to context, intonation, facial expressions, and movement of the body – thus: **a!**, **e!**, **i!**, **o!**, **y!**, **ай!**, **ей!**, **ой!**, **ій!**, **ах!**, **ех!**, and so on. Doubling of an interjection strengthens the expression of the emotion: **а-а!**, **еге-ге!**, **ну-ну!**

Other expessions of emotion will be clearly lexical (as some in the list above are), for example, **чудóво!** 'wonderful!', and – again – dependent on the context or meaning the speaker/writer wishes to impart.

1 SOUNDS AND SPELLING

1.0 A GENERAL GUIDE TO THE UKRAINIAN ALPHABET AND PRONUNCIATION

We begin with an informal presentation of the sounds of the Ukrainian language, which we will qualify in the subsequent more detailed examination. The outline in this chapter draws on works in the Bibliography.

The transcription which we use is that of the International Phonetic Alphabet. The approximate pronunciation equivalents given are also meant as a rough, preliminary guide. Wherever in the present book we make transliterations for purposes other than phonetic and phonological, we respectively replace [β/v, ε, jε, ʒ, ɪ, ɔ, t͡s, t͡ʃ, ʃ, ʃt͡ʃ] with [w/v, e, je, ž, y, o, c, č, š, šč], and the apostrophe and soft sign with an apostrophe.

THE UKRAINIAN ALPHABET – **Українська абе́тка**
LETTERS AND SOUNDS – **Лі́тери та зву́ки**

Printed	Hand-written	Name	Transcrip-tion	Approximate pronunciation[1]
А а	*A a*	**а**	[a]	*a* as in northern Engaish *bad*.
Б б	*Б б*	**бе**	[b]	*b* as in English *bed*.
В в	*В в*	**ве**	[β/v]	*v* as in English *vet* (but with perhaps more participation of *both* lips).
Г г	*Г г*	**ге**	[h]	close to English *h* in *house*, but with more voice and less aspiration (see the list of grammatical terms).
Ґ ґ	*Ґ ґ*	**ґе**	[g]	*g* as in English *get*; quite a rare sound in native Ukrainian words.
Д д	*Д д*	**де**	[d]	*d* as in English *debt*.
Е е	*Е е*	**е**	[ε]	*e* as in English *get*. May become **и**-like when unstressed (see below).
Є є	*Є є*	**є**	[jε]	*ye* as in English *yet*.
Ж ж	*Ж ж*	**же**	[ʒ]	*s* roughly as in English *pleasure* (keep your voice low and push out your lips).

З з	З з	зе	[z]	z as in English zen.
(И) и	И и	и	[ı]	somewhat between English i in sit and the very beginning of the a in gaze, usually transliterated as y. May become e-like when unstressed (see above).
І і	I і	i	[i]	ee as in English seen or i as in English machine.
Ї ї	Ї ї	ї	[ji]	yea as in English yeast.
Й й	Ŭ ŭ	йот	[j]	y as in English soya.
К к	К к	ка	[k]	k as in English skittle (with minimal aspiration).
Л л	Л л	ел	[l]	l as in English look.
М м	М м	ем	[m]	m as in English money.
Н н	Н н	ен	[n]	n as in English near.
О о	О о	о	[ɔ]	o as in English got, not as in English more. May become y-like when unstressed (see below).
П п	П п	пе	[p]	p as in English spot (with minimal aspiration).
Р р	Р р	ер	[r]	r as in Spanish caro.
С с	С с	ес	[s]	s as in English sit.
Т т	Т т	те	[t]	t as in English stop (minimal aspiration).
У у	У у	у	[u]	oo as in English hoot.
Ф ф	Ф ф	еф	[f]	f as in English fan.
Х х	Х х	ха	[x]	ch as in Scottish English loch (but pronounced without too much rasping).
Ц ц	Ц ц	це	[t͡s]	ts as in English bits.
Ч ч	Ч ч	че	[t͡ʃ]	ch as in English church (not as in cheer; push out your lips).
Ш ш	Ш ш	ша	[ʃ]	sh as in English shoot (keep your voice low and push out your lips).
Щ щ	Щ щ	ща	[ʃ͡t͡ʃ]	sh ch as in English fresh chicken (without a pause).
(Ь) ь	ь			the 'soft sign' м'який знак, it follows consonants and indicates that they are to be pronounced palatalized.
Ю ю	Ю ю	ю	[ju]	you as in English you.
Я я	Я я	я	[ja]	ya as in English yahoo.

'	апо́стро́ф	apostrophe (usually to separate a consonant, which then remains hard, from a following [j]).

It can also be useful to be able to transliterate the Ukrainian alphabet, that is to write out Cyrillic using Latin letters. A standard transliteration remains to be decided upon. Here we give a simplified 'non-linguistic' system, in the order of the letters of the alphabet (the final element in parentheses is the Cyrillic equivalent; if there is more than one element in parentheses, the first represents alternative transliterations of the letter concerned).

a (**а**)	b (**б**)	v (**в**)	h (**г**)
g (**ґ**)	d (**д**)	e (**е**)	ie (je, ye[†]) (**є**)
zh (ž) (**ж**)	z (**з**)	y (**и**)	i (**і**)
ï (ji, yi[†]) (**ї**)	i (j, y) (**й**)	k (**к**)	l (**л**)
m (**м**)	n (**н**)	o (**о**)	p (**п**)
r (**р**)	s (**с**)	t (**т**)	u (**у**)
f (**ф**)	kh (x, ch) (**х**)	ts (c) (**ц**)	ch (č) (**ч**)
sh (š) (**ш**)	shch (šč) (**щ**)	'* (**ь**)	iu (ju, yu[†]) (**ю**)
ia (ja, ya[†]) (**я**)	' (')		

[†] = *ye, yi, yu, ya*, if used, are restricted to the very beginning of a word or following a vowel word-internally.
* = may be omitted (it most often is, in titles and bibliographies).

Although they are not separate letters of the alphabet, in that they do not have their own sections in dictionaries, the combinations **дж, дз**, and **дзь** (including **дзю, дзя**) are to be pronounced as one sound each, namely [d͡ʒ], [d͡z], and [d͡zʲ]: **Ходжу́** [xɔd͡ʒ'u] 'I walk', **джи́нси** [d͡ʒ'ɪnsɪ] 'jeans', **дзе́ркало** [d͡z'ɛrkɑlɔ] 'mirror', **дзво́ник** [d͡zv'ɔnɪk] 'little bell', and **дзьоб** [d͡zʲɔb] 'beak'.

Sometimes they do represent two sounds, namely at morpheme juncture, and are pronounced as respective sequences of [d] + [ʒ], [z], [zʲ]: **піджива́ти** 'to be refreshed', **віджи́лий** 'obsolete', **підзе́мний** 'underground', **підзира́ти** 'to observe secretly'.

Note 1: There are not many words in Ukrainian with **ґ** [g], and in some publications (especially older, Soviet-era ones) the letter **г** will still be found to cover both [h] and [g]. In the following words we have [g]:

ґа́нок balcony	**ґра́ти** grating (compare **гра́ти** 'to play')
ґа́ва crow	**аґрусі́вка** gooseberry brandy
ґу́дзик button	**ґедзь** gadfly

Note 2: The sound [t͡s] is almost always soft when word- and syllable-final: **карбо́ванець** 'rouble', and in suffixes, for example, **-цьк-, -ець, -ць**:

туре́цький Turkish	**америка́нець** American
робітни́ць of the workwomen	

Exceptions are isolated words (usually borrowings), for example,

пала́ц palace   **абза́ц** paragraph, indentation

It is always soft before [i], and often before [a], [ɔ], [u]:

працівни́ця workwoman   **віко́нця** little window (G.*sg.* n.)
однокла́сницю classmate (A.*sg.* f.)   **п'ятна́дцять** fifteen
ву́лиця street   **цьому́** this (D.*sg.* m./n.)

Note:

цэр tear   **цап** goat
цу́кор sugar   **цура́тися** to avoid
цуценя́ puppy   **цо́кати** to clink

But [t͡s] is always hard before [ɛ], [ɪ]: **Кравце́ві**, dative of the surname **Краве́ць** 'Taylor'. Compare:

озе́рце small lake   **віко́нце** small window
се́рце heart   **цитри́на** lemon
цита́та quotation

[t͡sʲ] can also come about as a result of the combination -ть + ся in verbs, in which case [t͡sʲ] is long:

доведе́ться will have to   **зупи́няться** they will stop

Note 3: The sound [t͡ʃ] is hard in Ukrainian, except before [i] and when lengthened:

о́чі eyes   **обли́ччя** face.

Note 4: The letters **я**, **ю**, **є** either represent [j] + [a, u, ɛ] or the vowels alone after a soft consonant. The vowel **ї** always represents [j] + [i]:

я́блуко apple   **ю́ний** youthful
п'є́са play, drama   **Євге́н** Eugene
весі́лля wedding (feast) **любо́в** love
лле́ться flows   **їдки́й** biting, tart
істо́рії stories

They represent two sounds at the very beginning of a word or within a word after a vowel or after an apostrophe or soft sign:

м'яки́й soft   **м'я́та** mint
юрба́ crowd   **інтерв'ю́** interview
мої́ my/mine (nom. *pl.*) **пої́хати** to set/drive off
поєдна́ння accord   **об'єдна́ння** union
сім'я́ family   **зв'язо́к** link, tie

Although the apostrophe is meant to indicate that a preceding consonant is
hard, in practice one might occasionally hear a soft articulation; see **1.1.8**.

1.1   THE PRONUNCIATION AND SOUND SYSTEM OF UKRAINIAN

1.1.1   PREAMBLE

The preceding paragraphs begged a few questions on, among other things,
stress, the role of the soft sign, the use of the apostrophe, the opposition of
voiced and voiceless consonants, the opposition of hard and soft consonants,
consonantal and vocalic alternations, the assimilation and simplification of
consonantal groups, and intonation. We treat these after a general presentation of the sound system, or phonology, of Ukrainian, starting with a sche-
matic outline of the phonemes.

1.1.2   THE VOWEL SYSTEM

	Front	*(Central)*	*Back*
High/close	i		u
High-mid	ɪ		
Open-mid	ɛ		ɔ
Low/open		a	

The vowels as given are phonemes, but using the phonetic symbols which
correspond most closely to their predominant phonetic incidence, i.e. as chief
allophones. The major areas of variation apply to unstressed [ɪ, ɛ]. These two
tend to approximate to each other. Moreover, unstressed [ɔ] before stressed
[u] (and at times even [i]) may narrow to [u] or [ɔw] or, perhaps better, to [o].
Otherwise pronunciation is essentially as given, with variation consisting in
accommodation to contiguous sounds. The phoneme [ɪ] is occasionally also
symbolized as [ɨ], which is however properly a high central vowel, as in Russian, and hence misleading.

Given that it is meaningful to isolate phonemes, as above, then this needs to
be given some measure of justification. There is no problem with /a, ɔ, u, i/, in
that they can stand as independent words. The phoneme /ɛ/ can be justified by
adducing minimal pairs, for example, **пáра** 'pair' – **пéра** 'feathers', 'pens'.
This leaves /ɪ/. Put most simply, this candidate seems weaker since it cannot be
an independent word and never occurs at the very beginning of a word. So,
given that /i/ occurs word-initially and after soft consonants, while /ɪ/ occurs
only after hard consonants, we might seem to have a case of complementary
distribution, with [ɪ] an allophone of a phoneme /i/. Again, we might say that
certain people pronounce [i] after hard consonants (i.e. where **i** alternates
with **o**) and palatals (or certain soft consonants), for example, **ніс** 'nose',

синій 'blue', безкраїй 'endless'. But more important, given the arguable status of such data, would be (i) the phonetic difference between [i] and [ɪ], given that the latter is in fact much closer phonetically to [ɛ] than to [i] (we see this particularly when [ɛ] and [ɪ] are unstressed), and (ii) the fact that [i] and [ɪ] contrast after consonants which do not participate in the hard/soft distinction, for example, Кинь! 'Throw!' – кінь 'horse', Бий! 'Hit!' – бій 'battle'. Ukrainian, therefore, arguably has six vocalic phonemes.[2]

1.1.3 THE CONSONANT SYSTEM

Place of articulation

Model/manner of articulation		Bilabial	Labio-dental	Dental		Palatal	Velar	Glottal
Obstruents								
	Plosives	p		t	tʲ		k	
		b		d	dʲ		g	
	Fricatives		f	s	sʲ	ʃ	x	
				z	zʲ	ʒ		h
	Affricates			t͡s	t͡sʲ	t͡ʃ		
				d͡z	d͡zʲ	d͡ʒ		
Sonorants								
	Fricatives	[w]	β–v			j		
Stops								
	Nasal	m		n	nʲ			
	Lateral			l	lʲ			
	Vibrant			r	rʲ			

We give [w], a phonetic feature, because it is salient and, for reasons given below, currently recommended. One should note that /β–v/, as an allophone of which [w] occurs, does not contrast with /f/; /β–v/ is a weak sort of /v/, articulated with the lower lip behind the upper teeth (/f/, and English /v/, are articulated with the lower lip in front of the upper teeth). Something close to English /v/ might occur half-soft before /i/, for example, віз 'conveyed (masc.)'. Some commentators would contrast this, where the i alternates with e, i.e. везла 'carried (fem.)', with віз 'cart', which arguably has a hard [v] before the [i] which alternates with o, for example, воза 'cart (G.sg.)'. However, we have to see this nowadays as a dialectal feature and, whatever the dialectal reality, we have the complication of the в in везла being hard anyway. We are left with questions of chronology. Less problematic is the soft в in such words as вітер 'wind', where the i arises from *ě and would have always remained soft, but where there is no alternation.

The horizontal axis in the above diagram represents place of articulation (where constriction or blockage of the oral cavity occurs); the vertical axis represents mode or manner of articulation (the extent or type of constriction of the oral cavity). The two vertical pairs in certain columns are respectively voiceless and voiced. The horizontal pairs within certain columns represent respectively hard or non-palatalized and soft or palatalized consonants. The small superscript [j] indicates softness or palatalization, that is the articulation, simultaneous with the articulation of the consonant, of a palatal element. The consonants as given are phonemes; each one also has a phonetic reality as a sole or chief allophone as appropriate; several also have subsidiary allophones. Arguably, the representation of the phonemes in this manner is misleading, in that it suggests some phonetic reality; however, our experience is that from a practical point of view such a representation is both generally accessible and also to some extent represents the speakers' psychological reality.

What may surprise is that the labials, labio-dentals, palatals (except for [j]), and velars are not paired for palatalization in the table. Essentially they are seen only to occur in a semi-soft variant, before [i]; however, at least [βʲ] might be felt to contrast with [β], for example, **сват** 'kinsman', 'matchmaker' – **свят-** 'holy'. (Note that ULVN indicates the preferred pronunciation of the initial sequence **св-** here as **с'в'**, i.e. as [sʲβʲ]). One opinion, conveyed by Shevchenko 1993: 55, is to see this whole series as a 'peripheral subsystem'; such *adhoc*kery is often resorted to, though it is unnecessary. Finally, we know that a good number of Ukrainian consonants occur as long consonants. These may be quite straightforwardly seen as geminates and hence as sequences of two consonants.

1.1.4 STRESS

The acute accent placed over certain vowel letters marks the primary stress; a grave accent marks a secondary stress, restricted to compound words. We will not mark the stress on monosyllabic words. It is not in any case ever marked in normal written Ukrainian, except in grammars, courses, and where a word's meaning depends on the stress, for example,

за́мок castle	замо́к lock
о́бід circle, hoop	обі́д lunch
пла́кати to weep	плака́ти posters (N.A.*pl.*)
пе́ра feathers, pens (N.A.*pl.*)	пера́ of the feather, pen (G.*sg.*)
во́ди waters (N.A.*pl.*)	води́ water (G.*sg.*)
наси́пати to pour in (perf.)	насипа́ти to pour in (imperf.)[3]

In the transcription, which we use sparingly, we denote the stress by a superscript short vertical (secondary stress by a subscript short vertical), inserting it into monosyllables as appropriate. On the whole we place the stress mark immediately before the stressed vowel; another approach places the stress before the consonant or consonants (groups including sonorants may be split) preceding the stressed vowel, in other words roughly indicating syllable rather than vowel stress.

There is no general rule as to where the stress falls in a Ukrainian word; you must learn it as you go along, and be prepared to find it moving from syllable to syllable in some words (where there seems to be variation or a choice, we give two stresses for a word). It is worth noting that there is a tendency in modern Ukrainian to transfer the stress of three- or more-syllable first-declension nouns (ending in -a) to the endings in the plural, for example,

ма́ківка – маківки́ (а́м, а́ми, а́х) poppy head/flower

Others are:

на́ймичка maid	**ма́ківочка** small poppy head/flower
ла́стівка swallow (dim.)	**ла́стівочка** swallow (dim.)
я́гідка small berry	**това́ришка** comrade (fem.)

This may even be found in a few two-syllable nouns:

ху́стка neckerchief	**ді́вка** girl
кни́жка book	**рі́чка** river

The vowels [a] and [o] are pronounced clearly whether stressed or unstressed. However, before [u] and [i] (particularly but not always stressed) an unstressed [o] may acquire a [u]-like quality:

ону́ком grandson (I.*sg.*)	**дові́датися** to find out
полу́мисок platter	**нотува́ти** to note down
ми побі́гли we ran off	**своїм** one's (I.*sg.* m./n.)

When unstressed, the vowel [ɛ] may be pronounced somewhat like [ɪ] and the vowel [ɪ] may approximate to [ɛ]:

мене́ me (A.G.)	**мені́** me (D.L.)
сестра́ sister	**перемо́га** victory
університе́т university	**техні́чний** technical
меха́нік mechanic	**медици́на** medicine

1.1.5 VOICED AND VOICELESS CONSONANTS, ASSIMILATION

In Ukrainian, as in many other languages, there are voiced and voiceless consonants. It is possible to classify them in pairs. Thus:

[p]	–	[b]	=	п	–	б
[f]	–	[v]	=	ф	–	в (but see **1.1.3** and below)
[t]	–	[d]	=	т	–	д
[tʲ]	–	[dʲ]	=	ть	–	дь
[s]	–	[z]	=	с	–	з

[sʲ]	–	[zʲ]	=	сь	–	зь
[ʃ]	–	[ʒ]	=	ш	–	ж
[t͡s]	–	[d͡z]	=	ц	–	дз
[t͡sʲ]	–	[d͡zʲ]	=	ць	–	дзь
[t͡ʃ]	–	[d͡ʒ]	=	ч	–	дж
[ʃt͡ʃ]	–	[ʒd͡ʒ]	=	щ	–	ждж
[k]	–	[g]	=	к	–	ґ
[x]	–	[h]	=	х	–	г

Those given with a final soft sign stand for palatalized consonants preceding either a soft sign or one of the vowels я, ю, і, є in the spelling. Note that at the very end of a word and syllable voiced consonants remain voiced in Ukrainian, as in English but different from such languages as German and Russian.

A few examples:

швúдше [ʃvˈɪdʃɛ] more quickly
їжте [jˈiʒtɛ] eat
рóзталь [rˈɔztalʲ] thaw (weather)
швúдко [ʃβˈɪdkɔ] quickly
ніж [nʲˈiʒ] knife
рúбка [rˈɪbka] little fish
кáзка [kˈazka] tale – **кáска** [kˈaska] helmet
зáлюбки [zalʲubkˈɪ] with pleasure
мед [mˈɛd] honey
скрізь [skrˈizʲ] everywhere, always

Note that in a sequence of voiceless + voiced consonant, assimilation does take place, and is not reflected in the spelling:

вокзáл [vogzˈal] railway station   **молотьбá** threshing [mɔlɔdʲbˈa]
якбú [jagbˈɪ] if   **анекдóт** anecdote [anɛgdˈɔt]
хóч би [xˈɔd͡ʒbɪ] no matter what

The consonants [n], [m], [l], [r] are voiced but do not participate in this correlation; in other words, a voiceless consonant in front of any of them remains voiceless, for example:

при [prɪ] beside, near (not *[brɪ])

Before voiceless consonants the only voiced consonants to devoice are [z] (when in a prefix) and [h] in the middle of a word. Thus:

розписáти to distribute (writing)   **розсúпати** to strew, scatter (perf.)
безплáновий without a plan   **безплáтний** free (of charge)
вóгко damp   **нíгті** nails (on fingers)
кíгті claws

but **лéгкий** 'easy' may have both [x] and [h], and **могтú** 'to be able' and **лягтú** 'to lie down' have [h].

Before voiced consonants, voiceless consonants are voiced:

про́сьба request	**бороть́ба** struggle
молоть́ба threshing	**клять́ба** curse

Note too that the prefix **з-** may be fixed in the spelling and pronunciation as **с-** [s] before some voiceless consonants, namely **к, п, т, х, ф**:

схо́дити, but with its perfective	**зійти́** to rise, descend
спита́ти to enquire	**збити** to fasten
схопи́ти to seize	**згорі́ти** to burn/be burnt
сфотографува́ти to photograph	**звести** to lead down, mislead

With the prefixes **роз-, без-, від-** (**од-**)**, над-, під-, об-, між-, перед-, воз-, понад-, пред-, через-** the voiced character of the final consonant is retained (and conveyed in the spelling):

розколо́ти to split	**безпере́чний** incontestible
відпусти́ти to let go	**підбі́гти** to run up to

1.1.5.1 The consonant [β/v]

At the beginning of a word before a consonant, in the middle of a word after a vowel before a consonant, and at the end of a word after a vowel the consonant [β/v] is pronounced as a sound intermediate between [v] and [u] (it is sometimes asserted that it is a straight labio-dental when soft before [i], for example, as in **він** [vʲin] 'he'). The lips may be round and protrude, i.e. it is bilabial, or we have the lower lip behind the upper teeth. At the end of a word we should not have [f] for this sound, though one cannot but admit that it is heard. In other words, [w] is prescribed:

сказа́в said (masc.)	**любо́в** love
зроби́в did (masc.)	**впе́внений** assured, made certain
по́вний full	

1.1.6 HARD AND SOFT CONSONANTS

The hard/soft pairs which we find in Ukrainian are as follows (first those which are accepted as phonemic, second those which are rather restricted, on the whole to the position before **i** [i], where they tend, even then, to be minimally palatalized, and are thus peripherally phonemic):

[t]	–	[tʲ]	=	т	–	ть
[d]	–	[dʲ]	=	д	–	дь
[s]	–	[sʲ]	=	с	–	сь
[z]	–	[zʲ]	=	з	–	зь
[t͡s]	–	[t͡sʲ]	=	ц	–	ць
[d͡ʒ]	–	[d͡ʒʲ]	=	дз	–	дзь

[n]	–	[nʲ]	=	н	– нь
[l]	–	[lʲ]	=	л	– ль
[r]	–	[rʲ]	=	р	– рь
[b]	–	[bʲi]	=	б	– бі
[p]	–	[pʲi]	=	п	– пі
[β]/[w]	–	[vʲi]/[βʲi]	=	в	– ві
[f]	–	[fʲi]	=	ф	– фі
[m]	–	[mʲi]	=	м	– мі
[k]	–	[kʲi]	=	к	– кі
[h]	–	[hʲi]	=	г	– гі
[x]	–	[xʲi]	=	х	– хі
[ʒ]	–	[ʒʲi]	=	ж	– жі
[ʃ]	–	[ʃʲi]	=	ш	– ші
[t͡ʃ]	–	[t͡ʃi]	=	ч	– чі
[ʃt͡ʃ]	–	[ʃt͡ʃʲi]	=	щ	– щі
[d͡ʒ]	–	[d͡ʒʲi]	=	дж	– джі
[ʒd͡ʒ]	–	[ʒd͡ʒʲi]	=	ждж	жджі

For the first group, the spelling of the soft consonant with a following soft sign is purely a convention for the purposes of the table. In the actual spelling, as we shall see in the examples, a soft consonant can be identified by its being followed by one of the following letters: я, є, і, ю, and ь either on its own or followed by o as ьо. The special letters serve simply to indicate that the preceding consonant is soft. If a vowel, an apostrophe, or nothing precedes я, є, ю, then they represent [j] + [ɑ, ɛ, u]. As for і, it is only ever [i]; should there be a preceding [j], then the letter ї (which is always [ji]) is used. We might symbolize this as follows:

Soft-series vowel (after soft consonant or nothing)	[j] + vowel (after vowel, apostrophe, or nothing)	Hard-series vowel (after hard consonant or nothing)
я	я	a
є	є	e
і	ї	-
–	–	и only after hard consonant
ьо	йо after consonant or nothing	o
ю	ю	у

It might be noted that consonants were originally soft or half-soft before e and и.

We can on the whole divide the consonants up as follows as regards hardness and softness:

HARD-ONLY: [b, p, β/v, m, f], [ʒ, t͡ʃ, ʃ, d͡ʒ], [g, k, x], [h]

Final labial consonants and final **p** are always hard in Ukrainian:

го́луб pigeon, dove	**кров** blood
верф wharf	**степ** steppe
сім seven	**звір** (wild) animal

These and the rest of this group may soften slightly before [i] and before **я, ю** in foreign words and a few Ukrainian words:

бі́лий white	**мі́сто** town, city
бюро́ office	**пюре́** purée
збі́жжя grain	**кло́ччя** tow, oakum
Запорі́жжя Zaporizhia	

SOFT-ONLY: [j]

HARD AND SOFT: [d, dʲ, t, tʲ, z, zʲ, s, sʲ, t͡s, t͡sʲ, l, lʲ, n, nʲ, r, rʲ, d͡z, d͡zʲ]. They are soft:

(i)   Before the soft sign:

жо́втень October	**сьо́мий** seventh

(ii) Before **i**:

сіль salt	**дім** house, home
ніч night	

(iii) Before the vowel letters **я, ю, є**:

ляка́ти to frighten	**люби́ти** to love, like
си́нє blue (N./A.*sg.*N.)	**дзюркота́ти** to murmur, gurgle

(iv) Immediately before soft consonants:

майбу́тнє the future	**сього́дні** today
радя́нський Soviet	

Here are a few more examples:

ти [t'ɪ] you	**ті** [tʲ'i] those
дя́кую [dʲ'ɑkuju] thank you	
сад [s'ad] garden	**сядь** [sʲ'adʲ] sit down
пала́ц [pal'at͡s]	**хло́пець** [xl'ɔpɛt͡sʲ] boy
дзвін [d͡zʲβʲ'in] bell (nom. *sg.*)	**дзво́на** [d͡zβ'ɔna] bell (gen. *sg.*)
ра́са [r'asa] race, breed	**ря́са** [rʲ'asa] cassock

For the second group in the list at the beginning of this section we have given the letters followed by **i** because this is the commonest environment we come across. Some examples:

бíлий [bʲ'ilɪj] white   **вів** [vʲ'iβ] led
кінь [kʲ'inʲ] horse   **шість** [ʃʲ'isʲtʲ] six
ножí [nɔzʲ'i] knives   **уночí** [unɔt͡ʃʲ'i] at night

What has been said above does not refer to sequences of two consonants, of which the second is soft. In such cases the general rule is that the first is pronounced soft too unless it is a labial. So:

у місті [um͡ʲ'isʲtʲi] in the town   **одній** [ɔdʲnʲ'ij] one (D.L.*sg.* f.)
сніг [sʲnʲ'ih] snow

and after the labials, namely **б, п, в, ф, м**:

я люблю [j'a lʲublʲ'u] I love.
конóплі [kɔn'ɔplʲi] hemp (G.*sg.* f.)
вонѝ графлять. [vɔn'ɪ hraflʲ'at'] They draw lines.
вонѝ кóрмлять. [vɔn'ɪ k'ɔrmlʲatʲ] They feed.

Remember that in Ukrainian consonants are hard before **e**:

теáтр theatre   **лéбідь** swan
Невá the Neva (river)   **серенáда** serenade
день day   **дзéркало** mirror

Note the suffixes **-ськ-, -зьк-, -цьк-**:

росíйський Russian   **рѝзький** of Riga
козáцький cossack

Do not confuse these with cases where we are not dealing with the same suffixes:

плáскѝй flat   **різкѝй** harsh, sharp
в'язкѝй adhesive

The soft sign is never written after **ж, ч, ш, щ**, and these consonants are hard, except when lengthened before **я, ю, є**, and, slightly softened, before **i**.

1.1.7   THE SOFT SIGN

The soft sign palatalizes an immediately preceding consonant. One might see it extremely approximately as symbolizing the palatal *par excellence*, namely a *y*-sound, which is to be incorporated as well as possible into the preceding consonant. This *y*-sound appears also in our transcription of **є, ї, ю, я**; of these only the first one and last two occur regularly immediately after consonants, and their first component, the *y*, has the same effect as the soft sign (in the 1870s one hopeful reformer of the Ukrainian spelling system, M. Drahomanov, even suggested replacing them after a consonant with ь + е, і, у, a). It is worth stressing that the soft sign itself is not a sound, in spite of the crude approximation given above; it tells us something about the preceding sound. In other words, the noun **українець** 'Ukrainian (man)' is a consonant-final noun, and the final consonant is soft.

It is written after soft **д, т, з, с, ц, н, л** at the end of a word or word-internally before a hard consonant:

в'язень prisoner	**відповідь** answer, reply
мить sudden moment	**переписуватись** to correspond (with)
олівець pencil	**паморозь** hoarfrost
молотьба threshing	**сильний** strong
вчитель teacher	

Note that it frequently occurs in word-formational suffixes: **-ськ-, -цьк-, -зьк-, -еньк-, -оньк-, -есеньк-, -ісіньк-, -юсіньк-,** for example:

панський lord's, splendid	**козацький** cossack
вузький narrow	**гладенький** very smooth/sleek
голівонька pretty little head	**малісінький** extremely small
малюсінький very small	

It is not written:

(i)   After consonants which occur hard only: **б, п, в, м, ф, ж, ч, ш, щ,** and word-final **р**. But: **Горький** 'Gorky' (the author), as a Russian name, retains the soft sign as it is in Russian; compare the related Ukrainian adjective **гіркий** 'bitter'.

(ii)   Between soft consonants (except for **л**), including lengthened consonants:

волосся hair

(iii) After **н** before **ж, ч, ш, щ, -ськ-, -ств-**:

кінчик end (dim.)	**менший** smaller
інший other	**кінський** horse (adj.)
панство distinction, nobility	

1.1.8 THE APOSTROPHE

The apostrophe is inserted to separate a hard consonant from a following **є, ї, ю, я**. In other words, it serves to convey the sound [j] after hard consonants and before the vowels of letters **я, ю, є, ї**:

п'ятниця Friday	**Лук'янов** Lukjanov (surname)
м'якота soft flesh	

If the consonant before the apostrophe is a prefix or a part of a prefix, then it may be softened by the [j], for example:

під'їхати to drive up to (not softened)
з'їзд congress   **з'явитися** to appear (both softened)

Thus it is used after the labials (**п'ять** 'five'), after **р** at the end of a syllable (**бур'ян** 'weed(s)', **кур'єр** 'courier'), after a prefix or the first component of a compound word (**з'їхати** 'to come down', **дит'ясла** 'crèche'), and in foreign words (**комп'ютер** 'computer', **ад'ютант** 'adjutant').

If there is no [j], there is no apostrophe: **свято** 'holiday', 'feast', **цвях** 'nail', **морквяний** 'of a carrot (**морква**)' – we note that the consonant here is a labial, and the consonant before it belongs to the root. We find the same in foreign words (especially from French):

бюро́ office   **пюпі́тр** reading desk
фюзеля́ж fuselage

Before [ɔ] the jot ([j]) is conveyed by **й** or **ь** (or even both), so here there is no need for the apostrophe:

Воробйо́в (family name)   **серйо́зний** serious
бульйо́н bouillon

Here are a few more examples:

ти б'єш [t'ı bj'ɛʃ] You beat   **об'єкт** object
від'їзд [vʲidjʹizd] departure   **п'ять** [pjatʲ] five
п'ю. [pjʹu] I drink.   **здоро́в'я** [zdɔrʹɔvja] health
ф'юкати [fjʹukatı] to whistle, hiss   **м'який** [mjakıʹj] soft
з ма́тір'ю [z͡m'atʲirju] with mother

1.1.9   CONSONANT ALTERNATIONS[4]

One of the initial difficulties in learning Ukrainian is the need to build up vocabulary; this task can be aggravated if one is not aware of certain quite regular changes which occur in many common words and are reflected in the spelling. Here we mention three important consonantal alternations.

(i)   [k] – [t͡ʃ], [h] – [ʒ], [x] – [ʃ] = к – ч, г – ж, х – ш

рік – річни́й – річни́ця   year – annual – anniversary
бік – бічни́й – боч́астий   side – lateral – with large sides
слуга́ – служи́ти – слу́жба   servant – to serve – service
кни́га – кни́жка – кни́жник   book – book – bibliophile
друг – дру́же – дружи́на   friend – friend (voc.) – wife
страх – страши́ти – страшни́й   dread, very – to frighten – terrible
дух – души́ти – ду́шно   soul, spirit – to strangle – hot, close

(ii)   [k] – [t͡sʲ], [h] – [zʲ], [x] – [sʲ] = к – ц, г – з, х – с

The second of each pair appears before [i] **i**, something which is an important feature of the declension of nouns:

кни́жка – кни́жці	book (nom. – dat./loc.*sg.*)
нога́ – нозі́	foot/leg (nom. – dat./loc.*sg.*)
свекру́ха – свекру́сі	mother-in-law (nom. – dat./loc.*sg.*)
рок – у ро́ці	year (nom.*sg.*) – in . . . year (loc.*sg.*)
універма́г – в універма́зі	store (nom.*sg.*) – in the store (loc.*sg.*)
ву́хо – у ву́сі	ear (nom.*sg.*) – in the ear (loc. *sg.*)

Note that the alternation **ц – ч** can occur as well:

хло́пець – хло́пче! – хлопчи́на	boy – boy! (voc.) – boy
форте́ця – форте́чний	fortress – of a fortress

(iii)   A much broader range of consonantal alternations is as follows:

[t]	–	[t͡ʃ]	=	т	–	ч
[d]	–	[d͡ʒ]	=	д	–	дж
[s]	–	[ʃ]	=	с	–	ш
[z]	–	[ʒ]	=	з	–	ж
[k]	–	[t͡ʃ]	=	к	–	ч
[h]	–	[ʒ]	=	г	–	ж
[kh]	–	[ʃ]	=	х	–	ш
[p]	–	[pʲ]	=	п	–	пль
[b]	–	[bʲ]	=	б	–	бль
[m]	–	[mʲ]	=	м	–	мль
[f]	–	[fʲ]	=	ф	–	фль
[n]	–	[nʲ]	=	н	–	нь
[l]	–	[ʲ]	=	л	–	ль
[r]	–	[rʲ]	=	р	–	рь
[st]	–	[ʃt͡ʃ]	=	ст	–	щ
[zd]	–	[ʒd͡ʒ]	=	зд	–	ждж

These alternations are found in a wide number of forms. Their regularity helps us relate **земля́** 'earth' to **земни́й** 'earthly', without the soft **л**, and **кра́пати** 'to drip', to **кра́пля** 'drop'. These alternations are extremely common in the verb, and they are a function of the stem type to which each particular verb belongs. The following are a number of first-conjugation infinitives (see **6.3.1.1**) in which the basic consonant is present (on the left of each pair), while throughout the present tense we have the transformed consonant (on the right). Thus:

хоті́ти	to want	я хо́чу, ми хо́чемо, вони́ хо́чуть	I/we/they . . .
писа́ти	to write	я пишу́, ми пи́шемо, вони́ пи́шуть	I/we/they . . .
пла́кати	to weep	я пла́чу, ми пла́чемо, вони́ пла́чуть	I/we/they . . .

| могти́ | to be able | я мо́жу, ми мо́жемо, вони́ мо́жуть | I/we/they . . . |
| боро́тися | to wrestle | я борю́ся, ми бо́ремося, вони́ бо́рються | I/we/they . . . |

Note, however, that in the last example, which can stand for all the few such verbs where the last consonant is **н**, **л**, **р**, that consonant is soft only in the first-person singular and the third-person plural. In the first conjugation there are also verbs where no alternation occurs, for example:

бра́ти	to take	я беру́, ми беремо́, вони́ беру́ть	I/we/they . . .
жи́ти	to live	я живу́, ми живемо́, вони́ живу́ть	I/we/they . . .
нести́	to carry	я несу́, ми несемо́, вони́ несу́ть	I/we/they . . .

When in a second-conjugation verb the consonant before the infinitive ending **-ити** falls into this group, the change occurs only in the first-person singular, except where the consonant is a lip (labial) consonant (see, **6.3.2.1**, for example). Thus:

плати́ти	to pay	я плачу́, ми пла́тимо, вони́ пла́тять	I/we/they . . .
ходи́ти	to go	я ходжу́, ми хо́димо, вони́ хо́дять	I/we/they . . .
говори́ти	to speak	я говорю́, ми говори́мо, вони́ гово́рять	I/we/they . . .
пусти́ти	to let go	я пущу́, ми пу́стимо, вони́ пу́стять	I/we/they . . .

Note that these changes occur in passive participles too:

збере́жений (зберегти́) saved, preserved
зобра́жений (зобрази́ти) depicted
пе́чений (пекти́) baked
оголо́шений (оголоси́ти) announced
підтве́рджений (підтве́рдити) confirmed
скоро́чений (скороти́ти) shortened, abridged
об'ї́жджений (об'ї́здити) driven around
відпу́щений (відпусти́ти) released

Observe that second-conjugation verbs whose stem-final consonant is a labial have an inserted **л** in both the first-person singular and the third-person plural, and in the passive participle:

гублю́ – гу́блять (губи́ти) to lose
топлю́ – то́плять (топи́ти) to melt, sink
ловлю́ – ло́влять (лови́ти) to catch
соро́млю – соро́млять (соро́мити) to put to shame
роблю́ – ро́блять to do
ломлю́ – ло́млять to break

And participles:

| загу́блений | уто́плений |
| зло́влений | присоро́млений |

1.1.10 THE ALTERNATIONS [ɔ] – [i], [ɛ] – [i]

One of the characteristic features of Ukrainian is that there are many words where the vowel **i** is in a relationship with either the vowel **o** or the vowel **e**. In the simplest terms, we have **i** before a single consonant which belongs to the same syllable. Typically this will occur in grammatical forms (mostly of nouns, but also some past-tense verb forms) in which a zero ending alternates with a vocalic ending, triggering the **o–i** or **e–i** alternation; thus:

рік year   but   G.*sg.* **póку**

which have the syllable division (using '/' to separate syllables):

рік/   but   **рó/ку/**

and:

він ніс he carried	but	**вонá неслá** she carried
ніс nose (N.*sg.*)	but	**нóса** (G.*sg.*)
шість six (N.)	but	**шестú** (G.)
кінь horse (N.*sg.*)	but	**коня** (G.*sg.*)
Кúїв Kyiv (N.*sg.*)	but	**Кúєва** (G.*sg.*)

and, the other way round:

сіл villages (G.*pl.*)	but	**селó** (N.*sg.*)
гір mountains (G.*pl.*)	but	**горá** (N.*sg.*)

And we may find that the word regularizes itself so as to have the same vowel throughout. Thus:

доріжка path (N.*sg.*)	but	**доріжóк** (G.*pl.*)
кінця end (G.*sg.*)	but	**кінéць** (N.*sg.*)[5]

i does not always alternate with **o/e** (the last two are examples of this; others include **ліс** 'forest', **лíто** 'summer', **сíла** 'she sat down', **бíлий** 'white'[6]) and, as in the penultimate set of examples, **o/e** do not always alternate with **i**. These exceptions include:

(i)   **-оро-, -ере-, -оло-, -еле-** between consonants:

морóз frost   **мóлот** mallet
бéрег bank, shore   **шéлест** rustling, lisping
гóлод famine

(ii)   **-ор-, -ер-, -ов-** between consonants:

горб hump
вовк wolf

(iii)   Where there is a vowel–zero alternation (zero alternation affects **o**, **e**), typically in the declension of many nouns when a vocalic ending appears:

сон – сну sleep   чéрвень – чéрвня June
земля́ – земéль land   пíсня – пісéнь song
день – дня day   куто́к – кутки́ corner

(iv)   In some words of a 'bookish' or formal nature:

наро́д – наро́ду people   зако́н – зако́ну law

(v)   In the prefix воз- and the suffix -тель:

возвели́чити to extol   вчи́тель teacher

(vi)   In the genitive plural of deverbal nouns in -ення:

зна́чення – зна́чень meaning

(vii)   In the second-person singular non-past and the imperative:

іде́ш. You go.   Прихо́дь Come!
Дозво́льте Allow!   but Сті́йте Stop!

(viii) In many suffixes:

Шевче́нко Shevchenko   голу́бонько pretty little dove
мале́нький small

(ix)   In foreign words:

педаго́г pedagogue   о́рден order, decoration

Unless they are older and have been absorbed, for example:

шко́ла – шкіл school   ко́лір – кольорі́в colour

(x)   In non-Ukrainian surnames and other proper names in -ов, -ев, -єв, and
in words formed from them:

Суво́ров (surname)   Лук'я́нов (surname of Russian origin)
росто́вський Rostov (adj.)

There are also instances of analogy:

осно́ва – осно́в basis   імена́ – іме́н (first) names

1.1.11 CONSONANT GROUPS: ASSIMILATION

Perhaps the most notable assimilation (= becoming similar) of consonant
groups in Ukrainian relates to the sequence of the hushing consonants ж, ч,
ш and the soft hissing consonants зь, ць, сь. Here the hushing consonant
assimilates to the hissing consonant, giving a long hissing consonant (note
that a voiced hushing consonant remains voiced). Thus:

кни́жка [knˈɪʒka] book (N.*sg.*) – кни́жці [knˈɪzʲt͡sʲi] book (D.L.*sg.*)
дочка́ [dɔt͡ʃkˈa] daughter (N.*sg.*) – дочці́ [dɔt͡sʲt͡sʲˈi] daughter (D.L.*sg.*)

Ти чита́єш. [tɪ t͡ʃɪt'ajɛʃ] You read – **Ти смієшся.** [tɪ s͡ʲmʲij'ɛsʲsʲa] You laugh.
до́шка [d'ɔʃka] board (N.*sg.*)   – **до́шці** [d'ɔsʲt͡sʲi] board (D.L.*sg.*)

In spite of this, one does often hear a spelling pronunciation in the above groups.

Hissing consonants before hushing consonants within a word assimilate:

безжа́лісний [ʒ:] pitiless   **без ша́пки** [ʃ:] without a cap
підрі́сши [ʃ:] having grown up

Hissing consonants in one word which precede hushing consonants beginning the next word without a pause assimilate to the hushing consonants, optionally even in voice:

без ша́пки [bɛʃ ͡ʃ'apkɪ] without a cap (not the expected [bɛʒ ͡ʃ'apkɪ])

It should be admitted that these assimilations do not always take place; this may be due to the influence of Russian or of the spelling.

Something which does on the whole always happen is that dental plosives assimilate to following hissing/hushing consonants (this is not noted in the spelling):

кімна́тці little room (D.L.*sg.*)   **неві́стці** daughter-in-law (D.L.*sg.*)
крава́тці necktie (D.L.*sg.*)   **борі́дці** short beard (D.L.*sg.*)

All the above have [t͡sʲt͡sʲ]. Similarly:

людськи́й human = [d͡zʲsʲ], **солда́тський** soldier (adj.) = [t͡sʲsʲ]

Assimilation in the formation of possessives derived from personal names is not reflected in the spelling either:

Пара́ска – Пара́счин   Они́ська – Они́сьчин

Sometimes the spelling does change, reflecting a mutation of the consonants brought on (historically) by the nature of a following suffix:

-цьк-	+ -ин(а) > -чч-	коза́цький – коза́ччина
-с(ь)к-	+ -ин(а) > -щ-	віск – вощи́на
		полта́вський – Полта́вщина
-шк-	+ -ан-/-ян- > -щ-	до́шка – доща́ний
-ск-, -ст-	in verbs > -щ-	ве́реск – вереща́ти
		прости́ти – проща́ти
-зк-	in verbs > -жч-	бря́зк – бряжча́ти
-ськ-	in names > -щ-	Васько́ – Ваще́нко/Ващу́к
-зьк-	in names > -жч-	Кузько́ – Кужче́нко
г, ж, з	+ -ш(ий) > -жч-	дороги́й – доро́жчий
		ду́жий – ду́жчий
с	+ -ш(ий) > -щ-	висо́кий – ви́щий

Meanings: 'cossack's' – 'cossack state', 'wax' – 'honeycomb', 'of Poltava' – 'the Poltava region', 'board' – 'of a board', 'shriek' – 'to shriek', 'to forgive' (perf. – imperf.)', 'jingle' – 'to jingle', '(personal) names', '(family) names', 'dear', 'expensive' – 'dearer', 'tough', 'strong' – 'tougher', 'high', 'tall' – 'higher'

Summary of changes:

$[s] + [\int] \rightarrow [\int:]$: проні́сши having carried along

$[z] + [\int] \rightarrow [ʒ\int]$: підві́зши having given a lift

$[z] + [ʒ] \rightarrow [ʒ:]$: безжу́рний carefree

$[z] + [\widehat{t\int}] \rightarrow [ʒ\widehat{t\int}]$: безче́сний dishonest

$[z] + [\widehat{dʒ}] \rightarrow [ʒ\widehat{dʒ}]$: з джа́зу (lit.) from jazz

$[\int] + [s] \rightarrow [s^j:]$: сміє́шся you laugh

$[\int] + [\widehat{ts}] \rightarrow [s^j\widehat{ts^j}]$: у пля́шці in a bottle

$[ʒ] + [\widehat{ts}] \rightarrow [z^j\widehat{ts^j}]$: у ло́жці in a spoon

$[\widehat{t\int}] + [\widehat{ts}] \rightarrow [\widehat{ts^j}:]$: у нетерпля́чці in impatience

$[d] + [ʒ]/[\widehat{t\int}]/[\int] \rightarrow [\widehat{dʒ}]$: відшкодува́ти to make good damage, відчепи́ти to unhook, віджи́влювати to revive

$[d] + [z]/[\widehat{ts}]/[s] \rightarrow [\widehat{dz}]$: підзе́мний underground, підско́чити to jump up, відцідити to strain off

$[t] + [s] \rightarrow [\widehat{ts}]$: бага́тство riches

$[t] + [\int] \rightarrow [t\int\int]$: коро́тшати to become shortened

$[t] + [t\int] \rightarrow [t\int:]$: вітчи́зна fatherland

1.1.12   CONSONANT GROUPS: SIMPLIFICATION

In a group of three consonants the middle one will generally fall out, even in the spelling. There will also be simplification in larger groups. Thus:

вість – ві́сник	news – messenger
ко́ристь – кори́сний	profit/advantage – useful
честь – че́сний	honour – honest
пе́рстень – пе́рсня	ring (N. – G.)
при́страсть – при́страсний	passion – passionate
о́бласть – обласни́й	province/district (noun – adj.)
ра́дість – ра́дісний	joy – joyful
ща́стя – щасли́вий	luck/happiness – lucky/happy
ко́ристь – кори́сли́вий	profit/advantage – covetous
стели́ти – сла́ти	to make a bed, spread
ти́ждень – ти́жня – тижне́вий	week (N.*sg.* – G.*sg.* – adj.)
ви́їзд – виїзни́й	departure – departing/on the point of departure

проїзд – проїзний	passage – ticket (= adjectives with the root -їзд-)
брязк – бря́знути	loud metallic sound – to fall noisily/metallically
блиск – бли́снути	splendour/light – flash
бри́зка – бри́знути	splash – to splash
плюск – плю́снути	splashing – to splash
писк – пи́снути	squealing – to squeal
тиск – ти́снути	press/throng – to press/squeeze
тріск – трі́снути	cracking sound – to crack/split
ма́сло – масни́й	butter – fat/greasy
мисль – уми́сний	thought/idea – intentional
ремесло́ – ремісни́к	trade – tradesman

And note:

се́рце – серде́ць	heart (N.*sg.* – G.*pl.*)
ченця́ – черне́ць	monk (G.*sg.* – N.*sg.*)

In the following words the letter т is written but not pronounced:

шістна́дцять sixteen   **шістдеся́т** sixty
шістсо́т six hundred

This also happens in foreign words expanded by -ськ-, -ств- (the т is kept in the spelling, but not pronounced):

студе́нтський student (adj.)
студе́нтство students
аге́нтство agency

There are also foreign words where the т is pronounced, though rather feebly, for example,

аванпо́стний outpost (adj.)   **компо́стний** compost (adj.)
контра́стний contrast(ing) (adj.)   **форпо́стний** advance post (adj.)

In such words there may be variation in spelling.

And there are a few native words where т, к are both written and pronounced, for example,

зап'я́стний wrist (adj.)   **кістля́вий** bony
пестли́вий soft, delicate   **хвастли́вий** boastful
то́скно sadly   **скна́ра** miser
випускни́й issue (adj.) (and other adjectives in -пуск-)
бре́зкнути to become flabby

Thus we note that groups of three or more consonants are usually simplified by the deletion of one of them, usually internal to the group; the deletion is often reflected in the spelling, but it may lead to a change not reflected in the spelling:

жди – жн:	ти́ждень – ти́жня week
зди – зн:	проі́зд – проі́зний passage – ticket
стн – сн:	при́страсть – при́страсний passion – passionate
стл – сл:	стели́ти – сла́ти to make up a bed
скн – сн:	тиск – ти́снути pressure – to squeeze
зкн – зн:	бри́зка – бри́знути splash – to splash
нт + ськ → [nʲsʲk]:	студе́нтський of students
ст + ськ → [sʲk]:	тури́стський of tourists
нт + ст → [nst]:	аге́нтство agency
ст + ц → [sʲt͡sʲ]:	солі́стці soloist (D.L.*sg.*)
ст + д → [zd]:	шістдеся́т sixty
ст + → [s:]:	шістсо́т six hundred

In some words there is no simplification:

кістля́вий bony	пестли́вий tender, delicate
хвастли́вий boastful	випускни́й of something that comes out
рискну́ти to take a risk	

1.1.13 GEMINATION AND LENGTHENING OF CONSONANTS

These are found exclusively between vowels:

подру́жжя wedlock, marriage	новосі́лля house-warming
обли́ччя face	ті́нню shadow (I.*sg.*)

Compare:

ща́стя happiness, luck   ра́дістю joy (I.*sg.*)

Note the pronunciation (and spelling) of the present tense of ли́ти (also derivatives):

ллю, ллєш, лле, ллємо́, ллєте́, ллють

It should be borne in mind that the following consonants never lengthen, but remain combined with [j]: [b], [p], [β], [m], [f], [r], namely the labials and [r]:

з любо́в'ю with love	ве́рф'ю dockyard (I.*sg.*)
пі́р'я feather(s)	сім'я́ family

Lengthening is conveyed in the spelling by doubling or gemination. This occurs on morpheme boundaries:

prefix + root:	**беззу́бий** toothless, **відди́чити** to recompense, **роззу́тий** barefooted
two prefixes:	**возз'єдна́ти** to reunite
root/stem + suffix	
(most often adjectives):	**докорі́нно** fundamentally, **непи́сьме́нний** illiterate, **щоде́нний** everyday, daily
root/stem + postfix **-ся** (in verbs):	**ні́сся** rushed
compound	
(including truncated) words:	**міськкко́м** city committee (but the lengthening is not present in the pronunciation)

And there is lengthening of $[t, z, s, \widehat{ts}, l, n, ʒ, \widehat{tʃ}, ʃ]$ between two vowels:

життя́ life	**знання́** knowledge
гілля́ branches	**коло́сся** ears (of corn)
роздорі́жжя crossroad	**десятирі́ччя** period of ten years
ті́нню shadow (I.*sg.*)	**рілле́ю** ploughed field (I.*sg.*)
воста́ннє for the last time	

Namely:

(i)   Before **я** and other case endings, but not the genitive plural (because of the nature of the ending), in very many neuter nouns, for example:

   зна́чення meaning (G.*pl.* **зна́чень**)

(ii)   Before **я** in some masculine and feminine nouns (and all the case endings in -**і**, -**е**, -**ю**, -**я**, but not genitive plural -**ей**), for example:

   стаття́ article, **суддя́** judge

(iii)   Before -**ю** in the instrumental singular of feminines whose nominative singular ends in a soft sign or a husher, for example:

мить – **ми́ттю** sudden moment	**сіль** – **сі́ллю** salt
вісь – **ві́ссю** axle	**річ** – **рі́ччю** thing

(iv)   In forms of the verb **лити**: **ллю**, and so on.

(v)   In a few adverbs, for example:

   спросо́ння while asleep

(vi)   In the reinforcing and (im)possibility adjectival suffixes -**енн**-, -**анн**-, -**янн**-, for example:

здорове́нний very robust/healthy	**нездійсне́нний** unrealizable
незрівня́нний incomparable	

(vii)   A few Church Slavonic words, for example:

свяще́нний holy	**благослове́нний** blessed

1.2 A FEW NOTES ON PROBLEM AREAS IN SPELLING

1.2.1 o AND e AFTER HUSHERS AND [j]

Both are possible in Ukrainian. One tends to find **e** before a soft or historic-ally soft consonant, and **o** before a historically hard consonant or before a syllable with [a, ɔ, u, ɪ]:

жени́тися – жона́тий	to marry – married (of a man)
че́тверо – чоти́ри	four
копі́єчка – копійо́к	copeck (N.*sg.* of dim. – G.*pl.* of non-dim.)

книжо́к of the books	**до́чок** of the daughters
бджола́ bee	**пшоно́** millet
чого́ of what	**щока́** cheek
його́ him, it	**знайо́мий** friend, acquaintance

However, analogy may intervene:

на ве́чорі – ве́чора/ве́чору	evening (**ве́чір**)
сві́жості – мо́лодості	freshness – youth
пи́шемо – пи́шете	write
пе́чений/спе́чено – зро́блений/зро́блено	baked – done

Note: **грошови́й** 'money' (adjective), **бойови́й** 'fighting'

The vowel **e** is retained in the suffixes **-ечк-**, **-енк(о)** and certain others, and also in ancient bookish and borrowed words:

до́щечка small board	**Шевче́нко** (family name)
пече́ра cave	**же́ртва** victim
шеф chief	**чемпіо́н** champion

Other spellings are established by convention or tradition:

черво́ний red	**чека́ти** to wait
шепоті́ти to whisper	**ще́дрий** generous

Note particularly the convention of **e** in nominal endings, but **o** in pro-nominal and adjectival ones:

ста́нцією – на́шою – коли́шньою station – our – erstwhile/former (I.*sg.* f.)

1.2.2 VELARS PLUS [ɪ, i]

[i] occurs, both in the orthography and pronunciation, after velars in Ukrain-ian in instances of alternation with [ɔ, ɛ] (here the velar is pronounced either soft or hard) and in the nominative-accusative plural of adjectives and pro-nouns. Thus:

кінь horse	гірка hillock
глухíм deaf/dull/thick (L.*sg.* m./n.)	такíй such (D.L.*sg.* f.)
недолýгі weak (N.A.*pl.*)	легкí light, easy (N.A.*pl.*)
глухí deaf (N.A.*pl.*)	всякí every (N.A.*pl.*)

[ɪ] occurs in the genitive singular and nominative-accusative plural of first-declension nouns, the nominative-accusative plural of second-declension nouns, and the nominative-accusative singular masculine of adjectives and pronouns and the oblique cases of the plural of adjectives and pronouns:

рукú of the hand	ногú of the leg
свекрухú mothers-in-law	рýки hands
нóги legs	свекрýхи of the mother-in-law
берегú banks, shores	чоловікú husbands
кожухú sheepskin coats	
недолýгий weak	всякий every
глухúй deaf	
недолýгих weak	легкúми light
глухúми deaf	всякими every

1.2.3 THE ALTERNATIONS [u – w – v/β], [i – j] IN SPELLING

We find these alternations both at the beginning of a certain number of words and in the corresponding conjunction and preposition. Thus:

вчúтель – учúтель teacher	ітú – йти to go/walk
він і вонá he and she	вонá й онýка she and (her) granddaughter
сів у крíсло sat in the chair	сíла в автóбус got on the bus

The vowels [i, u] are both pronounced and noted in the orthography by the appropriate letters, in principle, at the beginning of a phrase before consonants (**у Кúєві** 'in Kyiv'), after a word ending in a consonant (**Івáн і Оксáна** 'Ivan and Oksana'), or between words, one of which ends, and the other begins, in a consonant (**Він у кýхні** 'He's in the kitchen'). Otherwise we have [j, w, v/β]. Note that Ukrainian **у/в** are one preposition (thus uniting the two original prepositions). Ukrainian **в, й** convey consonants and asyllabic vowels which occur between a vowel and a consonant at word juncture and after a vowel at the end of a word.

1.2.4 FOREIGN WORDS

In most instances the meanings of the following words are clear.

Many older loanwords are completely assimilated, and are unlikely to be recognized as borrowings:

борщ beetroot soup   пала́ц palace
цибу́ля onion

But quite a few words remain clearly foreign:

Words with [f]: **фо́то, фе́єрве́рк, фо́рма**
Words beginning with [a, ɛ]: **арти́ст, ескімо́с, ампермéтр, архітéктор**
Words with the foreign **уа, іа: будуа́р, павіа́н, діало́г, діа́метр**
Words with unusual consonantal groups: **ма́йстер, консéнсус, інстру́кція, абстра́ктний, конста́нта**

Many foreign words assimilate to Ukrainian consonantal (less frequently vocalic) alternations:

еле́ктрик electrician – електри́чний
специ́фіка – специфі́чний
Пари́ж – пари́зький
Лéйпциг – лéйпцизький

And there are indeclinables (see **2.1.3.3** on foreign words and **2.3.4** specifically on indeclinables):

таксі́   жабо́
кенгуру́

Regarding the pronunciation of foreign words, we should note:

[l]: may be hard or soft before [a, ɔ, u]:

бала́нс, со́ло   пляж, алюмі́ній

but hard before [ɛ]:

лéкція   еле́ктрик
елемéнт   елéгія
елега́нтний

[h, g]: traditionally = **г** [g] (though in proper names the orthography permits **ґ**):

гра́фік   геоло́гія
гекта́р   гектолі́тр
герба́рій   горизо́нт
Гельсінгфо́рс   Гава́на

In a few English words we have **x**:

хавбéк   хокéй
хол

[f, θ] are usually conveyed in Ukrainian by [f]:

фо́рма	катастро́фа
фі́зика	орфогра́фія

Foreign double consonants are not usually retained (certainly not in pronunciation):

баро́ко	беладо́на
браві́симо	грип
клас	інтерме́цо
кому́на	су́ма
шасі́	

But in certain situations a double consonant is possible, even in the pronunciation:

(i)   On the morpheme boundary:

імміґра́ція	апперце́пція
сюрреалі́зм	

(ii)   In a few words, for example:

мі́рра	бру́тто
ва́нна	ма́нна
не́тто	пе́нні
то́нна	бі́лль
бу́лла	ві́лла

(iii) In proper names:

Андо́рра	Голла́ндія
Маро́кко	Ні́цца

The apostrophe is very widely used, to convey, for example, the separate pronunciation of [j]:

(i)   Before я, ю, є, ї after б, п, в, м, ф and г, к, х, ж, ч, ш:

комп'ю́тер	кар'є́ра
п'єдеста́л	

(ii)   After an original prefix ending in a consonant:

ад'юта́нт	ін'є́кція
кон'юнкту́ра	

French words with the vowels conveyed by я, ю are an exception here:

бюро́	пюре́
кюве́т	рюкза́к

The consonants here are soft.

Softness may be conveyed by the soft sign. If there is no [j], then the soft sign is not written (but the softness remains):

конферансьє́	ательє́
марсельє́за	мілья́рд
бульйо́н	медальйо́н
каньйо́н	віньє́тка
нюа́нс	ілю́зія
мадя́р	

For **и** and **і** the 'rule of nine' often applies, namely **и** usually after д, т, з, с, ц, ж, ч, ш, р:

ди́спут	ти́тул
зигза́г	симфо́нія
цикло́н	жира́ф
речитати́в	ши́на
ринг	

This does not extend to foreign proper names, where **і** may be written after all consonants:

Грі́г	Ші́ллер
Чика́го	Ді́ккенс
Ле́йпциг	

But:

Рим	Брита́нія
Атла́нтика	А́рктика
Кита́й	Париж
Рига	

The letter **і** is written (i) after consonants other than the nine:

гіпс	лінгві́стика
ні́кель	пірамі́да

(ii)   At the beginning of words:

інтерва́л	ізю́м

(iii)   Before vowel letters and **й**:

діале́кт	революці́йні

(iv)   At the end of indeclinable words:

парі́	жюрі́

2 THE NOUN

2.0 GENERAL REMARKS

In this chapter we describe the characteristics of the Ukrainian noun: gender, number, and case; these are followed by an overview of the syntactic properties of the noun (such as case government, occurrence with prepositions), and a presentation of the most productive processes of nominal word formation.

2.1 GENDER

All Ukrainian nouns have gender: that is, they are identified as either 'masculine', 'feminine', or 'neuter', as is the case in German, Russian, Latin, Greek, *et al.* Some nouns will be 'masculine' or 'feminine' because they refer to male or female biological entities (such as **дочка́** 'daughter'); this phenomenon is termed 'natural gender'. A small number can refer to males or to females while being grammatically 'feminine'; compare **дити́на** 'child', **люди́на** 'person'. The vast majority of nouns have 'grammatical gender', as they are marked for gender without a biological basis; thus, for example, **стіл** 'table', is masculine but does not represent a male being. All nouns carry a 'gender marker'; it is the last sound (not necessarily letter) of a word in the nominative case (the 'dictionary' or 'citation form') that will generally indicate to which grammatical gender it is assigned. Some of these markers are unambiguous, such that the gender of the noun in question is immediately clear, while others can signal two possible genders; in the latter instance, semantic clues (if a person is being represented) or particular suffixes can give hints as to which gender is involved (as a rule one gender per suffix).

The gender of a significant number of nouns borrowed from non-Slavonic languages can be opaque: as a rule, those ending in a consonant are masculine, while those in -a are feminine; all others, especially those involving final vowels other than -a, vary from instance to instance. All of the possible patterns of gender distribution, including borrowings, are outlined in the following sections.

2.1.1   NOUNS ENDING IN A CONSONANT

2.1.1.1   Hard consonants, almost all masculine

All nouns ending in a consonant are declinable, including words of foreign origin. Thus:

буди́нок	building
кия́нин	Kievan (male person)
курс	course, year (at university)
робітни́к	worker (male)
син	son
стіл	table
студе́нт	student (male)
това́риш	comrade

A number of nouns ending in a hard consonant, most of which refer to people and are ultimately borrowings from other European languages, may be described as 'common gender' (**спі́льного ро́ду**): in other words, although they may be grammatically masculine, they will refer to both sexes in practice. In such instances, an accompanying form that reflects the gender of the noun, for example, a past tense verb form, will reflect the true gender of the individual:

Президе́нт був/була́ . . .	The president was . . . (masculine or feminine depending on the individual)
Прем'є́р-міні́стр прибу́в/ прибула́.	The prime minister arrived.

Other words of this kind:

адвока́т	lawyer, barrister, attorney
депута́т	deputy (e.g. member of parliament or a political congress)
диплома́т	diplomat
етно́граф	ethnographer
інжене́р	engineer
кандида́т	candidate
капіта́н	captain (military)
лі́кар	doctor (of medicine)
посо́л	ambassador
профе́сор	professor
член	member (of an organization)
юри́ст	lawyer, jurist

A large number of consonant-final nouns referring to people, whether in relation to their profession or their place of origin, are as a rule only masculine: this is a function of the presence of one of a number of suffixes, for which feminine equivalents also exist (see **2.5** on suffixal word formation). Thus, for example, **киян-ин, робіт-ник, регот-ун** ('one who laughs'), and so on, are masculine by virtue of the presence of the suffixes **-ин, -ник, -ун**. When faced with a compound title, like **інженер-будівельник**, lit. 'engineer-builder', the former element – which can refer to either gender – takes precedence; the new compound can refer to men and women, while **будівельник** on its own is less likely to do so. This rule of thumb is broken in very specific circumstances, notably when professional ranks or positions are involved; thus, **науковий співробітник** 'a scientific collaborator', can refer to male or female persons, although **співробітник** on its own will tend to be masculine. We shall mention these suffixes only in passing for the moment, only as they relate to or indicate gender; they are described in a comprehensive manner in **2.5** ('word formation').

2.1.1.2 *Forms in a final hard labial (б, п, в, м, ф) or ш, ч, щ, ж (all hard) can be masculine or feminine*

In the course of the development of the Ukrainian sound system, final labial consonants and **ш, ч, щ, ж** hardened: for example, at an early stage in the language 'blood' was written **кровь**, but [vʲ] hardened to [v], and, as a result, the soft sign **ь** was no longer written at the end of the word. This might suggest that **кровь** is masculine, as there are also masculine nouns with final labials and **ш**, and so on, and the feminine nouns must be learnt as they are encountered; the best way to assimilate such words as 'feminines' is to learn them together with their G.*sg.* form (see **2.3.1.4**). The following are examples of such forms:

кров	blood
ніч	night
подорож	journey
річ	thing, object

Compare the following masculines:

викладач	lecturer
ніж	knife
плач	weeping, lamenting
плащ	overcoat
рукав	sleeve

There are, naturally, occasionally suffixal hints that indicate that a given form is masculine, for example, **-ач**, which expresses 'a male doer of X', or **-(т)ив**, found in numerous borrowings (**детектив** 'detective', **примітив** 'primitive (painting)'); more on these elements is to be found in **2.5**.

2.1.1.3   Soft consonants can be masculine or feminine

Two extremely common suffixes referring to human beings express the 'male-ness' of the person (and therefore of the noun) in question: **-ець**, often associating a person with a place, and **-тель** occurring with verbal roots to express 'a male doer of X' (compare **-ач** above):

англíєць	Englishman
мрéць	corpse, dead body
полтáвець	man from Poltava (but also **полтавчáнин**)
украíнець	Ukrainian
хлóпець	boy
читéць	one who reads out loud (neutral: **читáч**)
вчúтель	teacher
мислúтель	thinker, etc.
просúтель	petitioner (but also: **прохáч**)

Other nouns, including some very common ones, are not so marked and must be learnt as they are encountered (again, learning the G.*sg.* will assist in the process); those that are very common, such as the second example below, are used in many everyday expressions, and will thus be assimilated without great difficulty. The following are all masculine:

біль	ache, pain
день	day (**дóбрий день, добрúдень** hello, good day)
гість	guest
квíтень	April
кінь	horse
мíсяць	month, moon
нíкель	nickel (the metal)
ýчень	pupil

Feminine nouns ending in a soft consonant fall into the same two categor-ies: with and without specific identifying suffixes. The most common suffix that occurs is **-ість**, one that most often occurs with abstract nouns, very much like English *-ness* or *-tion*; such nouns will have an identifiable root to which the suffix is appended (compare the masculine example **гість** above, which does not have an identifiable root if one takes away the element **-ість**: **-ість** is not a suffix in this example):

мóлодість	youth, youthfulness
паровидáтність	evaporation (scientific term)
самíтність/самóтність	loneliness
стáрість	old age
свíжість	freshness

All other feminines of this type (see **2.3.1.4**) must be learned individually; as in the case of the masculines, there are a few basic nouns that fall into this category, such that their acquisition and assimilation will be accomplished with little extra effort on the part of the learner:

Брета́нь	Brittany
дань	tribute (also: **дани́на**)
лінь	laziness
о́сінь	Autumn
смерть	death
суть	being; essence
сіль	salt
тінь	shadow, shade

2.1.1.4   Personal names ending in a consonant

All but an extremely small number of personal names ending in a consonant, whether hard or soft, are masculine and refer to male beings:

Гео́ргій
І́гор
Іва́н
Васи́ль

Exceptions are few, for example, **Есфі́р** 'Esther', and are of foreign origin; a few are no longer used or are considered archaic and rare, such as **Юді́ф** 'Judith'.

2.1.2   NOUNS ENDING IN A VOWEL: -а/-я

2.1.2.1   The marker -a/-я is essentially feminine

Most non-abstract nouns with the final vowels -**a** or -**я** are feminine, and many of these will be naturally feminine:

вівча́рка	shepherdess
дочка́	daughter
до́шка	board, plank
ді́вчина	girl
жі́нка	woman, wife
земля́	land
карто́пля	potato; potatoes (collective)
маши́на	car, machine
нога́	foot, leg
рука́	hand, arm
сестра́	sister
сторона́	side

| студе́нтка | female student |
| цибу́ля | onion |

Some of the above-mentioned are marked as feminines by the presence of the suffix -ка; this is commonly found in feminines corresponding to the masculine -ин and -ець, for example, кия́нка, украї́нка, and others (compare the masculines above). Similarly, the suffix -ниця signals a feminine noun, and is the feminine element corresponding to masculine -ник:

| письме́нниця | authoress (cf. письме́нник) |
| робітни́ця | worker (female) |

Compare also the expressive suffix -уха, which can correspond to masculine -ун: реготу́ха 'merry person', 'one who laughs', masc. товсту́н 'fat (male) person', fem. товсту́ха 'fat (female) person'.

2.1.2.2 Common gender words ending in -а/-я

In addition to the words of 'common gender' ending in a consonant (see above), there is also a group of nouns in -а/-я that can be so described; a very few of these nouns can be based upon borrowings from other languages, but tend in the main to be native constructions:

замазу́ра	slovenly person
калі́ка	disabled person
коле́га	colleague
крути́голова	meddling, persistent person
листоно́ша	post(man)
невда́ха	failure
просторі́ка	garrulous, talkative person
п'яни́ця	drunkard
слуга́	servant
сірома́ха	poor, wretched person (also: сіро́ма)
тихо́ня	quiet person

Many nouns of this kind, especially those containing the suffixes -ха, -уха, are of an expressive nature (see **2.5** for a detailed inventory of suffixes); as language is constantly changing, so will this element of the vocabulary: it is productive and dependent on the spoken language. As such, this part of the vocabulary is open to constant expansion, change, and reassignment: one example that might be mentioned here is всезна́йка 'know-it-all', which is cited in one very recent source as a common gender noun in -а (HUM 1993). In two older sources, however, it is given as всезна́йко/усезна́йко (SUM and UAS), in addition to which it is identified as 'masculine', not 'common gender' or 'masculine/feminine' as one might expect; both forms are currently acceptable. Less expressive nouns, such as коле́га and слуга́, are less likely to experience such shifts; the reader is advised to consult the most up-to-date dictionaries where there is any doubt.

As in the case of consonant-final common gender nouns, context (a verb or other element that is required to show gender) will tell the reader which of the genders, masculine or feminine, is being expressed in any given instance.

2.1.2.3   Neuters in -а/-я

A very large body of neuter nouns is marked by the final marker -я. This set of nouns is not at all difficult to identify and set apart from those femi nines or nouns of common gender that have the very same ending: the neuter nouns, with only a very few exceptions, have a doubled consonant preceding -я (in other words, if one sees a noun with final -CCя, where C = consonant, then its gender is neuter). These nouns have all resulted from processes of derivation which are described in **2.5.1**. Compare:

весі́лля	wedding
життя́	life
лівобере́жжя	the area of Ukraine extending from the left bank of the Dniepr (**Дніпро́**) to the Caspian Sea (**Каспі́йське мо́ре**)
моделюва́ння	modelling
пита́ння	question
почуття́	feeling
покриття́	covering
полі́сся	low-lying forest region (and name of a region of Ukraine)
чита́ння	reading

The set of examples of this type of neuter noun could be extended for many pages, but it is important at this stage merely to note the pattern, which is extremely straightforward. The exceptions to the structural CCя rule are: those nouns in which -я is preceded by labial consonants (**в, б, м, п, ф**) and by **p**; these consonants resisted lengthening (represented in writing, as above, by doubled letters). Such nouns are also easy to identify, however, as they appear graphically as C'я:

здоро́в'я	health
подвір'я	courtyard, yard
правосла́в'я	Orthodoxy

Compare **ща́стя** 'happiness', in which the cluster -ст- also resists lengthening.

One special subgroup of nouns is not so easily identified purely by orthographic means, but can be recognized as neuters on semantic grounds: these are nouns that refer to the young of animals – including human beings:

дитинча́	infant (but дити́на is feminine)
гусеня́	gosling, young goose
каченя́	duckling
лисеня́	young fox
лоша́	colt
маля́	small child
порося́	piglet, suckling pig
теля́	calf
ведмежа́	bear cub

In addition to their meaning, another hint is offered by the place of stress: all of the above forms are stressed on the final -á or я́.

2.1.2.4   Personal names ending in -a/-я

The vast majority of personal names – first, patronymic, family – ending in -a or -я are feminine. There are two sets of names that look feminine but are in reality masculine, however. The first consists of masculine (non-diminutive) first names; three of the most common names for males are:

Оле́кса	Oleksa
Мико́ла	Mykola
Мики́та	Mykyta

When referring to people bearing these names, masculine forms will be used (pronouns, adjectives, verbs). The second consists of diminutive forms of otherwise clearly masculine names:

Васи́ль – Ва́ся	Basil – Basil (dim.)
Гео́ргій – Жо́ра	George – George (dim.)
Євге́н – Же́ня	Eugene – Gene

Many other masculine diminutives exist, many of which will end in -o (see below) or a consonant.

2.1.2.5   Indeclinable nouns ending in -a

The vast majority of nouns ending in -a (see above) are declinable. The few indeclinable forms encountered are borrowings from French:

амплуа́ (neuter)	repertoire of roles (theatrical term)
па-де-труа́ (masculine)	pas de trois (ballet term)

2.1.3   NOUNS ENDING IN A VOWEL: -o/-e

2.1.3.1   Most nouns in -o/-e are neuter

As a rule, all nouns whose final vowel is -o or -e are neuter; the exceptions to this rule are foreign borrowings, which may or may not be neuter. The following is a representative list of regular neuter nouns:

вікно́	window
колі́но	knee
мі́сце	place
мі́сто	city
пе́чиво	baking, pastry
плече́	shoulder (Note particularly that this is neuter in SUM but masculine in the older UAS.)
по́ле	field
пра́во	law
ра́бство	slavery
сло́во	word
тепло́	warmth
я́вище	phenomenon

2.1.3.2   Non-neuter native Ukrainian nouns ending in -o/-e

A significant number of non-neuter nouns is found with final -o, more rarely with -e. Among the former are counted some very common masculine words denoting people, including proper names and many diminutive forms:

ба́тько	father
ба́течко	father (dim.)
ба́тенько	father (dim.)
дя́дько	uncle
дя́дечко	uncle (dim.)
Валько́	Валенти́н (dim.)
Ванько́	Іва́н (dim.)
Васько́	Васи́ль (dim.)
Васи́лько	Васи́ль (dim.)
Дани́ло	Daniel
Дмитро́	Dimitri
Павло́	Paul
Петро́	Peter
Самі́йло	Samuel
Са́нько	Олекса́ндр (dim.)

A number of expressive nouns, primarily used in colloquial speech, can be either masculine or feminine, depending on the referent; some sources (such as UAS) may identify some of the following as 'masculine' only, but in practice both genders can be indicated:

базíкало	babbler
вайлó	sluggard, lazybones
ледáщо	lazy person, layabout
мурлó	coarse, rude person
убóїще	stubborn person

Some derivatives referring to animate beings, on the other hand, can be neuter and masculine, or neuter and feminine:

хлопчúсько	boy, big boy (masculine and neuter)
бáбище	big (old) woman (feminine and neuter)

Compare the following derivatives, which are considered to be neuter only:

дівчúсько	big (hefty) little girl
рибúсько	big fish

2.1.3.3 Borrowings ending in -o/-e

Foreign borrowings ending in -o/-e are readily recognizable as non-Ukrainian and do not decline (see 2.3.4 below); as a general rule, nouns denoting objects will be neuter, while those denoting people will be common gender (masculine or feminine). See 2.1.4 on feminine-only substantives.

Neuters:

кашнé	scarf, muffler
пюрé	purée
сабó	shoes with wooden soles (France, Belgium)
сотé	sautée
фрикасé	fricassée

Masculines (denoting animals):

дúнго	dingo
фламíнго	flamingo
шимпанзé	chimpanzee

Common gender:

протежé	protégé
інкóгніто	incognito
рантьé	*rentier*, one living on a private income
конферансьé	commentator

2.1.4   NOUNS ENDING IN VOWELS OTHER THAN -o/-e

The number of nouns in Ukrainian that end in vowels other than -a (-я), -o, -e (in other words, -i and -y/-ю) are few indeed; these are all borrowings from other languages and indeclinable. The assignment of gender to such words follows the general guidelines described in **2.1.3.3**, for example:

Neuter:

інтерв'ю́	interview
попурі́	potpourri
рев'ю́	revue, review
са́рі	sari

Masculine (animals):

зе́бу	zebu
какаду́	cockatoo
колі́брі	hummingbird
по́ні	pony

Common gender:

ре́фері	referee
парвеню́	parvenu(e)
ко́мі	Komi (a Finno-Ugric people in Russia)
саа́мі	'Saami' (also known as Lapp(s))

Many words referring to real-specific phenomena, such as forces of nature not occurring in Ukraine, may be assigned to the gender of the nouns which describe those phenomena. Thus, for example, specific kinds of wind will be masculine because **ві́тер** 'wind' is masculine (for example, **па́мперо, сола́но, сиро́ко, торна́до**). The same is true of language names that do not fit the Ukrainian adjectival pattern; thus, **аймара́, бенга́лі, на́вахо, пу́шту, у́рду, гі́нді, гуджара́ні, саа́мі** (the language, not the people), **і́диш, еспера́нто,** can all occur as feminines because they are classified as a **мо́ва** 'language'. Where there is ambiguity or uncertainty such words will be used together with the classifier **мо́ва**, thereby clarifying the gender problem. The same is true of many geographic names, which are provided with an unambiguous Ukrainian noun, such as **ріка́ Міссу́рі, о́зеро Тітіка́ка, ато́л Бікі́ні, гора́ Кіліманджа́ро,** *et al.*

Very few nouns are assimilated as feminines only; the following are identified as such on the basis of a feminine Ukrainian qualifying noun:

авеню́	avenue (feminine as Ukr. **ву́лиця** 'street' is understood)
штра́се	street (see the preceding entry)

| закýска-антрé | snack, bite to eat (here the Ukrainian noun is present in initial position) |

2.2   NUMBER

The vast majority of Ukrainian nouns have 'number'; that is, their endings reflect 'singularity' or 'plurality'. In this respect, Ukrainian is like all European languages, from English to French, Polish and Russian to Finnish: 'table' (singular), 'tables' (plural). The exceptions to this pattern are those words of foreign origin which, for reasons outlined in **2.3**, are indeclinable; as they cannot take part in the Ukrainian declensional system, they cannot reflect number either. In such nouns it is context alone (an accompanying adjective or verb form) that will indicate whether the given form represents just one or more than one item. Markers of number, singular *vs.* plural, are described for each noun type in **2.3**, in the context of the declensional system as a whole.

2.3   THE CASES: BASIC MEANINGS

The noun, adjective, pronoun, and numeral are declined in Ukrainian, as they are in German, Latin, Russian, and many other languages; this means that they have case endings which show the function of a particular word in a sentence (for example, as subject, object, and so on). The only nouns that will not decline are those listed in **2.1.3.3** and **2.1.4**. The basic meanings of the seven cases, listed below in English and Ukrainian ('case' відмíнок), are as follows:

nominative – **називнúй**	The case of the subject ('*I* read a book').
accusative – **знахíдний**	The case of the direct object ('I read *a book*'; 'I saw *him*').
genitive – **родовúй**	The case of possession ('the beginning *of the day*'; '*Ivan's* book').
dative – **давáльний**	The case of the indirect object ('I sent the letter *to Natasha*').
locative – **мíсцéвий**	The case of location or 'place where' ('He lives *in Kiev*').
instrumental – **орýдний**	The case of instrument or accompaniment ('*with* Ivan', '*by means of X*').
vocative – **клúчний**	The case used in addressing someone ('*Ivan!*' will have an ending here)

Note that in some grammars the locative is termed the prepositional, as it is only used in conjunction with a preposition (compare Russian *предло́жный падéж* 'prepositional case'); as the Ukrainian name for this case does in fact mean locative (**мíсце** 'place', 'location'), we have chosen to retain the corresponding term in English. The use of the cases is described in **2.4.1** below.

2.3.0   DECLENSION: INTRODUCTION

All Ukrainian noun paradigms are ordered here according to grammatical gender, as all Ukrainian nouns are either masculine, feminine, or neuter (compare the same phenomenon in German, Russian, and Latin). Each gender is subdivided into groups of paradigms whose major phonological features bind them together: (1) the palatalization or non-palatalization of stem-final consonants, and (2) stress patterns within each paradigm. Stress patterns are described as follows:

SS: 'stem stress' in the singular and the plural.

SE: 'stem stress' in the singular, and 'end stress' in the plural.

EE: 'end stress' in the singular and plural.

ES: 'end stress' in the singular and 'stem stress' in the plural.

+:   The addition of a '+' mark after either element (e.g. E + S, SE +) indicates that there is a stress shift of some kind within that part of the paradigm in addition to the basic 'end stress' or 'stem stress' pattern.

The stress patterns provided do not include phenomena that occur in certain well-defined contexts, such as when used with other parts of speech: thus, for example, when used with numerals (specifically with two, three, and four), there are rules that govern the place of stress in a given noun. This information is found in the discussion of the use of numerals.

For every declensional type we provide first the endings themselves, followed by examples; the markers of gender are described in each pertinent section below. Note that the abbreviations for English case names are given on the left, with their Ukrainian equivalents on the right. The ordering of case forms (N.–G.–D.–A.–I.–L.–V. where there is a special vocative form, N.–G.–D.–A.–I.–L. when there is not) conforms to the ordering found in Ukrainian (and most Western) books. Note particularly that there is no separate vocative ending in the plural, thus V.*pl.* = N.*pl.*

2.3.1   DECLENSION OF FEMININE NOUNS

Feminine nouns can end either in a vowel (**-a**), or in a consonant; these two major types are further subdivided according to the 'soft' or 'hard' nature of the final consonant, whether it is alone in final position or preceding final -**a** (on hard and soft consonants, see **1.1.6**).

2.3.1.1   Feminine declensions ending in a vowel (-a): hard stems

		Singular	Plural	
N.		-a	-и	Н.
G.		-и	-Ø	Р.
D.		-і	-ам	Д.
A.		-у	-и	З.
I.		-ою	-ами	О.
L.		-і	-ах	М.
V.		-о	= N.	Кл.

This stem-type is so termed because the consonant preceding the final -**a** of the nominative is hard; note that '-ø' means 'zero ending', or 'no vowel following the stem-final consonant'. The following examples reflect different stress patterns within the hard stem paradigm, beginning with the common E + S type.

STRESS E + S: **водá** 'WATER'

	Singular – *Однина*	Plural – *Множина*	
N.	водá	вóди	Н.
G.	водѝ	вод	Р.
D.	водí	вóдам	Д.
A.	вóду	вóди	З.
I.	водóю	вóдами	О.
L.	водí	вóдах	М.
V.	вóдо!	= N.	Кл.

Like **водá** the following decline in the same way: **рукá** 'hand'/'arm', **ногá** 'foot'/'leg', **головá** 'head', **дочкá** 'daughter'. Note the special characteristics of this type of noun in Ukrainian: stress can shift in any paradigm, but will do so almost always when it is stressed on the final vowel (as in the case of **водá**) typically in the A. and V. singular, but throughout the plural individual nouns may vary, and exceptions are noted in dictionaries.

Now compare 'daughter', with the same stress pattern; note the consonant alternation in the D. and L. singular, as described in **1.1.9**:

	Singular – *Однина*	Plural – *Множина*	
N.	дочка́	до́чки	Н.
G.	дочки́	до́чок	Р.
D.	дочці́	до́чкам	Д.
A.	дочку́	до́чок	3.
I.	дочко́ю	до́чками	О.
L.	дочці́	до́чках	М.
V.	до́чко!	= N.	Кл.

Note that in **вода́**, the A *pl* is identical to the N *pl*; this is the case in all nouns denoting inanimate (non-living) beings. For animate beings, e.g. 'daughter' here, the A.*pl.* = G.*pl.* (this is also the case for masculine nouns; see **2.3.2**).

STRESS SE: **кни́жка** 'BOOK'

The stress pattern of the following paradigm must be noted: the basic form does not have final stress, but stress shifts in the plural (the opposite direction to what is found in **вода́** above).

	Singular – *Однина*	Plural – *Множина*	
N.	кни́жка	книжки́	Н.
G.	кни́жки	книжо́к	Р.
D.	кни́жці	книжка́м	Д.
A.	кни́жку	книжки́	3.
I.	кни́жкою	книжка́ми	О.
L.	кни́жці	книжка́х	М.
V.	кни́жко!	= N.	Кл.

Like **кни́жка** the following decline in the same way: **жі́нка** 'wife', **до́шка** 'board', 'plank'. There will be many words without stress shifting in the plural (see **брига́да** below); most of the latter will either be borrowings from a West European language (or at least based on Latin or Greek roots) or, very simply, they will be long words, the product of word-formational processes and often denoting abstract notions (in simplistic terms: the more syllables, the less the tendency to shift stress).

STRESS SS: **брига́да** 'BRIGADE'

Брига́да is an example of a feminine noun with no shifting stress whatsoever (stress is stable in this instance because it is a borrowing):

	Singular – Однина	*Plural – Множина*	
N.	брига́да	брига́ди	Н.
G.	брига́ди	брига́д	Р.
D.	брига́ді	брига́дам	Д.
A.	брига́ду	брига́ди	3.
I.	брига́дою	брига́дами	О.
L.	брига́ді	брига́дах	М.
V.	брига́до!	= N.	Кл.

2.3.1.2 *Feminine declensions ending in a vowel (-a): soft stems*

	Singular	*Plural*	
N.	-я	-і	Н.
G.	-і	-Ø (-ей)	Р.
D.	-і	-ям	Д.
A.	-ю	-і	3.
I.	-ею	-ями	О.
L.	-і	-ях	М.
V.	-е	= N.	Кл.

Stem-final consonants of the nouns of this declension are always soft. Below are four sample types, in which final -**a** is preceded by -l'-, -n'-, -j-, and finally by -c'- (**ць**). In comparison with the hard stems, there is less shifting of stress in this group of feminine nouns:

STRESS E + S: **земля́** 'EARTH/LAND'

	Singular – Однина	*Plural – Множина*	
N.	земля́	зе́млі	Н.
G.	землі́	земе́ль	Р.
D.	землі́	зе́млям	Д.
A.	зе́млю	зе́млі	3.
I.	землє́ю	зе́млями	О.
L.	землі́	зе́млях	М.
V.	зе́мле!	= N.	Кл.

To be noted are the V.*sg.*, in which we see the same retraction of stress as in the hard stems, and the stress pattern of the plural: the latter is identical to the pattern of **вода́**, except that there is a fleeting vowel in the G.*pl.* that attracts the stress away from the initial syllable (for more on fleeting vowels, refer to Chapter 1).

STRESS EE: **стаття́** 'ARTICLE'

	Singular – *Однина*	Plural – *Множина*	
N.	стаття́	статті́	Н.
G.	статті́	статей	Р.
D.	статті́	стаття́м	Д.
A.	статтю́	статті	З.
I.	статте́ю	стаття́ми	О.
L.	статті́	стаття́х	М.
V.	–	–	Кл.

The stability of stress in this example is governed by the phonological structure of the word, *viz.* -ССя́, where C = consonant.

STRESS SE: **пі́сня** 'SONG'

	Singular – *Однина*	Plural – *Множина*	
N.	пі́сня	пісні́	Н.
G.	пі́сні	пісе́нь	Р.
D.	пі́сні	пісня́м	Д.
A.	пі́сню	пісні́	З.
I.	пі́снею	пісня́ми	О.
L.	пі́сні	пісня́х	М.
V.	пі́сне!	= N.	Кл.

STRESS SS: **наді́я** 'HOPE'

	Singular – *Однина*	Plural – *Множина*	
N.	наді́я	наді́ї	Н.
G.	наді́ї	наді́й	Р.
D.	наді́ї	наді́ям	Д.
A.	наді́ю	наді́ї	З.
I.	наді́єю	наді́ями	О.
L.	наді́ї	наді́ях	М.
V.	наді́є!	= N.	Кл.

The following noun (**робітни́ця** 'female worker') is also stem-stressed throughout; it is an example of a form with soft -ц:

	Singular – *Однина*	Plural – *Множина*	
N.	робітни́ця	робітни́ці	Н.
G.	робітни́ці	робітни́ць	Р.
D.	робітни́ці	робітни́цям	Д.
A.	робітни́цю	робітни́ць	З.
I.	робітни́цею	робітни́цями	О.
L.	робітни́ці	робітни́цях	М.
V.	робітни́це!	= N.	Кл.

2.3.1.3   Feminine declensions ending in a vowel (-a): mixed stems

	Singular	Plural	
N.	-a	-i	Н.
G.	-i	-Ø	Р.
D.	-i	-ам	Д.
A.	-y	-i	З.
I.	-ею	-ами	О.
L.	-i	-ах	М.
V.	-e	= N.	Кл.

This nominal type is often termed 'mixed' because the paradigm is considered to be composed of case endings of the hard declension as well as of the soft declension. This is the result of the historical development of the consonant preceding the final vowel, which was originally soft, but now phonetically hard. Note that such consonants can be positionally softened by the ending -i, for example:

плóща 'square'

	Singular – *Однина*	Plural – *Множина*	
N.	плóща	плóщі	Н.
G.	плóщі	плóщ	Р.
D.	плóщі	плóщам	Д.
A.	плóщу	плóщі	З.
I.	плóщею	плóщами	О.
L.	плóщі	плóщах	М.
V.	плóще!	= N.	Кл.

Nouns ending in -ша, -ча, -жа (**кáша, дáча, бíржа**) are declined according to the same pattern. Although stress will be the stable SS type in the majority of mixed stems, there will be exceptions (or at least forms with two accepted stress patterns), as in **тúсяча** 'thousand':

	Singular – *Однина*	Plural – *Множина*	
N.	тúсяча	тисячí	Н.
G.	тúсячі	тúсяч	Р.
D.	тúсячі	тисячáм	Д.
A.	тúсячу	тисячí	З.
I.	тúсячею	тисячáми	О.
L.	тúсячі	тисячáх	М.
V.	(тúсяче!)	= N.	Кл.

Both the expected pattern SS and SE are acceptable; note that in the case of G.*pl.* the lack of a final vowel means that there is only one G.*pl.* form, as -я- is not stressed.

2.3.1.4   *Feminine declensions ending in a consonant: soft stems*

	Singular	*Plural*	
N.	–(ь)	-і	Н.
G.	-і	-ей	Р.
D.	-і	-ям	Д.
A.	–(ь)	-і	З.
I.	-ю	-ями	О.
L.	-і	-ях	М.
V.	-е	= N.	Кл.

Large numbers of feminine nouns end in a palatalized consonant. Note the case forms that differ from those seen to this point: A.I.*sg.* (zero ending and -ю, respectively) and G.*pl.* (-ей instead of zero). The G.*sg.* as seen here is the same as in the soft and mixed -a feminines; in older books, however, the reader may in fact come across the now-archaic variant -и, which is the hard stem form. Likewise, this variant is sometimes used in current Ukrainian publications; however, the most recent orthographic dictionaries (1997, for example) still prescribe -i. Stress among these nouns tends to be extremely stable, such that the vast majority will be classified as belonging to the SS type; in spite of such stability, there will always be exceptions, as in the first example below.

STRESS SS +: **по́вість** 'TALE'

	Singular – Однина	*Plural – Множина*	
N.	по́вість	по́вісті	Н.
G.	по́вісті	повісте́й	Р.
D.	по́вісті	повістя́м	Д.
A.	по́вість	по́вісті	З.
I.	по́вістю	повістя́ми	О.
L.	по́вісті	повістя́х	М.
V.	по́вісте!	= N.	Кл.

STRESS SS: **сіль** 'SALT'

The example **сіль** has the same endings as **по́вість**, but there are two differences: (i) there is an alternation i–o (the latter appears in the root when a vowel immediately follows the final consonant: see Chapter 1 for a reminder), and (ii) before I.*sg.* -ю a single consonant is doubled, in which case the preceding vowel remains -i-:

	Singular – Однина	*Plural – Множина*	
N.	сіль	со́лі	Н.
G.	со́лі	соле́й	Р.

D.	сóлі	сóлям	Д.
A.	сіль	сóлі	З.
I.	сíллю	сóлями	О.
L.	сóлі	сóлях	М.
V.	сóле!	= N.	Кл.

Note the vowel alternation (**i–o**), as described in Chapter 1. One large set of nouns always has this alternation, *viz.* those with the abstract noun suffix -**ість**, as in **слáбість** 'weakness':

	Singular – *Однина*	Plural – *Множина*	
N.	слáбість	слабостí	Н.
G.	слабостí	слабостéй	Р.
D.	слабостí	слабостям	Д.
A.	слáбість	слабостí	З.
I.	слáбістю	слабостями	О.
L.	слабостí	слабостях	М.
V.	(слáбосте!)	= N.	Кл.

We see here that the two-consonant sequence -**ст**- cannot geminate (double) in the I.*sg.*, and the preceding vowel is still -**i**-. The vocative is technically possible, but unlikely to be used for an abstract noun.

Finally, compare the form **óсінь** 'autumn', in which there is an **i–e** alternation:

	Singular – *Однина*	Plural – *Множина*	
N.	óсінь	óсені	Н.
G.	óсені	óсеней	Р.
D.	óсені	óсеням	Д.
A.	óсінь	óсені	З.
I.	óсінню	óсенями	О.
L.	óсені	óсенях	М.
V.	óсене!	= N.	Кл.

2.3.1.5   *Feminine declensions ending in a consonant: mixed stems*

		Singular	Plural	
	N.	-Ø	-i	Н.
	G.	-i	-ей	Р.
	D.	-i	-ам	Д.
	A.	-Ø	-i	З.
	I.	-ю	-ами	О.
	L.	-i	-ах	М.
	V.	-е	= N.	Кл.

As in the 'mixed' declensions seen in **2.3.13** above, there are 'mixed' stems among feminines ending in a consonant.

STRESS SS +: **ніч** 'NIGHT', **річ** 'THING'

In the following two examples (both with root vowel alternations), hard final -**ч** occurs in the N.A.*sg.* and throughout the plural paradigm, but this sound is slightly softened by the vowels in the remaining cases in the singular:

	Singular – *Однина*	Plural – *Множина*	
N.	ніч	ночі	Н.
G.	ночі	ночей	Р.
D.	ночі	ночáм	Д.
A.	ніч	ночі	З.
I.	ніччю	ночáми	О.
L.	ночі	ночáх	М.
V.	ноче!	= N.	Кл.

	Singular – *Однина*	Plural – *Множина*	
N.	річ	речі	Н.
G.	речі	речей	Р.
D.	речі	речáм	Д.
A.	річ	речі	З.
I.	річчю	речáми	О.
L.	речі	речáх	М.
V.	рече!	= N.	Кл.

2.3.1.6 Irregular feminine nouns

(A) Very few feminine nouns decline irregularly or somehow contrary to expectations; the most commonly cited of these is the word for 'mother', **мáти**:

	Singular – *Однина*	Plural – *Множина*	
N.	мáти	матері	Н.
G.	мáтері	матерів	Р.
D.	мáтері	матерям	Д.
A.	мáтір	матерів	З.
I.	мáтір'ю	матерями	О.
L.	мáтері	матеряx	М.
V.	= N.	= N.	Кл.

The syllable -**ер**- appears in all forms of the root outside of the N.V.*sg.*, and a vowel alternation takes place in the A.I.*sg.*; note that -**р**- is not doubled in the I.*sg.* (unlike other consonants above), and is also not softened (hardness is indicated by the presence of the apostrophe; compare **1.1.6**).

(B) The nouns **двéрі** 'door' and **рáдощі** 'joy' occur only as plural forms in Ukrainian (stress pattern S + and S, respectively); we can include them here because they were originally feminine, although to a speaker of Ukrainian they are unlikely to have any gender associated with them:

Plural – Множина

N.	двéрі	Н.
G.	дверéй	Р.
D.	двéрям	Д.
A.	двéрі	З.
L.	двéрях	М.
I.	двéрмѝ, дверѝма	О.
V.	= N.	Кл.

Plural – Множина

N.	рáдощі	Н.
G.	рáдощів	Р.
D.	рáдощам	Д.
A.	рáдощі	З.
L.	рáдощах	М.
I.	рáдощами	О.

(C) The last two nouns that need to be considered here are extremely important, as they are amongst the most commonly used nouns in the language: **людѝна** 'person', and **дитѝна** 'child'. They decline as feminines in the singular (ending in -a, as in **2.3.1.1**), and are feminines for purposes of agreement and/or reference in that number; they are anomalous, however, with soft variant endings in most cases of the plural; as the plural stem differs from that of the singular, we may refer to these two as 'semi-suppletive' forms. Note the stress pattern in the plural in both paradigms:

	Singular – Однина	*Plural – Множина*	
N.	людѝна	лю́ди	Н.
G.	людѝни	людéй	Р.
D.	людѝні	лю́дям	Д.
A.	людѝну	людéй	З.
I.	людѝною	людьмѝ	О.
L.	людѝні	лю́дях	М.
V.	людѝно!	= N.	Кл.

	Singular – Однина	*Plural – Множина*	
N.	дитѝна	ді́ти	Н.
G.	дитѝни	дітéй	Р.
D.	дитѝні	ді́тям	Д.
A.	дитѝну	дітéй	З.
I.	дитѝною	ді́тьмѝ	О.
L.	дитѝні	ді́тях	М.
V.	дитѝно!	= N.	Кл.

2.3.2 DECLENSION OF MASCULINE NOUNS

Like feminine nouns, masculine stems can be described as hard or soft; the vast majority of such nouns end in a consonant (hard or soft). There are a few, however, that end in final -**a**; we shall treat these first.

2.3.2.1 *Masculine nouns ending in a vowel (-**a**)*

It is important to remember that gender is usually grammatical and not natural; in other words, a 'city square' **плóща** is feminine, but not female (there are exceptions, of course, in the form of nouns like **жíнка** 'wife', where feminine = female). A few masculine words look like feminines, but denote male persons; they decline exactly as feminine nouns do, in other words, according to their form and not to their grammatical gender. The only time we notice a difference between these two groups is when they are modified by adjectives, which must carry appropriate gender markers for the nouns they describe (see **3.4**).

STRESS SS OR SE: **стáроста** 'ELDER', 'GO-BETWEEN' (MASCULINE)

	Singular – Однина	*Plural – Множина*	
N.	стáроста	стáрости, -й	Н.
G.	стáрости	стáрост, -ів*	Р.
D.	стáрості	стáростам, -áм	Д.
A.	стáросту	стáрост, -ів*	З.
I.	стáростою	стáростами, -áми	О.
L.	стáрості	стáростах, -áх	М.
V.	стáросто!	= N.	Кл.

* In this example there are two possible stress patterns in the plural, depending on the meaning of the word: SS (with zero ending in the G.*pl.*) when it means 'chief', 'elder'; SE (with the masculine G.*pl.* ending) when it means 'go-between'.

There are also soft-stem variants, such as **суддя́** 'judge':

STRESS E + S

	Singular – Однина	*Plural – Множина*	
N.	суддя́	сýдді	Н.
G.	судді́	сýддів	Р.
D.	судді́	сýддям	Д.
A.	суддю́	сýддів	З.
I.	суддéю	сýддями	О.
L.	судді́	сýддях	М.
V.	сýдде!	= N.	Кл.

There are also masculine nouns that end in -o: although they end in a vowel (as do the examples shown in this section), they decline like masculines in a consonant and are discussed under **2.3.2.2.1**.

2.3.2.2 *Masculine nouns ending in a consonant: hard stems*

The masculine declensions are more diverse in the singular than the feminine, in that some of the cases admit more than one ending. Frequently one also finds paradigms in which two or more cases have the same ending; there will be no confusion in practice, however, as the contexts in which such forms occur clarify which case is meant. The full range of hard-stem possibilities is as follows:

	Singular	*Plural*	
N.	-Ø	-и	Н.
G.	-а, -у	-ів	Р.
D.	-у, -ові	-ам	Д.
A.	-Ø, -а	-и, -ів	З.
I.	-ом	-ами	О.
L.	-і, -у, -ові	-ах	М.
V.	-е, -у	= N.	Кл.

Note especially the variation allowed within the L.*sg*. The choice of ending is not entirely haphazard; there are some rules of thumb regarding the various endings possible for the G.D.L. cases, but they must be understood as such: there are always exceptions.

GENITIVE SINGULAR   People, city names, scientific terminology, leisure activities, units of time, weights and measures tend to take -a, while objects, substances, phenomena and places in nature ('snow', 'forest'), abstract notions, organizations, emotions, and river/country names tend to take -y. As always, a dictionary should be consulted in cases of uncertainty, as the G.*sg*. is always provided; the following sample forms illustrate the principle:

-a
робітникá worker
чоловíка husband
Івáна Ivan
Чернíгова Chernigov
Кúєва Kyiv
лóба forehead
грáма gramme
дня day

-y
лíсу forest, woods
піскý sand
інститýту institute
снíгу snow
мéду honey
дощý rain
прогрéсу progress
ідеáлу ideal

ве́чора evening	**оптимі́зму** optimism
кіломе́тра kilometre	**гні́ву** anger
листопа́да November	**Кавка́зу** Caucasus
тені́си́ста tennis player	**те́нісу** tennis
емі́ра Emir	**еміра́ту** Emirate
пентаго́на a pentagon	**Пентаго́ну** the Pentagon
бика́ bull	**футбо́лу** football

The pairs 'tennis – tennis player' and 'Emirate – Emir' are good examples of the distribution of **-a** *vs.* **-y**. Notice, in 'pentagon', an instance of one word having two forms to differentiate their meanings: in the **-a** form we are dealing with a geometric shape (following the pattern of measurements, *et al.*, with this ending), while the **-y** form indicates the reification of the shape in reference to the organization.

DATIVE SINGULAR   One generally finds **-ові** for animates, **-y** for all others; some sources prefer the former for all nouns to reduce the level of ambiguity, but both endings are certainly encountered and ought to be noted. Compare the following list of examples:

-ові	*-y*
ді́дові grandfather	**сте́пу** steppe
робітнико́ві worker	**гекта́ру** hectare
си́нові (-y) son	**столу́** table

LOCATIVE SINGULAR   **-y** is found with most words containing the suffixes **-ок**, **-ак**, **-ик**, **-ник**, while **-ові** generally occurs with animates (although **-y** and **-i** are possible as well), and **-i** with other (non-suffixed) stems. The alternation of velar consonants does not take place if the ending is **-y** or **-ові**.

-ові	*-y*	*-i*
робітнико́ві worker	**буди́нку** building	**база́рі** bazaar
ба́тькові father	**істо́рику** historian	**Ки́єві** Kyiv
студе́нтові student	**попе́реднику** predecessor	**ро́ці** year
си́нові son	**степу́** steppe	**лі́сі** forest

The following are all also possible, however: **істо́рикові, попере́дникові, си́ну, робітнику́, студе́нту**. The stress patterns of the following paradigms require special attention, as they can be as varied as they are in the feminine declensions.

STRESS E + E: **стіл** 'TABLE'   This is a typical masculine declension (note the i–o alternation):

	Singular – *Однина*	Plural – *Множина*	
N.	**стіл**	**столи́**	Н.
G.	**стола́**	**столі́в**	Р.

D.	столу́	стола́м	Д.
A.	стіл	столи́	З.
I.	столо́м	стола́ми	О.
L.	столі́	стола́х	М.
V.	сто́ле!	= N.	Кл.

There is basically no shifting of stress, but one form requires the shift, *viz.* the V.*sg.* (it is important to note that this is the same phenomenon that occurs among feminine nouns, such as вода́, земля́, because features that cut across gender lines are otherwise rare).

STRESS SE: **дід** 'GRANDFATHER'

	Singular – Однина	*Plural – Множина*	
N.	дід	діди́	Н.
G.	ді́да	діді́в	Р.
D.	ді́дові	діда́м	Д.
A.	ді́да	діді́в	З.
I.	ді́дом	діда́ми	О.
L.	ді́дові	діда́х	М.
V.	ді́ду!	= N.	Кл.

We note again from the forms of the A. that this is an animate noun; note especially the forms of the G.D.L.V.*pl.* We can already see from these examples alone that there are clear similarities between the masculine and feminine declensions, embracing almost the whole of the plural paradigm; specifically, the basic N.*pl.* ending is the same (-и), as are the D.L.I.*pl.* forms, while A. = N. for inanimates, and A. = G. for animates (compare the feminine plurals).

STRESS SE: **до́ктор** 'DOCTOR' (NOT MEDICAL)   The following paradigm is morphologically almost identical to that of дід, with the exception of the V.*sg.* ending:

	Singular – Однина	*Plural – Множина*	
N.	до́ктор	доктори́	Н.
G.	до́ктора	докторі́в	Р.
D.	до́кторові	доктора́м	Д.
A.	до́ктора	докторі́в	З.
I.	до́ктором	доктора́ми	О.
L.	до́кторові	доктора́х	М.
V.	до́кторе!	= N.	Кл.

STRESS SS: **ра́нок** 'MORNING'   Note in extreme instances, as in this example, identical forms can represent three different cases.

	Singular – *Однина*	Plural – *Множина*	
N.	ра́нок	ра́нки	Н.
G.	ра́нку	ра́нків	Р.
D.	ра́нку, -ові	ра́нкам	Д.
A.	ра́нок	ра́нки	З.
I.	ра́нком	ра́нками	О.
L.	ра́нку, -ові	ра́нках	М.
V.	ра́нку!	= N.	Кл.

STRESS S + E: **степ** 'STEPPE'   Sometimes the place of stress can differentiate case forms that are otherwise identical; thus, here in the G.D.L.*sg.*:

	Singular – *Однина*	Plural – *Множина*	
N.	сте́п	степи́	Р.
G.	сте́пу	степі́в	Н.
D.	степу́, -о́ві	степа́м	Д.
A.	сте́п	степи́	З.
I.	сте́пом	степа́ми	О.
L.	степу́	степа́х	М.
V.	сте́пе!	= N.	Кл.

STRESS EE (E + E): **робітни́к** 'WORKER'

	Singular – *Однина*	Plural – *Множина*	
N.	робітни́к	робітники́	Н.
G.	робітника́	робітникі́в	Р.
D.	робітнико́ві (-у́)	робітника́м	Д.
A.	робітника́	робітникі́в	З.
I.	робітнико́м	робітника́ми	О.
L.	робітнико́ві (-у́)	робітника́х	М.
V.	робітни́че! (-нику́!)	= N.	Кл.

Worthy of note are the competing endings (= more than one possible) in three of the cases, D.L.V.*sg.*; note the stress shift in the V.*sg.* when the ending is -**e**.

Note also that where a sequence of two datives occurs, for instance in a phrase consisting of two masculine nouns or noun + a name, one of the competing dative endings (*viz.* -**y** or -**ові**, -**ю** or -**еві**, -**єві** in the soft or mixed stems: see below) will occur with one form, the other with the accompanying form:

дідові Сергі́ю
това́ришеві Па́влу

2.3.2.2.1   Masculine nouns ending in a vowel (-o)

A few masculine nouns in Ukrainian have the N.*sg.* marker -o; although they look like neuters (see **2.1.3**), they decline like masculine hard-stem nouns in a consonant. The most common noun of this sort is 'father':

STRESS SE: **бáтько** 'FATHER'

	Singular – *Однина*	Plural – *Множина*	
N.	бáтько	батькѝ	Н.
G.	бáтька	батькíв	Р.
D.	бáтькові	батькáм	Д.
A.	бáтька	батькíв	З.
I.	бáтьком	батькáми	О.
L.	бáтькові	батькáх	М.
V.	бáтьку!	= N.	Кл.

Ukrainian personal names in -o are declined in the same way, *viz.* **Дмитрó**, **Дмитрá**, and so on; see Declension of personal names at **2.1.2.4** and **2.3.5**.

2.3.2.3   *Masculine nouns ending in a consonant: soft stems*

The soft-stem masculine paradigms are just as prone to variation as the hard stems described above. The following table contains all the possible endings used with these nouns:

	Singular	Plural	
N.	-Ø (-ь)	-і, -ï	Н.
G.	-я,-ю	-ів/-їв, -(ей)	Р.
D.	-ю, -еві/-єві	-ям	Д.
A.	-Ø (-ь), -я	-і, -ів/-їв, -(ей)	З.
I.	-ем/-єм	-ями	О.
L.	-і, -ю, -еві/-єві	-ях	М.
V.	-ю, -е	= N.	Кл.

The apparent proliferation of endings is in fact not quite as dramatic as this table makes it out to be, as all endings that contain -ï- or -є- merely indicate the presence of a [j] at the end of the stem. They are not, then, independent endings, but are included above as graphic variants of -i- and -e-. Examine the following paradigms, and you will note that the general rules of thumb regarding the G.*sg.*, D.*sg.*, and L.*sg.* encountered for hard stems applies equally to the soft stems.

In the G.*pl.* most masculine nouns will have the ending -ів; -ей is encountered in a very few forms (see p. 76).

STRESS SS: хло́пець 'BOY', 'YOUNG MAN'

	Singular – Однина	Plural – Множина	
N.	хло́пець	хло́пці	Н.
G.	хло́пця	хло́пців	Р.
D.	хло́пцеві	хло́пцям	Д.
A.	хло́пця	хло́пців	З.
I.	хло́пцем	хло́пцями	О.
L.	хло́пцеві	хло́пцях	М.
V.	хло́пче!	= N.	Кл.

It must be remembered that **ц** can be soft in Ukrainian (hard before **e**), especially when it occurs word-finally; this paradigm illustrates the principle, as does **робітни́ця** above. In this instance we have no competing endings for each case, and stress is fixed. The V.*sg.* must be noted, however: **ц** alternates with **ч** before the V.*sg.* **-e** (**ц** arose out of an original **k*, which normally alternated with **ч** before **-e**). Compare **молоде́ць** 'young fellow', 'lad' – V.*sg.* **моло́дче!** with the anticipated E + E stress shift.

STRESS SE: учи́тель/вчи́тель 'TEACHER'   The following example illustrates a declensional pattern (seen in the hard stems as well), in which stress shifts to the ending in the plural; **вчитель** 'teacher' is animate, as is clear from the A.*sg./pl.*:

	Singular – Однина	Plural – Множина	
N.	вчи́тель	вчителі́	Н.
G.	вчи́теля	вчителі́в	Р.
D.	вчи́телеві,-ю	вчителя́м	Д.
A.	вчи́теля	вчителі́в	З.
I.	вчи́телем	вчителя́ми	О.
L.	вчи́телі,-еві	вчителя́х	М.
V.	вчи́телю!	= N.	Кл.

STRESS SE: лі́кар 'PHYSICIAN'

	Singular – Однина	Plural – Множина	
N.	лі́кар	лікарі́	Н.
G.	лі́каря	лікарі́в	Р.
D.	лі́кареві (-ю)	лікаря́м	Д.
A.	лі́каря	лікарі́в	З.
I.	лі́карем	лікаря́ми	О.
L.	лі́кареві (-і)	лікаря́х	М.
V.	лі́карю!	= N.	Кл.

The declension of this, and other nouns ending in **-p**, is not transparent if the N.*sg.* is the point of departure (see the G.*sg.* in the dictionary, as usual);

during the development of the Ukrainian language, final soft -рь was hardened, but the softness usually reappears in the presence of a vocalic ending other than -e. Compare **кобзáр** below.

The following (**день** 'day') is also representative of those soft-stem masculines that do not admit variation within the paradigm (note, however, the vowel–zero alternation, the vowel appearing only when there is no vocalic ending):

	Singular – Однина	*Plural – Множина*	
N.	дéнь	дні́	Н.
G.	дня́	дні́в	Р.
D.	дню́	дня́м	Д.
A.	дéнь	дні́	З.
I.	днéм	дня́ми	О.
L.	дні́	дня́х	М.
V.	(день!)	= N.	Кл.

The stress pattern of this particular noun does not allow it to be classified as 'stem-stressed' or 'end-stressed' in the strictest sense, as there is only ever a stem vowel or an ending vowel present: that vowel carries the stress.

STRESS E + E: **кобзáр** 'KOBZA PLAYER'

	Singular – Однина	*Plural – Множина*	
N.	кобзáр	кобзарі́	Н.
G.	кобзаря́	кобзарі́в	Р.
D.	кобзарéві, -ю́	кобзаря́м	Д.
A.	кобзаря́	кобзарі́в	З.
I.	кобзарéм	кобзаря́ми	О.
L.	кобзарéві, -і́	кобзаря́х	М.
V.	кобзáрю!	= N.	Кл.

Note the expected retraction of stress in the V.*sg.*; other nouns that decline in the same way are **воротáр/воротаря́** (EE) 'gatekeeper', **ключáр/ключаря́** (EE) 'steward', 'doorkeeper', *et al.* A word like **бібліотéкар/бібліотéкаря** (SS) 'librarian' has the same paradigm, except that – because stress precedes the suffix **-ар** – stress is stable throughout, including the vocative.

STRESS E + S: **кінь** 'HORSE'

	Singular – Однина	*Plural – Множина*	
N.	кі́нь	кóні	Н.
G.	коня́	кóней	Р.
D.	конéві (-ю́)	кóням	Д.
A.	коня́	кóней	З.
I.	конéм	кі́ньми (кóнями)	О.
L.	коні́ (-éві)	кóнях	М.
V.	кóню!	= N.	Кл.

Кінь 'horse' has (a) an **i–о** alternation, (b) animacy (note the A.*sg./pl.*) reflecting the rarer G.*pl.* ending **-ей**, (c) two possible forms in the D.L.*sg.* and I.*pl.*, and (d) a vocative form. Note the stress pattern in **кінь**, as stress is essentially final in the singular (but, as seen elsewhere, it retracts in the V.*sg.*), and it retracts in the plural; this parallels the pattern found in end-stressed feminines, compare **вода́**, **голова́**.

STRESS SE +: **гість** 'GUEST'

	Singular – *Однина*	Plural – *Множина*	
N.	гість	го́сті	Н.
G.	го́стя	гостей	Р.
D.	го́стеві, -ю	го́стям	Д.
A.	го́стя	гостей	З.
I.	го́стем	го́стями	О.
L.	го́стеві, -і	го́стях	М.
		гістьми, гістьми́	
V.	го́стю!	= N.	Кл.

It is not atypical for nouns to exhibit several different forms (as seen in masculine hard stems, for example) or acceptable places of stress. In this instance there is clear vacillation throughout the plural outside the N.A.G.: note especially the four possible variants in the I.*pl.* Sometimes one particular form is preferred for a set phrase: **бу́ти у го́стях** 'to be visiting'.

Stems ending in **-й** decline essentially like those soft stems seen to this point, but it is useful to note them separately from the standpoint of their orthography; here we shall examine inanimates *vs.* animates, and the three possible stress patterns, SS, SE, and E + E.

STRESS SS: **геро́й** 'HERO'

	Singular – *Однина*	Plural – *Множина*	
N.	геро́й	геро́ї	Н.
G.	геро́я	геро́їв	Р.
D.	геро́єві, -ю	геро́ям	Д.
A.	геро́я	геро́їв	З.
I.	геро́єм	геро́ями	О.
L.	геро́єві, -ї	геро́ях	М.
V.	геро́ю!	= N.	Кл.

STRESS SE: **чай** 'TEA'

	Singular – *Однина*	Plural – *Множина*	
N.	ча́й	чаї́	Н.
G.	ча́ю	чаї́в	Р.
D.	ча́ю	ча́йм	Д.

A.	чай	чаї	З.
I.	ча́єм	чая́ми	О.
L.	чаї́	чая́х	М.
V.	ча́ю!	= N.	Кл.

Край 'edge', 'land' declines in exactly the same manner.

STRESS E + E: **водій** 'DRIVER'

	Singular – *Однина*	Plural – *Множина*	
N.	водій	водії́	Н.
G.	водія́	водії́в	Р.
D.	водіє́ві, -ю́	водія́м	Д.
A.	водія́	водії́в	З.
I.	водіє́м	водія́ми	О.
L.	водіє́ві	водія́х	М.
V.	воді́ю!	= N.	Кл.

2.3.2.4   Masculine nouns ending in a consonant: mixed stems

All remarks regarding mixed-stem endings in other declensions apply here as well; note the mixture of 'hard' and 'soft' stem endings in the following masculine nouns.

STRESS E + E: **чита́ч** 'READER'

	Singular – *Однина*	Plural – *Множина*	
N.	чита́ч	читачі́	Н.
G.	читача́	читачі́в	Р.
D.	читачє́ві, -у́	читача́м	Д.
A.	читача́	читачі́в	З.
I.	читачє́м	читача́ми	О.
L.	читачє́ві, -і́	читача́х	М.
V.	чита́чу!	= N.	Кл.

As expected, stress retracts to the stem in the V.*sg.*, as in the following, **ніж** 'knife':

	Singular – *Однина*	Plural – *Множина*	
N.	ні́ж	ножі́	Н.
G.	ножа́	ножі́в	Р.
D.	ножу́, -є́ві	ножа́м	Д.
A.	ні́ж	ножі́	З.
I.	ножє́м	ножа́ми	О.
L.	ножі́, -є́ві	ножа́х	М.
V.	но́же!	= N.	Кл.

STRESS SE: **това́риш** 'COMRADE', 'COMPANION'

	Singular – Однина	Plural – Множина	
N.	това́риш	товариші́	Н.
G.	това́риша	товаришíв	Р.
D.	това́ришеві (-у)	товаришáм	Д.
A.	това́риша	товаришíв	З.
I.	това́ришем	товаришáми	О.
L.	това́ришеві (-і)	товаришáх	М.
V.	това́ришу!	= N.	Кл.

The next noun could easily be included in the E + E type described above, but it merits separate consideration because of the nature of the stem-final consonant. We noted, among the soft-stem nouns, those in which a historically soft final -рь was hardened in absolute final position. There is a body of masculine nouns in which this hardened -р has spread to other forms beyond just the N.*sg.*:

STRESS E + E: **повістя́р** 'STORY TELLER', 'NOVELIST'

	Singular – Однина	Plural – Множина	
N.	повістя́р	повістярí	Н.
G.	повістярá	повістярíв	Р.
D.	повістярéві (-ý)	повістярáм	Д.
A.	повістярá	повістярíв	З.
I.	повістярéм	повістярáми	О.
L.	повістярéві (-í)	повістярáх	М.
V.	повістя́ре!	= N.	Кл.

Thus we note the hardness of -р throughout the singular, although some of the case endings (D.*sg.*, L.*sg.*) are clearly soft-stem variants; the clearest indication of the stabilization of hardened -р in the paradigm is in the A./G.*sg.* and D.L.I.*pl.* Declined in identical fashion are **маля́р** 'painter' (EE or SS: G.*sg.* ма́ляра/малярá), **гуса́р** 'hussar' (SS: G.*sg.* гуса́ра), and others.

2.3.2.5   Pluralia tantum nouns; nouns in -ин

(A) There are few nouns that may be said to be irregular among the masculines. One such noun, **штани́** 'trousers' (E type stress), is similar to the feminines **две́рі** and **ра́дощі**: in other words, they are not truly irregular but only exist as plural forms, and as such the V. = N./A.

	Plural – Множина	
N.	штани́	Н.
G.	штанíв	Р.
D.	штанáм, шта́ням	Д.

A.	штани́	3.
I.	штана́ми, штаньми́, шта́нями	О.
L.	штана́х	М.

(B) A special declensional type exists for the naming of 'masculine denizens of place X' (often referring to nationality); the properties of this type are dictated by the presence of the suffix -а́нин, -я́нин in the singular, as in росія́нин 'a Russian':

	Singular – Однина	*Plural – Множина*	
N.	росія́нин	росія́ни	Н.
G.	росія́нина	росія́н	Р.
D.	росія́нинові, -у	росія́нам	Д.
A.	росія́нина	росія́н	3.
I.	росія́нином	росія́нами	О.
L.	росія́нинові	росія́нах	М.
V.	росія́нине!	= N.	Кл.

Датча́нин 'a Dane', городя́нин 'townsman', 'inhabitant of a town' and all other nouns of this type will decline in exactly the same way. The declension of these forms in the plural in particular must be noted, as the element -ин is lost throughout; note also that stress is stable.

2.3.3   DECLENSION OF NEUTER NOUNS

The majority of case endings for neuter nouns will be exactly the same as those occurring with the masculines (whether hard, soft, or mixed stems). Contrary to the N.*sg.* marker *par excellence* among masculines (a consonant), the N.*sg.* ending of neuter nouns is always a vowel, usually -o or -e; a significant number have the final vowel -я (and, as will be seen, are easily recognizable as neuters), while irregular forms exist as well. The major differences between neuters and masculines are: (i) A. always = N. and (ii) there is no separate vocative form, thus V. = N. Variation and competition between two or more identical case endings – on the scale of what occurs among masculines – is unknown; in those instances when a given case can be expressed by two possible endings, this (with the exception of a very small number of nouns) will be limited to the I.*pl.*

Stress patterns among neuter nouns are very much like those of the feminines, hard as well as soft stems.

2.3.3.1   *Neuter nouns: hard stems*

The following may be considered to represent the quintessential neuter hard-stem paradigm. Note the following points: there is no separate vocative ending in the neuter gender – singular or plural – and it is therefore not included in our tables (V. = N.); apart from the place of stress in many neuters, the N.*pl.* will look like the G.*sg.* (the latter phenomenon is well-known among feminine nouns as well):

	Singular	Plural	
N.	-о	-а	Н.
G.	-а	-Ø	Р.
D.	-у	-ам	Д.
A.	-о	-а	З.
I.	-ом	-ами (-ьми)	О.
L.	-і	-ах	М.

STRESS SE: мі́сто 'CITY'

	Singular – Однина	Plural – Множина	
N./V.	мі́сто	міста́	Н./Кл.
G.	мі́ста	міст	Р.
D.	мі́сту	міста́м	Д.
A.	мі́сто	міста́	З.
I.	мі́стом	міста́ми	О.
L.	мі́сті	міста́х	М.

STRESS ES: вікно́ 'WINDOW'

	Singular – Однина	Plural – Множина	
N./V.	вікно́	ві́кна	Н./Кл.
G.	вікна́	ві́кон	Р.
D.	вікну́	ві́кнам	Д.
A.	вікно́	ві́кна	З.
I.	вікно́м	ві́кнами	О.
L.	вікні́	ві́кнах	М.

In this particular form, note the fleeting vowel that appears in the G.*pl.* (i.e. in the presence of a zero-ending: вікн- > ві́кон-).

The following paradigm is morphologically in agreement with the other examples seen to this point, but note the vowel alternation e–i in the G.*pl.*:

	Singular – Однина	Plural – Множина	
N./V.	село́	се́ла	Н./Кл.
G.	села́	сіл	Р.
D.	селу́	се́лам	Д.
A.	село́	се́ла	З.
I.	село́м	се́лами	О.
L.	селі́	се́лах	М.

The following example reflects a pattern of stable stress, but note the variation possible in the I.*pl.*:

STRESS SS: **коліно** 'KNEE'

	Singular – Однина	*Plural – Множина*	
N./V.	коліно	коліна	Н./Кл.
G.	коліна	колін	Р.
D.	коліну	колінам	Д.
A.	коліно	коліна	З.
I.	коліном	колінами, колíньми	О.
L.	коліні	колінах	М.

All nouns formed with the suffix **-ство** have stable stress; compare the following example:

STRESS SS: **товари́ство** 'SOCIETY', 'ASSOCIATION'

	Singular – Однина	*Plural – Множина*	
N./V.	товари́ство	товари́ства	Н./Кл.
G.	товари́ства	товари́ств	Р.
D.	товари́ству	товари́ствам	Д.
A.	товари́ство	товари́ства	З.
I.	товари́ством	товари́ствами	О.
L.	товари́стві	товари́ствах	М.

One final stress pattern, unlike those seen in previous examples, must be noted; this pattern is of the SS type, except that stress shifts to the right within the stem for the plural paradigm:

STRESS SS + 1: **ко́лесо** 'CIRCLE', 'RING'

	Singular – Однина	*Plural – Множина*	
N./V.	ко́лесо	колéса	Н./Кл.
G.	ко́леса	колíс	Р.
D.	ко́лесу	колéсам	Д.
A.	ко́лесо	колéса	З.
I.	ко́лесом	колéсами (колíсьми, rarer)	О.
L.	ко́лесі	колéсах	М.

Note the G.*pl.*, in which the zero ending triggers the vowel alternation **e–i** within the stem.

2.3.3.2 Neuter nouns: soft stems

The following endings are with one exception merely the soft variants of the forms seen above in the hard stems; the exception is the G.*pl.*, in which there are two possibilities:

	Singular	Plural	
N./V.	-е	-я	Н./Кл.
G.	-я	-ів, -Ø	Р.
D.	-ю	-ям	Д.
A.	-е	-я	З.
I.	-ем	-ями	О.
L.	-і	-ях	М.

STRESS SE: **мо́ре** 'SEA'

	Singular – *Однина*	Plural – *Множина*	
N./V.	мо́ре	моря́	Н./Кл.
G.	мо́ря	морі́в	Р.
D.	мо́рю	моря́м	Д.
A.	мо́ре	моря́	З.
I.	мо́рем	моря́ми	О.
L.	мо́рі	моря́х	М.

STRESS SE: **по́ле** 'FIELD' (a very similar paradigm to **море** 'sea')

	Singular – *Однина*	Plural – *Множина*	
N./V.	по́ле	поля́	Н./Кл.
G.	по́ля	полі́в/піль	Р.
D.	по́лю	поля́м	Д.
A.	по́ле	поля́	З.
I.	по́лем	поля́ми	О.
L.	по́лі	поля́х	М.

The one form to note here is again the G.*pl.*: two possible forms are used, one with the expected ending, and the zero ending which calls for the internal vowel alternation **о–і**.

STRESS SE: **мі́сце** 'PLACE'

	Singular – *Однина*	Plural – *Множина*	
N./V.	мі́сце	місця́	Н./Кл.
G.	мі́сця	місць	Р.
D.	мі́сцю	місця́м	Д.

A.	мі́сце	місця́	З.
I.	мі́сцем	місця́ми	О.
L.	мі́сці	місця́х	М.

STRESS SE: **се́рце** 'HEART'

	Singular – Однина	*Plural – Множина*	
N./V.	се́рце	серця́	Н./Кл.
G.	се́рця	серде́ць	Р.
D.	се́рцю	серця́м	Д.
A.	се́рце	серця́	З.
I.	се́рцем	серця́ми	О.
L.	се́рці	серця́х	М.

The G.*pl.* draws our attention here as before: in this instance a -д-, historically present in the stem but lost in pronunciation in the presence of the following ц, reappears before the vowel of the G.*pl.*

2.3.3.3   *Neuter nouns: soft stems in -я*

This class of nouns is extremely large in Ukrainian, as it includes all those nouns formed from verbal stems: these are 'deverbal nouns' (compare the verb **пита́ти** 'to ask' in the present instance), the formation of which is described in sections 2.5.1 and 2.5.2 on word formation. The majority of these forms will end in **-ння**, and their stress pattern is always stable.

	Singular	*Plural*	
N./V.	-я	-я	Н./Кл.
G.	-я	-Ø, -ів	Р.
D.	-ю	-ям	Д.
A.	-я	-я	З.
I.	-ям	-ями	О.
L.	-і	-ях	М.

STRESS SS: **пита́ння** 'QUESTION', 'PROBLEM'

	Singular – Однина	*Plural – Множина*	
N./V.	пита́ння	пита́ння	Н./Кл.
G.	пита́ння	пита́нь	Р.
D.	пита́нню	пита́нням	Д.
A.	пита́ння	пита́ння	З.
I.	пита́нням	пита́ннями	О.
L.	пита́нні	пита́ннях	М.

Note the exceptional forms of this declensional type: N.A.G.*sg.* and N.A.*pl.* are identical, something that is never encountered in other neuter paradigms (or either of the other genders, for that matter). Also exceptional is the I.*sg.*: -ям *vs.* -ем, -ом elsewhere.

Compare another such noun, in which -я is preceded by a different consonant:

STRESS EE: **життя́** 'LIFE'

	Singular – Однина	*Plural – Множина*	
N./V.	життя́	життя́	Н./Кл.
G.	життя́	житті́в	Р.
D.	життю́	життя́м	Д.
A.	життя́	життя́	З.
I.	життя́м	життя́ми	О.
L.	житті́	життя́х	М.

There is one major difference to note between this form and those with the formant -н- (as above): the G.*pl.* is not zero, but the masculine-type -і́в. This is explained by the stress pattern of such words: with stem stress zero is the norm in the G.*pl.*, while end-stress requires, as it were, the presence of an ending to carry that stress.

STRESS SS/SE: **весі́лля** 'WEDDING'

	Singular – Однина	*Plural – Множина*	
N./V.	весі́лля	весі́лля/весілля́	Н./Кл.
G.	весі́лля	весі́ль/весілли́в	Р.
D.	весі́ллю	весі́ллям/весілля́м	Д.
A.	весі́лля	весі́лля/весілля́	З.
I.	весі́ллям	весі́ллями/весілля́ми	О.
L.	весі́ллі	весі́ллях/весілля́х	М.

Here we see an ideal example of the role of stress in the choice of G.*pl.* ending: stem-stress zero, end-stress і́в.

As described in Chapter 1, not all consonants geminate (double) stem-finally; this is a function of the phonetic properties of the final consonant: thus, a labial or р will resist gemination, while л will geminate (compare the feminine I.*sg.* ма́тір'ю above, *vs.* сі́ллю). Such nouns are often formed from other parts of speech, such as adjectives:

STRESS SS: **здоро́в'я** 'HEALTH'

	Singular – Однина	
N./V.	здоро́в'я	Н./Кл.
G.	здоро́в'я	Р.
D.	здоро́в'ю	Д.

A.	здоро́в'я	З.
I.	здоро́в'ям	О.
L.	здоро́в'ї	М.

Depending on its meaning, there may or may not be a plural (or, while theoretically possible, its use in the plural would not make sense, as in the present instance). Note the form of the L.*sg.*, in which we clearly see the presence of phonetic [j], as **ї** = [ji].

2.3.3.4   Neuter nouns: mixed stems

STRESS SS: **прі́звище** 'SURNAME'

	Singular – Однина	*Plural – Множина*	
N./V.	прі́звище	прі́звища	Н./Кл.
G.	прі́звища	прі́звищ	Р.
D.	прі́звищу	прі́звищам	Д.
A.	прі́звище	прі́звища	З.
I.	прі́звищем	прі́звищами	О.
L.	прі́звищі	прі́звищах	М.

STRESS EE + /ES +: **плече́** 'SHOULDER'

	Singular – Однина	*Plural – Множина*	
N./V.	плече́	плéчі	Н./Кл.
G.	плеча́	плечéй (пліч)	Р.
D.	плечу́	плéча́м	Д.
A.	плече́	плéчі	З.
I.	плече́м	плечи́ма (плеча́ми)	О.
L.	плечі́	плéча́х	М.

This noun has a degree of variation in the plural, with two possible stress patterns in two of the forms, and two instances of variation in ending: G.*pl.* (a zero ending with concomitant vowel alternation **e–i**, or **-ей**), and I.*pl.*

The following noun is anomalous in its declensional pattern: from its N.*sg.* form one would expect it to be a hard-stem noun, but it clearly belongs here based on the plural paradigm:

STRESS SE +: **о́ко** 'EYE'

	Singular – Однина	*Plural – Множина*	
N./V.	о́ко	о́чі	Н./Кл.
G.	о́ка	очéй	Р.
D.	о́ку, о́кові	оча́м	Д.
A.	о́ко	о́чі	З.
I.	о́ком	очи́ма	О.
L.	о́ці, о́кові	оча́х	М.

Attention must be paid to the two alternations: к–ц in the L.*sg.* and the replacement of к by ч throughout the plural. Compare this declensional pattern with that of вýхо 'ear', which has become a regular hard-stem neuter without a consonant alternation between the singular and plural (N.*pl.* вýха, G.*pl.* вух, and so on).

2.3.3.5 *Neuter nouns: mixed stems in -я: hidden consonant stems*

There is one further body of neuter nouns that end in -я or -а; in comparison with the soft-stem forms seen above, this is a smaller (indeed, limited) body of words. The hidden consonant emerges outside of the N.A.*sg.*, and will be either -н- or -т-; the latter all refer to the young of a species, not just animals. The forms of the plural are all clearly hard, while some of those in the singular paradigm are clearly soft.

STRESS E + E: **ім'я** '(FIRST) NAME'

	Singular – Однина	*Plural – Множина*	
N./V.	ім'я́	імена́	Н./Кл.
G.	íмені, ім'я́	іме́н	Р.
D.	íмені	імена́м	Д.
A.	ім'я́	імена́	З.
I.	íменем, ім'я́м	імена́ми	О.
L.	íмені	імена́х	М.

We note first the stress pattern, *viz.* shifting to the stem within the singular paradigm. Second, there is vacillation in this form between the G.I.*sg.* forms typical of the -я stems in general, and forms which agree with the rest of this particular paradigm: in other words, there is pressure for the paradigm to agree as a whole, with -н- appearing throughout, away from the -я stem norm. Compare this paradigm with the following pattern:

STRESS SE (SS): **плéм'я** 'RACE', 'TRIBE', 'CLAN'

	Singular – Однина	*Plural – Множина*	
N./V.	плéм'я	племена́	Н./Кл.
G.	плéмені, плéм'я	племе́н	Р.
D.	плéмені	племена́м	Д.
A.	плéм'я	племена́	З.
I.	плéменем, плéм'ям	племена́ми	О.
L.	плéмені	племена́х	М.

Here we see the same tendency noted above: the -я type forms in the G.I.*sg.* are vying with forms containing -н- under pressure of the paradigm as a whole. Ukrainian sources indicate a preference for the SE pattern, but SS may be found as well.

The following are examples of the 'hidden -т-' type:

STRESS SS: теля́ 'CALF'

	Singular – Однина	*Plural – Множина*	
N./V.	теля́	теля́та	Н./Кл.
G.	теля́ти	теля́т	Р.
D.	теля́ті	теля́там	Д.
A.	теля́	теля́т, теля́та	З.
I.	теля́м	теля́тами	О.
L.	теля́ті	теля́тах	М.

STRESS SS: дівча́ 'YOUNG GIRL'

	Singular – Однина	*Plural – Множина*	
N./V.	дівча́	дівча́та	Н./Кл.
G.	дівча́ти	дівча́т	Р.
D.	дівча́ті	дівча́там	Д.
A.	дівча́	дівча́т, дівча́та	З.
I.	дівча́м	дівча́тами	О.
L.	дівча́ті	дівча́тах	М.

STRESS SS: курча́ 'CHICK'

	Singular – Однина	*Plural – Множина*	
N./V.	курча́	курча́та	Н./Кл.
G.	курча́ти	курча́т	Р.
D.	курча́ті	курча́там	Д.
A.	курча́	курча́та, курча́т	З.
I.	курча́м	курча́тами	О.
L.	курча́ті	курча́тах	М.

Three points to note here are: (i) the G.*sg.* ending is not the soft variant -i, but the hard variant -и; (ii) as these forms are neuters (even 'young girl'), the A.*pl.* can = N.*pl.*; the animacy inherent in these nouns can, however, allow the use of the G.*pl.* for the A.*pl.*; (iii) although -н- of the 'н-type' nouns appears in all cases but the N.A. in the singular, the -т- does not appear in the I.*sg.*

2.3.4 INDECLINABLE NOUNS

Foreign borrowings ending in a final consonant or in -a (with the exception of French-based loans with the very un-Ukrainian final sequence -ya < *-ois*) are assimilated as regular Ukrainian nouns, and are therefore declined as such; nouns in all other vowels (-e, -i, -o, -y) are not declined. The following nouns have been listed according to their gender in **2.1**, but are repeated here together as a representative (but not exhaustive) list of such forms.

авеню́	avenue
ди́нго	dingo
жюрі́	jury
зе́бу	zebu
інко́гніто	incognito
інтерв'ю́	interview
какаду́	cockatoo
кашне́	scarf, muffler
кенгуру́	kangaroo
колібрі́	hummingbird
ко́мі	Komi (a Finno-Ugric people in Russia)
конферансьє́	commentator
парвеню́	*parvenu(e)*
по́ні	pony
попурі́	potpourri
протеже́	protégé
пюре́	purée
рантьє́	*rentier*, one living on a private income
рев'ю́	revue, review
ре́фері	referee
саа́мі	Saami (Lapp(s))
сабо́	shoes with wooden soles (*sabots*) (France, Belgium)
са́рі	sari
соте́	sautée
таксі́	taxi
фламі́нго	flamingo
фойє́	foyer
фрикасе́	fricassée
шимпанзе́	chimpanzee
штра́се	street

2.3.5 DECLENSION OF PROPER NAMES (PEOPLE)

In this section we will examine names of people only; proper place names
follow the familiar nominal declensional patterns.

The declension of first names and patronymics is identical to that of regular non-proper nouns; thus, both elements of **Óльга Петрíвна** will decline in
the same way as **ногá**, **Івáн** declines like **студéнт**, and the patronymic
Петрóвич like the masculine mixed-stem type **читáч** (i.e. as animate masculine nouns). Masculine first names in -**a** (such as **Микóла**) decline as feminines, while those in -**o** (**Дмитрó**, for example) decline as masculines
(**Дмитрó**, **Дмитрá**, **Дмитрóві**, and similar). Surnames behave differently,
however. All names that look like adjectives, i.e. having the final adjectival
markers -**ий** (**Швúдкий**, **Бíлий**), feminine -**a** (**Швидка**, **Бíла**), or the soft

variants **-ій**, **-я**, including the considerable number of names ending in **-ський**, **-цький**, **-ська**, **-цька**, decline as adjectives throughout the singular and plural; the adjectival declensions are described in Chapter 3.

2.3.5.1 Declension of masculine surnames

The first three surnames described below all have an **i–е** or an **i–о** alternation in the suffix; most masculine surnames will decline as they do, however, with or without such an alternation. Note, in particular, the following characteristics of the pattern: (i) the singular is identical to any other non-proper noun with the exception of the instrumental, which has an adjectival ending (**-им** *pro* **-ом**); (ii) the plural forms are all adjectival in form, with the exception of the N.*pl.*, which reflects the nominal ending (**-и** *pro* **-i**: see Chapter 3 for comparison); (iii) there is no separate vocative in either singular or plural.

	Singular – Однина	*Plural – Множина*	
N./V.	Лéсів	Лéсеви	Н./Кл.
G.	Лéсева	Лéсевих	Р.
D.	Лéсеву	Лéсевим	Д.
A.	Лéсева	Лéсевих	З.
I.	Лéсевим	Лéсевими	О.
L.	Лéсеві	Лéсевих	М.

	Singular – Однина	*Plural – Множина*	
N./V.	Андрíїв	Андрíєви	Н./Кл.
G.	Андрíєва	Андрíєвих	Р.
D.	Андрíєву	Андрíєвим	Д.
A.	Андрíєва	Андрíєвих	З.
I.	Андрíєвим	Андрíєвими	О.
L.	Андрíєві, -у	Андрíєвих	М.

	Singular – Однина	*Plural – Множина*	
N./V.	Данúлів	Данúлови	Н./Кл.
G.	Данúлова	Данúлових	Р.
D.	Данúлову	Данúловим	Д.
A.	Данúлова	Данúлових	З.
I.	Данúловим	Данúловими	О.
L.	Данúлові, -у	Данúлових	М.

Standard grammars of Ukrainian can differ with respect to the form of the L.*sg.*: some sources published in Ukraine cite the ending -у only, while other, Western, sources prefer -i. This is an instance where both are possible and the choice of form is made by the individual author or speaker.

According to the established rules of Ukrainian orthography, names in **-ів** are expected to have an **i–е** or **i–о** alternation, as seen in the examples given above; in practice, however, the 'rule' is often flouted. In other words, the norms of the language are changing, and the retention of -i- in all case forms is becoming more widespread (KUM 1990):

	Singular – Однина	Plural – Множина	
N./V.	Лу́ків	Лу́кови, Лу́ківи	Н./Кл.
G.	Лу́кова, Лу́ківа	Лу́кових, Лу́ківих	Р.
D.	Лу́кову, Лу́ківу	Лу́ковим, Лу́ківим	Д.
A.	Лу́кова, Лу́ківа	Лу́кових, Лу́ківих	З.
I.	Лу́ковим, Лу́ківим	Лу́ковими, Лу́ківими	О.
L.	Лу́кову, Лу́ківу	Лу́кових, Лу́ківих	М.

As a result of long contact between Russian and Ukrainian, names ending in **-ов** are also common: the variant **-ів** is more common in West Ukraine, while **-ов** is more characteristic of East Ukraine. The following is the most Ukrainian variant (compare Russian **Ивано́в** or **Ива́нов**):

	Singular – Однина	Plural – Множина	
N./V.	Іва́нів	Іва́нови	Н./Кл.
G.	Іва́нова	Іва́нових	Р.
D.	Іва́нову	Іва́новим	Д.
A.	Іва́нова	Іва́нових	З.
I.	Іва́новим	Іва́новими	О.
L.	Іва́нову	Іва́нових	М.

The next type is uncontroversial, as there are no alternations; the **-ин** suffix is not uncommon in Ukrainian names, but will be especially familiar to readers acquainted with Russian history (Rus. **Ле́нин, Ста́лин,** Ukr. **Ле́нін, Ста́лін**) and literature (Rus. **Бу́нин, Карамзи́н,** Ukr. **Бу́нін, Карамзі́н**):

	Singular – Однина	Plural – Множина	
N./V.	Степани́шин	Степани́шини	Н./Кл.
G.	Степани́шина	Степани́шиних	Р.
D.	Степани́шину Степани́шинові	Степани́шиним	Д.
A.	Степани́шина	Степани́шиних	З.
I.	Степани́шиним	Степани́шиними	О.
L.	Степани́шинові Степани́шину Степани́шині	Степани́шиних	М.

More widespread in Ukrainian, however, are names with the suffixes **-енко** and **-чук**; the declension of names in **-чук** follows the same pattern characteristic of those with the suffix **-ин**. Names such as **Шевче́нко** need to be noted, however: (i) they are masculines ending in **-о**, (ii) they decline in the singular as regular masculine nouns throughout the singular and the plural; in the I.*sg.*, the form which stands out is the nominal ending **-ом**, not **-им**; overall, it is declined according to the pattern of **ба́тько**:

	Singular – **Однина**	*Plural –* **Множина**	
N./V.	Шевче́нко	Шевче́нки	Н./Кл.
G.	Шевче́нка	Шевче́нків	Р.
D.	Шевче́нкові	Шевче́нкам	Д.
	Шевче́нку		
A.	Шевче́нка	Шевче́нків	З.
I.	Шевче́нком	Шевче́нками	О.
L.	Шевче́нкові	Шевче́нках	М.
	Шевче́нку		

Note that Ukrainian surnames that are historically short-form adjectives or past passive participles have lost their connection to the adjectival declension, and are treated as regular nominal forms, in the singular as well as the plural: **Михайло Петро́вич Глух, Миха́йла Петро́вича Глу́ха**, and so on, *pl.* **Глу́хи, Глу́хів**, and similar, **Миха́йло Іва́нович Коха́н, Миха́йла Іва́новича Коха́на**, and likewise, *pl.* **Коха́ни, Коха́нів**, and so on.

Also note a special reminder regarding the use of masculine first/Christian names + patronymic in the dative case. Because there are two dative singular endings in the masculine noun (**-ові** and **-у**), the pattern must be: **Степа́нові Бори́совичу.**

2.3.5.2   *Declension of feminine surnames*

Feminine surnames need little comment, as most are feminine variants of names seen above, for example, **Ле́сева, Іва́но́ва, Іваниши́на**, and so on, and are declined as feminine adjectives throughout. However, it is important to note the following:

(1) Masculine surnames of the type **Ле́сів, Іваниши́н** can have two corresponding feminine forms: **Ле́сева, Іваниши́на**, which decline as described, as well as the unchanged masculine-looking variants **Ле́сів, Іваниши́н**. If a name appears as **Ольга Іва́нів, Окса́на Іваниши́н**, then the surname is not declined: **Ольга Іва́нів, Ольги Іва́нів**, and such, **Окса́на Іваниши́н, Окса́ни Іваниши́н**, and so on.

(2) Feminine surnames ending in a consonant are in general indeclinable; names containing the suffix **-чук** will be among the most visible of these: **А́нна Ме́льничук, А́нни Ме́льничук**, and so on.

(3) This is also true of surnames that are historically short-form adjectives or past passive participles: whereas the masculine surnames **Глух, Коха́н, Мо́лод**, and so on will decline as masculine nouns, the feminine variants lack an overt feminine marker, and will not decline: **Га́нна Мо́лод, Га́нни Мо́лод**, and similar, **Марі́я Глух, Марі́ї Глух**, and such.

(4) The common suffix **-енко** follows the same pattern: although declined for males, surnames in **-енко** denoting females will not be declined, as in **Галина Шевче́нко, Галини Шевче́нко**, and so on. This is in fact true of all

names ending in -o: **Дмитро́ Соро́ко**, **Дмитра́ Соро́ка**, and similar, but **Га́нна Соро́ко**, **Га́нни Соро́ко**, and so on.

2.4 SYNTAX OF THE NOUN

2.4.1 THE CASES

In this section we examine the occurrence of the noun in all seven cases first without the presence of specific elements (such as prepositions or verbs) that require the use of a particular non-accusative case. As the occurrence of the accusative is most commonly tied to the presence of a verb (and the majority of transitive verbs will involve the accusative case rather than the oblique cases), we must treat the construction 'verb + accusative noun' here: in other words, they are 'unmarked', and basic to the definition of the accusative case. All other cases that are dependent upon the presence of a particular verb are described in the context of the 'Syntax of the Verb'.

2.4.1.1 The nominative case

The nominative case is the case of the subject; it is the naming case, as the English and Ukrainian terms indicate: Eng. *nomin-* < Lat. *nomen, nominis* 'name', Ukr. **назив-** < the Ukrainian verb 'to name', 'to call'.

(1) A noun-subject is free to occur either before or after a verb because the nominative marker prevents misunderstanding or ambiguity. English, on the other hand, requires fixed word order because the declensional system characteristic of Old English was lost over the centuries: 'The cat saw Peter' does not = 'Peter saw the cat', whereas Ukrainian allows:

Петро́ поба́чив во́вка.
and
Во́вка поба́чив *Петро́*.   Petro saw the wolf.

Although the word order can change, the subject is still 'Petro', as this form is in the nominative case. However, even though the basic idea is the same, a change in word order does shift the emphasis: the second version is more likely to mean 'It was Petro who saw the wolf'; i.e. new or significant information is placed last.

(2) The lack of overt definite/indefinite articles in Ukrainian ('a' and 'the' in English) does not mean that such differentiation cannot be made; indeed, placement of the subject (nominative element) first or last in an utterance makes this possible:

Студе́нт сту́кнув у две́рі.   The student knocked at the door. (The student is a known quantity, what he is doing is new information.)

У двéрі стýкнув *студéнт*.   A student knocked at the door. (The
                                 student is new information.)

(3) A noun in the nominative can appear as a thought on its own, with the
verb 'to be' understood:

Зимá.   (It is/was*) winter.
Лíто.   (It is/was*) summer.

*depending on context.

(4) A subject (noun or pronoun) can be equated with or defined by
another noun simply by means of a dash, implying the presence of the verb
'to be' (as in X = Y):

Кúїв – столúця Украïни.   Kyiv is the capital of Ukraine.
Шевчéнко (Він) – творéць   Shevchenko (He) is the creator (father)
сучáсної украïнської   of the modern Ukrainian literary
літератýрної мóви.   language.
Івáн – геóлог.   Ivan is a geologist.
Ми – і рядовí, . . . і генерáли We – privates (army), . . . and generals,
– солдáти.   are soldiers.
                                     (О. Єфíмов)

The hyphen is replaced by suitable forms of **бýти** 'to be' for like expressions in
the past or future. When a form of this verb is present, the second, or defin-
ing, noun can also appear in the instrumental case depending on style; the
instrumental can imply a more temporary state – especially with professions
(see 'Verbs governing the instrumental case' at **6.4.7.3**; see also **8.1.3.3**
footnote):

Шевчéнко був *поéт/поéтом*.   Shevchenko was *a poet*.
Ахмáтова не булá *росіянка/росіянкою*. Akhmatova was not *Russian*.
Íгор був *студéнтом*.   Ihor was *a student*.

(5) Finally, a phenomenon that is widely found is that of double-barrelled,
hyphenated nouns. The two nouns will always agree in case, number, and
gender with one another, whether as subjects or other elements of a statement; this pattern is an economical way to provide information (without the
use of conjunctions or relative clauses), as the second element more closely
defines or identifies the first element:

генерáл-полкóвник, генерáл-майóр   brigadier-general, major-general
послáнник-нýнцій   envoy, but no ordinary envoy, *viz.*
                                        the Papal nuncio
швейцáр-бородáч   a doorman who has a long beard
                                        (lit. 'doorman-man with a long
                                        beard', Ь. Олíйник)

This is just a small sampling of possible combinations; needless to say, the number of possible pairs is theoretically infinite ('worker' + 'bald man' = 'The worker who is/was bald').

2.4.1.2   The accusative case

The accusative case is first and foremost the case of the direct object: the case ending (where there is one that differs from the nominative) indicates that its bearer is the object of the verbal action. The English and Ukrainian terms for this case are more opaque than those of the nominative, but both indicate that something is being done to the object: Eng. *accusat-* < Lat. *accuso* 'blame', 'charge (with)', Ukr. **знахід-** 'find', 'discover', 'come upon'.

THE ACCUSATIVE OF AN INANIMATE OBJECT

Учи́тель написа́в *кни́жку* (nom. кни́жка).	The teacher wrote a book.
Наш гість диви́ться *телеві́зор.* (nom. телеві́зор)	Our guest is watching television.
О́льга відчиня́є *вікно́.* (nom. вікно)	Ol'ha is opening a window.

Among these examples we see that only the feminine singular has a peculiarly accusative marker, *viz.* -**у**; word order (A does B to C) and common sense (in this instance A are animate beings, C are not) dictate that 'television' and 'window' are the direct objects, hence in the accusative rather than the nominative. In the plural, of course, there is no differentiation of any kind between the nominative and accusative of inanimate nouns:

Учи́тель написа́в *кни́жки́.*	The teacher wrote the *books*.
Він купи́в *телеві́зори.*	He bought the *televisions*.
О́льга відчиня́є *ві́кна.*	Ol'ha is opening *windows*.

THE ACCUSATIVE OF AN ANIMATE OBJECT

Учи́тель поба́чив *хло́пця.* (nom. хло́пець)	The teacher saw the *boy*.
Наш гість зна́є *І́горя.* (nom. Ігор)	Our guest knows *Ihor*.
А́нна розбуди́ла *діду́ся.* (nom. діду́сь)	Anna woke *grandfather*.
Ми поба́чили *швейца́ра-бородача́.*	We saw the *doorman who has a long beard*.

An important point to note is that inanimate objects will also occasionally favour the genitive case as an accusative marker. Thus, **Іва́н написа́в/писа́в листа́** 'Ivan wrote/was writing a letter'; the use of the accusative in such instances will not be seen as incorrect, however. In the plural, however, we find the expected accusative almost exclusively: **Іва́н написа́в/писа́в листи́** 'Ivan wrote/was writing letters'. Compare the following quotation from a

Ukrainian folk tale, in which one accusative form is clearly marked as a genitive (**воза** from N.*sg.* **віз**):

Візьми во́за, са́ни й чо́вен/чо́вна́.   Take a waggon, sleigh, and boat.

In the singular only masculine animates are marked for animacy; note that this marker is the same as the genitive singular ending, and it will occur with both parts of a noun pair, as in the last example cited. In the plural, however, animacy is marked for all living (animate) beings, be they male, female, or animal. Nouns can be of all three genders, including a few common neuters; the ending is that of the genitive plural. Compare the following plural animate examples (given in the singular as well as the plural):

Зна́ю хло́пця – зна́ю хло́пців.   I know a/the boy/boys.
Зна́ю ді́вчину – зна́ю дівча́т.   I know a/the girl/girls.
Зна́ю дівча́тко – зна́ю дівча́ток.   I know a/the girl/girls.

These constructions are naturally dependent on the function of the particular verb in question; as verbs can require the use of other cases as well, we return to this syntactic point in our discussion of the use of the verb (see **6.4**). One further pattern to note is the use of the accusative (clearly evident only among animate direct objects) in 'passive' constructions involving the past passive participle of the verb, something that is unexpected from a grammatical point of view, as a passive implies the lack of a direct object; this is a function of the verb, however, and is examined in the context of the appropriate participles in **6.4.4**.

ACCUSATIVES IN TIME EXPRESSIONS   The accusative is used in expression not of 'time when' (compare the genitive below), but 'time during'; an entire phrase is said to be in the accusative, although this is not always apparent as a masculine inanimate noun, with its modifier(s), will appear to be in the nominative:

Ці́лий ти́ждень **він працюва́в.**   He worked (for, during) the entire
                             week.
Ці́лий рік . . .   . . . the whole year.
Ці́лий мі́сяць . . .   . . . the entire month.
Ці́лий день . . .   . . . the entire day.

The modifier can be left out here, losing the sense 'entire', but the unit of time will still be in the accusative on its own. Compare these constructions with the following, containing a feminine noun, in which the accusative is plainly evident:

Ко́жну хвили́ну . . .   Every moment/minute, continually . . .
Перемо́вчати хвили́ну.   To be silent (for) a minute/moment.
Яку́сь хвили́ну . . .   For a certain/short length of time . . .
Всю ніч . . .   . . . all night.

Note again that the unit of time can stand on its own in the accusative, or appear with a modifier. Essentially the presence of a word like **цíлий** or **кóжний** will lead to the use of the accusative; note, however, that (for **кóжний**, for example) the genitive is also possible or even preferred (see below).

The accusative also occurs in time expressions involving the use of prepositions; these are addressed in **2.4.2.2.2.**

2.4.1.3 The genitive case

The genitive case is often described as the case of possession, as it is this case that will occur in phrases such as the English 'Ivan's book', 'the book *of Ivan*'. It is more than that, of course, just as English 'of' will appear in many phrasal units that do not involve possession *per se*. The name of the case is equivalent in English and Ukrainian: Eng. *gen-* (< Lat. *genus, generis* 'kind'), Ukr. **род-** 'birth', 'origin', 'lineage', 'generation', and so on; in other words, this case tells us 'of what kind', 'of what relation', 'to what group' a word belongs.

POSSESSION   In the most general terms, one might describe the use of the genitive as a means of indicating the relation of one object or person to another. Compare the following examples, illustrating true possession as well as purely relational constructions:

кни́жка *профéсора*	the *professor's* book
брат *Óльги*	*Ol'ha's* brother
почáток *війни́*	the beginning *of the war*
кінéць *дня*	the end *of the day*
незалéжність *Украї́ни*	the independence *of Ukraine*

We note that each of these cases is more or less equivalent to English 'of' or ''s' constructions, and that the word in the genitive (the possessor, or object/idea about which specific information is being given) occurs second: it does not begin the phrase, unlike English 'apostrophes' ('the *professor's* book').

GENITIVE IN TIME EXPRESSIONS   Just as the prepositionless accusative can be used in time expressions to express duration, the genitive is used to focus on a point in time, for example, 'time when (X took/takes place)'; unlike the accusative, however, genitive constructions will require the presence of a modifier ('this', 'last', 'next'):

цього́ ро́ку	this year
мину́лого ти́жня	last week
насту́пного ро́ку	next year
одного́ ра́зу	once, one time

It is also possible for Ukrainian equivalents of such phrases, for example, 'last year', to be expressed using a prepositional construction with the locative case; this option is described under **2.4.2.2.4**.

THE PARTITIVE USE OF THE GENITIVE   The genitive is frequently used with the direct object when that object is a substance (mass, uncountable, or indivisible matter) in order to express 'some', 'some of', rather than the item or substance as a whole; the genitive is still used when an element indicating a particular measure is present ('litre of', 'bottle of'). Compare:

Да́йте *хлі́ба*!	Give (me) (some) *bread*!
Він хо́че пи́ти *води́*.	He wants to drink (some) *water*.
Він хо́че ви́пити *води́*.	He wants to have a drink of (some) *water*.
скля́нка *ча́ю*	a glass of *tea*
літр *горі́лки*	a litre of *horilka* (= Ukrainian vodka)

Compare these examples with the following accusative phrases, which refer to the totality of the substance:

Переда́йте *цу́кор*!	Pass the *sugar*! (the whole sugar bowl)
Вона́ з'ї́ла *хліб*.	She ate (up) the (loaf, piece of) *bread*.

In the last example the use of a perfective verb indicates the totality of the action (she ate it all up), as does the accusative of the object. It is certainly possible to have an imperfective verb with a genitive object (**Вона́ з'ї́ла хлі́ба, Він хо́че ви́пити води́**): this is one of those instances in which two speakers of Ukrainian may give two different answers to the question 'which aspect?' (see **6.4.3**).

THE GENITIVE OF NEGATION   The genitive can also occur as the case of the direct object, if the action is negated: in 'I did not X (verb) Y (object)' Y will appear in the genitive unless the object is accompanied by an element identifying it as definite; if the object is a person's name (that is, as definite as it can be), then only the accusative will be used:

Він прода́в *стіл*.	He sold a *table*.
Він не прода́в *стола́*.	He did not sell a *table*.
Він не прода́в *цей стіл*.	He did not sell *this table*.
Лі́кар прописував *лі́ки*.	The physician prescribed *medicine*.
Лі́кар не прописував *лі́ків*.	The physician did not prescribe *medicine*.
Лі́кар не прописував *ці лі́ки*.	The physician did not prescribe *this* medicine.
Ми не ба́чили *Марі́йку*.	We did not see *Marijka*.
but compare:	
Ми нія́кої *Марі́йки* **не ба́чили**.	We did not see any *Marijka* at all (no one of that name).

The use of the genitive is only possible (and in fact obligatory) in the last example because of the presence of the negative pronoun **ніякий** 'none', 'not any' (see **4.5.3**, negative pronouns).

As noted above (see 'the accusative' p. 95) some words, when direct objects, will tend to occur in the genitive in positive statements, where neither negation nor partitivity are expressed. This is the exception rather than the rule, however.

2.4.1.4   The dative case

The concept inherent in the meaning of the dative case is that of motion/ direction (real or figurative) to or towards; the etymology of the case name expresses this notion, as it is derived from the verb 'to give (*to*)': in English (from the Latin *dare–datum*) as well as in Ukrainian (from the Ukrainian **давáти–давáльний**).

THE INDIRECT OBJECT   The indirect object is the recipient of the direct object (= Ukrainian accusative); in English this recipient is accompanied by the preposition 'to': 'Give the book *to me!*' The preposition can also be implied in English: 'Give (*to*) *him* the book!' In Ukrainian it is the dative case that is used to express the indirect object:

відправля́ти поси́лку *дідусе́ві*	to send a package to *Grandfather*
дарува́ти *Іва́нкові* кни́жку	to give a book to *Ivanko* (as a present)
переда́ти *ма́мі* сіль	to pass the salt to *Mum*

йому́ віддаю́ть солда́ти ша́ну
   як *геро́єві*.
	The soldiers glorify (render honour
	   to) him as a *hero* (as to a hero).

These dative forms can be replaced by the construction **до** + genitive (see **2.4.2**, 'Prepositions'), without change in meaning. The dative will also be used to express English 'for (someone)', as in the following examples:

купува́ти *Мико́лі* крава́тку	to buy a tie *for Mykola*
діста́ти *си́нові* квито́к	to obtain a ticket *for (one's) son*

This use of the dative can be replaced by the prepositional construction **для** + genitive (see section); it is felt that the use of the latter renders a statement more personal or individual. Finally, a direct object need not be present if a given verb requires the use of the dative (for example, **Він не телефонува́в ба́тькові** 'He did not phone/ring father', 'did not make a phone call *to* father'). As this is a function of the verb, however, such constructions are examined in the context of the use of the verb (see **6.4.7.2**).

FIGURATIVE 'TO'   The dative of a noun can express 'to', 'for (the purpose of)' in the presence of another noun, without a verb:

па́м'ятник *Франко́ві*	monument to (Ivan) *Franko*
сла́ва *наро́ду*!	glory/praise *to the people*!
Сла́ва *Бо́гу*/*Бо́гові*!	Thank *God*! (lit. 'glory *to God*')
Спаси́бі *ба́тькові* за . . .	Thanks to father for . . .
(or the verb дя́кую 'I thank' + dative)	
при́клад *і́ншим хло́пцям*	(as an) example *to other boys*
Що *хло́пцеві* роби́ти?	What can the boy do? (What is there *for the boy* to do?)

Note particularly that nouns can require the use of the dative case if they are deverbal, i.e. formed from verbs that require the dative.

EXPRESSION OF AGE   One's age is expressed using the dative; in other words 'to him is/are X years':

Іва́нкові (бу́де/було́) шість ро́ків.	Ivanko is (will be/was) six years old.
Дити́ні (бу́де/було́) два ро́ки.	The child is (will be/was) two years old.
А́нні (бу́де/був) оди́н рік.	Anna is (will be/was) one year old.

IMPERSONAL CONSTRUCTIONS   Extremely common in the Slavonic languages, including Ukrainian, is the impersonal construction. In general these might be described as conditions (physical, mental, emotional) that are seen as imposed on one (hence the person is in the dative case) from the outside: implicit in this is the idea of one's lack of control over the situation.

Physical:

Си́нові хо́лодно.	(My) son is cold.
Сестрі́ тепло́, жа́рко.	(My) sister is warm, hot.
О́льзі до́бре/недо́бре/пога́но.	Ol'ha is fine, unwell, feeling badly.
Ба́тькові незру́чно.	Father is (feeling) uncomfortable (this can be physical or mental).

Mental, Emotional:

Бори́сові байду́же, . . .	It's all the same to Borys . . .
шкода́, що . . .	Borys is sorry that . . .
приє́мно, що . . .	Borys (finds it) pleasant that . . .
неприє́мно, що . . .	Borys (finds it) unpleasant that . . .
су́мно, що . . .	Borys is sad that . . .
тя́жко	Borys is *very* unhappy (= It weighs heavily on . . .)
до́сить	Borys (has had) enough.
було́ стра́шно	Borys was afraid.

Notice that most of the words in question are derived from adjectives, but they appear in the neutral form, as adverbs: '*It* is hot *to/for* someone'. Were one to say **Він жаркий** 'He is hot', it would be taken to refer to his temperament rather than his perception of temperature.

Modals – permission, possibility, necessity:

Ба́тькові ва́рто . . . (+ verb)	It is worth (it) for father to . . . (+ verb)
можли́во . . .	It is possible (physically) for father . . .
мо́жна . . .	It is possible/permissible for father . . .
не мо́жна . . .	Father is not allowed . . .
заборо́нено . . .	It is forbidden (for father . . .)
неможли́во . . .	It is not possible (physically) for father . . .
слід . . .	Father ought to/should . . .
тре́ба . . .	Father must/has to . . .

It is clear from these three sets of examples alone how vital impersonal constructions are to Ukrainian, whether in writing or in speaking. Note that the person (and therefore the dative) need not be indicated, if one is making a general statement, 'Here it is cold, one may not . . .', and so on. These constructions are close in status to adverbs, and are therefore treated in **7.1.2** and **7.8** as well.

Impersonal constructions: -ся verbs:

The last set of impersonal constructions involves the use of reflexive verbs (see **6.4.2.4**); they are included here as they involve the use of the dative case and are classed as impersonals, rather than as verbs that govern the dative case. These, as with the adverbial forms above, do not agree with the person in question, but appear in their 'neutral' ('it') form, *viz.* the 3*sg.* of the non-past, the neuter of the past. Note that they express a wide range of meanings, from how one feels or is able to function, to ability/permissibility.

(Вам) не годи́ться так говори́ти.	You/one should not talk like that.
Як до́чці спа́лося?	How did (your) daughter sleep?
Робітнико́ві не працю́ється.	The worker doesn't feel like working.
Оле́ксі хо́четься ї́сти.	Oleksa feels like (having something to) eat.
Оле́ксі хо́четься води́.	Oleksa would like to have (a drink of) water (+ genitive of substance).

Note that the use of the impersonal construction in the last two examples softens the sense of the sentences in comparison with the non-reflexive **хоті́ти** in similar contexts: **Він хо́че ї́сти** 'He wants to eat'. There are other -ся verbs that require the dative, but these are not impersonals and are therefore examined later on (see **6.4.7.2**).

THE ETHIC DATIVE (*PRO* THE GENITIVE) The dative can be used where an English speaker might expect a genitive, specifically in constructions involving motion '(in)to/(on)to' part of a person or a person's clothing:

Ма́ма ста́ла засо́вувати огірки́ зно́ву *Ко́стикові* в кише́ні.* (М. Носов)
Mama again started shoving cucumbers into *Kostyk's* pockets.

*(Although this example was taken from a Ukrainian book – produced in Ukraine – one native reader preferred: **Ма́ма ста́ла засува́ти огірки́ зно́ву до кише́нь.**)

А́ся покла́ла ру́ку *бра́тові* на плече́.
Asya placed her hand on her *brother's* shoulder.

2.4.1.5   The locative case

The locative case (Ukr. *місце́вий* 'locative = pertaining to location') is only used with prepositions: hence the alternative name of this case in English, the 'prepositional'.

2.4.1.6   The instrumental case

The instrumental is very widely used. As its English name implies, this can be the case of 'instrument', indicating that the object/person in this case is the instrument of a given action. The Ukrainian name expresses much the same sense: **ору́дний**, **ору́дник** 'instrumental', colloquial **ору́ддя** 'tool(s)', 'instrument(s)'. This case includes a wide range of meanings above and beyond that of the 'instrument' of an action, however; let us examine this particular usage first.

'INSTRUMENT', 'BY MEANS OF', 'WITH'   When English 'with' means 'by means of', then the Ukrainian instrumental is required, without a preposition (there is a preposition 'with' that requires the instrumental as well, but it refers to 'accompaniment': see **2.4.2.2.5**).

писа́ти *олівце́м*	to write *with* a pencil
ї́хати *авто́бусом*	to go/travel *by* bus
працюва́ти *рука́ми*	to work *with* one's hands
ї́сти *виде́лкою*	to eat *with* a fork
забива́ти цвях *молотко́м*	to hammer a nail *with* a hammer
говори́ти *телефо́ном*	to speak *by* telephone
Зубреня́ . . . сту́кнуло лісни́чого *ло́бом.*	The young bison struck the forester *with* its forehead/brow. (Я. Зазека)

Close in meaning – and identical in structure – to this pattern is the use of the instrumental with a substance (real or implied) of some kind, rather than with an instrument: for example 'to fill a glass with water' ('*with*' will again usually be present in the English equivalent). Such constructions are *not* described as 'verbs requiring the instrumental case' because the verb can often occur without the instrumental complement; in other words, 'to fill a glass' is possible without naming the substance:

Хатинка разом і світлом-огнем освіщається, і димом сповняється. (Марко Вовчок)

The little cottage all at once is illuminated by a fiery light (lit. 'light-fire'), and is filled *with smoke*. (Note particularly that modern Ukrainian prefers **вогонь** for **огонь** 'fire'.)

Ранки покривають усе рясними та холодними росами. (Ю. Збанацький)
The mornings cover all *with* (a) thick and cold dew (here in the plural).

Кожний її рух наллятий чавунною вагою. (О. Донченко)
Her every movement (was) filled with (lit.) 'the weight of iron' (i.e. she moved with great difficulty/slowness of speed).

Листівки . . . кожна з яких починалася закликом « . . . ». (В. Соснін)
Leaflets . . . each of which began *with* the appeal ' . . . '.

'BY' (AGENTIVE INSTRUMENTAL)   The agent of an action, crucial for passive constructions, is expressed by means of the instrumental case (X was done *by* Y):

стаття, написана *професором*	an article written *by* the professor
закон, затверджений *міністром*	the law, approved by the minister
слова, забуті *хлопцем*	the words, forgotten *by* the boy

Passive constructions are rare in spoken Ukrainian, but do occur in the literary language. Other ways of expressing the passive, without the use of the instrumental, are described in 6.4.4.

MOVEMENT 'THROUGH/ACROSS' SPACE   The instrumental on its own is frequently used with nouns indicating places across, along, or through which motion is taking place:

ходити лісом	to walk through a forest
бігати полями	to run across (the) fields
іти/їхати дорогою до . . .	to walk/ride along the road to . . .
Ледве помітною стежкою . . . ішла дівчинка. (О. Донченко)	A girl walked along a scarcely perceptible forest path.

TIME EXPRESSIONS   A number of prepositionless time expressions (functioning adverbially) involve the instrumental case; while some still feel like instrumental noun forms to Ukrainian speakers, others are distinctly adverbial. Conceptually some of these constructions are close to the expressions of motion through space, as they can mean 'during time X' rather than simply 'at time X':

зимою	in the winter (of X year, or by itself)
весною	in the spring (of X year, or by itself)
літом	in the summer (of X year, or by itself)
часом, часами	at times, sometimes

да́вніми часа́ми	in the old(en) days
тим ча́сом	meanwhile (lit. 'during that time')
ра́нком	in the morning
ве́чером	in the evening
ні́ччю	at night, in the night
ноча́ми	nights, for (many) nights
ци́ми дня́ми	during those days

Some Ukrainian informants see a number of these forms as having entered the language under the influence of Russian; nevertheless, they are provided as forms that are encountered. There are other variants for many of these adverbialized instrumentals, which are described in Chapter 7 (**7.2**, but see especially **7.3** for time expressions as a whole).

INSTRUMENTAL OF MANNER   A widely used construction is one that we might call the instrumental of 'manner': this is a construction which describes, sometimes comparing or equating a subject X with another noun; it answers such questions as 'how?', 'in what manner?', 'like/as a what?':

говори́ти ні́жним го́лосом	to speak in/with a soft voice
Со́нце . . . припіка́ло ко́сим промі́нням.	The sun was scorching hot (with its) slanting rays. (Н-Л)
диви́тися во́вком	to look angrily (at) (lit. 'to look as a wolf')
леті́ти стріло́ю	to fly as (straight as an) arrow
Он жо́втими пуши́нками вже пла́вають на чи́стім плесі каченя́та ди́кі.	There, (as/in) little yellow tufts, the wild little ducklings already swim on the clear surface of the river. (Л.У.)
Зли́ва звали́лася йому́ на плечі холо́дною ма́сою води́.	The torrential rain fell on his shoulders in/as a cold mass of water. (О. Донченко)
Се́рце озива́ється до ньо́го ра́дісним тре́петом.	(His) heart answers him with (a) joyful trembling. (О. Донченко)

It is also possible for nouns or noun phrases to appear in a particular case (and this might be any case) with no verb present; in such instances the case may actually be dependent on a verb or preposition in a previous sentence: an author may choose to end a sentence by means of a full stop while carrying over the thought of the previous sentence, as one would do in the spoken language, with the full stop reflecting a speaker's pause or hesitation. Thus, in the following example:

Льо́ня Ушако́в – гео́логом, Стьо́па Кучере́нко – моряко́м, Ва́ля Ча́йка – медсестро́ю . . . (Д.Ткач)

Lyonya Ushakov – a geologist, Styopa Kucherenko – a sailor, Valya Chayka – a nurse . . .

the instrumentals are all dependent on the previous sentence:

... **вони́ зга́дували й зга́дували, хто ким став. Льо́ня Ушако́в – гео́логом, ...**

... they kept on recalling who had become what ('who'). Lyonya Ushakov – a geologist, ...

The verb **ста́ти** requires the instrumental (see **6.4.7.3**); without this pivotal preceding sentence, the instrumental could not occur in the way that it does above, and one might instead expect **Льо́ня Ушако́в – гео́лог** 'Lyonya Ushakov *is* a geologist', and so on.

2.4.1.7   The vocative case

The vocative case is described as that form which occurs with names of persons or words designating persons/things being addressed: 'John!' 'Kolya!' 'Anna!' will all be marked as 'vocatives' in Ukrainian. As a rule, foreign names (such as 'John') are not marked, but there is nevertheless a tendency to do so, especially in the spoken language. Thus:

А́нно!	Anna!
Па́вле!	Pavlo!
Іва́не!	Ivan!
ба́тьку!	Father!
Джо́н(е)!	John!

The vocative is not limited to contexts in which the person is addressed directly, however; the name of a person mentioned in the middle or at the end of an utterance (almost parenthetically) will also be in the vocative:

Іді́ть сюди́, О́льго Сергі́ївно.	Come here, Ol'ha Serhijivna.
Що ти сказа́в, Воло́дю?	What did you say, Volodya?
Це я, Бори́се, твій брат.	It is I, Borys, your brother.

2.4.2   SYNTAX OF CASE: THE PREPOSITION

The presence of a preposition in conjunction with a noun (as with other declinable elements) requires the noun to appear in the particular case which that preposition governs; Ukrainian prepositions may govern any case except the vocative and the nominative. The following is a virtually complete alphabetical list of Ukrainian prepositions and the cases they govern; this list is followed by subgroups of prepositions according to the case which each governs, with definitions, and followed by examples.

2.4.2.1   Alphabetical list of Ukrainian prepositions

Many Ukrainian prepositions can govern more than one case. The vast majority of prepositions that govern only one case govern the genitive. We explore instances – and meanings – of multiple governance in the relevant sections of **2.4.2.2**. Where a list is provided of prepositions governing one case only, examples of only a few selected ones will suffice, especially when several are synonymous (this is especially true of the genitive prepositions). Where prepositions govern more than one case, examples are cited for each. The following list includes historically simple prepositions (such as **y**), formations consisting of two prepositions (for example, **з-за**) or three prepositions (such as **з-пóнад**) acting as one, prepositional constructions involving a frozen case form (like **позáду**), as well as those resulting from other word-formational processes (for example, **завдяки́**). It does not include constructions such as **пóруч з**, in which the case of an accompanying noun or noun phrase is determined by the second element (here the preposition **з**); such constructions are numerous in Ukrainian, and quite transparent in their usage and meaning. English meanings for each preposition are given as of **2.4.2.2**.

Preposition	*Case(s) governed*
без	G.
біля	G.
близько	G.
в = у	G., A., L.
вдовж = удовж	G.
вздовж = уздовж	G.
від (**од**: archaic)	G.
віддалік = оддалік	G.
вподовж = уподовж	G. (cited in SUM)
впоперек = упоперек	G.
впродовж = упродовж	G.
всередині	G.
вслід = услід	D.
всупереч = усупереч	D.
для	G.
до	G.
довкола (довкіл)	G.
(**ід = до**, dial.	D.)
з, зі, зо	G., A., I.
за	G., A., I.
з-за, із-за	G.
завдяки	D.
замість	G.

заради	G.
збоку	G.
(зверх, зверху, rare	G.)
ззаду	G.
з-перед	G.
з-під	G.
з-поміж (з-помежи)	G.
з-понад	G.
з-попід	G.
з-посеред	G.
з-проміж	G.
(к: archaic	D.)
коло	G.
край	G.
крізь	A.
крім	G.
між (rarely: межи, меж)	G., A., I.
мимо	G. (cited in SUM)
на	L., A.
навколо (навкіл)	G.
навпроти	G.
над	I., A.
накрай	G.
налад	G.
напередодні	G.
наперекір	D.
неподалік	G.
насупроти (less common than навпроти)	G.
о	L., A.
об	L., A.
обабіч	G.
обік	G.
обіч	G.
од: see від	
оддалік (віддалік)	G.
опріч	G.
перед	I., A.
перше	G. (rarely as a preposition but cited in SUM)
під	I., A.
після	G.
по	L., A., (D.)
побіля	G.

побіч	G.
поблизу	G.
поверх	G.
повз (dial. **поз, поуз**)	A., G.
повздовж	G. (rare, SUM)
подовж (dial. **подовш**)	G.
поза	I., A.
позад	G.
позаду	G.
поздовж	G.
поміж (**помежи**)	I., G., A.
понад (variants **понаді, понадо**)	I., A.
поперед	G., I., A.
попереду	G.
поперек	G.
попід	I., A.
попри	A., L., G.
поруч	G.
поряд	G.
посеред	G.
при	L.
про	A.
проміж (**промежи, промеж**)	I., G., A.
проти (**против** dial.)	G.
протягом	I.
ради = **заради**	G.
серед	G.
спереду	G
супроти (**супротив**, dial.)	G.
у = **в**	G., L., A.
уздовж = **вздовж**	G.
упоперек = **впоперек**	G.
услід = **вслід**	D.
усупереч = **всупереч**	D.
через	A.

A great many prepositions live a double life as adverbs: for example, **вздовж** 'along (something)', or simply 'along', **всупереч** 'in spite of (something)', or just 'to the contrary'. Good dictionaries will indicate both usages for such forms, but some may mention only the adverbial usage (in other words, this will be the more common or primary usage) when it can in fact also be found as a preposition; just one such example is **позаду**, which in many sources is described as an adverb only, while SUM describes it as a preposition as well.

2.4.2.2   Case government of Ukrainian prepositions

2.4.2.2.1   Prepositions governing the genitive

Preposition	*Meaning*
біля	close to, near
близько	near
в = у	at, near, from, among, to have
вдовж = удовж	along
вздовж = уздовж	along
від (од. archaic)	from, since, than (with a comparative)
вподовж = уподовж	along
впоперек = упоперек	across
впродовж = упродовж	along
всередині = усередині	inside
для	for
до	to, until, up to, before
довкола (довкіл)	around (rare, cited as an adverb in SUM)
з, зі, зо, із	from, off, of
з-за, із-за	from behind, through
замість, замісто	instead of, in place of
збоку	alongside, by the side of
зверх, зверху	on top of, beyond (more than)
ззаду	from the rear of, behind
з-перед	from in front of, from before
з-під	from under, from beneath
з-поміж (з-помежи)	from among
з-понад	from above
з-попід	from under, from beneath
з-посеред	from the midst of
з-проміж	from among
коло	around, near, by
край	near, by
крім	except (for), besides
мимо	past
навколо (навкіл)	around, round
навкруч (навкручи)	around
навпроти	directly opposite
накрай	at the end/edge of
налад	according to, in the form/shape of
напередодні	a short time before (an action or event)
насупроти	opposite
неподалік	not far from
обабіч	on/from both sides of

обік	side by side, near
обіруч	on all sides, from all sides (rare)
обіч	beside, by
од: see **від**	
округ (округи)	around
опріч	except, besides
(перше, rare, coll.	before (in time))
після	after
побіля	nearby, close by (to)
поблизу	near, close to
поверх	over, on, above
повз	past
повздовж	along
подовж	along
позад	behind, after
позаду	behind, at a certain distance behind
поздовж	along
попереду	before (temporally and spatially)
поперек	across, through the centre of
поруч	next to, alongside
поряд	near, close to, along with
посеред	in the middle of, amongst, among
проти (против dial.)	against, opposite
ради	for the sake of, on account of
серед	in the middle of, amongst, among
спереду	in front of, before
супроти (супротив, dial.)	against, opposite, in the face of
у: see **в**	
удовж: see **вдовж**	
уздовж: see **вздовж**	
уподовж: see **взподовж**	
упоперек: see **впоперек**	
упродовж: see **впродовж**	
усередині: see **всередині**	

This list clearly contains many synonymous (or nearly so) prepositions; compare, for example, the set 'along', which can be expressed by **вздовж, вдовж, вподо́вж, впродо́вж, подо́вж, повздо́вж, поздо́вж**. The key element in all of these particular prepositions is the root **-довж-** (< **довг-**) 'long'. Another large group of this kind expresses 'near', but not all of these forms are based on the same root. Some items may be considered by individual sources to be adverbs only (and then will be used with an unambiguous preposition, as in **неподалі́к від** 'not far from'); all forms listed here may, however, occur as *bona fide* prepositions and are included for the sake of completeness. Examples:

без су́мніву	without doubt, doubtlessly
без цу́кру	without sugar
вздовж бе́рега	along(side) the bank (e.g. of a river)
від Мико́ли	from Mykola
для Петра́	for Petro
до мі́ста	to the city
до прихо́ду профе́сора	before the arrival of the professor
з-за де́рева	from behind the tree
за́мість горі́лки	instead of *horilka* (Ukrainian vodka)
ко́ло університе́ту	near the university
навпро́ти магази́ну	opposite the store
пі́сля відпу́стки	after the holiday
посере́д студе́нтів	among the students

The form **про́тягом** 'during the course of', 'during' functions either as a preposition or as an adverb; as a preposition it governs the genitive:

про́тягом но́чі	during the night

PREPOSITIONS GOVERNING THE GENITIVE IN ADDITION TO OTHER CASES

в = у + G.: 'in', 'at', 'from' (with verbs of 'taking'), 'with', 'among', 'to have'; see **2.4.2.2.4** on **в** + L., A.

у бра́та	at (one's) brother's (place)
в украї́нців	among the Ukrainians . . .
Це я взяв у Іва́на.	I got that from Ivan.
В О́льги нема́є грошей.	Ol'ha has no money.
В ме́не є . . .	I have . . .

з, зі, із + G.: 'from', 'since'; see **2.2.4.2.5** on **з, зі, із** + I., A.

з Ки́єва	from Kyiv
з то́го ча́су	from/since that time
зі стола́	from off of the table (or any surface)
зі шко́ли	from school
із книжо́к	from (out of) books

In conjunction with certain adjectives or verbs (**дово́лі, до́сить, ви́стачить,** this preposition + G. can express a sense of 'having one's fill of' something; however, such phrasal units occur almost exclusively with pronouns (and then generally of the first person: **до́сить з ме́не**) rather than with nouns.

за + G.: 'during (time)', 'at (time)', 'in (time)'; see **2.4.2.2.5** on **за** + I., A.

за часі́в револю́ції	during the time of the revolution
за Хмельни́цкого	during the time of Khmel'nytskyj

повз (dial. **поз, поуз**) 'by', 'past', 'along'; more rarely with the G. than with the A. (see **2.4.2.2.2**)

повз пшениці густої	past the dense wheat (growing in the fields) (Ковінька, cited in SUM, more common now with the A. See **2.4.2.2.2.**)

попри 'in spite of', 'contrary to', 'in addition to'/'besides' (see **2.4.2.2.2** on A., **2.4.2.2.4** on L.)

Попри сили, була в ньому й доброта.	In addition to strength, there was also kindness in him.

The remaining prepositions occur with I. and A. in addition to G.; all of the following occur more rarely with the G. than with the I. and A., however (see **2.4.2.2.5** on I., A.):

між (rarely: **межи, меж**) 'between', 'among', this form and:

між веселих людей	among cheerful people
між гір	between the mountains (more often: **між горами**)

поміж (**помежи**) 'among', 'between'

поміж моряків	among the seamen
поміж дівчат була мовчанка.	(lit. 'There was silence among the girls.')

поперед temporally or spatially before something or someone

Поперед Анни йшов її знайомий.	(lit. 'Ahead (in front) of Anna was walking her acquaintance.')

проміж (**промежи**) 'among', 'between' (sometimes in contexts indicating 'motion to' a place)

проміж робітників	among the workers
Ліг спати проміж двох собак.	He lay down to sleep between two dogs.

2.4.2.2.2   Prepositions governing the accusative

крізь 'by', 'through'

Ми пройшли крізь ліс.	We walked through the forest.
крізь усе життя	through (one's) entire life
Крізь шум почулися голоси.	Through the noise one could hear voices.

про 'about', 'concerning', 'for'

Він співав про дитину.	He was singing about the child.
Знайдеться робота про Івана?	lit. Will there be work (found) for Ivan? (colloq.)
про всяку пригоду	(in preparation) for any eventuality

че́рез 'across', 'through', 'over', 'by means of', 'in'/'after' (time), 'because of'

Íхали че́рез усе́ село́.	They rode through the whole village.
Вона́ сиді́ла че́рез стіл.	She sat across the table (from . . .).
Вони́ говори́ли че́рез перекладача́.	They spoke through an interpreter.
Усього́ дося́гнеш че́рез пра́цю.	You (will, can) attain everything by means of (hard) work.
че́рез ти́ждень	In/after a week('s time)
че́рез ці́ле життя́	(one's) whole life through
че́рез Бори́са заги́нув діду́сь.	Grandfather perished because of Borys.

PREPOSITIONS GOVERNING THE ACCUSATIVE IN ADDITION TO OTHER CASES
Note that **без** + A. is possible in dialect but not in literary usage; the constructions with **о** below are considered generally archaic by native informants, but are included here as they can be encountered in older Ukrainian literature.

о 'about', 'on', 'at', 'upon', 'over', 'for'

о цю по́ру	at about/during that time (approximation)
О во́ду про́сить.	He/she is asking for water. (rare, SUM)
Скля́нка розби́лася о ка́мінь.	The glass broke (apart) on/against the rock. (archaic, SUM)
о пів на п'я́ту	at half past four
о три ро́ки моло́дший	younger by three years (dial., SUM) (but preferable: **на три ро́ки**)

об (rare, archaic) 'concerning', 'about', 'on', 'against' (at times = **о**, see preceding entry)

об цю по́ру	at/during that time
сту́кати об сті́ну	rap on the wall
обпе́ртися об сті́ну	lean against the wall (for support).
Його́ взяла́ об ру́ку.	She took him by the hand. (rare)

по 'up to', 'as far as', 'down to' (motion implied), 'along', 'each' (distributive meaning)

по той бік	along that side (indicates motion or location of action, usually with words such as **бік**, **сторона**)
іти́ по лі́каря	to go for the doctor
іти по молоко́	to go for the milk
сніг по колі́на	the snow (is) up to the knees
по п'ять ра́зів	five times (each)

ходи́ли по че́тверо	They walked (in groups of) four/four at a time.
з бе́резня по ве́ресень	from March through September
від війни́ по на́ші дні	from the war up to the present day
з 1 по 9 квітня	from the 1st to the 9th of April (inclusive)

повз 'along', 'by', 'past', 'across'

ходи́ти повз двір	to walk across the courtyard
Вона́ пройшла́ повз відчи́нене вікно́.	She walked past the open window.
рік повз рік	from year to year (continuously) (more dialect than literary, preferred: **рік за ро́ком**)
повз пшени́цю густу́	past the dense wheat (growing in the fields)

по́при 'along', 'past (dial.)', 'besides', 'in spite of'

| по́при всі намага́ння | in spite of all (one's) efforts |

See sections **2.4.2.2.1** on без, повз, по́при + G.; **2.4.2.2.3** on по + D.; **2.4.2.2.4** on по, о, об, по́при + L. A number of prepositions that may occur with the accusative also govern the instrumental or prepositional; the two contexts dictating which of these cases is required are usefully described together on semantic grounds, thus за, з (зі, із), над, пе́ред, під, по́за, пона́д, по́під + accusative are examined in **2.4.2.2.5**, while на and у (в) + accusative are described in **2.4.2.2.4**.

2.4.2.2.3   Prepositions governing the dative

вслід = услід 'after' (in the direction of)

| Ба́тько дити́ні вслід крича́в «Стоп!». | Father shouted 'Stop!' after the child. (Note that here it functions as a postposition, as it follows the noun.) |

всу́переч = усу́переч 'in spite of', 'without regard for', 'contrary to'

| всу́переч усі́м зако́нам | contrary to all laws |

завдяки́ 'thanks to'

| завдяки́ його́ допомо́зі | thanks to his help |
| завдяки́ ба́тькові | thanks to father |

ід = до, dialect   'to', 'as far as'

к: archaic   towards, to

| **Іди́ к бі́су** | Go to the devil. |

напереќір 'in spite of', 'contrary to'

напереќір усі́м тру́днощам	in spite of all the difficulties
напереќір її бажа́нням	contrary to her wishes

PREPOSITIONS GOVERNING THE DATIVE IN ADDITION TO OTHER CASES **По** is cited by some sources as a preposition + D. used to express 'according to', for example in **по-мо́єму** 'in my opinion'; such a construction ought instead to be considered a frozen expression, i.e. thought of as an adverb rather than as a viable preposition (it can be used in the speech of Ukrainians under the influence of the Russian language in which it is employed in contexts expressed by other means or cases in Ukrainian). See **2.4.2.2.4** on **по** + L., **2.4.2.2.2** on **по** + A.

2.4.2.2.4   Prepositions governing the locative

There is only one such preposition, but it is extremely important and widely used. Some of the examples below show just how difficult it is to translate into English; the reader is advised to assimilate sample patterns and not to rely too heavily on English equivalents.

при 'beside', 'by', 'at', 'in the presence of' (spatially and temporally), 'during'

при вхо́ді до кімна́ти	by/at the entrance to the room
при само́му Дністрі́	(right) by/along the river Dniester
при на́шому інститу́ті є ка́федра . . .	at our institute there is a department of . . .
при захо́ді сонця	at (the time of) sunset
при поча́тку XX ст.	at the beginning of the twentieth century
при О́льзі	at/during the time of Ol'ha
Він прибу́в у фо́рмі при всіх о́рденах.	He arrived in (his) uniform (with) all of his medals/orders.
Хай бог її де́ржить при здоро́в'ї.	May God keep her in (good) health. (Л.У.)
При здоро́в'ї він мав такі́ си́ли.	When he was healthy, he had such strength(s).
При мізе́рному лиці́ бра́та, Іва́сько здава́вся щасли́вим та здоро́вим.	(Given/in the presence of) the miserable/sickly face of his brother, Ivas'ko appeared happy and healthy.
Він живе́ при ма́тері.	He lives with his mother (in her presence).
бу́ти при сме́рті	To be on the verge of death.

PREPOSITIONS GOVERNING THE LOCATIVE IN ADDITION TO OTHER CASES   Of the following prepositions, **на** and **в** (**у**) are by far the most common, as they are used in a wide variety of contexts, most of which are temporal and spatial. It is the spatial constructions in particular that make their joint presentation with the L. and A. necessary: use with the L. commonly expresses location 'in', 'on', 'at', while the corresponding use with the A. expresses motion *to* that location (in addition to **до** + G.).

SPATIAL CONSTRUCTIONS

на + L. 'on', 'at' (a location), generally used with words denoting outdoor or uncovered locales, or surfaces of objects (e.g. street, floor, roof . . .); some words must simply be learnt as '**на**' words, as English equivalents may require 'in'.

бу́ти на ста́нції	be at the station (implied: outdoor, platform)
бу́ти на ву́лиці	be on the street
бу́ти на тротуа́рі	be on the pavement
бу́ти на база́рі	be at the market, bazaar
бу́ти на мо́рі	be at the sea
бу́ти на чужині́	be in a foreign land
на глибині́ 200 ме́трів	at a depth of 200 metres

на + A. 'to', 'onto' (a location); motion can also be figurative.

ї́хати на ста́нцію	go to the station (implied: outdoor, platform)
іти́ на ву́лицю	go (out) onto the street
іти́ на тротуа́р	go onto the pavement
іти́ на база́р	go to the market, bazaar
ї́хати на мо́ре	go to the sea
ї́хати на чужину́	go to a foreign land

у = **в** + L. 'in' (a location, situation, or state)

бу́ти в (у) кімна́ті, ха́ті	be in the room, cottage (house, hut)
бу́ти в Украї́ні	be in Ukraine
бу́ти в (у) журбі́	be in sorrow
бра́ти у́часть у святкува́нні	take part in the celebration (of . . .)
у ро́лі Га́млета	in the role of Hamlet
сад у росі́	a garden in (covered with) dew
дра́ма в 4 ді́ях	a drama in four acts
крича́ти во гніві́	shout in anger (very elevated style)
жи́ти в дру́жбі	live in friendship (harmoniously)

y = в + A. 'into' (a location); in certain expressions motion can be figurative
(cf. до + G.).

іти́ в (у) кімна́ту, ха́ту	go into the room, cottage (house, hut)
їхати в Украї́ну	go to Ukraine
іде́я прийшла́ мені́ в го́лову	an idea came into my head
леті́ти у вікно́	fly into/through the window
сту́кати у две́рі	knock on the door
вдава́тися в ту́гу	become/enter into melancholy
узя́ти в поло́н	to take prisoner, into captivity
в ім'я́ свооо́ди	ın the name ol' freedom
іти́ в го́сті	go visiting

TEMPORAL CONSTRUCTIONS

на + L. less common: 'at', 'during'; see в + L. below.

на тім ти́жні	(during) that week
На днях хо́дитч	to be in the last days of pregnancy

на + A. 'on', 'for', 'per'

захо́дь до ме́не на хвили́нку	come to (see) me for a minute
їхати в Оде́су на весну́	go to Odessa for the spring
на дру́гий день	the next day
на п'я́ту ніч	on the fifth night
на той/цей час	at that/this time
два ра́зи на день	twice a day

в + L. 'in', 'during'

в че́рвні	in June
в молоди́х літа́х	in one's youth
в мої́х літа́х	at my age

в + A. 'on', 'at', 'during'

у п'я́тницю	on Friday
в таку́ ніч	on such a night
у цю по́ру	at (during) this time
В його́ три́дцять ро́ків він усти́г . . .	In/during the course of his thirty years, he managed/succeeded in (doing X, inf.).
в одну́ мить	at one (sudden) moment . . .
з лі́та в лі́то	from summer to summer

OTHER CONSTRUCTIONS USING *в* AND *на*: These two prepositions occur in many contexts that are difficult to describe satisfactorily in a systematic way; sources such as SUM do devise numerous sub-categories into which examples can be made to fit, but these are in many cases artificial. Therefore we will simply list their most common (non-temporal, non-spatial) occurrences.

в + L. and A. (including a number of set expressions):

в п'ятй кіломе́трах від . . .	(at a distance of) five kilometres from . . .
у неду́зі лежа́ти	be ill
відда́ти в на́йми	rent out, lease something to
ви́йти в лю́ди	become somebody
у ві́дповідь	in answer (to)
поцілува́ти когóсь в ру́ку	kiss someone on the hand
кімна́та у три вікна́	a room with three windows
у три ра́зи бі́льше	three times as large
убива́ти комýсь у же́ртву	sacrifice to . . . (lit. 'kill in/as a sacrifice to . . .')

на + L. and A.:

ві́рити на слóво	take (someone) at his word
попа́сти на óчі комýсь	come into someone's view
попа́сти на слід . . .	find/come upon the trail of . . .
перекла́сти на англі́йську мóву	translate into English
бýти на самоті́	be in solitude
жи́ти на картóплі	live on potatoes
на па́м'ять	as a memento (lit. 'for memory')
на честь комýсь	in honour of . . .
мука́ на хліб	flour for (the making of) bread
на бі́са . . .	to hell with . . .
погляда́ти на кóгось	look at someone
на шви́дку ру́ку	in haste
бра́ти на се́бе	to take upon oneself
іти́ на вóрога	go against the enemy
на знак	as a sign
ма́ти на ду́мці	to have/bear in mind
лежа́ти комýсь на се́рці	to be dear to someone (used of things, ideas)

The list of expressions with **на** could be much longer, but the examples here suffice to give the learner an idea of its use. Many other contexts in which this preposition can be found are cited in the better dictionaries, and of course it occurs now as an integral part of many set phrases and sayings (some of the examples cited in the list above fall into this category); it is advisable to make note of individual usages as they are encountered in reading or in speech.

The last three prepositional sets involving the L. are **по**, **о**, **об**, and **попри**; of these prepositions **по** is the most common, and attention should be paid to its many varied uses (temporal, spatial, and relational):

по + L. 'about', 'along', 'after', 'by', 'throughout', 'on'

Жили́ по Дніпру́.	They lived along(side) the Dniepr.
Вона́ ходи́ла по кімна́ті.	She walked about/around the room.
уда́рити по голові́	hit (someone) about/on the head
по війні́, о́біді	after the war, lunch
по трьох ро́ках	after three years
по те́плій пого́ді	(during, at the time of) warm weather (X action takes place)
поноча́х	at nights (something regularly happens)
годи́на по годи́ні	hour after hour
рік по ро́ці	year after year
пізна́ти по го́лосі	recognize by (one's) voice

Many other constructions of this kind (for example, **това́риш по шко́лі** 'school comrade', **транслюва́ти по ра́діо** 'broadcast on/by radio') may be seen as Russianisms, or as due to the influence of Russian; they will be heard in the speech of a considerable number of Ukrainians, but will not necessarily be found in literary Ukrainian. Thus a construction like **Вони́ прийшли́ по ді́лу** 'They came on business' might be considered less Ukrainian than **Прийшли́ у спра́ві**.

о + L. 'at' (time on the clock); all other meanings with the L. are considered archaic or dialectal, e.g. 'about' (= 'concerning') but may be found in works of literature.

о дев'я́тій (годи́ні)	at nine o'clock
о тій порі́, коли́	at that time, when . . . (rarer)

об + L. 'at approximate time when' or 'during', 'about', 'in physical proximity to'

об 11 годи́ні	at about 11 o'clock
об о́біді	at the time of, during lunch (rare)
Було́ об Іллі́.	It was around the time of St Illya. (archaic, SUM)
ва́лянці об нога́х	felt boots about/on the feet (rare)

по́при + L. 'in the presence of' (= **при**)

по́при осо́бі на́шого тетра́рха	in the presence of the person of our tetrarch (Л.У.)

2.4.2.2.5   Prepositions governing the instrumental

It will be noted from the master list of prepositions that none is used exclusively with the instrumental. All prepositions that govern the instrumental also occur with the accusative, while three occur with the genitive as well as the instrumental and accusative; their use with the genitive is described in **2.4.2.2.1**. As in the case of prepositions governing the locative, the reason for treating these prepositions together here has to do with the expression of spatial relationships: most of the following, when used with the instrumental, refer to the specific position of one object in relation to another object (X is over, under, behind, in front of . . . Y); when used with the accusative, it is movement *into* that position that is being expressed (X is going into position over, under, behind, in front of . . . Y). The use of particular prepositions, for example, **з**, together with other prepositions or adverbs (such as **поруч**) is not reflected in the examples below, as the meaning of such phrasal units is evident from their constituent parts.

з, зі, зо + I.: 'with', 'together with'

Я подружив з колéгою.	I made friends with a colleague.
проблéми з начáльством	problems with those in authority
Ми говорúли з мáтір'ю.	We spoke with mother.
Він пішóв з парасóлькою в руцí.	He set off with an umbrella in his hand.
з виїздом президéнта . . .	upon (with) the departure of the president . . .
з повáгою	lit. 'with respect'; 'respectfully yours' (in letters)
Чекáли з рáдістю.	They (a)waited with (in a state of) happiness.
Чекáли з óстрахом.	They waited with/in dread, great fear.
Президéнт приїхав з візúтом.	The president arrived for a visit (came to visit).
три з половúною днí	three and a half days
Що з Óльгою?	What's with Ol'ha?
кáва з цýкром та молокóм	coffee with sugar and milk
Я згóден з Оксáною.	I agree with Oksana.

Phrasal examples of the last type, i.e. in conjunction with adjectives that imply an attitude towards closeness to a person or a position (here: **згоден з**), are common and easily understood on the basis of the adjective in question.

з, зі, зо + A. expression of approximation

з годúну	about one hour
з мíсяць	approximately one month
з п'ять фýнтів	about five pounds

за + I. 'by means of', 'through', 'after', 'at', 'by', 'on', 'for', 'outside', 'beyond'

за обідом	at lunch
за кавою	at (over, while having) coffee
день за днем	day after day
Батько бігає за дітьми.	Father runs after the children.
Черга за нами.	It is our turn. (lit. 'The queue is after/behind us.')
за горами	beyond the mountains
За роботою неможлйво . . .	Because of work it is impossible to . . .
за його прикладом	by (after) his example
Ми за нашим лідером!	We are behind/follow our leader!
за редакцією X-ого	under the editorship of X

за + A. 'in the course of (time)', 'behind', 'beyond', 'after (temporally and spatially)', 'for', 'in exchange for', 'from', 'than' in comparative constructions (see **3.2.1.4**).

Сісти за стіл.	Sit down at the table.
За дві години написав . . .	During the course of two hours he wrote . . .
за розмовою	during the conversation
За місяць приїде.	He/she will come in a month.
Дякую за хліб.	Thank you for the bread.
Я за правду.	I am for the truth.
за батьківщину . . .	for one's country (e.g. to give one's life)
далеко за південь	long (lit. 'far') after noon
Вона була за шістдесят.	She was past sixty (in years).
за сто кілометрів від . . .	at a distance of 100 kilometres from . . .
питати, говорити за нього	ask, speak about (lit. after) him
Мені страшно за Івана.	I am afraid for Ivan.
Це я купив за 100,000 гривень.	I bought that for 100,000 hryvni.
віддати дочку за когось	give one's daughter (in marriage) to someone
уважати когось за генія	consider someone (to be), take as, a genius

між (rarely: межи, меж) + I. 'among', 'between', 'amid'

між Києвом і Одесою	between Kyiv and Odessa
між горами	in the middle of, amid the mountains
між сином та батьком	between son and father
між солдатами	among the soldiers
Яка разниця між X та X?	What's the difference between X and X (where both X's are in the I.)?

між (rarely: межи, меж) + A. 'motion, corresponding to the spatial relationships expressed by між + I.

вдáрити когóсь між óчі	hit someone between the eyes
ітѝ між дерéва	go between the trees

над, пóнáд + I. 'over', 'above', 'beyond', 'on', 'upon' (понад: also 'along')

над мíстом	above the city
над полямѝ	over the fields
робóта над кнѝжкою	work on the book
пóнáд рíчкою	along (at a height above) the river
Птах летíв пóнáд водóю.	The bird flew (just) above the water.
Літератýра – пóнáд політикою.	Literature is above (unconnected to) politics.

над + A. motion corresponding to над + I.; expression of the time of an action; in comparison, but not necessarily with comparative adjectives (see 3.2.1.4).

Птах літáє над вóду.	The bird flies (into position) over the water.
над зáхід сóнця	at the time of sunset (an action took place)
Заснýла над рáнок.	She fell asleep at/by morning.
Тебé люблю́ над життя́.	I love you more than (over) life (itself).
давáти продýкцію над план	produce over the plan (= overfulfil the quota)

пóнáд + A. 'motion (just) above', 'more than', 'above' (figuratively), 'near' (in time)

дивѝтися на когóсь пóнáд окуляри	look at someone over one's spectacles
пóнáд три тѝжні, годѝну	over/more than three weeks, an hour
Булó вже пóнáд рáнок.	It was already approaching morning.
пóнáд сто студéнтів	over/more than 100 students
вѝпустити Х пóнáд план	produce X beyond the quota/planned amount
Він герóй пóнáд усíх герóїв.	He is a hero above all heroes (a hero of heroes). (Л.У.)

пéред + I. 'before' (temporally and spatially), 'in front of', 'ago', 'in the face of'

пéред дóмом, хáтою	in front of the house, cottage/home
пéред нарóдом	before the people/nation
Пéред áрмією булó тяжкé діло.	The army was faced with a difficult task (matter).
пéред рáнком	(just) before morning, daybreak

перед + A. motion corresponding to **перед** + I.

прийти́ пе́ред дім	come (to a place) in front of the house

під, по́під + I. 'under', 'beneath', 'below', 'near', 'along', 'towards' (with motion)

під Льво́вом	near L'viv
під столо́м	under the table
під впли́вом	under the influence (of)
Пи́ше під і́менем « Х ».	He/she writes under the name X.
Під цим сло́вом розумі́ю . . .	By this word I understand (= I understand it to mean) . . .
під руко́ю	at hand
під керівни́цтвом	under the direction (of)
під зву́ки полоне́зу	to (while hearing) the sounds of a polonaise
по́ле під пшени́цею	a field of wheat (under = sown with)
під нарко́зом	under (the influence of) a narcotic
по́під водо́ю та земле́ю	under water and earth
під, по́під гора́ми	under (at the foot of) the mountains
по́під стіно́ю	along, alongside, under the wall

під, по́під + A. motion corresponding to **під, по́під** + I.; 'near', 'along', 'towards', 'almost' (time)

прийти́ під керівни́цтво	come under the direction (of)
під ра́нок, ве́чір	towards morning, evening
Їй під три́дцять.	She is almost thirty.
сі́сти під сті́ну	sit down near the wall
Пішли́ під зе́млю.	They went underground.
Прийшли́ під на́шу ха́ту.	They came towards our house.
під той ві́тер	in such a (strong) wind (as in: X went somewhere under such bad conditions.)
потра́пити під вплив . . .	fall under the influence of . . .
карто́плю сади́ти під плуг	plant potatoes with, by means of the plough
під стра́хом сме́рті	in fear of death
під нови́й рік	(on the eve of) the new year
під час пере́рви	during the interval
диви́тися по́під стіл	have a look under the table
ходи́ти по́під сті́ну	go up to, near the wall
трава́ по́під ру́ки	grass up to (as high as) one's hands

по́за + I. 'beyond', 'behind', 'after'

по́за дверми́	behind the door
по́за ціє́ю кімна́тою	beyond this room
по́за війно́ю	after the war

пóза + A. 'to the outside of', 'outside', 'a certain time before'

ітú пóза двéрі	go out, beyond the door
пóза ці стíни	(go) beyond these (four) walls

2.5   SUBSTANTIVAL WORD FORMATION

Word formation refers to the processes by which new words are constructed from the pool of linguistic elements (roots, prefixes, suffixes) present in the language. Thus, the English word 'formation' is made up of the verbal element '(to) form' + the suffix '-(a)tion' on the pattern of such verb-noun pairs as 'generate-generation', 'obligate-obligation', etc.; this process is not in fact originally an English one, but one adopted from Latin: *formare* – N.sg. *formatio*, G.sg. *formationis*, *obligare* – N.sg. *obligatio*, G.sg. *obligationis*, and so on. When we refer to such processes of word formation, it is customary to specify the nature of the building blocks: thus, a 'desubstantival' noun is one 'built from a noun or nouns'; similarly, the terms 'deadjectival', 'deverbal' mean that a given form is based upon adjectival or verbal stems, respectively. A familiarization with the elements that are used in word formation, and with their general meanings, makes the process of acquiring vocabulary (especially elements of more sophisticated lexicon) easier and more systematic. However, just knowing the origin of the elements of a word does not guarantee that the meaning of a derived form will equal the sum of its parts. Thus, for example, **о-бач-ення** could be segmented as 'look + around', but in fact means 'consideration', 'care': i.e. 'looking around' in a figurative sense; knowing the processes of word formation therefore gives us linguistic tools which must be handled with care.

In the following sections we shall examine the major patterns of substantival word formation typical of the Ukrainian language: prefixation, suffixation, and compounding. The ultimate source of every example is not always described, as it can often have different interpretations: thus, for example, 'desubstantival' forms may be based on a substantive that is itself derived from an adjective (for example, **без-ум-н-ість** < **ум-н-ість** < **-ум-н-ий** < **-ум-**, in which the progression is one of substantive > adjective > substantive > substantive). For our purposes, forms are identified as 'deadjectival' only where the source is clearly only or originally adjectival.

2.5.1   SUFFIXAL WORD FORMATION

The formation of new substantives (from other substantives) using suffixes only is very common; new prefixed forms typically involve the presence of suffixes as well, therefore suffixation is introduced first. Suffixes borrowed from West European languages that are clear to the learner (for example,

-ад(а) '-ade' in 'colonnade', 'blockade', and so on, -аж '-age' in 'massage', and similar) are not included.

-áк, -я́к 'pertaining to one's profession', 'place of habitation', 'ethnic group': a marker of masculine persons, in reference to the quality expressed by a source adjective, the action expressed by a source verb, or an action associated with a source noun. Deadjectival and deverbal nouns with this suffix can in many cases be considered very colloquial, and even as sub-standard by some speakers.

desubstantival: **моряк** 'seaman', **сибіряк** 'a Siberian', **земляк** '(fellow-) countryman', **подоляк** 'native of Podolia'.

deadjectival: **бідак** 'poor fellow', **дивак** 'strange person', **срібняк** 'silver coin', **мертвяк** 'corpse' (= мрець, see -ець below).

deverbal: **вожак** 'leader', **співак** 'singer', **лежак** 'layabout'.

-áка, -я́ка see preceding entry, much less frequent, for example,

deverbal: **гуляка** 'reveller', 'one who makes merry' (better: **гультяй**)

-ан(ь) formations (mostly from nominal roots) refer to a person's activities or to the presence in that person of particular traits or characteristics (compare -ач below).

desubstantival: **головань** 'person with a large head', **лобань** 'blockhead', **стариган(ь)** 'stout old man', **бородань** 'bearded man'.

deadjectival: **білань** 'fair-haired person'.

-áнин, -я́нин 'pertaining to one's geographical and/or ethnic origin', for male persons. Compare also the adjectival suffix -ин (Chapter 3).

росіянин 'a Russian', **киянин** 'person from Kyiv', **волжанин** 'one from the Volga region' (note the consonant mutation г > ж), **галичанин** 'one from Galicia'.

-áнка, -я́нка 'pertaining to one's geographical and/or ethnic origin', for female persons.

росіянка 'a Russian woman', **киянка** 'woman from Kyiv', **волжанка** 'woman from the Volga region' (note the consonant mutation г > ж), **галичанка** 'woman from Galicia'.

-áнка, -я́нка deadjectival (including passive participles) formation, principally denoting female persons exhibiting characteristics of the adjective in question (rare). See also -ка below.

обідранка = **обшарпанка** 'woman in tatters, rags', **вигодованка** 'girl brought up at another's expense'.

-ар, -яр very common, most frequently in desubstantival formations: denotes a masculine person engaged in activities associated with the base noun; rarely with verbs and adjectives. Compare (i) forms borrowed from West European languages (i.e. with non-Slavonic roots), for example,

ветеринар, резервуар, санітар, and so on (ii) deverbal nouns whose root contains the same sequence, such as **пивовар** 'brewer', < **пиво + вар-ити**.

> *desubstantival:* **бондар** 'cooper', **шахтар** 'miner', **вівчар** 'shepherd', **словникар = лексигограф** 'lexicographer', **книгар** 'bookseller', 'stationer', **цегляр** 'brickmaker', **бджоляр** 'beekeeper', **газетяр** 'journalist', and so on.
>
> *deverbal:* **дзвонар** 'bellringer', **писар** 'clerk', 'scribe', **бунтар** 'mutineer'.
>
> *deadjectival:* **крутар** 'cheat', 'deceitful person' (= **крутій**)

-арка, -ярка see **-ка** below.

-а́(та), -я́(та) in desubstantival formations, denoting the young of animals or small children. In the singular one individual is designated by the presence of this suffix (**-а**), while the full suffix (plural **-ата**) is used to designate either simple plurality or the category as a whole; in other words, it then becomes a collective noun.

внук > внуча(та) 'little grandchild(ren)', **гусь > гусеня(та)** 'gosling(s)', **циган > циганча(та)** 'little/young gipsy/gipsies', **козеня(та)** '(goat) kid(s)', **вовченя(та)** 'wolf young', **жереб'я(та)** 'colt', and so on.

-атина, -ятина formed from some animal names to denote their meat; note that this suffix is in turn derived from **-а́(та), -я́(та)** above. See also **-ина** below for derivations based on non-derived nouns.

> **курятина** chicken meat
> **гусятина** goose meat
> **телятина** veal

-а́ч Desubstantival (unproductive) and deadjectival (rarer) formations refer to a person's activities or to the presence in that person of particular traits or characteristics; deverbal forms are productive, and denote one who performs the action in question, or an instrument used in that action.

> *desubstantival:* **трубач** 'trumpeter', **бородач** 'bearded man', **циркач** 'circus performer', **головач** 'one with a big head', **силач** 'wrestler', 'athlete' (lit. 'strongman'), **горбач** 'hunchback'.
>
> *deadjectival:* **багач** 'wealthy man'.
>
> *deverbal:* **глядач** 'spectator', **викладач** 'lecturer', **ткач** 'weaver', **розвідач** 'explorer', 'researcher', **розповідач** 'narrator', **шукач** 'searcher', 'investigator', **вимикач** 'electric switch', **радіоприймач** 'radio receiver'.

-(ь)ба realized either as **-ьба** or as mutated consonant + **ба**, more rarely **-оба**. This is one suffix used (unproductively) to form new nouns from verbal roots.

різьба 'carving', 'sculpture', **служба** 'service', **стрільба** 'firearm', **дружба** 'friendship', **ходьба** 'walking about', 'continual walking', **боротьба** 'fight', 'combat', **жалоба** 'sorrow', **хвороба** 'illness'.

-бищ(е): see **-ищ(е)** below.

-еність: see **-ість** below.

-ець, -єць, including the (ultimately deadjectival) compounds **-анець, -янець, -енець, -инець, -лець, -овець, -івець**.

-ець, -єць is an extremely common suffix in Ukrainian, and occurs in desubstantival, deadjectival, as well as deverbal constructions, primarily to denote the origin, characteristics, or activities of male persons.

> *desubstantival:* **горець** 'man from the mountains', 'highlander', **кавказець** 'man from the Caucasus', **українець** '(a) Ukrainian', **комсомолець** 'male member of the Komsomol', **партієць** 'male member of the Party', **італієць** 'an Italian'.
>
> *deadjectival:* **мудрець** 'wise man', **старець** 'aged man', **щасливець** 'fortunate person'.
>
> *deverbal:* **боєць** 'fighter', **борець** 'boxer', 'wrestler', **їздець** 'horseman', 'rider', **читець** 'reciter'.

-анець, -янець occurs in some words denoting nationality (again, of male persons): **американець** 'American', **мексиканець** 'Mexican', also in forms reflecting one's philosophical leanings: **кантианець** 'a Kantian', **гегельянець** 'a Hegelian' (but note: these forms consist in fact of an initial international element '-ian-', such as 'Hegelian', + **ець**).

-енець is found in derivatives of abstract nouns with the suffix **-ння** (see below): **переселенець** 'emigrant', **уродженець** 'a native of (place X)'.

-инець 'native of place X', as in: **кубинець** 'Cuban', **сочинець** 'one from Sochi', **ялтинець** 'one from Yalta'.

-лець occurs occasionally in deverbal formations reflecting the activity (or result of the activity) expressed by the verb in question: **пожилець** 'lodger', **страждалець** (= **страдник**) 'martyr', 'one who has suffered'.

-овець, -івець is used in forms denoting geographical provenance or organizational membership; the base forms can themselves be new compounds: **донбасівець** 'one from the Donbass', **кузбасівець** 'one from the Kuzbass', **райкомівець** 'member of the Rajkom (regional committee)'.

-знь is extremely rare, occurring in some abstract nouns: **боязнь** = **боязність** 'timidity', **водобоязнь** 'hydrophobia', **приязнь** = **приязність** 'goodwill', 'friendliness'. See **-ість, -ність** below.

-изн(а) is unproductive; it is found in some nouns reflecting the characteristics of the base (usually adjectival) form: **новизна** 'novelty', **білизна** 'linen', 'washing'.

-ик, including the compound suffixes **-ник, -льник, -овник, -евник, -євник**, is extremely common in Ukrainian. On its own, **-ик** can form diminutive/affectionate forms of base substantives (see first entry below); compounds **-ник** and so on are formed from base adjectives and denote persons working in a field described by the adjective in question.

> **-ик: братик** little brother, **котик** little cat, **дощик** fine rain.

deadjectival formations: **водник** 'a person working in the field of water transport', **передовик** 'guide', 'leader', **харчовик** 'one involved with food provisions', **цілинник** 'one who works virgin land', **сезонник** 'seasonal worker', **стройовик** 'one who serves in a military unit' (**стройовий**).

-**ин**: see -**анин**, -**янин** above.

-**ина** has several different functions in Ukrainian, all of which, when treated individually, are unproductive. These are formations, (1) from verbs indicating the result of an action, (2) from names of animals referring to their meat, (3) from adjectives denoting a state or condition, (4) from substances expressing one element thereof, (5) from nouns making new (somewhat) diminutive forms.

(1) **западина** 'cavity', 'hollowness', **пробоїна** 'pothole', 'hole in the road', **зарубина** 'cut', 'incision'.
(2) **баранина** 'mutton', **свинина** 'pork', **козлина** 'goat meat or skin'.
(3) **вишина** 'height', 'altitude', **глибина** 'depth', **рівнина** 'level ground'.
(4) **горошина** 'one pea', **зернина** 'one grain', **картоплина** (coll.) 'one potato'.
(5) **хатина** 'little cottage', **хустина** 'kerchief'.

-**иння** occurs only in collective formations based on the names of plants, usually in reference to the leafy parts thereof: **картоплиння** 'leafy parts of a potato plant', **бурячиння** 'leaves of a beet plant'. See '-ССя' below on -**ання**, -**ення**.

-**иха** is relatively unproductive, and is found in a small number of nouns (i) referring to the occupation of a woman (felt to be colloquial) or the wife of a man in the occupation in question and (ii) designating the female of animal species: **ослиха** 'she ass' (more commonly **ослиця**), **слониха** 'female elephant'.

-**иця** has three main functions in Ukrainian, all of which are seen most commonly in desubstantival formations (some deadjectivals are possible as well): (1) to refer to female persons, the corresponding masculine forms of which have the suffix -**ик**; (2) rarely to refer to place or objects; (3) as a marker of a term of endearment or diminutive:

(1) **робітниця** female worker, **розумниця** witty, clever woman.
(2) **гірчиця** mustard, **гнилиця** wild pear, **світлиця** chamber, room.
(3) **сестриця** little sister, **водиця** water.

-**ич**, -**іч** occurs in a small number of masculine patronymics (compare -**ович** below) and in a few words indicating one's geographical provenance (for men only): (i) patronymics **Ілліч** 'son of Illya', **Савич** 'son of Sava'; (ii) **костромич** 'one from Kostroma', **москвич** 'one from Moscow'.

-**ищ**-, including the compounds -**бищ(е)**, -**лищ(е)**, -**овищ(е)**:

-**ищ(е)** is slightly more common than the preceding suffix, but nevertheless is also rare; it also imparts a feeling of great physical size, but the connotation can be negative: **ножище** 'large, ugly foot' (or 'knife'!), **ручище** 'large hand', **бородище** 'large beard'.

-**ищ(е)** can indicate a place or result of an action (especially if formed from verbs); compare -**бищ(е)** below. Thus: **сховище** 'shelter', 'hiding place', **збіговище** 'mob of people', **городище** 'former site of a city', 'ruins'.

-**бищ(е)** reflects a combination of -**б**- (compare -**ьба** above) and -**щ(е)**; formations with this suffix denote the place in which the action of the source verb takes or used to take place, rarely the notion itself. Thus: **лежбище** 'place in which herds (usually of animals) lie', **стрільбище** 'shooting gallery', **займище** 'site for a building', 'plot of land for construction', **водосховище** 'reservoir', **мольбище** 'former site of a temple'.

-**лищ(е)** is rare, and can refer to the place where an activity takes place: **училище** 'teaching institution', **судилище** 'tribunal'.

-**овищ(е)** is likewise unproductive, referring to location: **становище** 'position', 'station', **зимовище** 'storage for the winter' (= **зимівля**).

-**івка** forms a number of substantives referring to the meaning of the base word: **курсівка** 'official document giving one permission to stay, for example, at a sanatorium, to receive food and treatment', **листівка** 'postcard', **шумівка** 'brandy' (= **горілка**).

-**івна**, -**ївна** is the standard suffix for the formation of feminine patronymics: **Іванівна** 'daughter of Ivan', **Андріївна** 'daughter of Andrij'.

-**ій**- occurs infrequently in deverbal constructions expressing 'male doer of X': **водій** 'driver', **крутій** 'swindler'.

-**інь** is unproductive, and occurs in some deadjectival forms expressing abstract notions associated with the base words: **височінь** 'height', 'altitude' (= **висота, високість**), **широчінь** 'breadth', 'width' (= **широта**).

-**ість** is extremely common, especially in the literary language; it is used to form abstract nouns from adjectives and, more rarely, from passive participles of verbs.

deadjectival: **гордість** 'haughtiness', 'pride', **давність** 'antiquity', 'old times', **ніжність** 'tenderness', **співучість** 'melodiousness', **хоробрість** 'bravery', **швидкість** 'quickness'.

deverbal: **видимість** 'ability to see far into the distance', **стриманість** 'coolness', 'coldness (of character)', **вихованість** 'breeding', 'bringing up', **зніженість** 'sickliness'.

COMPOUND DERIVATIVES WITH -**ість**: -**ність**, -**еність** can occur in deverbal nouns in reference to qualitative conditions arising as a result of the action expressed by the base verb (the examples show the limited usefulness of this particular construction): **домовленість** 'agreement reached in prior conversations', **розжареність** 'the state of having been heated or cooked excessively'.

-к-а is frequently encountered in Ukrainian; in some words this suffix (**-к-** + ending **-a** in this instance) has clear semantic functions, while in others (especially those formed from verbs) it merely serves to produce new nouns reflecting the process or result of an action.

deverbal: **бійка** 'scuffle', 'fight', **знахідка** 'a find', 'something found', **чистка** (= **чищення**) 'cleaning', **заслінка** 'cover for cooker/stove', **зарубка** 'cut', 'incision' (compare **зарубина, зарубинка** 'incision', 'little incision' respectively), **закуска** 'snack'. In reference to people, the following express a degree of irony and occur (albeit infrequently) primarily in the spoken language: **писака** 'scribbler', **гуляка** (= **гультяй, гультяйка**) 'reveller'.

desubstantival: the suffix is used

(1) as a marker of a female person, often in place of or in addition to the masculine suffixes **-ець, -ин, -(ан)ич** (see above): **москвичка** 'woman from Moscow', **грузинка** 'a Georgian woman', **бельгійка** 'a Belgian woman', **німка** 'a German woman', **журналістка** 'female journalist'.

(2) as a marker of an individual piece of a substance or item: **шоколадка** 'a piece of chocolate', **таблетка** 'a tablet'.

(3) as a marker of a diminutive form or of endearment: **берізка** 'little birch tree', **доріжка** '(foot)path', **конячка** 'a bit of cognac', **ягідка** 'small berry'. Note the compounding of this suffix onto the suffix **-иця** (above) in the following: **водичка** diminutive of **вода, водиця**, **рукавичка** 'little mitten'.

(4) in forming a slightly pejorative variant of personal names: **Колька** < **Коля**.

deadjectival: the suffix is added to a small number of adjectival stems in reference to names of newspapers or everyday items whose full designations are made up of adjective + noun: **вечірка** 'evening newspaper', **літературка** 'literary newspaper', **електричка** '(a local service) electric train'.

COMPOUND SUFFIXES WITH **-к-а**: **-лка** expresses a tool used in a particular activity or the place in which it takes place; both of these are deverbal constructions: **вішалка** 'place to hang clothes or a coat' (more often **вішало**), **віялка** 'winnowing machine', **грілка** 'an apparatus for heating (objects, not living space)'; see **-льня** below.

-очка, -ечка is found in diminutive forms of nouns or names in **-ок, -ка**: **вазочка** 'little vase', **кісточка** 'small bone'.

-ки is a little-used suffix, found in two basic constructions formed primarily from verbs: (i) expressing the result of (or physical remains resulting from) an action and (ii) in names of games or events: **висівки** 'siftings', **недоїдки** 'leftovers (from a meal)', **ошурки** 'filings', 'dust from filing', жмурки 'blindman's buff', досвітки 'evening party (autumn or winter) for village youth activities', поминки 'commemoration of the dead', хованки 'hide-and-seek'.

-ко occurs infrequently in diminutives of neuter nouns, and as a marker of diminutives or endearment for animate nouns in general: блюдечко 'little plate', відерко 'small bucket', вушко 'small or dainty ear', яблучко 'little apple', зайченятко 'little rabbit', соловейко '(dear) little nightingale', матвійко '(dear) little Matvij'.

-лищ(е): see -ищ-.

-ло is unproductive in the language, but does occur in two contexts: (i) as a colloquial marker, in deverbal forms, reflecting an activity characteristic of the person in question; and (ii) in naming a tool or object used in the action expressed by the base verb: бурмило 'mutterer', зубрило (= зубрилка) 'one who studies mechanically', чудило (= чудій, дивачка) 'eccentric person', мило 'soap', шило 'awl', грузило 'lead used in fishing nets', сідло 'saddle'.

-льня occurs in deverbal nouns indicating the place of an action: спальня 'bedroom', читальня 'reading room', купальня 'bathroom' (not 'toilet').

-ник (<н-ик) is an extremely common suffix (most common as in (i) below), with a wide variety of functions and meanings.

(i)   In *deverbals* as a designator of a male person occupied with the activity expressed by the base verb, likewise in *deadjectivals* (the base forms of which are in turn ultimately based on nouns): зазивник 'one who appeals', зрадник 'traitor', керівник 'director', 'leader', провідник 'guide', 'leader', двірник 'janitor', 'courtier', ключник 'doorkeeper', 'butler'.

(ii)   In a few deverbal forms designating the tools with which an action takes place: накатник 'instrument (such as a brush) with which to spread paint, glue and other substances', підйомник (= підіймач, ліфт) 'a lift'.

(iii) In deadjectival/desubstantival formations referring to items relating to the base noun: градусник 'thermometer', нічник 'chamber pot ('thing for use at night'!), сірник 'match'.

(iv)   In reference to plants or the places in which they grow: малинник 'raspberry', 'place where raspberries grow', ялинник 'fir (tree) grove'.

(v)   As a designator of the place in which animals are kept: корівник 'cowshed', курник 'henhouse', 'chicken coop'.

COMPOUND SUFFIXES WITH -НИК: -льник is found in deverbal nouns expressing items used in the action in question, more rarely in reference to a person involved in the action: вішальник 'one who has been hanged', мовчальник (= мовчан, мовчун) 'taciturn person', будильник 'alarm clock ('waker')', світильник 'lamp', 'candlestick', холодильник 'refrigerator'.

-ництво: see -ство, -цтво below.

-ниця is commonly used to form nouns designating female persons (where the corresponding masculine marker is **-ник**), less commonly as a designator of objects associated with base nouns: **письменниця** 'authoress', **помічниця** 'female assistant', 'deputy', **робітниця** 'female worker', **працівниця** 'female worker', **віконниця** 'window frame', **гірчичниця** 'mustard pot', **попільниця** 'ashtray', **чорнильниця** 'inkwell'.

-ність: see -ість above.

-няк is unproductive, and occurs in a few words in reference to the whole or mass of a particular botanical or geological element: **бережняк** 'that which is cast upon the shores by waves (wood, plants, and similar)', **дубняк** (= **дубник**) 'oak forest', **залізняк** 'ferrous stone', **сосняк** (= **соснина, сосник**) 'pine forest'.

-ович, -йович form masculine patronymics for the majority of Ukrainian first names: **Олександрович** 'son of Oleksandr', **Павлович** 'son of Pavel', **Олексійович** 'son of Oleksij'.

-овищ(е)-: see -ищ-

-овство, -івство: see -ство, -цтво below.

-ок (including **-ток**) is very common and productive, with a variety of functions: in deverbal formations, to indicate (1) single occurrences of an action, (2) the action itself or the result of an action, and (3) the tool with which an action is carried out, (4) especially in desubstantival formations, as a marker of diminutives or of endearment. Thus:

(i)   **кивок** 'wink', 'nod of the head', **кидок** 'a throw'.

(ii)   **здобуток** 'acquisition', **відросток** 'offshoot'.

(iii) **мазок, помазок** 'small paintbrush', **скребок** 'an implement for scraping'.

(iv)   **синок** 'sonny', 'little son', **дідок** 'granddad', 'old man', **ручайок** 'little brook', **горішок** 'tiny nut'.

-онька, -енька, -енько is not productive but common especially in colloquial speech; it imparts a sense of endearment to nouns referring to persons, animals, and some objects/plants: **батенько** (= **батечко**) 'papa', 'daddy', **мамонька** (= **мамуся**) 'mummy', **лисонька** (= **лисичка**) 'little female fox', **кізонька** (= **кізочка**) 'little she goat', **берізонька** (= **берізочка**) 'little birch tree', **рученька** (= **рученя, ручиця**) 'tiny (for example, a child's) hand'.

-оньки, -еньки is rare, and occurs as a parallel variant of **-ят(а)**: **зубоньки** 'little teeth', **оченьки** 'little eyes'.

-ота is an unproductive suffix that nevertheless occurs in a number of abstract nouns, some of which are in common use (note the place of stress):

deadjectival: **біднота́** (= **бідність**) 'poverty', 'the poor' (colloq.), **доброта́** 'goodness', **повнота́** 'fullness', 'plenty', **теплота́** 'warmth', **чистота́** 'cleanliness'.

desubstantival: **дрімо́та** 'drowsiness', **скорбо́та** 'grief', 'sorrow', **сміхота́** (= **сміх, сміховище**) 'much laughter'. In a noun like **робо́та** 'work', the suffix is no longer recognizable as such or segmentable.

The suffix -ота (stressed on either syllable) is also occasionally found in colloquial speech imparting a sense of irony or disdain to the word in question. Doublets are rare but possible: compare **біднота́** (cited above) with the ironic or disdainful **бідно́та**.

-ство, -цтво is widely found in formations representing (i) collective groups of people (in reference to their occupations or social standing, from nouns), (ii) personal qualities (from nouns), and (iii) abstract notions or qualities (from verbs and adjectives):

(i)   **дворянство** 'aristocracy', **селянство** 'peasantry', **купецтво** 'merchants', 'merchant class', **учнівство** 'the state of being a schoolboy or -girl', 'immaturity', **юнацтво** 'young people', 'bravery'.

(ii)   **геройство** 'heroism', **авторство** 'authorship', **просвітництво** 'the Enlightenment', **акторство** 'the act of acting'.

(iii) **керівництво** 'directorship', **безумство** (= **безумність**) 'lunacy', 'folly', **багатство** 'riches', **лукавство** 'slyness', 'craftiness'.

-тель is rather uncommon in Ukrainian, occurring in a few deverbal formations designating 'male doer of action X', as in **вихователь** 'educator', 'tutor', **житель** (= **жилець, мешканець**) 'inhabitant', **вчитель** 'teacher'.

-уга, -юга occurs in desubstantival formations, and can be a mark (especially in colloquial Ukrainian) of disdain, coarseness, augmentation, or familiarity: **ледацюга** 'layabout'.

-уля, -юля imparts a negative sense to a few deadjectival nouns: **капризуля** 'capricious person', **чистюля** '(excessively) tidy person'; it is found slightly more often in desubstantival formations, denoting familiarity or endearment: *бабуля* (*бабуня, бабуся*) 'grandma', *мамуля* (*мамуся*) 'mummy'.

-ун forms (colloquially) nouns designating male persons, more rarely animals, or instruments associated with the meaning of the base word (usually a verb): **бігун** 'runner', 'racehorse', **брехун** (= **брехач**) 'liar', **хвастун** (= **хваст**) 'braggart', **скакун** 'leaper', **колун** 'axe', 'hatchet'.

-уня imparts a sense of endearment to a few nouns: **бабуня** 'granny', 'dear (little) grandmother', **мамуня** 'mummy'.

-уся, -усь as **-уня**, but with either masculine or feminine base nouns: **бабуся** (= **бабуня**), **мамуся** (= **мамуня**), **дідусь** 'dear (little) grandfather', **Петрусь** 'dear (little) Petro'.

-уха, -юха occurs in a few colloquial formations designating (i) female persons, (ii) names of illnesses, and (iii) objects or phenomena associated with the base forms (either deverbal or deadjectival):

(i)   **гладуха** 'fat woman', **шептуха** 'gossipy woman'.

(ii)   **жовтуха** (= **жовтяниця**) 'jaundice', **краснуха** 'children's disease, in which the skin breaks out in a red rash'.

(iii) **показуха** 'showing something as being better than it is in reality'.

-це forms diminutives from base neuter nouns: **віконце** 'little window', **дільце** 'small matter', 'thing', **сінце** 'a little hay', **слівце** 'a single word'.

-ця (-дзя) gives base nouns or names a sense of endearment: **кумця** 'dear (little) godmother', **Гандзя** 'Hanna' (affectionately used).

-чак is unproductive, and forms isolated nouns denoting male persons associated with the meaning of the base adjective: **весельчак** (= **веселун**, **сміхун**) 'jolly fellow', **смільчак** (= **сміливець**) 'daredevil', 'bold man'.

-чик, -щик denote a male person, in reference to his occupation or activities; they are not productive, and most such forms owe their existence or continued presence in Ukrainian to the influence of Russian: **банщик** 'one who works in a **баня** (sauna)', **льотчик** (= **пілот**) 'pilot', 'flier'. Isolated words can also designate tools or instruments used in the activity described by the base word: **тральщик** 'a fishing boat fitted with a dragnet (**трал**)'.

-чик is a marker of diminutives, and can impart a sense of endearment to base nouns: **костюмчик** '(cute) little suit (of clothing)', **стаканчик** (= **скляночка**) 'little glass'.

-чиця is the feminine marker corresponding to **-чик** (and as such is as rare as the masculine suffix): **льотчиця** 'woman pilot'.

-(CC)я, in which CC = 'geminated/lengthened consonant', the suffix is extremely common, as it is used in the formation of abstract and collective nouns from a variety of stems: verbal, adjectival (although these are the rarest formations), as well as substantival. The most common realizations of this formula are **-ння** from verbal stems; other possible formations are illustrated in the examples below (for example, **-лля**, **-ття**, **-сся**).

deverbal: **звертання** 'turning back', 'aside', **призначення** 'destination', 'fate', **викладання** 'lecturing', 'explaining', **досягнення** 'attainment', **представлення** 'introduction', **відганяння** 'driving away', **розбиття** 'ruin', 'shipwreck', **життя** 'life', **розлиття** 'shedding', 'overflowing', **почуття** 'feeling', 'perception'.

deadjectival: **мокряччя** 'something wet', 'swampy', **величчя** 'greatness', 'grandeur', **весілля** 'wedding'.

desubstantival: **картоплиння** 'potatoes', **підземелля** 'cave', 'underground place', **підпілля** 'underground', 'underground movement', **малоліття** 'minority (age)', **волосся** 'hair', 'head of hair', **різноголосся** 'discord', 'the sound of voices not singing together', **браття** 'brethren', **межиріччя** 'land between (two) rivers', **сторіччя** (= **століття**) 'century', **бездушшя** (= **бездушність**) 'soullessness', 'insensibility'.

Note particularly that in words in which the stem-final consonant is **p** or a labial (lip) consonant, such as **м, б, в, п**, the suffix is still **-я** but it is separated from the preceding single consonant by an apostrophe (see Chapter 1): **здоров'я** 'health', **межигір'я** 'valley between mountains'.

-яга is a colloquial marker of common gender nouns signifying (i) persons associated with the base form or (ii) the (over-) large size of the item in question, sometimes to be interpreted negatively; neither formation is very productive, and these forms will occur primarily in familiar speech:

(i) **бродяга** 'wanderer', 'vagabond', **добряга** 'good-natured person'.

(ii) **вітряга** (= **вітрюга**) 'powerful wind'.

-ятина is unproductive; used in colloquial speech, this suffix occurs in deadjectival formations to refer to substances relating to the base form, usually with negative connotations: **дохлятина** 'carrion', **кислятина** 'something very sour', **тухлятина** 'something musty or rotten'.

2.5.2   PREFIXAL WORD FORMATION

As in the case of suffixes, the presentation of prefixal elements used in word formation does not include prefixes borrowed from West European languages, as their meanings will be transparent to the reader (for example, **а-** 'not-' or 'un-', **анти-** 'anti-', **архи-** 'archi-', **де-, дез-** 'de-, des-', **дис-** 'dis-', **контр-** 'contra-', **про-** 'pro- (pro-communist), one who substitutes for another (pro-rector)', **ультра-** 'ultra-'). Most prefixes can occur word-formationally without the concomitant presence of suffixes; examples are cited first with prefixes only (wherever this is possible), then with a variety of suffixes as described in **2.5.1**. The reader will note that many of these prefixes are in fact also prepositions.

без- 'lacking something', 'without' (compare the preposition **без**). A great many of the formations involving **без-** also involve the presence of suffixes:

desubstantival: **безкрай** 'endless space', **безлад** 'disorder', **безлік, безліч** 'multitude', **безмір** 'vastness', **безпека** 'safety', 'security', **безрода** 'one without relations (family)', **безрух** 'lack of mobility', 'immobility', **безсмак** 'lack of taste', **безум** 'foolishness', 'folly', **безвітря** 'lack of wind', 'calm (at sea)', **безсилля** 'weakness', 'impotence', **безрукавка** 'sleeveless shirt', **безумець** 'lunatic', 'fool', **безумність** 'madness'.

в-, у- 'in', 'into' (compare the preposition **в, у**).

deverbal: **внесок** 'insertion', 'deposit', 'agreement', **вступ** 'section', 'paragraph', **вхід** 'entrance', **вступання** 'process of entering', **укладання** 'process of putting in order', **укладач** 'arranger', 'composer', **устаткування** 'installation'.

вз-, уз- 'motion upwards', 'location near', not very productive.

desubstantival: **узгір'я** 'rising ground', 'elevation', **узголів'я** 'bedside', 'head of the bed', **узлісок** 'edge of a forest', **узріччя** 'area near a river'.
deverbal: **узвар** 'stewed fruit', 'compote', **узвіз** 'driving up', 'ascension'.

ви- 'motion out of (real or figurative)', relatively productive.

deverbal: **виїзд** 'departure (by vehicle)', **вихід** 'exit', 'way out' (various senses), **вивіз** 'exportation', **вигнання** 'expulsion', **виведення** '(the act of) leading away', **вимовність** 'expressiveness', **викрутка** 'screwdriver', **вимочка** 'blotting paper', **висихання** 'drying out', 'wasting away'.

від- 'motion from (real or figurative)', relatively productive (compare the preposition **від**).

deverbal: **відзвук** 'resonance', 'echo', **відмова** 'refusal', **відділ** 'section', 'department', **відклик** 'recall', 'repeal', **відділення** 'separation', **відгук** 'a reply'.

воз- 'motion upwards' (real or figurative), 'location near', unproductive.

desubstantival: **возлісся** dial., = lit. **узлісся** (see entry above).
deverbal: **возвіз** dial. = lit. **узвіз** (see above), **Воздвиження** 'the Elevation' (Christian feast, the Elevation of the Cross), **возз'єднання** 'unification', **возз'єднувач** 'unifier'.

до- 'up to', 'until', 'as far as', 'before', 'in addition to' (compare the preposition **до**), very common.

desubstantival: **дозвілля** 'free time', 'leisure', **досвіт** 'daybreak'.
deverbal: **довіз** 'importation', **довіра** 'confidence', 'trust', **доказ** 'proof', **докір** 'reproach', **доступ** 'access', 'approach', **додавання** 'addition', **довершення** 'accomplishment', 'fulfilment', **докажчик** 'informer', **домішування** 'admixture', 'addition to mixture', **допитливість** 'curiosity', **досипка** 'surplus', 'over-measure'.

з- (**із-**, **зі-**), **с-**: two semantic sources, one meaning approximately 'together', 'with', the other 'from', 'out of', 'off of' (compare the preposition **з**, and so on); formations from verbs in which **з-** is now a purely perfectivizing element will have the original sense of the prefix obscured.

deverbal: **здих** 'expiration', 'last breath', **знос** 'wearing out', **змова** 'conspiracy ('talking together')', **зіскок** 'leap from a height', **зруб** 'cutting down', 'felling', **спуск** 'descent', **зголошення** 'readiness', 'agreement to do something', **здача** 'change (money)', **здиханка** 'sighing', 'last breath', **злиття** 'pouring into', **змішка** 'mixture', **змішування** 'mingling', 'confusion', **зрізування** 'cutting off', 'paring', **згінник** (dial., SUM) 'dealer in animals' (lit. 'one who drives animals together'), **зрубувач** 'one who fells (for example, trees)', **збиток** 'harm'.

за- 'beyond/behind', 'beginning', or semantically neutral depending on the source (usually a verb) in question. Very common, because verbs with this prefix are widely used (compare the preposition **за**).

desubstantival: **закарпаття** 'region beyond the Carpathians', **залісся** 'region beyond the forest', **заворіття** 'area beyond the gate(s)', **забережжя** 'the opposite bank (for example, of a river)', **заголовок** 'title (of a written work)', **запоясник** 'dagger'.

deverbal: **заїзд** 'gateway', **запит** 'inquiry', **захват** 'rapture', **завершення** 'perfection', 'accomplishment', **завдаток** 'deposit' (monetary), **заводчика** 'instigator', 'inciter', **заколотник** 'rebellious person', **застрільник** 'provoker', 'instigator', **заклинач** 'conjurer'.

між-, межи- 'between', 'inter-'; not very productive (compare the preposition **між, межи**).

desubstantival: **межиріччя** 'region between rivers', **міжгір'я** 'valley between mountains', **межичасся** 'between times', 'periods', **межигірець** 'one who lives in valley (between two mountains)'.

на- 'on (spatial)', 'onto', 'in addition to', also semantically neutral, depending on the source verb (compare the preposition **на**), very common.

desubstantival: **наголос** 'stress', 'accent', **наділ** 'recompense', **намисел** 'reflection (thought)', **нагір'я** 'highlands', **нагрудник** 'breastplate', **навушник** 'earring', **назимок** 'fatted calf', **наконечник** 'tip', 'point', **намордник** 'muzzle'.

deverbal: **набір** 'freight', 'load', **навал** 'multitude', **нажин** 'harvest', **наказ** 'command', **наїздник** 'invader', **наказник** 'one who orders', **накривало** 'cover', **наливка** 'infusion', **наливайко** 'one who pours', **наростання** 'increase', 'growing upon', **насмішка** 'derision', **наставлення** 'direction', 'tendency', **настоятель** 'chief', 'superior' (in a monastery).

над- 'over', 'beyond', 'super-', not extremely productive (compare the preposition **над**).

desubstantival: **надмір** 'excess', **надсистема** 'supersystem' (*vs.* **підсистема** 'subsystem'), **надвартість** 'extremely high worth', **надбережжя** 'coast', 'riverbank', **надгробник** 'tombstone', **надмор'я** 'coastal region', 'littoral'.

deverbal: **надріз** 'incision', **надзиск** 'excessive profit', **надбудівля** 'superstructure', **надходження** '(the act of) wearing out (by walking)', **надписування** '(the act of) making an inscription'.

не- 'not', 'un-', productive (compare the particle **не**).

desubstantival: **небіж** 'nephew', 'miser', **невдача** 'failure', **неволя** 'slavery', **неміч** 'illness', 'weakness', **неохота** 'reluctance', **непогода** 'bad weather', **неправда** 'a lie', 'untruth', **неспокій** 'disquiet', 'trouble'.

deverbal: **небажання** 'undesirability', **невіра** 'incredulity', **невідомість** 'ignorance', 'uncertainty (lack of information)', **невчення** 'ignorance (lack of learning)', **немовля** 'infant (one who lacks the ability to speak!)', **неук** 'ignorant person'.

недо- 'not as far as (expected)', 'insufficiently' (< не + до: compare the preposition/prefix до).

desubstantival: **недолюд** 'inhuman person', **недомір** 'thing of (unexpectedly) small size', **недопанок** 'little lord', **недорозум** 'lack of reason', 'absurdity', **недосіл** 'insufficient salting (of food)', **недоум** 'foolish person'.

deverbal: **недобір** 'deficit' (lit. 'insufficient amount taken'), **недозір** 'one with bad eyesight', **недокрів'я** 'anaemia', 'lack of blood', **недолік** 'shortage', **недоламок** 'partly-' or 'half-broken piece', **недомовка** 'omission', **недомовність** 'stuttering', 'lisping', **недоношениця** 'girl born prematurely', **недопивки** 'that which is left undrunk', **недоріс** 'adolescent', **недоспів** 'unfinished song'.

о-, об-, обі- 'around', 'something left/remainder after an action', this very common prefix can also be less definable semantically, again depending on the verb in question (compare the prepositions о, об).

deadjectival: **обнова** 'renovation', 'novelty'.
desubstantival: **огорода, обгорода** 'enclosure', 'fence', **обіч** 'slope', 'declivity', **обміжок** 'ridge between two fields'.
deverbal: **обвід** 'circumference', **оборот** 'turning', 'revolution', **огляд** 'examination', 'inspection', **обмова** 'slander', 'calumny', **осад** 'sediment', 'dregs', **обіг** 'revolution', 'circulation', **обід** or **обвід** 'circle', 'ring', 'enclosure', **обв'язка** 'binding', 'something that envelops', **обдуманність** 'circumspection', 'deliberation', **оберега** 'precaution', 'wariness', **обіхідка** 'unfenced house', **оглядач** 'inspector', **обмеженість** 'narrow-mindedness', **обрізок** 'cutting', 'paring', **огризок** 'remnants of (gnawed, picked) food', **окапини** 'droppings of wax from a candle', **обаченість** 'consideration', 'care'.

пере- 'across', 'cross-', 'over', 'trans-', 're-' or indicating an action of short duration, very common.

desubstantival: **перегорода** 'partition', **перегорок** 'hillock', **перегородження** 'separation (by a fence)', **переторг** 'sale by auction', **перереєстрація** 're-registration'.
deverbal: **перевезення** 'transport', **переїзд** 'crossing', 'passing through', **переклад** 'translation', **перекур** 'having a (quick) smoke', **перекуп** 'second-hand buying', **переміна** 'alteration', 'transformation', **перекупник** 'middle-man', **перекладач** 'translator', **перегрів** 'overheating', **перекуплення** 'the act of bribing', **перепродування** 'resale'.

перед- 'fore-', 'before', 'ante-', productive (compare the preposition **перед**).

desubstantival: **передвік** 'eternity', **переддень** 'eve', 'the day before', **передмова** 'foreword', **передісторія** 'prehistory', **передсвіт** 'just before daybreak', **передгір'я** 'land at the foot of mountains', **передвечір'я** 'time (just) before evening'.

deverbal: **передбачення** 'foresight', **передплата** 'subscription' (lit. 'pre-payment'), **передплатник** 'subscriber', **передчуття** 'presentiment', 'foreboding'.

під- 'under', 'sub-', relatively productive (compare **над** above and the preposition **під**).

desubstantival: **підбій** 'conquest', 'subjugation', **підтекст** 'subtext', **підштурман** 'assistant to steersman', 'pilot', **підборіддя** 'chin', **підворіття** 'area in front of a door or gate', **підмосков'я** 'area around/near Moscow', **підніжжя** 'base', 'pedestal'.

deverbal: **підвода** 'vehicle', 'conveyance', **підступ** 'deceit', 'cunning', **підхід** 'approach (various senses)', **підтримка** 'support', **підказувач** 'prompter', **підкладка** 'support (physical)', **підсипка** 'strewing'.

по- 'along (a place or region)', depending on the source verb in question, **по-** can also be semantically undefinable. Extremely common (compare the preposition **по**).

desubstantival: **помисел** 'idea', 'thought', **погір'я** 'slope', 'mountainous area', **поголос** 'rumour', 'hearsay', **побережжя** 'littoral', **полісся** 'low-lying forest region', **поріччя** 'river plain', **помор'я** 'littoral (along a sea)', **попутник** 'fellow traveller'.

deverbal: **поділ** 'lowland', **похід** 'procession', 'parade', **повід** 'rein', **погляд** 'look', **помазання** 'anointing', **посилка** 'package', 'something that is sent', **посилання** '(the act of) sending', **полюбовник** 'lover', **помилування** 'mercy', 'forgiveness', **поплавець** 'float (on a fishing line)'.

пред- historically 'fore-' (compare **перед** above), of Church Slavonic origin, not productive.

deverbal: **представлення** 'introduction (of people)', **пред'явник** 'presenter', **представник** 'representative'.

при- 'relating to', 'near to', 'in addition to', not productive (compare the preposition **при**).

desubstantival: **призвук** 'a sound accompanying another', 'main sound', **приземок** 'small man', 'boy', **прикорень** 'treestump', **примара** 'phantom', 'spectre', **присмак** 'seasoning', **примор'я** 'coastal region (near the sea)', **прибережжя** 'littoral', **прикордонник** 'border guard', **придуха** 'lack of fresh air'.

deverbal: **привід** 'motive/reason', 'leadership', **привіз** 'importation', **присід** 'one (single) sitting', **причіпка** 'quibble (with something)', **прибулець** 'one who has arrived', 'an arrival', **примирення** 'reconciliation', **примиритель** 'a reconciler', 'one who reconciles or makes peace'.

про- unproductive with adjectival stems (colours); common in deverbal nouns expressing 'through' (compare the preposition **про**), otherwise semantically opaque.

deadjectival: **прозелень** 'first green (of spring)', **прожовть** 'yellowish tinge of colour', **проглиб** 'depth', 'profundity', **прохолода** 'coolness', 'freshness'.

desubstantival: **просіл** 'salted fish', **провесінь** 'beginning of spring', **просвіт** 'opening (through which light comes in)', **протовп** 'passageway through a crowd', **прослава** 'great glory', **проміжжя** 'distance (between two places)'.

deverbal: **проліт** 'flight through', **пролаз** 'opening (through which to crawl)', **процвіт** 'blossoming', **протяг** 'draught (of air)', 'course (time)', **провал** 'abyss', 'precipice', **продаж** 'selling', **прохач** 'petitioner', **провадження** 'leading', 'conducting', **провірення** 'verification', **проповідник** 'preacher', **прочистка** 'thorough cleaning', **провгулок** 'narrow passage', **проникливість** 'keenness', 'capacity to penetrate (mentally)'.

проти- 'anti-', 'counter-', unproductive (compare the preposition **проти**).

deadjectival: **протилежність** 'extremity', 'oppositeness' (ultimately from the verbal root **леж-** 'lie', 'be lying').

desubstantival: **протигаз**, **протигазник** 'gas mask', **противага** 'counterweight', **противогневик** 'firewall'.

роз-, **розі-** approximately 'apart', 'dispersion', very common in deverbal formations.

deverbal: **розпал** 'kindling', 'shavings', **розкол** 'split', 'crack', **розквіт** 'flowering (plants)', **роздум** 'consideration', **розбір** 'selection', **розділ** 'division', 'section', **розклад** 'timetable', **роз'їзд** 'departure (of many)', **розліт** 'departure by flight (in various directions)', **розвідка** 'reconnaissance', **розв'язка** 'solution (to a problem)', **розпаковувач** 'one who unpacks', **розвиток** 'development', 'unfolding', **розвага** 'entertainment', 'deliberation', **розкрадання** 'stealing' (in many places), **розладдя** 'dissension', **розміщування** 'distribution of places', **розподільник** 'dispenser', 'distributor', **рознощик** 'distributor', **розповідання** 'story-telling'.

с-: see **з-** above.

спів- 'co-', 'fellow-'.

desubstantival: **співавтор** 'co-author', **співдружба** 'co-operation', 'harmony', **співжиття** 'life in common', **співчуття** 'sympathy', **співвласник** 'joint owner', 'co-partner', **співгромадянин** 'fellow-citizen', **співробітник** 'co-worker'.

су- indicates the presence, occurrence, admixture, or small measure of a substance or thing (expressed by the root to which it is prefixed); 'with-', 'co- (can = **с-**, **спів-**)', unproductive.

desubstantival: **сутінь** 'half shade', 'twilight', **супісок** 'sandy ground'.
deadjectival: **сукупність** 'totality', 'togetherness', **суспільність** 'society', 'commonwealth', **сучасність** 'the present times', 'contemporaneity', **суміжність** 'contiguity'.
deverbal: **супровід** 'accompaniment', **супровідник** 'accompanist'.

у-, **уз-**: see **в-**, **вз-** above.
через- 'cross-', 'across', very rare (compare the preposition **через**).

desubstantival: **черезплічник** 'something that is thrown or carried across the shoulder'.

2.5.3 COMPOUNDING

Thus far we have concentrated on two major processes of word formation, suffixation and prefixation: structurally, these can be described as:

prefix + stem + Ø
prefix + stem + suffix (+ suffix)
Ø   + stem + suffix (+ suffix)

Another common process of forming new nouns involves the addition of another 'stem' element, in other words, compounding. The new formations can have the following structures:

stem 1 + stem 2 + Ø
stem 1 + stem 2 + suffix

In such nouns, stem 1 is generally either a noun itself or an adjectival stem; stem 2 is then either another noun stem or a verbal stem (stem 1 is not likely to be a verbal stem). Under the rubric 'adjective' we include other forms that are adjective-like, such as forms of **сам-** 'self-', and ordinal numerals. In all nouns with this structure, there has to be a linking element between the two stems: in the vast majority of such forms, this element is the vowel **o** or its soft variant **e**; in adjectival formations, this can be interpreted as the adverbial marker. Other vowels are also possible: (i) in loanwords from Western languages, we may find an original **-a-**: **авіа** + **лінія**, **авіа** + **конструктор** (compare Eng. avia-tion, for example); (ii) more importantly, as a structural element, is the occasional occurrence of the genitive ending of stem 1 (here examples with suffixes):

п'ят-и-літ-ок five-year-old child (fem.)
п'ят-и-клас-ник fifth-grade pupil (masc.)

2.5.3.1 Compounding without suffixation

SUBSTANTIVE + VERB + Ø

землемір < **земл(я) – е – мір(яти)** land surveyor, geometer
рудовоз barge for the transport of mineral ore
листопад November (lit. 'leaf-falling')
вертоліт helicopter
криголам icebreaker
пилосос vacuum cleaner (lit. 'dust-sucker')
пивовар brewer
лісоруб woodcutter

SUBSTANTIVE + SUBSTANTIVE + Ø

лісостеп forest steppe
залізобетон reinforced concrete
лісопарк forest (woody) park
автозавод car factory
складоподіл division into syllables (grammatical term)
бронетранспортер armoured transport
звукооператор sound operator (film)
законопроект legal draft, bill
конов'яз(ь) post to which a horse is tied

ADJECTIVE + SUBSTANTIVE + Ø, ADJECTIVE + VERB + Ø

самохід car (lit. 'self-goer')
чорнозем, чорноземля black earth, soil
першоджерело original source
білоемігрант one who emigrated after the October socialist revolution (lit. 'white' emigrant)
самоконтроль control over, checking of one's own work
далековид spyglass

2.5.3.2 Compounding with suffixation

SUBSTANTIVE + VERB + SUFFIX

м'ясорубка meat grinder
вогнегасник fire extinguisher
соломорізка agricultural machine for cutting straw
картоплесховище place where potatoes are stored

бомбокидальник bomber (person)
нафтовидобуток the acquisition of petroleum
українознавство Ukrainian studies
книготоргівля book trade
звуконаслідування onomatopoeia (lit. 'following sounds')
машинобудування machine building
кровопролиття shedding of blood
братовбивця fratricide (murderer of one's brother)
цілеспрямованість orientation towards one's goal
метробудівець metro (underground) builder

SUBSTANTIVE + SUBSTANTIVE + SUFFIX

лісопромисловість forest(ry) industry
лісогосподарство ownership of a forest

ADJECTIVE + SUBSTANTIVE + SUFFIX, SUBSTANTIVE + ADJECTIVE + SUFFIX

червоногвардієць Red Army guard
короткохвильовик short-wave radio enthusiast
великодержавник imperialist
взаємозв'язок mutual relations
самодержавство autocracy (= **самовлада**)
правобережжя the right bank (region)
пустоцвіт sterile flower
чотирикутник quadrangle, square
багатоженство polygamy
холоднокровність cold-bloodedness
першокласник a first-grade pupil
вогнетривкість fire-resistance

ADJECTIVE + VERB + SUFFIX

низькопоклонник one who fawns on, is deferential to, another
головнокомандувач commander-in-chief
самовбивця a suicide (the person)
голосномовник loudspeaker

ADJECTIVE + ADJECTIVE + SUFFIX

доброзичливість benevolence
взаємозалежність interdependence (lit. 'mutual dependence')

2.5.3.3   *Compounds incorporating abbreviations*

One final method of compounding involves the use of abbreviations: abbreviations for stem 1 are modifiers (adjectives); stem 2 can also be an abbreviation, in this case of a base substantive. Both constructions became extremely common during the Soviet period; while many such formations will be encountered in older writings, most are falling into disuse.

фізкультура physical culture (physical education) < **фізична культура**
фізкультурник, фізкультурниця male, female lover of sports
держплан state plan(ning)
держбанк state bank
держбюджет state budget
соцстрах social security, insurance < **соціальне страхування**
Нарком < **народній комісаріат** people's commissariat (now only as a
   historical term, in reference to the early Soviet period)
сільрада rural council
компартія Communist Party
госпрозрахунок management of accounts, economy

3   THE ADJECTIVE

3.0   GENERAL

Adjectives are conventionally seen as words which describe or qualify nouns
and subdivided into qualitative and relative adjectives, to which one might
add possessive adjectives (those based on nouns we treat here, those on
pronouns are dealt with in Chapter 4), and ordinal numerals (dealt with in
Chapter 5). The last two might in certain respects be grouped with the relative
adjectives – this may be seen from some of the examples of relative adjectives
below. Giving adjectives in their citation form, the nominative singular masculine, we note that qualitative adjectives generally tell us something of the
inherent features of a person or thing, for example:

червóний red	слабúй sick, weak
весéлий happy	солóдкий sweet, lovely
мýдрий wise	висóкий high

Relative adjectives are derived from, and thus relate to, other things, in other
words describe something in terms of something else, thus:

дерев'яний wooden, of wood (= дéрево wood, tree, з дéрева (made) of
  wood)
ведмéжий of a bear (= ведмíдь bear)
сьогóднішній today's (= сьогóдні today)
місцéвий local (= мíсце place)
сóтий hundredth (= сто hundred, an ordinal, but formally an adjective)
сéстрин sister's (= сестрá sister)

See **3.3** on the formation of adjectives.

Relative adjectives do not normally permit the derivation of abstract nouns,
and do not have comparative and superlative forms.

From the tables below it will be clear that Ukrainian adjectives share one
set of endings, but that these endings are added to a stem terminating either
in a hard consonant or in a soft consonant, with consequences for spelling
(and pronunciation).[7] The only special group, entirely a consequence of spelling and pronunciation, is formed by those whose stem terminates in **-ц-**,
namely the adjective **кýций** 'short(-tailed)' and compound adjectives in
-лúций '(-)faced' (see **3.14**). Soft-stem adjectives are characterized by **-ій** in the
citation form and are almost exclusively relative adjectives, ending in **-ній**,

including a large number of adjectives in **-жній** and **-шній** derived from adverbs (also vice versa) but not always relative, for example:

весі́нній spring (adj.)
майбу́тній future (adj.)
поро́жній empty
коли́шній former, erstwhile (= **коли́сь** formerly)
зо́внішній external (= **зо́внішньо** outwardly)
спра́вжній genuine

There are a number of compounds in stems terminating in **-й** (with orthographic consequences), for example:

безкра́їй boundless (= **без** without + **край** country, limit)
довгоши́їй long-necked (= **до́вг(ий)** long + **ши́я** (stem **ший-**) neck)

some possessive-like adjectives, for example:

бра́тній brotherly, fraternal, i.e. like a **брат** brother

and the adjective **си́ній** 'blue'.

Hard-stem adjectives are characterized by the ending **-ий** in the citation form as regards the vast majority, and may be either qualitative or relative, for example:

молоди́й young	**нови́й** new
сві́жий fresh	**теля́чий** calf's, of veal

Hard also are possessive adjectives in **-ів** (**-їв** after a vowel or apostrophe) and **-ин** (**-їн** after a vowel or apostrophe), such as **Андрі́їв** 'Andrew's', **ба́тьків** 'father's' (the vowel of the suffix alternates respectively with **-є-** and **-о-**), and **Марі́їн** 'Maria's', **се́стрин** 'sister's' (no alteration) – note zero ending of the citation form and the capitalization where the derivation is from a name.

We must also mention the so-called short adjectives, all hard-stem and restricted to the nominative and masculine (thus they look like the possessives mentioned above, but do not have case, number, or gender). Some handbooks give relatively long lists of such forms, but it makes sense only to mention those most frequently encountered:

варт worth (+ G. for worth something, worthy of something)
ви́нен guilty, owe (+ D. for what one is guilty of or the person to whom one owes something, the something going in the accusative, e.g. **я ви́нен тобі́ бага́то гроше́й** I owe you a lot of money)
(**зго́ден** agree (+ **з** + inst. for what one agrees to/with or whom one agrees with)
дрі́бен small, trifling
жо́ден no, not a, no one
здоро́в healthy, hale (limited use, in idioms)

зéлен green
кóжен each, every, everyone
лáдéн disposed, ready
лáскав kind
мóлод young
пéвен sure, certain
пóвен full (+ G. = of)
повúнен should, ought, must (duty or obligation)
потрíбен necessary (+ D. of the person who needs something, the something being the grammatical subject)
рад glad (+ D. = for)
слáвен renowned, glorious
ясен clear

As adjectives, these forms are all used predicatively, i.e. in the structure 'X is/ was . . . ready', never attributively (see **3.4** for some examples). This is conveyed by their having only the nominative form, i.e. they can refer to and agree with only the grammatical subject of the sentence, which is in the nominative case. Two of them, **кóжен** and **жóден**, may be found attributively, for example, **кóжен день** 'every day', and as pronouns with the meaning 'anyone', 'everyone', 'no one', 'none'. They all have more or less optional, and usually preferred, long (= 'normal') forms, namely (but not exhaustively):

вáртий	**вúнний**	**згóдний/згíдний**
готóвий	**живúй**	**дрібнúй**
здорóвий	**зéлений**	**кóжний**
лáдний	**ласкáвий**	**молодúй**
пéвний	**пóвний**	**повúнний**
потрíбний	**рáдий**	**слáвний**
яснúй		

The most common of these, functioning more or less as verbs or, perhaps preferably, 'predicative words' (preceded by appropriate tense forms of **бýти** 'to be' as necessary), are:

варт	**вúнен**	**згóден**
здорóв	**лáден**	**пéвен**
пóвен	**повúнен**	**потрíбен**

with **здорóв** and **ласкáв** common in the set expressions **Будь здорóв!** 'Hello!', 'Goodbye!', 'Bless you!' (in response to a sneeze)' (lit. 'Be healthy!') and **Будь ласкáв!** 'Please!' (lit. 'Be kind!'). These are, needless to say, the masculine singular forms; feminine or plural forms are used when appropriate.

In comparison with the masculines, the nominative feminine, neuter, and plural forms of the adjective look 'short' (here both hard and soft adjectives are given):

молода́ – коли́шня   молоде́ – коли́шнє
молоді́ – коли́шні

They are in fact what is referred to as 'full contracted forms', as distinct from the nominative singular masculine, молоди́й – коли́шній, which is a 'full uncontracted form'. Full uncontracted forms do exist for the nominatives other than masculine, but tend to be restricted to folklore and poetry and are not recommended for the standard language. Examples would respectively be:

молода́я – коли́шняя   молоде́є – коли́шнєє
молоді́ї – коли́шнії

In northern dialects one also encounters a full contracted form for the nominative singular masculine, for example, молоди́ – коли́шні.

3.1 DECLENSION

3.1.1 GENERAL

In Chapter 2 we saw that the Ukrainian noun possesses a complex declensional system, involving gender, number, and case. Ukrainian adjectives agree in gender, number, and case with the noun they qualify. As will be seen from the following tables, which aim to be reasonably comprehensive, this has the consequence that the Ukrainian adjective has separate forms for each gender in the singular. This does not apply in the plural, presumably partly because the noun itself does not have clear gender distinctions there. It will also be seen that the masculine and neuter singular forms largely overlap, and that there is some measure of identity between different case forms. In the tables the locative forms given in parentheses are less frequently found alternatives, and '= nom. or gen.' for the accusative singular masculine and accusative plural indicates that the genitive form is selected where animate nouns are qualified, and the nominative form otherwise (compare the noun). The vocative is not mentioned separately, as it is identical with the nominative.

3.1.2 HARD-STEM ADJECTIVES

Га́рний 'beautiful', 'fine', 'nice'

	Masculine	Neuter	Feminine	Plural	
N.	га́рний	га́рне	га́рна	га́рні	Н.
G.	га́рного		га́рної	га́рних	Р.
D.	га́рному		га́рній	га́рним	Д.
A.	= nom. or gen.	= nom.	га́рну	= nom. or gen.	З.
I.	га́рним		га́рною	га́рними	О.
L.	га́рному (га́рнім)		га́рній	га́рних	М.

Вели́кий 'big', 'large', 'great'

	Masculine	Neuter	Feminine	Plural	
N.	вели́кий	вели́ке	вели́ка	вели́кі	Н.
G.	вели́кого		вели́кої	вели́ких	Р.
D.	вели́кому		вели́кій	вели́ким	Д.
A.	= nom. or gen.	= nom.	вели́ку	= nom. or gen.	З.
I.	вели́ким		вели́кою	вели́кими	О.
L.	вели́кому (вели́кім)		вели́кій	вели́ких	М.

3.1.2.1 Possessive adjectives

Бра́тів 'brother's'

	Masculine	Neuter	Feminine	Plural	
N.	бра́тів	бра́тове	бра́това	бра́тові	Н.
G.	бра́тового		бра́тової	бра́тових	Р.
D.	бра́товому		бра́товій	бра́товим	Д.
A.	= nom. or gen.	= nom.	бра́тову	= nom. or gen.	З.
I.	бра́товим		бра́товою	бра́товими	О.
L.	бра́товому (бра́товім)		бра́товій	бра́тових	М.

Андрі́їв 'Andrij's'

	Masculine	Neuter	Feminine	Plural	
N.	Андрі́їв	Андрі́єве	Андрі́єва	Андрі́єві	Н.
G.	Андрі́євого		Андрі́євої	Андрі́євих	Р.
D.	Андрі́євому		Андрі́євій	Андрі́євим	Д.
A.	= nom. or gen.	= nom.	Андрі́єву	= nom. or gen.	З.
I.	Андрі́євим		Андрі́євою	Андрі́євими	О.
L.	Андрі́євому (Андрі́євім)		Андрі́євій	Андрі́євих	М.

О́лин 'Olja's'

	Masculine	Neuter	Feminine	Plural	
N.	О́лин	О́лине	О́лина	О́лині	Н.
G.	О́линого		О́линої	О́линих	Р.
D.	О́линому		О́линій	О́линим	Д.
A.	= nom. or gen.	= nom.	О́лину	= nom. or gen.	З.
I.	О́линим		О́линою	О́линими	О.
L.	О́линому (О́линім)		О́линій	О́линих	М.

Марі́їн 'Marija's'

	Masculine	Neuter	Feminine	Plural	
N.	Марі́їн	Марі́їне	Марі́їна	Марі́їні	Н.
G.	Марі́їного		Марі́їної	Марі́їних	Р.
D.	Марі́їному		Марі́їній	Марі́їним	Д.

A.	= nom. or gen. = nom.	Маріїну	= nom. or gen.	3.
I.	Маріїним	Маріїною	Маріїними	О.
L.	Маріїному (Маріїнім)	Маріїній	Маріїних	М.

3.1.3 SOFT-STEM ADJECTIVES

Колишній 'former', 'erstwhile'

	Masculine	Neuter	Feminine	Plural	
N.	колишній	колишнє	колишня	колишні	Н.
G.	колишнього		колишньої	колишніх	Р.
D.	колишньому		колишній	колишнім	Д.
A.	= nom. or gen. = nom.		колишню	= nom. or gen.	3.
I.	колишнім		колишньою	колишніми	О.
L.	колишньому (колишнім)		колишній	колишніх	М.

Безкраїй 'boundless', 'unlimited'

	Masculine	Neuter	Feminine	Plural	
N.	безкраїй	безкрає	безкрая	безкраї	Н.
G.	безкрайого		безкрайої	безкраїх	Р.
D.	безкрайому		безкраїй	безкраїм	Д.
A.	= nom. or gen. = nom.		безкраю	= nom. or gen.	3.
I.	безкраїм		безкрайою	безкраїми	О.
L.	безкрайому (безкраїм)		безкраїй	безкраїх	М.

3.1.4 ADJECTIVES IN -ц-

Білолиций 'white-faced'

	Masculine	Neuter	Feminine	Plural	
N.	білолиций	білолице	білолиця	білолиці	Н.
G.	білолицього		білолицьої	білолицих	Р.
D.	білолицьому		білолицій	білолицим	Д.
A.	= nom. or gen. = nom.		білолицю	= nom. or gen.	3.
I.	білолицим		білолицьою	білолицими	О.
L.	білолицьому (білолицім)		білолицій	білолицих	М.

3.1.5 THE ADJECTIVAL DECLENSION OF SURNAMES

Note that patronymics decline like nouns and are dealt with in Chapter 2. It might be noted in reinforcement here that their dative singular masculine tends to have the ending **-y**, essentially because sequences of **-ові/-еві** are avoided, the recommendation being to restrict that ending to the first in a series, and patronymics tend not to come first.

Surnames come in many forms. Those which are clearly adjectives decline as is to be expected: **Груше́вський, Груше́вська, Груше́вські**. Those in **-ів/-ева, -їв/-єва, -ов/-ова, -ин/-ина, -ін/-іна, -їн/-їна** have adjectival declension in the feminine (in West Ukraine they do not decline) and the adjectival ending **-им** in the instrumental singular masculine: **Кова́лів – Кова́левим – Кова́лева** – except for non-Slavonic surnames in **-ов, -ин, -ін**, which have nominal **-ом**, thus: **Да́рвін – Да́рвіном** (feminine like the masculine, but indeclinable). For a complete description of these surnames, for women's surnames, and surnames in **-ко**, see **2.3.5.1** and **2.3.5.2**.

3.2 COMPARISON

3.2.1 COMPARATIVES

We have divided adjectives below into regular, irregular, and compound. However, one may bring the first two together as a 'simple' form, leaving aside the 'compound' form, which is created from practically any adjective using the word **більш** 'more' or **менш** 'less' in front of the basic form of the adjective (see **3.2.1.3**). One can also precede the plain adjective with **більш-менш**, but there is no sense of comparison, rather one of approximation, i.e. 'more or less'.

Not all adjectives have comparative and superlative forms. Most often this is for semantic reasons, which may occasionally be overridden. Such adjectives include those relating to colour and those having an attenuative or augmentative suffix, thus respectively:

(a) **-ав-/-яв-, -уват-/-юват-**
(b) **-ущ-/-ющ-, -енн-, -езн-**

Adjectives with prefixes such as **пре-, архі-, ультра-** also belong here. See **3.3** for examples.

3.2.1.1 Regular comparatives

Adjective (– -**ий** ending) + -**іший**[8]	*Adverb* (– -**о/е** ending) + -**іше**
холодні́ший colder	**холодні́ше**
теплі́ший warmer	**теплі́ше**
ціка́віший more interesting	**ціка́віше**

3.2.1.2 Irregular comparatives

First, we have a few suppletive comparatives:

Simple adjective/adverb	Predicative/adverb	Attributive
вели́кий	бі́льш(е)	бі́льший
га́рний, га́рно	кра́ще	кра́щий
га́рний, га́рно	гарні́ше	гарні́ший
мали́й, ма́ло	ме́нш(е)	ме́нший
до́брий, до́бре	кра́ще, лі́пше	кра́щий, лі́пший
	добрі́ше	добрі́ший kinder
пога́ний	гі́рше	гі́рший

Meanings: 'big', 'good', 'pretty/beautiful', 'small', 'good/kind', 'bad', respectively.

Second, adjectives (and adverbs) with the suffixes -к-, -ок-, -ек- lose the suffixes and take a simplified comparative formant (it is mainly these adjectives which have the suffix -ш-), so we get:

дале́ко/дале́кий	да́льший (not *далекі́ший) – note да́лі
ле́гко/легки́й	ле́гший (not *легкі́ший) – ле́гше
шви́дко/швидки́й	шви́дший (not *швидкі́ший) – шви́дше
глибоко/глибо́кий	гли́бший – гли́бше
ви́соко/висо́кий	ви́щий – ви́ще
ни́зько/ни́зький	ни́жчий – ни́жче
ву́зько/вузьки́й	ву́жчий – ву́жче
ши́роко/широ́кий	ши́рший – ши́рше
то́нко/тонки́й	то́нший – то́нше
бли́зько/близьки́й	бли́жчий – бли́жче

The meanings are, respectively: 'far', 'light/easy', 'fast', 'deep', 'high', 'low', 'narrow', 'wide/broad', 'fine/slim', 'near'.

Similarly note:

ду́жий strong, powerful, healthy – **ду́жчий**
до́рого/дороги́й dear, expensive – **доро́жчий**
стари́й old – **ста́рший**
молоди́й young – **моло́дший**
деше́вий cheap – **деше́вший**
важки́й heavy, difficult – **ва́жчий**
тяжки́й heavy, difficult – **тя́жчий**
до́вгий long – **до́вший**

3.2.1.3   The analytic or compound comparative

In addition to the synthetic comparative, there is an analytic or compound comparative, formed by preceding the plain adjective with **більш** 'more' (or **менш** 'less'). This form is used primarily with polysyllabic adjectives (basically, those whose stems contain more than two syllables), and then only optionally. Its optionality may be extended to more or less all adjectives. An example:

бíльш/менш симпати́чна люди́на
a more/less likeable person

3.2.1.4 Usage and 'than'

'Than' after comparative adjectives is rendered by one of the following:

(a) **ніж**	+	thing/person compared (no change in case)
(b) **від**	+	genitive of the thing/person compared
(c) **про́ти**	+	genitive of the thing/person compared
(d) **за**	+	accusative of the thing/person compared
(e) **як**	+	thing/person compared (no change in case)
(f) **над**	+	accusative of the thing/person compared

The comparative may also be qualified by various adverbs, such as **зна́чно** 'considerably', **незрівня́нно** 'incomparably', **ще** 'even', 'yet', **дале́ко** 'far', **бага́то** 'much', **ге́ть то** 'far and away'.

In the following few examples of usage, you will note that the comparative agrees in case, number, and gender with the noun or noun phrase to which it refers, whether its role is attributive or predicative. As predicate it may occur in the instrumental case, but this is atypical and tends to be limited to usage with pseudo-copulas like **здава́тися** 'to seem', **вважа́тися** 'to be regarded, considered', and **уявля́тися** 'to appear'.

Він ви́брав ще ни́жчий стіле́ць, ніж інші ді́ти, бо не хоті́в, щоб його́ ба́чили.
He chose an even lower chair than the other children, because he didn't want to be seen.

Ки́ївські хмарочо́си незрівня́нно бі́льші, від тих у Нью-йо́рку.
The skyscrapers of Kyiv are incomparably higher than those in New York.

Моя́ сестра́ вважа́ється всіма́ ще розумні́шою від брати́в.
Everyone considers my sister to be even more sensible than her brothers.

Мину́лого ти́жня книжки́ в тому́ магази́ні були́ доро́жчі, ніж у вели́кій книга́рні в це́нтрі мі́ста.
Last week the books in that shop were more expensive than in the big bookshop in the town centre.

Ста́рша ді́вчина, з гли́бшої ба́лки, я не ба́чив нічо́го кра́щого за це.
The older girl, from the deeper valley, I've seen nothing more beautiful than that. (Syn: 65)

3.2.2   SUPERLATIVES

The superlative is formed synthetically, by prefixing **най-** to the comparative or, where the comparative is formed analytically, by preceding the plain adjective by **найбíльш** 'most' (or **наймéнш** 'least'). The synthetic form may be reinforced by the prefixation of **як-** or **що**, such as **щонайкрáщий** 'the (very) best'. (For the 'absolute' superlative, i.e. roughly 'a most . . .', 'very', and so on, see **3.4.4**.)

To render 'of' after a superlative, as in 'the best of . . .', one may use the following prepositions:

(a)   **з**   + genitive
(b)   **сéред**   + genitive
(c)   **за**   + accusative
(d)   **вiд**   + genitive
(e)   **мíж** among   + instrumental
(f)   **з-пóмíж** from among   + instrumental

In the case of (c) and (d) the phrase will normally include a form of **увéсь**:

Сергíй – це студéнт гíрший за всíх.
Serhij is the worst student.

One may also form the superlative by using the comparative followed by a 'than' phrase including the pronoun **увесь**.

Superlatives agree in case, number, and gender just like comparatives, with the occasional use of the instrumental case after pseudo-copulas, again as with comparatives.

Here are a few examples:

Найбíльш промислóві райóни знахóдяться у схíдній Украïні.
The most industrial regions are to be found in eastern Ukraine. (Such a comparative would not always be approved, since the adjective is relative.)

У цій грамáтиці говóриться за особлúвості та найбíльш уживáні констрýкції украïнської мóви.
In this grammar the features and most used constructions of Ukrainian are discussed.

Сéред усíх батькíв вонú найсимпатичнíші.
Of all the parents they are the most likeable.

3.3   THE FORMATION OF ADJECTIVES

Individual prefixes naturally go along with suffixes, the latter being essential in the creation of adjectives except in the case of many body parts, where the adjectival ending may be added directly to the stem, зуб 'tooth' – беззу́бий 'toothless'. In the ordering of the suffixes an initial component и (though it never begins a word in Ukrainian) precedes і, ї, й.

3.3.1 SUFFIXES

In many of the pairs of suffixes given below, the second occurs after soft consonants terminating stems. All other variants are commented upon.

Suffixes	Notes	Examples
-ав-, -яв-, -ляв-	Denominal and deadjectival. Sense of great quantity or, less often, incompleteness.	діря́вий 'full of holes', кістля́вий 'bony', 'nothing but bones', жовта́вий 'yellowish'
-альн-, -іальн-	Denominal (borrowed nouns).	геніа́льний 'of genius', норма́льний 'normal', 'related to the norm', документа́льний 'documentary'
-ан-, -ян-	Denominal, quite frequent. Refers to material source or material used for something.	дерев'я́ний 'wooden', лляни́й 'flaxen', 'linen', водяни́й 'using water', e.g. млин 'mill', торф'яни́й 'made of'/'using peat'
-анн-, -янн-	Participial (past participle passive). Evaluative and superlative sense, with prefix не-.	невблага́нний 'implacable', 'inflexible', незрівня́нний 'incomparable', 'unique'
-анськ-, -янськ-, -іанськ-	Denotes belonging to the deriving word.	америка́нський 'American'
-аст-, -яст-	Denominal. The -с- may be inserted and related to the following suffix. May have intensive sense, sense of 'like the deriving noun', or simply being the adjectival form of the deriving noun.	зуба́(с)тий 'toothy', 'with large teeth', миша́стий 'mouse-coloured', 'like a mouse', клітча́стий 'made up of squares/cells' (note -к- > -ч-: клі́тка 'square', 'cell').

Suffixes	Notes	Examples
-ат-	Also occurs as -уватий, -юватий, -чатий. Denominal (parts of the body) – intensive or simply possession.	борода́тий 'bearded', 'with a beard', борода́ 'beard', крила́(с)тий 'winged' (крило́ 'wing')
-ач-, -яч-	Denominal (possessive sense) or original present participle active (second conjugation).	ко́зячий 'goat's' (коза́ 'goat'), коро́в'ячий 'cow's (коро́ва 'cow'), бродя́чий 'itinerant', вися́чий (замо́к) 'padlock' (lit. 'hanging lock') – also with other nouns.
-ащ-, -ящ-	Church Slavonic version of preceding suffix – quite rare.	підходя́щий 'appropriate', 'suitable' (also, and less Russian, підходя́чий, підхо́жий)
-езн-, -елезн-	Colloquial, evaluative: majorative, possible slight coarsening. See also -енний.	довже́зний 'very/quite long' (from до́вгий 'long'), товстеле́зний 'very fat'
-ен-	Participial origin (past passive participle). Refers to effect of action of deriving verb. Also derives adjectives from reflexive verbs.	жа́рений 'roasted', 'baked' (from жа́рити 'to roast', 'bake'), кра́шений 'coloured', 'dyed' (from кра́сити 'to colour', 'dye'; зневі́рений 'desperate', 'despondent' (from зневі́ритися 'to give up hope').
-енн-	Evaluative, intensive (negative), colloquial.	довже́нний 'very/quite long', товсте́нний 'very/quite fat', широче́нний 'very/quite wide' (from широ́кий 'wide'). See -(ел)езн- above.
-енськ-	Geographical.	пе́нзенський 'of/relating to Penza'

Suffixes	Notes	Examples
-еньк-	Evaluative: affectionate, attenuative (very common).	біле́нький 'white' (from бі́лий 'white'), кругле́нький 'round' (from кру́глий 'round'), багате́нький 'rather rich' (from бага́тий 'rich'), глибоче́нький 'quite deep' (from глибо́кий 'deep')
-есеньк-	Colloquial. Evaluative: very affectionate and rather intensive. See -еньк- above.	біле́сенький 'lovely and white', гарне́сенький 'really lovely' (doubly derived from га́рний 'lovely', 'beautiful')
-есн-	Denominal. Ancient and unproductive.	небе́сний 'heavenly' (from не́бо 'sky'), словесний 'oral', 'verbal' (from сло́во 'word')
-ив-	Denominal, denoting presence of, capacity for, or inclination to in the person described of the particular quality. Also deverbal, indicating inclination or capacity related to the action described by the deriving verb. Also occurs with -лив-.	ліни́вий 'lazy' (from лінь 'laziness'), розсу́дливий 'prudent', 'reasonable' (from розсу́джувати/розсуди́ти 'to decide', 'judge', 'consider')
-им-	Participial (present participle passive), Church Slavonic. Conveys ability, permissibility.	припусти́мий 'admissible', 'supposed', несходи́мий 'limitless', 'immeasurable'
-ин-, -ін-	Denominal (first-declension personal names and the noun ма́ти). Note the consonantal alternations. Rare with animals, where the genitive or the suffix -ач- is more likely.	доччи́н (дочка́), ма́терин (ма́ти), О́льжин (О́льга). Note орли́ний – орля́чий.

Suffixes	Notes	Examples
-инськ-	Quite rare, derives from geographical names and **ма́ти**.	**баки́нський** 'of Baku', **матери́нський** 'maternal', 'motherly'
-ист-, -іст-	Denominal, deadjectival, deverbal. Denominals are somewhat colloquial and emphasize great quantity. Deadjectivals are similar (filtering through to a source noun). Deverbals are rare and suggest an inclination.	**баси́стий** 'bass (-player)', **голоси́стий** 'loud-voiced', **піща́нистий** 'with lots of sand' (from **піща́ний** 'sandy')
-ит-	Unproductive.	**масти́тий** 'dignified', **імени́тий** 'noble', 'respectable (colloquial)'
-ичн-, -ічн-	Forms adjectives covering international scientific terms. Also derived from numerals.	**артисти́чний** 'artistic', **циклі́чний** 'cyclic', **п'ятери́чний** 'fivefold'
-инн-	Derived from ordinal numerals.	**перви́нний** 'primary', 'initial' (from **пе́рвий = пе́рший** 'first')
-ів-, -їв-	Denominal (human reference, personal names).	**учи́телів** 'teacher's', **Олексі́їв** 'Oleksii's'
-івськ-, -ївськ-, -овськ-	Deadjectival (creating relative adjectives). Creates adjectives from male animates, with sense of 'like', 'peculiar to', from inanimates, with a sense of 'relating to', from geographical names, and from initial or truncated compounds.	**бальза́ківський** 'relating to Balzac', **ба́нківський** 'relating to a bank', **дніпро́вський** 'relating to the Dniepr', **ву́зівський** 'relating to a Higher Education/university establishment'

Suffixes	Notes	Examples
-ійськ-	Geographical, not productive.	альпíйський 'Alpine', чілíйський 'Chilean'
-ісіньк-, -юсіньк-	Deadjectival, very frequent. Evaluative (positive and affective). Colloquial.	малю́сíнький 'very little', 'wee', 'titchy', новíсíнький 'spanking new', свíжíсíнький 'really fresh'
-и- (-j-)	Quite rare: possessives, peculiarities, and relating to products made from the pelt or skin of animals. Note the consonantal alternation.	во́вчий 'wolf's', 'lupine', ове́чий 'sheepskin'
-к-	Deverbal and denominal. May convey inclination.	верткúй 'active', 'restless', пухкúй 'soft', 'tender', 'plump'
-л-	Participial (second past active or л participle). Resultative.	в'я́лий 'faded', 'withered', пу́хлий 'swollen', 'bloated'
-льн-	Deinfinitival. Sense of to be used for something.	гладúльний 'for ironing', читáльний 'for reading'
-н- (soft)	Particularly temporal and spatial. Note the common derived suffix -шній (see below).	весíнній 'springtime' (adj.), вчорáшній 'yesterday's'
-н- (hard)	Found as final component of several compound suffixes. Denominal, denumerical (rare), and deverbal.	залíзний 'iron', четвертнúй 'made of four identical parts', 'quadruple' (also via verbs: подвíйний 'double'), складнúй 'complicated'
-ов-, -ев-	Denominal (possessive – animals). Also from inanimate nouns and (arguably) from verbs.	бере́зовий 'of a birch', торго́вий 'of a market'

Suffixes	Notes	Examples
-уват-, -юват-	Deadjectival (qualitative) and denominal, giving respectively an attenuative nuance (-ish) and an idea of rough similarity.	**блакитнува́тий** 'blueish' (from **блаки́тний** 'blue'), **голкува́тий** 'like a needle', 'prickly' (from **го́лка** 'needle'), **лантухува́тий** 'awkward', 'clumsy' (from **ла́нтух** 'coarse linen sheet', 'heavy hempen sack')
-овит-	Denominal, with a slight majorative sense, e.g. 'rather . . .'	**ділови́тий** 'active', 'serious' (from **ді́ло** 'deed', 'act'), **хвалькови́тий** 'inclined to boasting', 'rather boastful' (perhaps from **хвалі́й** 'boaster')
-овн-, -евн-	Not productive. Denominal.	**плаче́вний** 'weeping', 'tearful' (from **плач** 'weeping', 'tears')
-онн-	Denominal (borrowed words). Very rare – more common as **-ійний**.	**дивізіо́нний** 'relating to a cavalry division'
-ськ-, -зьк-, -цьк-	Denominals with senses of possession (rare), intention ('meant for'), characteristic of. Also geographical terms and names of nations.	**а́вторський** 'author's', **учи́тельський** 'teacher's', 'for a teacher', **геро́йський** 'heroic', 'like a hero', **украї́нський** 'Ukrainian', **ки́ївський** 'of Kyiv'. Note alternations, as mentioned in Chapter 1.
-т-	Participial (past participle passive). Resultative.	**відкри́тий** 'open', **мо́лотий** 'threshed'
-тн-	Unproductive and rare, formed from simplex verbs.	**зна́тний** 'notable', 'distinguished', 'eminent'

Suffixes	Notes	Examples
-уч-, -юч-	Participial (present participle active, first conjugation). Sense of inclination or appropriateness to a particular action, sometimes simply qualitative, and it may also function as a participle, though this is rare. It may be denominal. Finally, it may be evaluative with an intensive nuance.	повзу́чий 'creeping' (from повзти́ 'to creep'), палю́чий 'burning', 'scorching' (from пали́ти 'to burn'), балаку́чий 'talkative', 'garrulous' (from балака́ти 'to prattle'), відпочива́ючий 'rooting' (from відпочива́ти 'to rest'), жагу́чий 'ardent', 'passionate' (from жага́ 'thirst', 'yearning'), кислю́чий 'very sour', 'tart'
-ущ-, -ющ-	Participial (present participle active, first conjugation), Church Slavonic, sense of inclination (slightly intensive) or intensive with a scornful nuance. It may overlap with the preceding suffix.	видю́щий 'very apparent', 'visible', злю́щий 'very irate', 'bad'
-ч-	Denominal and deverbal.	будівни́чий 'builder', 'architect (noun)' (from будівни́к, with the same meaning), ви́борчий 'electoral' (from вибира́ти 'to elect', 'choose')
-част-	Denominal (rare). Sense of great quantity.	клітча́стий 'in squares', 'divided into cells'
-ш-, -іш-	Comparative formant.	бі́льший 'bigger', ме́нший 'smaller', ціка́віший 'more interesting'
-шн- (soft)	Adjectival form of expressions of time and space. See -н- (soft) above.	за́втрашній 'tomorrow's', зо́внішній 'external', 'outward'

3.3.2 PREFIXES

Prefixes	Notes	Examples
а-	negates, synonym of не-	аполітичний 'apolitical'
анти-	opposition – 'anti-', close to проти-	антифашистський 'anti-fascist'
архі-	enhancing, rare	архіважливий 'very important'
без-	dePP., absence	бездомний 'homeless', беззубий 'toothless'
внутрі/ внутрішньо-	dePP., 'inside', 'internal'	внутрішньочерепний 'intracraneal'
до-	dePP., close to перед-, під-, opposite of після-, 'pre-'	довоєнний 'pre-war', допетровський 'pre-Petrine'
за-	dePP., 'beyond'; 'excessive'	застолітній 'over a hundred years old', завеликий 'too big'
між- (межи- rare)	dePP., 'inter-'	межирічний 'between rivers', міжнародній 'international'
на-	dePP., 'on' something	настінний 'wall-mountable', настільний 'table-', 'on the table'
над-	dePP., 'above', 'super-', 'extreme', 'excessive', 'beyond', 'somewhat'	наднормовий 'above the norm', надрічний 'on the riverbank' (= 'above the river')', надприродний 'supernatural', надскладний 'extremely complex', надмірний 'excessive', надлімітний 'beyond the limit(s)'
най-	deadjectival, superlative, 'the most', also intensive or absolute щонай-, якнай-	найкращий 'the best', якнайшвидший 'extremely fast', 'as fast as possible'

Prefixes	Notes	Examples
не- (its status as a prefix might be disputed)	negation, opposition, absence	непога́ний 'not bad', невесе́лий 'unhappy'
перед-	dePP., 'before', 'pre-'	передгі́рний 'at the foot of (= 'before') the mountain(s)', передвечі́рній 'before the evening'
під-	dePP., 'near', 'under', 'subject to'	підру́чний 'near at hand', 'subordinate', підземе́льний 'subterranean', підцензу́рний 'subject to censorship'
після-	dePP., 'after'	післявоє́нний 'postwar'
по-	dePP.: 'near', 'along', 'after', 'each', deverbal: 'inclined to', 'subject to', 'used in . . .'	поворотки́й 'agile ('inclined to turn')', полиня́лий 'faded ('subjected to fading')', пошивни́й 'sewing ('used in sewing')'
поза-	dePP., 'beyond', 'outside'	позашкі́льни́й 'outside school', позаєвропе́йський 'outside Europe'
понад-	'beyond', 'above', often alternative to над-	понадбуде́нний 'out of the ordinary', понаднормо́вий 'extra', 'additional'
пре- (rare)	enhancing (slightly ironic or familiar)	превесе́лий 'very happy', пречудо́вий 'marvellous', 'most wonderful'
при-	dePP., 'near'	припо́люсний 'near the Pole', примо́рський 'by the sea coast'
проти-	dePP., 'anti-', 'against'	протира́ковий 'anti-cancer'
роз-	deverbal adjectives and deverbal denominal adjectives, rather abstract, a sense of dispersal	розливни́й 'overflowing'

ультра-	'ultra-', 'extreme', often synonymous with **над-**	**ультракоро́ткий** 'ultra-short', **ультрафіоле́товий** 'ultra-violet'
через-	dePP., rather rare, 'across', 'over'	**черезплі́чний** '(carried) over the shoulder'

3.3.3   PREFIX + SUFFIX

Prefix-suffix	Notes	Examples
небез- + **-н-** (hard)	denominal, 'not un-'	**небезуспі́шний** 'not inefficient', 'not unsuccessful', **небезкори́сний** 'not without profit'
про- + **-ськ-/-зьк-/ -анськ-/-н-** (hard)	denominal, 'pro-'	**профранцу́зький** 'pro-French', **проза́хідний** 'pro-West'
спів- + **-н-** (hard)	denominal, 'co-'	**співря́дний** 'equal'
су- + **-н-** (hard)	denominal, characterizes source noun, unproductive	**суча́сний** 'modern', 'of the time'
транс- + **-н-** (hard)/ **-ов-/-ськ-/-ійськ-**	denominal (place-names), 'trans-'	**трансполя́рний** 'transpolar'

Note that derivation can be more complex and the prefixation/suffixation need not be simultaneous, for example, **співробі́тни́к** 'collaborator', 'fellow-worker' may be seen as an established stem (itself a derived noun: see **2.5**), from which **співробі́тни́цький** 'collaborative' may be derived. There is no word **пе́ка** underlying **безпе́ка** 'safety', 'security', so here we do not really have the prefix **небез-** in **небезпе́чний** 'dangerous' (**безпе́чний** 'safe'). What we have is the prefix or particle **не-** and a root or stem **-безпе́к-**, plus an ending **-а**, thus **безпе́ка** 'safety'. See **3.3.2**. Remember too that certain suffixes trigger consonantal alternations.

3.3.4   COMPOUND ADJECTIVES

Some compound adjectives reflect coordination of their lexical elements; the elements are sometimes quite independent of each other, sometimes more closely linked, without being clearly subordinate to each other. Thus:

істо́рико-філологі́чний факульте́т history and language-and-literature faculty (independent)

торгове́льно-морськи́й флот merchant navy (lit. 'trading-maritime fleet') (more closely linked, with hyphen)

яскра́во-си́ній bright blue (the same, typical of shades of colour and of taste)

сві́тло- bright-, light-

те́мно- dark-

сі́ро-зеле́ний grey-green

ки́сло-соло́дкий sweet-and-sour

Where a hyphen is written one might consider the stress on the first component to be secondary. The hyphen may be missing in such cases too (the rule would be that a hyphen is present where the compound is less integrated, thus the first of the two examples below is in a sense two colours, while the second, without a hyphen, is one), for example,

жо̀вто-блаки́тний yellow-blue

жо̀втогаря́чий fire-yellow

and where the first component comes from **зага́льний** 'common', 'general', 'universal', for example,

зага̀льновжива́ний generally accepted/used

зага̀льнообов'язко́вий binding on all

Similar to the more tightly linked compounds are those which are often considered subordinate, where the first element may be seen as syntactically dependent on the second. If the second element is a part of the body, such compound adjectives are suffixless, for example:

бі́лоли́ций white-faced   **по̀внови́дий** chubby (lit. 'full-faced')

си́ньоо́кий blue-eyed

Otherwise we find a suffix, as in **ву̀зькогля́дний** 'narrow-minded', **чо̀рноморськи́й** 'Black-Sea'. These two types of compound adjectives are both made up of an adjective followed by a noun. We find also sequences of noun and adjective, noun and verb, and numeral and noun, each suffixed unless a part of the body is involved, for example:

жѝттєраді́сний buoyant, jovial   **во̀гнепа́льний** capable of being fired/

шѐстикри́лий six-winged   shot

кі̀лькаповерхо́вий multi-storeyed   **двòмо́вний** bilingual

The first component may be an adverb, for example:

гу̀стонасе́лений densely populated

or a form of **все, сам, свій** with suffixation, for example:

всеукраї́нський all-Ukrainian   **своєрі́дний** original

'Half-' is conveyed by **пів-** or **напів-**, for example:

піврі́чний six-months-old, half-yearly   **напівди́кий** half-wild

We might also mention compounds whose second component is **-ви́дний** or **-поді́бний**, for example:

гру̀шови́дний pear-like/shaped   **людѝноподі́бний** like a person

3.4 USING ADJECTIVES

3.4.1 GENERAL

Regarding position relative to the qualified noun or noun phrase, the attributive adjective as a rule precedes, although it may follow when emphatic or for stylistic reasons.

Adjectives are more often than not 'used' – they say something about other words, typically nouns, which themselves may be independent or dependent, say, when a noun is in a case determined by a governing verb or preposition, thus:

стара́ ха́та an old house
у старі́й ха́ті in the old house
Вона́ ви́йшла сухо́ю з води́. She got off scot-free.
Він ви́знав себе́ ви́нним. He admitted his guilt (lit. 'confessed himself guilty').
молоди́й/молода́ сирота́ a young orphan (Note that with epicenes (common-gender nouns) the adjective takes the gender of whom the noun refers to.)

So adjectives are mostly subordinate to other words and constructions. In this respect one might note that there are, too, adjectives which function as nouns, for example:

лісни́чий forester	**Рі́вне** Rivne (city)	**мину́ле** the past
майбу́тнє the future	**хво́рий** a sick person	**молоди́й** a young person, groom

The last two exemplify the universal potentiality of semantically appropriate adjectives to refer to a person, man, or woman, or people without the actual use of the noun proper.

3.4.2   ADJECTIVES CONSTRUCTED WITH CASES AND PREPOSITIONAL PHRASES

How do we translate situations equivalent to English 'capable of', 'ready for', and similar expressions? Here we can see the adjective as controlling the construction. Here are a few such constructions (drawing substantially on Rusanovskij *et al.* 1986: 273–5) – note that the translations are necessarily occasionally approximate, since much will depend on context:

3.4.2.1   *Adjective + genitive*

ва́ртий worthy of	**Не ва́рте ню́ху таба́ки.** It's not worth a fig.
гі́дний worthy of	**Він не гі́дний пова́ги.** He's not deserving of respect.
пе́вний certain of	**Вона́ зо́всім не пе́вна цього́.** She's not at all certain of it.
по́вний full of	**Філіжа́нка по́вна води́.** The cup is full of water.
свідо́мий aware/informed of	**Він нічо́го не свідо́мий.** He doesn't know a thing.

3.4.2.2   *Adjective + dative*

близьки́й near to	**близьки́й се́рцю** near to one's heart
вдя́чний grateful to	**вдя́чний ба́тькові (за гро́ші)** grateful to father (for the money)
ви́нен guilty, at fault	**Він сам тому́ ви́нен.** He himself is to blame for that.
ви́нен owe	**Я ви́нен тобі́ гро́ші/життя́.** I owe you money/my life. (but **Я завдя́чую тобі́ життя́м.** I owe you my life.)
відо́мий known/famous to	**відо́мий лю́дям** known to people
воро́жий hostile to	**воро́жий наро́дові** hostile to the people
дороги́й dear to	**дороги́й ма́тері** dear to mother
потрі́бний necessary to	**потрі́бний лю́дям** needed by people
протиле́жний opposite to	**протиле́жний по́глядам** opposite/contrary to (my) views
рад glad of	**Вона́ була́ ду́же ра́да нам.** She was really pleased to see us/gave us a good reception.
рі́вний equal to	**Вона́ не ма́є собі́ рі́вної.** She doesn't have her equal.
шкідли́вий harmful to	**шкідли́вий лісо́ві** detrimental to the forest

3.4.2.3   *Adjective + accusative*

вúнен owe   **Я вúнен йому́ бага́то гроше́й.** I owe him a lot of money. (Note
(above) the dative for the person to whom something is
owed.)

3.4.2.4   *Adjective + instrumental*

важлúвий significant in   **важлúвий вúсновками** significant as regards
                                 the conclusions that can be drawn
відо́мий known for   **відо́мий у́спіхами** known for her success
сúльний strong in   **сúльний ду́хом** strong in spirit

3.4.3   ADJECTIVES CONSTRUCTED WITH PREPOSITIONAL PHRASES

Or the adjective can be linked, as in English, with an explicit preposition, the
preposition in turn governing a particular case – from the meanings of the
following examples, by no means exhaustive, it will be clear that some are
productive (usable with any semantically appropriate noun or noun phrase),
while others are set expressions.

3.4.3.1   *Genitive*

Adjective + **до** + genitive:

байду́жий до проха́нь	indifferent to requests
беру́чкий до робо́ти/всього́	assiduous in/inclined to work
блúзький до оригіна́лу	close to the original
ввíчливий до діте́й	considerate to children
вимо́гливий до се́бе	demanding on himself
гото́вий до випро́бувань	ready for testing/experiments
заборо́нений до ввезе́ння	prohibited for import
зда́тний до робо́ти	capable of work
ла́ден/ла́дний до п'є́си	keen on the play
охо́чий до казо́к	keen on fairy tales
прида́тний до вúкористання	fit for/good for use/utilization
привíтний до дру́зів	kind to friends
ува́жний/ува́жливий до люде́й	attentive to people
мо́крий до нúтки	soaked to the skin
смíлий/смілú́вий до безме́жності	infinitely courageous
схúльний до пра́ці	inclined to (the) work

The last two but one are really a set and an adverbial expression respectively.

Adjective + **від** + genitive:

далéкий від розумíння	far from understanding
протилéжний від сóнця	opposite the sun
блідúй від перевтóми	pale with exhaustion
мóкрий від дощý	wet with rain
солóдший від мéду	sweeter than honey
стáрший від брáта	older than his brother

The last two are examples of comparison.

Adjective + **для** + genitive:

близькúй для читачá	close for the reader (= comprehensible)
важкúй для розумíння	important for comprehension
дорогúй для друзíв	dear for friends
знайóмий для ýчнів	familiar to the pupils
корúсний для людúни	useful to man/a person
придáтний для аналíзу	suitable for, capable of, analysis
старáнний для людéй	attentive to people
шкідлúвий для органíзму	damaging to the organism

Almost all constructions involving **для** are synonymous with constructions of the type 'adjective + dative', for example, **знайóмий ýчням, корúсний людúні**.

Adjective + **з** + genitive:

рáдий з ýспіхів	overjoyed with the success
найвúщий з хлóпців	the tallest of the boys
найтеплíше з морíв	the warmest of (the) seas

The last two demonstrate superlative constructions.

3.4.3.2 Accusative

Adjective + **за** + accusative:

відповідáльний за робóту	responsible for the work
пéвний за людéй	sure of the people
рáдий за дітéй	pleased for the children

Adjective + **на** + accusative:

згóден на пропозúцію	agree(d) to a proposal
здáтний на пóдвиг	capable of, fit to achieve a feat
хвóрий на грип	ill with the flu
вúдний на всі бóки	visible on/from all sides
відóмий на всю респýбліку	known/famous throughout the republic

вищий на метр	higher by a metre
старший на рік	a/one year older
невеликий на зріст	small of stature/in height
терпкий на смак	sour/bitter/tart in taste
схожий на батька	similar to (his/her . . .) father
бридкий на дотик	repugnant to the touch

3.4.3.3   Instrumental

Adjective + з + instrumental:

близький з автором	close to the author (figurative)
ввічливий із друзями	polite with, considerate to friends
дружний/дружній з колективом	friendly/getting on well with the team
згодний з висновком	agreeing with, in harmony with the conclusion
знайомий з робітником	acquainted with the worker
паралельний з вулицею	parallel to the street

Adjective + за + instrumental:

близький за роллю	close/similar in role
далекий за значенням	remote in meaning/significance
подібний за формою	similar in form

Adjective + між + instrumental:

| відомий між людьми | well-known among folk |

Adjective + перед + instrumental:

| винен перед батьком | guilty in respect of one's father |

3.4.3.4   Locative

Such constructions are on the whole adjunctive rather than complementary, i.e. they are optional adverbial extensions, with the preposition more autonomous. Thus:

близький у поглядах	close in one's opinions
охайний у побуті	neat and tidy in one's way of life
потрібний у житті	required in/necessary to life
непомітний у темряві	unnoticeable in the darkness
яскравий на сонці	dazzling in the sunlight
відвертий при зустрічі	honest/open on meeting
потрібний при перекладі	needed in translation

The following are closer to being complementary constructions:

ви́нен/ви́нний у по́милці	guilty of a mistake
пе́вен/пе́вний у перемо́зі	sure of victory
рі́вний у си́лі	equal in strength
протиле́жний у по́глядах	opposite views
ува́жний у ста́вленні	attentive/considerate in attitude/treatment

3.4.4 ADJECTIVES CONSTRUCTED WITH INFINITIVES AND ADVERBS

Adjectives may also govern infinitives and be qualified by adverbs, for example:

безси́лий боро́тися	powerless to struggle
гото́вий допові́сти	ready to make a report
зда́тний працюва́ти	capable of working
зго́ден акомпанува́ти	willing/ready to accompany
зобов'я́заний закінчи́ти	obliged to finish
ла́дний відпочи́ти	ready to take a rest
охо́чий ме́шкати там	keen to live there
ра́ди́й стара́тися	pleased to try
схи́льний перебі́льшувати	prone/inclined to exaggerate
ду́же приві́тний	very friendly
абсолю́тно задові́льни́й	absolutely satisfactory/satisfying
надмі́рно рухли́вий	excessively active/quick
неймові́рно строка́тий	incredibly variegated/capricious
ма́йже спі́лий	almost ripe
зо́всім зеле́ний	quite/entirely green
мікроскопі́чно мали́й	microscopically small
(за)на́дто відве́ртий	too open/frank/sincere
по-дру́жньому дба́йливий	attentive/concerned in a friendly way
по-півде́нному зати́шни́й	peaceful/pleasant in a 'midday sort of way'
математи́чно то́чний	mathematically precise
техні́чно доскона́лий	technically perfect
за́вжди́ сві́жий	always fresh

3.4.5 'TOO X'

One may indicate 'too' by prefixing за-, although not to every adjective; it is best to note which adjectives admit this prefix (in particular those describing physical properties), for example:

замали́й	too small
завели́кий	too large
зашоро́кий	too wide
завиcо́кий	too tall/high

A useful adverb is **на́дто**, and it will be quite appropriate to use, say, **ду́же** 'very', 'considerably', **неймові́рно** 'incredibly'. See also **3.2.1.4** and **3.4.4**.

4 THE PRONOUN

4.0 GENERAL

Trask (1993: 221–2) defines pronouns as 'The lexical category, or a member of this category, whose members typically function as noun phrases in isolation, not normally requiring or permitting the presence of determiners or other adnominals, and whose members typically have little or no intrinsic meaning or reference', and he divides them into personal, reflexive, demonstrative, indefinite, interrogative, and relative. In discussing pronouns it is also useful to refer to their role as anaphors, in that they may refer to, or 'take their interpretations from, other items in the same sentence or discourse' (*ibid.*, p. 15): 'John saw the book' – 'He saw it', and as deictics, in that they may 'make crucial reference to such factors as the time or place of speaking or the identity or location of the speaker, the addressee or other entities' (*ibid.*, p. 75): 'this', 'that' (in the context of pronouns). The vocative, insofar as it might be needed, is identical with the nominative.

4.1 PERSONAL PRONOUNS

We note that the personal pronouns for the first and second persons are declensionally quite anomalous (as often happens in languages), the first persons being suppletive as between the nominative and the other cases. The third-person pronouns too are suppletive, the nominatives having been supplied from the distal demonstrative *он of Proto-Slavonic, still surviving in certain Slavonic languages or in set phrases in others. The endings of the non-nominative case forms are not anomalous, and reflect those found in the adjective, given that the Ukrainian adjective is historically (in its non-short form) composed of the nominal short adjective, to which the third person pronoun was added (the original nominative shows up here). Note that the first- and second-person plural pronouns are not strictly the actual plurals of the first- and second-person singular pronouns, but for the first person an inclusive form and for the second a form which may or may not include anyone but the first person. We capitalize the second-person plural pronouns (some native speakers recommend capitalization of the second-person singular pronouns too, something which we occasionally do in examples).

Though there is a certain amount of variation, it is possible to generalize that the nominative case forms of the personal pronouns are normally actually expressed, even though the verbal non-past endings make it absolutely clear, if only for the first- and second-persons singular, who the subject is. Perhaps the pronouns are expressed because this does not work for the third person and not entirely for the first- and second-persons plural, and because of the need, but not obligation, for the subject pronouns to be expressed in the past tense, conditional mood, and passive forms. In informal speech these pronouns are more readily dropped, and in any event would certainly be dropped in a string of verbs with an identical subject, as in English: **Я сиджу́ та чита́ю** 'I sit and read'.

On the question of address, we note that **ти** is used to address a single addressee who is a close friend, a child, an animal, or God. **Ви** is used for all plural addressees, or in singular address where politeness or formality is appropriate.

Here is a full paradigm for the personal pronouns:

	I (1sg.)	*You (2sg.)*	*He/it*	*It*	*She/it (3sg.)*	
N.	я	ти	він	воно́	вона́	Н.
G.	ме́не́	те́бе́	його́/ньо́го		її́/не́ї	Р.
D.	мені́	тобі́	йому́		їй	Д.
A.	ме́не́	те́бе́	його́/ньо́го		її́/не́ї	З.
I.	мно́ю	тобо́ю	ним		не́ю	О.
L.	мені́	тобі́	ньо́му (нім)		ній	М.

	We (1pl.)	*You (2pl.)*	*They (3pl.)*	
N.	ми	Ви	вони́	Н.
G.	нас	Вас	їх/них	Р.
D.	нам	Вам	їм	Д.
A.	нас	Вас	їх/них	З.
I.	на́ми	Ва́ми	ни́ми	О.
L.	нас	Вас	них	М.

There are no strict rules on the position of personal pronouns. The subject pronoun will certainly normally come before the verb, any other position being emphatic or at least stylistically marked. The object pronoun may come after the verb or before it. Needless to say, a pronoun will be fixed in relation to a governing preposition:

Я їх не зна́ю ог **Я не зна́ю їх.**
I don't know them. (Both relatively neutral.)

Він їм ничо́го не сказа́в. ог **Він нічо́го не ска́зав їм.**
He didn't say a thing to them. (Both relatively neutral.)

До них вона́ посла́ла дочку́.
They were sent her daughter. (lit. 'She sent (her) daughter to them.') (It is not possible to separate **до** and **них**.)

Stress retracts one syllable left (1st-2nd persons accusative-genitive: мене́ – до ме́не, тебе́ – у те́бе) and an initial **н-** appears in the third-person forms when they are immediately governed by a preposition (accusative-genitive, locative), thus: його́ – до ньо́го 'it – to it', у ньо́му 'in it'.[9] In this connection note (a) the spelling changes, particularly as regards її – не́ї, (b) that the instrumental and locative forms always have the initial **н-**, and (c) the recommended absence of such a form for the dative, given the rarity of prepositions governing the dative and the tendency for such sequences to be restricted to set expressions. It might be borne in mind that in texts and dialects one may occasionally come across forms where the initial **н** is expected, but absent. Also, as regards pronunciation, one may, again dialectally, come across a pronunciation of він with a hard **в** (because it alternates with **о**), and even a pronunciation of ї as if [јı], for example, їх [јıx]. Very occasionally, after a preposition, one may encounter an accusative singular feminine **ню**.

Себе́ 'self' (reflexive) declines like ти, but has no nominative form, since it is only used to refer back to the grammatical subject. Note the stress retraction in the accusative-genitive when immediately governed by a preposition.

G.	себе́	P.	
D.	собі	Д.	
A.	себе́	З.	
I.	собо́ю	О.	
L.	собі	M.	

За́втра ми пове́рнемося до се́бе.
Tomorrow we'll return home.

Сестра́ Ната́лка така́ га́рна з се́бе.
My sister Natalka is so very pretty.

Пе́ред собо́ю я ра́птом поба́чив старо́го дру́га.
Suddenly, before my very eyes, I saw an old friend.

In connection with себе́ we can mention the reflexive particle -ся (after consonants and commonly after vowels), -сь (sometimes after vowels and, optionally, sonorants), now firmly attached to the verb in its 'reflexive form' (see пове́рнемося above). Formerly, and still in south-western dialects, this particle was enclitic, in the forms ся and си (also first-person singular м'я – ми, second-person singular тя – ти, and third-person accusative-genitive singular masculine-neuter го, dative singular masculine-neuter му) and not attached to the verb. We still have Як ся ма́єш? 'How are you?'

It is appropriate to mention the reciprocal pronoun, namely 'each other', 'one another'. This is conveyed by оди́н о́дного (for two males), одна́ одну́ (for two females), and одне́ о́дного (for male and female). Note that the first component, as one might expect, occurs in the nominative singular and is invariable; the neuter singular first component (see **5.0**) for 'male and female' is perhaps striking. The second component goes in whatever case the syntax of the sentence requires – the forms for males and mixed as given indicate animate accusative; if a preposition is involved, then it immediately precedes the second component. For 'male and female', note that the masculine is selected for the second component. Note finally the stress of the second component, fixed on the first syllable. Thus:

Мені здається, що вони майже завжди розмовляють одне з одним.
It seems to me that they're almost always talking to one another. (mixed)

Ми розмовляли один про одного.
We were talking about each other. (males)

Щовечора вони телефонують одна до одної.
They telephone each other every evening. (females)

Коли жінка нарешті отримала розлучення, вона зрозуміла, що вони з чоловіком зовсім не знали одне одного.
When his wife finally obtained a separation, she understood that she and her husband didn't know each other at all. (mixed)

Note from the last example how one conjoins subjects, namely, and normally, by using the plural pronoun, adding the other component of the subject (pronoun or noun) via the preposition з + instrumental, thus **ми з братом** 'my brother and I', **Ви з нею** 'you and she'.

4.2   POSSESSIVE PRONOUNS

Note first of all that these are adjectival in form and agree in case, number, and gender with what they possess. On the whole they precede the noun or noun phrase they qualify, but may, for emphasis or stylistic reasons, follow. They function both as possessive pronouns, i.e. 'mine', 'yours', and so on and as possessive adjectives, i.e. 'my', 'your', and so on.

My/mine

	Masculine	*Neuter*	*Feminine*	*Plural*	
N.	мій	моє	моя	мої	Н.
G.	мого		моєї	моїх	Р.
D.	моєму		моїй	моїм	Д.
A.	= nom./gen.	= nom.	мою	= nom./gen.	З.
I.	моїм		моєю	моїми	О.
L.	моєму (моїм)		моїй	моїх	М.

Твій 'your/yours' (singular familiar/informal) and **свій** 'one's', 'my/mine', and so on decline like **мій**. Occasional alternative forms for **мого, моєму, моєї, моєю** are respectively (and generalizing to **твій, свій**) **мойого, мойому/мойму/мому, меї, мею**. The first two are dialectal and poetic; the others are more narrowly local.

Our(s)

	Masculine	Neuter	Feminine	Plural	
N.	наш	на́ше	на́ша	на́ші	Н.
G.	на́шого		на́шої	на́ших	Р.
D.	на́шому		на́шій	на́шим	Д.
A.	= nom./gen.	= nom.	на́шу	= nom./gen.	3.
I.	на́шим		на́шою	на́шими	О.
L.	на́шому (на́шім)		на́шій	на́ших	М.

Ваш 'your/yours' (singular formal, plural) declines like **наш**. Note particularly the instrumental singular feminine ending **-ою**; in a noun with a similar
stem ending (soft consonant), husher, **ц**, [j], we have **-ею/-єю**, for example,
земля́ – земле́ю 'land', **вівця́ – вівце́ю** 'sheep', **ка́ша – ка́шею** 'gruel',
стая́ – ста́єю 'shepherd's hut', 'sheepfold'. Adjectives too have **-ою**. See the
pertinent sections in Chapters 2 and 3.

The genitives of the third-person forms function as indeclinable, and completely invariable, possessives, thus: **його́, її, їх** 'his/its', 'her(s)/its', 'their(s)'.
For 'their(s)' we also have the more common **їхній**, declined as a soft adjective
and agreeing as normal with what is possessed. None of them ever attracts
the initial **н-**.

їхній 'their(s)'

	Masculine	Neuter	Feminine	Plural	
N.	їхній	їхнє	їхня	їхні	Н.
G.	їхнього		їхньої	їхніх	Р.
D.	їхньому		їхній	їхнім	Д.
A.	= nom. or gen.	= nom.	їхню	= nom. or gen.	3.
I.	їхнім		їхньою	їхніми	О.
L.	їхньому (їхнім)		їхній	їхніх	М.

Свій is used for all the possessive pronouns when what is possessed is possessed by the grammatical subject of the sentence or clause:

Я взяв свою́ валі́зку.
I took my suitcase.

Він взяв свою́ валі́зку.
He took his (own) suitcase.

Він взяв його́ валі́зку.
He took his (another male's) suitcase.

Він попроси́в мене́ взя́ти свою́ валі́зку.
He asked me to take my suitcase.

Він попроси́в мене́ взя́ти його́ валі́зку.
He asked me to take his suitcase.

Я попросив його взяти свою валізку.
I asked him to take his suitcase.

Я попросив його взяти його валізку.
I asked him to take his (another male's) suitcase.

and particularly:

Він попросив його взяти свою валізку.
He asked him to take his suitcase.

Він попросив його взяти його валізку.
He asked him to take his suitcase.

where in the first **свою** refers to **його**, the underlying subject of **взяти**, and in the second **його**[1] refers to **він**.

One may freely use the possessives as adjectives, but Ukrainian uses them less frequently than English, especially where there is little or no possibility of ambiguity, such as with kinship terms. See Chapter 3 (**3.1.1**) for possessive adjectives formed from personal names and kinship terms.

4.3   INTERROGATIVE AND RELATIVE PRONOUNS

4.3.1   'WHO?' AND 'WHAT?'

хто? 'who?' **що?** 'what?'

N.	хто	що	Н.
G.	кого	чого	Р.
D.	кому	чому	Д.
A.	кого	що	З.
I.	ким	чим	О.
L.	кому	чому (чім)	М.

Note that stress retraction after prepositions is applicable to these two pronouns. Note too that the accusative of **що** is **що**, and that after prepositions this often manifests itself as **віщо** (it may even fuse orthographically with the preposition), as in **Навіщо?** 'Why, for what reason?', **По віщо він пішов туди?** 'What did he go there for?' **Що** is also used as the basic subordinating conjunction after declaratives, and in a particular construction in relative clauses (see Chapter 8, **8.1.3.2**, and **4.3.1.1**). Here are a few examples:

Хто це такий?
Who's that?

Що це таке?
What's that?

Хто не був у Ки́єві, той не зна́є, яке́ це га́рне мі́сто.
Whoever has not been to Kyiv doesn't know what a fine town it is.

Що це за лю́ди?
What sort of people are they?

Що за краса́!
What beauty!

(Note the nominative of the noun in these two phrases. The reason is that we have a loan from German through Polish, with **за** actually going with **що**, which is in the expected accusative case. Compare German *Was ist das für ein Mann?* 'What sort of a man is that?')

4.3.1.1 що *in relative clauses*

In the following examples we see the use of **що** functioning as a marker of relative clauses (compare **4.3.3**). This is counter to what one might expect as a speaker of English and other languages, in which the element – in reference to persons – is 'who' and not 'what'. The second and third examples are especially worthy of note, as 'with whom' and 'to whom' are expressed by preposition(s) and/or relevant case(s) following the element **що**, with no change in **що**:

Там сиди́ть ді́вчина, що ме́шкає в Оде́сі.
The girl who lives in Odessa is sitting there.

Он той чолові́к, що з ним я розмовля́в у це́нтрі мі́ста.
That's the man with whom I was talking in the town centre.

Я не зна́ю люди́ни, що їй я дав кни́жку.
I don't know the person to whom I gave the book. (Note that **люди́на** refers to both sexes, but has feminine gender – occasionally errors occur! The form here is the genitive, after the negative verb.)

4.3.2   'WHOSE?'

чий? 'whose?'

	Masculine	*Neuter*	*Feminine*	*Plural*	
N.	**чий**	**чиє́**	**чия́**	**чиї́**	Н.
G.	**чийо́го**		**чиє́ї**	**чиї́х**	Р.
D.	**чийо́му**		**чиї́й**	**чиї́м**	Д.
A.	= nom./gen.	= nom.	**чию́**	= nom./gen.	З.
I.	**чиї́м**		**чиє́ю**	**чиї́ми**	О.
L.	**чийо́му/чиє́му** (**чиї́м**)		**чиї́й**	**чиї́х**	М.

Чий is used in direct and indirect questions:

Чия це кімната?
Whose room is this?

Я спитав його, чия це кімната.
I asked him, whose room this was.

4.3.3 'WHAT SORT OF?' – 'WHICH?'

Який 'what kind of', also the most common relative pronoun, namely 'who', 'which', and **котрий** 'which?' (rather restricted; most often identifying something particular or in reference to a series, for example, in telling the time), are declined as adjectives:

який 'what kind of?'; 'who', 'which', '(that)'

	Masculine	Neuter	Feminine	Plural	
N.	який	яке	яка	які	Н.
G.	якого		якої	яких	Р.
D.	якому		якій	яким	Д.
A.	= nom. or gen.	= nom.	яку	= nom. or gen.	З.
I.	яким		якою	якими	О.
L.	якому (якім)		якій	яких	М.

котрий 'which?'

	Masculine	Neuter	Feminine	Plural	
N.	котрий	котре	котра	котрі	Н.
G.	котрого		котрої	котрих	Р.
D.	котрому		котрій	котрим	Д.
A.	= nom. or gen.	= nom.	котру	= nom. or gen.	З.
I.	котрим		котрою	котрими	О.
L.	котрому (котрім)		котрій	котрих	М.

Both may be used in direct and indirect questions. A few examples, starting with the equivalents of sentences given above:

Там сидить дівчина, яка мешкає в Одесі.
The girl who lives in Odessa is sitting there.

Он той чоловік, з яким я розмовляв у центрі міста.
That's the man with whom I was talking in the town centre.

Я не знаю людини, якій я дав книжку.
I don't know the person to whom I gave the book.

Вона ще не знає, яке в неї буде помешкання наступного року.
She still doesn't know what sort of flat she'll have next year.

Я хотів би зна́ти, о котрі́й (годи́ні) вони́ бу́дуть у Ки́єві.
I wonder at what time they will be in Kyiv.

Яки́й is used in the genitive case to convey 'whose', 'of whom', 'of which' in relative clauses (one tends not to get **чий** here):

Óн та люди́на, си́нові яко́ї ми да́ли ко́шика.
That's the person to whose son we gave the basket. (Note the position of **яко́ї** and the direct object, **ко́шик**, in the genitive case.)

4.3.4 'HOW MUCH?' 'HOW MANY?'

скі́льки 'how much/many'

N.	скі́льки	Н.	
G.	скілько́х	Р.	
D.	скілько́м	Д.	
A.	скі́льки/скілько́х	З.	
I.	скількома́	О.	
L.	на скілько́х	М.	

сті́льки 'so much'/'so many'

N.	сті́льки	Н.	
G.	стілько́х	Р.	
D.	стілько́м	Д.	
A.	сті́льки/стілько́х	З.	
I.	стількома́	О.	
L.	на стілько́х	М.	

Скі́льки too can be used in direct and indirect questions. The preposition given with the locative above is purely for illustration. Note that both **скі́льки** and **сті́льки** are, when in the nominative or inanimate accusative, constructed with the genitive singular or plural of what is quantified, as appropriate; if nominative, the verb will be third-person singular and, if not non-past, then neuter. For the animate accusative and the other cases, there is agreement between the pronoun and the noun or noun phrase. Thus:

Скі́льки Вас там було́?
How many of you were there?

Вона́ бої́ться стілько́х екза́менів.
She's afraid of so many exams.

4.4 DEMONSTRATIVE PRONOUNS

On the whole these pronouns precede the noun or noun phrase they qualify, if any.

4.4.1 'THIS' AND 'THAT'

цей 'this'

	Masculine	*Neuter*	*Feminine*	*Plural*	
N.	цей	цé	ця́	ці́	Н.
G.	цьо́го		ціє́ї	цих	Р.
D.	цьому́		цій	цим	Д.
A.	= nom. or gen.	= nom.	цю́	= nom. or gen.	З.
I.	цим		ціє́ю	цими	О.
L.	цьо́му (цім)		цій	цих	М.

Цей also appears as **оце́й**, where the meaning is somewhat reinforced by initial **о-**. **Ціє́ї** and **ціє́ю** may appear, in dialects and poetry, respectively as **цéї/ції́** and **цéю/ці́ю**.

The identically declined and synonymous pronoun **сей** is obsolescent and may be considered restricted to set expressions, such as **сього́ ро́ку** 'this year', **сього́дні** 'today', **сю ніч** 'tonight', and compounds, for example, **сьогобі́чний** 'on this side of a river', **сьоголі́тній** 'of this summer', **сьогорі́чний** 'of this year', **сьогосві́тній** 'earthly', **сьогоча́сний** 'present', 'contemporary', **сьогоча́сність** 'present times'.

той 'that'

	Masculine	*Neuter*	*Feminine*	*Plural*	
N.	то́й	тé	та́	ті́	Н.
G.	то́го		тіє́ї/то́ї	тих	Р.
D.	тому́		тій	тим	Д.
A.	= nom. or gen.	= nom.	ту́	= nom. or gen.	З.
I.	тим		тіє́ю/то́ю	тими	О.
L.	то́му (тім)		тій	тих	М.

Той also appears as **ото́й** (with a slightly reinforced meaning) and, rare and typical of the west, the 'remoter' **тамто́й**, as in **тамто́й світ** 'the other world' (= lit. 'that world yonder, faraway'). **Тіє́ї** and **Тіє́ю** may appear, in dialects and poetry, respectively as **то́ї/ті́ї/тéї** and **то́ю/ті́ю** (**то́ю** is quite frequent). Rarer and more localized are the forms **тот**, **то́та**, **то́те** respectively for **той**, **та**, **те**.

Note that there is retraction of stress one syllable to the left in the genitive and locative singular masculine and neuter and animate accusative singular masculine when immediately preceded by a preposition.

A couple of examples:

Ця/Та кни́жка не моя́, а його́.
This/That book is not mine, but his.

У цьо́му о́фісі працю́є мій та́то.
My dad works in this office.

4.4.2 'THIS IS', 'THAT IS'

The invariable **це** and **то**, which function much as French *ce* or German *das* in *c'est, ce sont, das ist, das sind*, have no referential value, and may serve as present copula or 'presenter':

Микóла – це мій брат.
Mykola's my brother (lit. 'Mykola that's my brother'). (Note the dash.)

То бýдуть батьки́ на́ших дрýзів.
Those'll be our friends' parents

Similarly we might mention the deictic particles or 'pointers' **ось, от,** and **он**. Literally they suggest respectively 'Here is/are', 'There is/are', and 'Yonder is/are', but they float somewhat, and may be reinforced by, say, **там** 'there', and may seem to be simply emphatic, even interjections:

От люди́на! *Ecce homo!*
Ось вона́. Here she is.
Ось там, вгорі́. Up there.
Он як. That's how. (**як** how)
Óсьде. That's where (**де** where)

4.5 INDEFINITE, NEGATIVE, AND DISTRIBUTIVE PRONOUNS

4.5.1 'ALL'

весь 'all'

	Masculine	*Neuter*	*Feminine*	*Plural*	
N.	весь/увéсь/ввесь	все/усé	вся/уся́	всі/усі́	Н.
G.	всьóгó		всіє́ї	всіх	Р.
D.	всьомý		всій	всім	Д.
A.	= nom./gen.	= nom.	всю	= nom./gen.	З.
I.	всім		всіє́ю	всіма́	О.
L.	всьóму (всім)		всій	всіх	М.

Here too we have retraction of stress one syllable to the left in the genitive singular m./n., locative singular m./n., and accusative singular masculine animate when immediately preceded by a preposition, for example, **на всьóго**. Variant forms in dialects and poetry are, for **всіє́ї** and **всіє́ю**, respectively **всéї/всéї** and **всéю/всію**. More localized are at least **усі́ми** for **усіма́** and **усéй** for **увéсь**.

Весь tends to precede the noun or noun phrase it qualifies, if any, but to follow a personal pronoun:

увесь місяць	all month
Ми всі пішли додому.	We all went home.

Всенький is a diminutive of **увесь**.

4.5.2   INDEFINITES AND DISTRIBUTIVES

The true indefinites of Ukrainian are very varied and resistant to concise treatment. They are formed using the suffixes **-сь, -будь, -небудь**, and the prefixes **де-, аби-, будь-, казна-, хтозна-**. The least indefinite, thus with a sense of something real and actually rather definite but simply not known, are those in **-сь** and **де-**, with the latter being less indefinite. Thus:

дехто, деякий, дещо: a clear sense of 'someone, a certain, something' (the last in particular has also a sense of 'somewhat', 'a little', or of something being concealed), for example,

Ми дечого не сказали.
There was a thing or two we didn't say.

A preposition may come between де- and the pronoun:

Я де з ким/з деким розмовляв.
I was talking to a certain person (or persons).

The forms with **-сь** may be slightly more indefinite:

якийсь чоловік a certain man, some man or other
у котрімсь місці in some/a certain place

We can quite readily create these forms, for example, **чийсь – дечий, котрийсь – декотрий, хтось, щось**. Such creations are not restricted to pronouns, thus **десь** 'somewhere', 'approximately', not to mention **де-де** 'somewhere', 'here and there', 'somewhere or other'.

The particles **будь-, -небудь** have senses of 'any-', 'any- at all' respectively, thus **будь-що, що-небудь**.

The prefix **аби-** has senses of 'no matter', '-ever', for example,

Аби з ким вони працювали.
They worked with anyone. (**аби** otherwise means 'in order that'/'to', with a negative verb an optative 'lest').

Будь- has a sense of 'any (at all)', for example,

Будь-яке місце буде добре.
Any place at all will be fine.

Казна- has a sense of 'the devil knows' and is consequently pejorative, for example,

Казна-що говорить. He says any old nonsense.

Хтозна- is similar, but rather an expressive 'God' than the devil:

Цей дріт приносить телеграми хтозна з якої далини.
This wire brings telegrams from heaven knows what distant places.

The ending '-ever' in such clauses as 'Whoever it might be' is conveyed as follows:

Хто б це не був, . . .

Finally, we might note the following additional adjective-like distributive pronouns which also fit in here, but present no particular difficulties of usage:

кожен/кожний 'each', 'every' (seldom **кождий**):

Кожен добре знає, як живуть в Україні.
Everyone has a good idea how people live in Ukraine.

жоден/жодний 'no', 'not a':

Не знаю жодного з них.
I don't know any of them.

всякий 'every', 'each', 'all manner of':

На базарі продаються всякі овочі.
All sorts of fruit are sold at the market.

інший 'other', 'another' (i.e. different):

Хтось інший буде там. Someone else will be there.
(For 'another' in the sense of 'yet another', **ще** 'still', 'yet' will be used.)

інакший 'other', 'another', 'different', 'another sort of' (**інак(ше)** 'otherwise', 'differently'):

Словників у книгарнях нашого міста є дуже багато, а я шукав зовсім інакший словник, такого, я тепер добре знаю, немає тут.
There are very many dictionaries in the bookshops of our city, but I was searching for one of a different kind, and such a dictionary, I now well know, simply is not to be found here.

усілякий 'of all sorts':

У тому парку є всілякі дерева.
There are all sorts of trees in that park.

самий 'same', 'close to', 'itself' (emphatic):

цей самий the same person
у самій квартирі in the very flat

сам/сама́/само́ (nominative plural **самі́**, and declines like an adjective, thus merging with **сами́й** above) 'alone', 'one's self', 'in person', for example,

Я заста́ла його́ само́го.
I caught him on his own/him himself.

Він сам на бі́лому сві́ті.
He's all alone in the world.

Річ га́рна сама́ по собі́.
The thing is good in itself.

Він сам не свій.
He's not himself, out of sorts.

бу́ти в воді́ по саму́ ши́ю
to be in water up to one's very neck

бу́ти в борга́х по самі́ ву́ха
to be up to one's ears in debt

4.5.3 NEGATIVE PRONOUNS

The negative pronouns **ніхто́, ніщо́** decline like **хто** (masculine singular), **що** (neuter singular), but prepositions occur between the prefix **ні-** and the declined form of **хто, що**, for example, **ні у ко́го, ні на ко́го, ні з ки́м, ні до чо́го**. The example given for the locative in the table is purely illustrative.

ніхто́ 'no-one'/**ніщо́** 'nothing'

N.	ніхто́	ніщо́	Н.
G.	ніко́го	нічо́го	Р.
D.	ніко́му	нічо́му	Д.
A.	ніко́го	нічо́го	З.
I.	ніки́м	нічи́м	О.
L.	ні на ко́му	ні на чо́му (чім)	М.

Thus:

Абсолю́тно ніхто́ не ціка́виться його́ пра́цею.
Absolutely no one is interested in his work.

Я ніко́му не да́м ві́дповіді.
I shan't give an answer to anyone.

У Льво́ві вона́ ні з ки́м не знайо́ма.
She doesn't know anyone in L'viv.

Ні про що́ ми не розмовля́ли.
We weren't talking about anything.

Note that there is a change of meaning when a preposition does not come in between:

Я купи́в це за ніщо́.
I bought this for nothing (= a mere trifle, or just nothing).

За ніщо́ не ку́пиш нічо́го.
Nothing is bought for nothing.

All the above negative forms also occur with the stress on **ні**. In this form they have a sense 'There isn't anyone/anything', i.e. as alternatively **нема́(є) кого́, нема́(є) кому́, нема́(є) з ким, нема́(є) про що, etc.**[10] These forms, in themselves impersonals, may also be rendered in a personal form, thus: **Я не ма́ю коли́ наї́стися.** I haven't the time to get a good feed'.

Here are a few examples (see Synjavs'kyj 1941):

Ні́кому да́ти цей підру́чник.
There's no one to give this textbook to.

Ні́ за що купи́ти хлі́ба.
There's nothing to buy bread for. (Compare: **Ні за що́ не ку́пиш хлі́ба.** You can't buy bread for love or money.)

Ні́ з ким працюва́ти.
There's no one to work with.

Ні́чого роби́ти.
There's nothing for it./Nothing can be done about it.

These forms are equivalent to negatives such as **ніде́, ніку́ди, ніко́ли** 'nowhere (to)', 'nowhere', 'never' and the impersonals **Ні́де, Ні́куди, Ні́коли, Ні́як** 'There's nowhere (to go)', 'There's no time', 'There's no way/ possibility', for example,

Ні́де пра́вди ді́ти.
The truth will out. (lit. 'There's no place to put (= hide) the truth.')

Мені́ ні́коли.
I haven't the time.

Ї́м ні́як поверну́тися.
They won't be able to come back.

Somewhat apart we have **ні́котрий** 'neither', 'none' and **нія́кий** 'none':

Нема́(є) нія́кого су́мніву. There's no doubt.

and there are a good deal of set phrases, for example,

Це нія́ка шту́ка.
It's no big deal, serious matter.

Це люди́на ні до чо́го.
He/she's a good-for-nothing.

Вона́ сього́дні яка́сь нія́ка.
She's not quite all right today. (See the preceding section for pronouns in
 -сь.)

5 THE NUMERAL

5.0 SUMMARY TABLE OF CARDINAL, COLLECTIVE, AND ORDINAL NUMERALS

	Cardinals	Collectives	Ordinals
1	оди́н, одна́, одне́ (одно́)	–	пе́рший
2	два (m./n.), дві (f.)	дво́є	дру́гий
3	три	тро́є	тре́тій
4	чоти́ри	че́тверо	четве́ртий
5	п'ять	п'я́теро	п'я́тий
6	шість	ше́стеро	шо́стий
7	сім	се́меро	сьо́мий
8	ві́сім	во́сьмеро	во́сьмий
9	де́в'ять	де́в'ятеро	дев'я́тий
10	де́сять	де́сятеро	деся́тий
11	одина́дцять	одина́дцятеро	одина́дцятий
12	двана́дцять	двана́дцятеро	двана́дцятий
13	трина́дцять	трина́дцятеро	трина́дцятий
14	чотирна́дцять	чотирна́дцятеро	чотирна́дцятий
15	п'ятна́дцять	п'ятна́дцятеро	п'ятна́дцятий
16	шістна́дцять	шістна́дцятеро	шістна́дцятий
17	сімна́дцять	сімна́дцятеро	сімна́дцятий
18	вісімна́дцять	вісімна́дцятеро	вісімна́дцятий
19	дев'ятна́дцять	дев'ятна́дцятеро	дев'ятна́дцятий
20	два́дцять	два́дцятеро	двадця́тий
30	три́дцять	три́дцятеро	тридця́тий
40	со́рок	–	сороко́вий
50	п'ятдеся́т	–	п'ятдеся́тий
60	шістдеся́т	–	шістдеся́тий
70	сімдеся́т	–	сімдеся́тий
80	вісімдеся́т	–	вісімдеся́тий
90	дев'яно́сто	–	дев'яно́стий
100	сто	–	со́тий
200	дві́сті	–	двохсо́тий
300	три́ста	–	трьохсо́тий
400	чоти́риста	–	чотирьохсо́тий
500	п'ятсо́т	–	п'ятисо́тий
600	шістсо́т	–	шестисо́тий

700	сімсо́т	–	семисо́тий
800	вісімсо́т	–	восьмисо́тий
900	дев'ятсо́т	–	дев'ятисо́тий
1000	ти́сяча	–	ти́сячний
2000	дві ти́сячі	–	двохти́сячний
1 million	мільйо́н	–	мільйо́нний
1 billion	мілья́рд	–	мілья́рдний

Note 1: Cardinal '1' is declined as an end-stressed pronoun (as in **той, та, те** – **Одно́** is the earlier form, **одне́** having arisen under the influence of the adjectival form, for example, **старе́**); ordinals are declined like adjectives (see **5.1.4**).

Note 2: The teens, tens (apart from 'ten'), and hundreds (apart from 'one hundred') are compound, i.e. written as one word – the hundreds are declined in both elements. Compound numerals and fractions are composite, i.e. written separately, as in **три́дцять сім** 'thirty-seven', **вісімсо́т п'ятдеся́т шість** '856', **дві ці́лі і чоти́ри п'я́тих** 'two point eight'.

Note 3: Note the use of the apostrophe and the soft sign, particularly the omission of the soft sign (when a nominative marker) word-internally (an omission not preventing word-internal declension of the hundreds).

Note 4: Note the stress difference between certain ordinals and cardinals, namely **де́в'ять** – **дев'я́тий** 'nine' – 'ninth', **де́сять** – **деся́тий** 'ten' – 'tenth', **два́дцять** – **двадця́тий** 'twenty' – 'twentieth', **три́дцять** – **тридця́тий** 'thirty' – 'thirtieth', **со́рок** – **сороко́вий** 'forty' – 'fortieth'.

Note 5: We can add **нуль** 'zero', genitive **нуля́**, which if constructed with a noun or noun phrase will place them in the genitive case.

5.1 THE CARDINALS AND COLLECTIVES

Cardinals may on the whole be used either on their own, in which case they are fully declined (see **5.14**) as required by the syntax of the sentence, for example:

До шести́ дода́ти сім.
Add six to seven.

Від чотирьо́х відня́ти три.
Subtract three from four.

Пятдеся́т – це ці́ле число́.
Fifty is a whole number.

Все одно́.
It's all the same.

Одні́ були́ вдо́ма, і́нші були́ в мі́сті.
Some were at home, others were in town.

Ім пощасти́ло, що вони́ знайшли́ одна́ о́дну в університе́ті вчо́ра.
They were lucky they found each other at the university yesterday.[11]

As such they might be interpretable as pronouns, since there will always be some sort of reference, even when used mathematically.

Or they are used together with nouns (or, more precisely, noun phrases), in which case the relations between the numeral and the noun phrase need explication. Thus:

5.1.1 Одѝн

The numeral **одѝн** agrees in case, gender, and as appropriate number with the accompanying noun phrase:

одѝн числі́вник one numeral.
в одні́й ха́ті in one house.
однѝм сло́вом in a word
одні́ две́рі one door (with pluralia tantum nouns)

It should not be seen as any sort of indefinite article (though this may be suggested by translation, as in the last but one example, of the set phrases above), and indeed its absence is often quite enough to indicate 'one'.

It also takes priority in compound numerals in that an accompanying noun phrase will 'agree with' it, for example:

два́дцять одна́ кни́жка twenty-one books
у ста пятдесяти́ одні́й краї́ні in 151 countries

In the masculine singular the animate accusative has the form of the genitive:

Я ба́чу одного́ хло́пця в авто́бусі. I can see one boy in the bus.

5.1.2 Два/дві, три, чоти́ри AND обѝдва/обѝдві

The numerals **два – двí, три, чоти́ри,** and **обѝдва – обѝдві** 'both' are constructed with the plural forms of the noun, with the qualification that if the stress of the nominative plural is different from that of the genitive singular, then the stress (but not the form, where the forms are different) of the genitive singular is taken. Thus:

	Nom. sg..	*Gen. sg..*	*Nom. pl.*	
два бра́ти	брат	бра́та	братѝ	two brothers
два села́	село́	села́	се́ла	two villages
двí головѝ	голова́	головѝ	го́лови	two heads
три мі́ста	мі́сто	мі́ста	міста́	three towns
чоти́ри кни́жки	кни́жка	кни́жки	книжкѝ	four books

A look at the masculine noun above confirms that it is the nominative plural, not the genitive singular, that occurs with such numbers. Other examples of masculines make this absolutely clear: **два дні** 'two days', **три буди́нки** 'three buildings', and likewise. A very few exceptions seem to exist: words in **-анин,** **-янин,** and **-ин** take the genitive singular, for example, **два/три/чоти́ри**

росіянина 'two/three/four Russians'. This applies in general to nouns whose plural stem is different from their singular stem, for example,

дві дитини two children (plural **діти**, singular **дитина**)
дві дівчини two girls (plural **дівчата**, singular **дівчина**)
два імені two (first) names (plural **імена**, singular **ім'я**)

One may find collectives with animates with such forms, for example, **двоє росіян** 'two Russians', **четверо дітей** 'four children'. One also finds the genitive singular where the noun refers to something occurring in pairs, though this arguably overlaps with the two-stem case, for example **два вуха** 'two ears', **три ока** 'three eyes', **чотири плеча** 'four shoulders' (nominative plural of the last two **очі**, **плечі** respectively, citation forms **око**, **плече**; note that, though these may refer to pairs, there is no restriction to using **два** with them).

One needs also to note that an adjective after these numerals will go either into the nominative plural or into the genitive plural, thus **два нові/нових будинки** 'two new buildings', **три нові/нових хати** 'three new houses', **чотири нові/нових села** 'four new villages'.

What was said above applied only when the syntax of the sentence requires the nominative case (or the inanimate accusative). When any other case is required, the numeral and noun phrase go into that case. This may seem to be a superfluous comment; however, it does reflect the special treatment of the adjective, and the use of the genitive form and genitive stress just mentioned. Thus, for example:

Я знаю тих двох молодих хлопців.
I know those two young boys.

Він дасть книжки тим ста шістдесятьом двом дівчатам.
He'll give the books to those 162 girls.

Note, from the last example, that a pronoun precedes the numeral and goes in the appropriate case – it is autonomous of the numeral, i.e. **ті дві людини** 'those two people' (this will be clearer immediately below, where we look at other numerals).

5.1.3 П'ЯТЬ AND ABOVE

Beyond **чотири**, in non-compound numerals, in compound numerals ending in anything but '1–4', and in collectives, we have the same situation where the genitive, dative, instrumental, locative, and, optionally, animate accusative are concerned, for example, **у двадцяти п'яти хатах** 'in twenty-five houses'. Where the nominative and inanimate accusative are concerned, however, the noun phrase goes into the genitive plural, for example, **п'ять нових будинків** 'five new buildings'. But note **усі п'ять нових будинків** 'all five new buildings', where the pronoun, standing outside the quantifier phrase, appears in the nominative plural.

A particular problem can be that of agreement between a subject quantifier phrase and a verb. The general rule will be to use the singular and, if the past or conditional, the neuter singular. However, the plural may be used with '2–4'. It may be more common where the verb comes first, as a way of introducing plurality, or where there is an emphasis on individuality, animacy, separateness. If a pronoun is expressed, as in **усі п'ять нових будинків** 'all five new buildings' as given above, then the unambiguous plural character of **усі** forces a plural verb form.

6.1.1 SELECTED PARADIGMS

The vocative is throughout identical with the nominative.

'One'

	Masculine	*Neuter*	*Feminine*	*Plural*	
N.	один	одно́/одне́	одна́	одні́	Н.
G.	одного́		однієї/одно́ї	одни́х	Р.
D.	одному́		одні́й	одни́м	Д.
A.	= nom. or gen.	= nom.	одну́	= nom. or gen.	З.
I.	одни́м		однією/одно́ю	одни́ми	О.
L.	одно́му (одні́м)		одні́й	одни́х	М.

'Two', 'three', 'four'

	2 Masc./Neut.	*2 Feminine*	*3*	*4*	
N.	два	дві	три	чоти́ри	Н.
G.	двох		трьох	чотирьо́х	Р.
D.	двом		трьом	чотирьо́м	Д.
A.	= nom. or gen.		= nom. or gen.	= nom. or gen.	З.
I.	двома́		трьома́	чотирма́	О.
L.	двох		трьох	чотирьо́х	М.

'Five', 'six', 'seven'

	5	*6*	*7*	
N.	п'ять	шість	сім	Н.
G.	п'яти́/п'ятьо́х	шести́/шістьо́х	семи́/сімо́х	Р.
D.	п'яти́/п'ятьо́м	шести́/шістьо́м	семи́/сімо́м	Д.
A.	= nom. or gen.	= nom. or gen.	= nom. or gen.	З.
I.	п'ятьма́/п'ятьома́	шістьма́/шістьома́	сьома́/сімома́	О.
L.	п'яти́/п'ятьо́х	шести́/шістьо́х	семи́/сімо́х	М.

'Eight', 'nine', 'ten'

	8	*9*	*10*	
N.	вíсім	дéв'ять	дéсять	Н.
G.	восьмú/вісьмóх	дев'ятú/дев'ятьóх	десятú/десятьóх	Р.
D.	восьмú/вісьмóм	дев'ятú/дев'ятьóм	десятú/десятьóм	Д.
A.	= nom. or gen.	= nom. or gen.	= nom. or gen.	З.
I.	вісьмá or	дев'ятьмá or	десятьмá or	О.
	вісьмомá	дев'ятьомá	десятьомá	
L.	восьмú/вісьмóх	дев'ятú/дев'ятьóх	десятú/десятьóх	М.

Eleven to nineteen, with fixed stress, decline like ten; twenty, thirty decline like ten.

	60	*100*	
N.	шістдеся́т	сто	Н.
G.	шістдесятú/шістдесятьóх	ста	Р.
D.	шістдесятú/шістдесятьóм	ста	Д.
A.	= nom. or gen.	сто	З.
I.	шістдесятьмá/шістдесятьóма	ста	О.
L.	шістдесятú/шістдесятьóх	ста	М.

Fifty, seventy, eighty decline like sixty. Forty, end-stressed, and ninety decline like one hundred.

	200	*500*	
N.	двíсті	п'ятсóт	Н.
G.	двохсóт	п'ятисóт	Р.
D.	двомстáм	п'ятистáм	Д.
A.	двíсті	п'ятсóт	З.
I.	двомастáми	п'ятьмастáми/п'ятьомастáми	О.
L.	двохстáх	п'ятистáх	М.

300 and 400 follow the pattern of 200 and 600–900 that of 500.

Note particularly that, of the variant pairs, the latter members are as a rule used only with animates.

Сóрок, дев'янóсто, and **сто** have the ending -**a** in all cases outside of the nominative and accusative (stressed in the case of **сóрок**). Two of the variants of 'both' (**обúдва** (masc./neut.) and **обúдві** (fem.)) decline like **двá**: gen. **обúдвох**. See **5.1.5**.

5.1.5 COLLECTIVES

The collective numerals decline like the cardinals in the genitive, dative, instrumental, locative, and, though it is optional, the animate accusative.

	2	*9*	
N.	двóє	дéв'ятеро	Н.
G.	двох	дев'ятьóх	Р.
D.	двом	дев'ятьóм	Д.
A.	= nom. or gen.	= nom. or gen.	З.
I.	двомá	дев'ятьомá	О.
L.	двох	дев'ятьóх	М.

	12	*30*	
N.	дванáдцятеро	трѝдцятеро	Н.
G.	дванадцятьóх	тридцятьóх	Р.
D.	дванадцятьóм	тридцятьóм	Д.
A.	= nom. or gen.	= nom. or gen.	З.
I.	дванадцятьомá	тридцятьóма	О.
L.	дванадцятьóх	тридцятьóх	М.

Note the stress patterns. That of **двóє** applies also to **трóє**, that of **дéв'ятеро** applies to four to ten and to **обóє** 'both', that of **дванáдцятеро** applies to the teens, and that of **трѝдцятеро** applies to that of **двáдцятеро**. In the instrumental one also encounters the ending **-ьмá**.

The collectives are quite widely used in Ukrainian, particularly from **двóє** to **чéтверо** and to some extent to **дéсятеро**. They are used in counting masculine human beings (though this is not a strict rule, most animates being candidates), if any other noun is included, or just human groups without a noun, thus **двóє брáтів** 'two brothers', **трóє бобрíв** 'three beavers', **Нас булó чéтверо** 'There were four of us'. Note that they are followed by the genitive plural when themselves in the nominative. When constructed with a noun, the normal cardinal is very frequent, for example, **два брáти** 'two brothers'. Otherwise, their major use is with *pluralia tantum*, for example, **чéтверо дітéй** 'four children' (there is, of course, a singular **дитѝна** 'child', but the relationship is suppletive; since it is suppletive, as we have seen above, **двí дитѝни** is quite acceptable!), **двóє нóжиць** 'two (pairs of) scissors' (**нóжиці** 'scissors'), **чéтверо окулярíв** 'four (pairs of) spectacles' (**окуляри** 'spectacles'), **двóє дверéй** 'two doors' (**двéрі** 'door').

A problem occurs in the case of compound numerals, where the collectives would not be used as final component, i.e. there is no **двáдцять трóє**. Here, in the cases other than the nominative and accusative inanimate one simply uses the ordinary cardinal; for the nominative and accusative inanimate one may use a quantifier, most often **штýка** 'piece' or **пáра** 'pair' (for animates the use of the normal cardinal is acceptable, as we saw for **дитѝна** above). Thus:

У тій крамнѝці я знайшóв трѝдцять три штýки такѝх окулярíв.
In that shop I came across thirty-three such pairs of spectacles.

Бíля всіх чотирьóх дверéй стоя́ли поліцéйські.
Policemen were standing by all four doors.

One may note set phrases such as **по дво́є** 'in pairs', 'two by two', **вдво́є** + comparative 'twice as . . .' (as = than . . .) (see Chapter 3).

5.1.6 APPROXIMATION

In order to express 'about', 'approximately' with numerals, we can use words such as the prepositions **бі́ля** + G., **бли́зько** + G., and **з** + A. 'about', or the indefinite adverb **десь** 'somewhere' in front of the quantity:

Марі́я чита́ла кни́жку бі́ля трьо́х годи́н.
Mariya was reading the book for about three hours.

Це ста́лося з де́сять ти́жнів тому́.
This happened about ten weeks ago.

Скі́льки? З два́дцять до́ларів.
How much? About twenty dollars.

Десь чоти́ри гра́дуси моро́зу було́ вночі́.
There were somewhere around four degrees of frost during the night.

Бли́зько трьо́х днів я був у Ки́єві.
I was in Kyiv for more or less three days.

For numbers above 'one', we can simply invert the order in which the numeral and the object occur: **сантиме́трів два-три** 'about two to three centimetres', **ро́ків чоти́ри** 'about four years'. If there is a preposition involved, the number will precede the preposition + noun phrase: **Він пішо́в годи́н на дві** 'He went for about two hours'. Note from these examples that the measurement will then appear in the genitive plural, no matter what the number is ('Of the set of "centimetres", we have the number X'); some speakers may nevertheless prefer to keep the noun in the case specified by the number (**годи́ни на дві**).

5.1.7 DISTRIBUTION

By 'distribution' we mean the construction which conveys 'one coat each', 'five apples each', and so on. The core of this construction is the preposition **по** plus the quantifier phrase conveying what each has. Where the quantity 'each' has is more than one, the quantifier phrase is expressed in the accusative (perhaps it is simpler to say 'nominative', since, were one to have 'two slaves each', the nominative would be used, i.e. there is no reflection of animacy, something which is hardly surprising given the meaning); where the quantity 'each' has is 'one', the quantifier phrase is expressed in the dative case. The possessor will be expressed as appropriate, with **ко́жен** 'each' not at all superfluous. Here are two examples:

У ко́жній кімна́ті по чоти́ри стільці́.
There are four chairs in each room.

У всіх восьми́ сесте́р по одно́му бра́тові.
All eight sisters have one brother each.

5.2 THE ORDINALS

The ordinals are straightforward, agreeing in case, gender, and number with the noun phrase which they qualify. They differ from adjectives only in the obvious way of not being able to be piled up in qualification of a single noun phrase, i.e. as one cannot say 'the seventh eleventh white house'. Where a compound ordinal is concerned, such as 'the 127th book', then in Ukrainian only the final component will take the ordinal form and agree as necessary; the preceding components will take the cardinal form and be indeclinable, for example:

сто два́дцять *сьо́ма* кни́жка the 127th book
со́рок *пе́рший* дом the 41st house

5.2.1 TIME EXPRESSIONS

Ordinal numerals are used in the expression of time and 'time when', including the time of day and expressions of the year and 'year when'.

5.2.1.1 Years

As in all other large ordinal numerals, only the last element is an ordinal and it is the only one to change its form. 'The Year X' is a nominative construction, while 'in the Year X' is a locative construction:

ти́сяча дев'ятсо́т дев'яно́сто *дев'я́тий* рік the year 1999
у ти́сяча вісімсо́т п'ятдеся́т *шо́стому* ро́ці in 1856

5.2.1.2 Hours (time of day)

Котра́ годи́на?	What time is it? (lit. 'Which hour?')
Во́сьма	(It's) eight (o'clock).
Двана́дцята	twelve
Тре́тя	three

Fractions of the hour are expressed by means of a number of constructions, most of which involve the use of prepositions: **на** + acc., **по** + loc., **за** + acc., **до** + gen. Compare:

Дéсять/чверть на шóсту. Дéсять/чверть по п'я́тій.	(It's) ten/quarter past five.
п'я́та дéсять, п'я́та п'ятнáдцять	Five ten, five fifteen
пів на десяту пів до десятої	half past nine (lit. 'half towards the tenth hour')
за дéсять п'я́та за хвили́ну п'я́та	ten to five a minute to five

'Time when' constructions can be identical to the above when fractions of the hour are involved, thus:

за дéсять п'я́та	at ten to five
пів на десяту	at half past nine
дéсять/чверть на шóсту	at ten/a quarter past five

The preposition **o** + loc. is used with the hour alone (**об** only with eleven):

о котрíй (годи́ні)?	at what time? when?
о шóстій	at six
о трéтій	at three
об одинáдцятій	at eleven

Optionally with **пів** 'half', and when the hour precedes the fraction:

(о) пів на сьóму	at half past six
о дев'я́тій двáдцять	at nine twenty

5.3 FRACTIONS

Many fractions will be restricted to scientific usage, with whole numbers conveyed by cardinals (optionally accompanied by the appropriate form of the adjective **ці́ла** (**части́на** 'part' understood)) and the fractional part conveyed by the appropriate ordinal preceded by the number of fractional parts. For single fractional parts the ordinal will qualify **части́на**, and a number consisting of a whole number or numbers and a fraction will be linked by **i** 'and'. For example:

однá і п'ять шóстих
one and five sixths

Я вже знáю деся́ту части́ну тогó, що трéба знáти.
I already know a tenth of what I need to.

однá ці́ла і двí деся́тих мільйóна квадрáтних кіломéтрів
1.3 million square kilometres

Чоти́ри п'я́тих поділи́ти на одну́ сьо́му.
Divide four fifths by one seventh (imperfective **поділя́ти**).

Сім деся́тих помно́жити на три дев'я́тих.
Multiply seven tenths by three ninths (imperfective **мно́жити**).

The numerals **пів** 'half', **півтора́** (m./n.) and **півтори́** (f.) 'one-and-a-half',
and **півтора́ста** '150' are indeclinable. They all totally agree with the counted
noun phrase when the dative, instrumental, and locative are required. For the
nominative, accusative, and genitive, **пів** and **півтора́/півтори́** are followed by
the genitive singular, while **півтора́ста** is followed by the genitive plural.
Animacy is unlikely to affect **пів** and **півтора́/півтори́**, and for **півтора́ста** the
accusative and genitive formally coincide. Thus, for example:

півтора́/півтори́, півтора́ста

N.A.	півтора́ сло́ва	півтори́ кни́жки	півтора́ста столі́в	Н.З.
G.	півтора́ сло́ва	півтори́ кни́жки	півтора́ста столі́в	Р.
D.	півтора́ слова́м	півтори́ книжка́м	півтора́ста стола́м	Д.
I.	півтора́ слова́ми	півтори́ книжка́ми	півтора́ста стола́ми	О.
L.	у півтора́ слова́х	у півтори́ книжка́х	на півтора́ста стола́х	М.

One must note the fractional nouns **чверть** (f.) 'quarter' and **полови́на** 'half',
'middle', the adverb **на́впіл** 'in half'. In the following examples note how one
says 'and a half, and a quarter', these components never changing. For
example:

Вона́ дала́ мені́ чверть книжо́к.
She gave me a quarter of the books.

сім із чве́ртю ро́кі́в
seven and a quarter years

дві з полови́ною годи́ни
two and a half hours

за чверть во́сьма
(at) a quarter to eight
(the hour goes in the nominative of the ordinal, with **годи́на** 'hour'
   understood)

(о) чверть по четве́ртій
(at) a quarter past four (**о** is optional in rendering 'at', **годи́ні** understood)

(о) пів до сьо́мої/на сьо́му
(at) half past six (**о** is optional in rendering 'at', **годи́ни/годи́ну** understood)

пів на пі́в
fifty-fifty

Ще пів біди.
That's not too bad.

Ні пів слóва!
Not a word!

5.4   INDEFINITE QUANTIFIERS

багáто 'much/many', небагáто 'not much', 'not many', кíлька 'some', 'several', 'a few', and декілька 'some', 'several', 'a few' decline as follows:

N.	багáто	кíлька	декілька	Н.
G.	багатьóх	кількóх	декількóх	Р.
D.	багатьóм	кількóм	декількóм	Д.
A.	= nom. or gen.	= nom. or gen.	= nom. or gen.	З.
I.	багатьмá	кількомá	декількомá	О.
L.	багатьóх	кількóх	декількóх	М.

Note that their declension is similar to that of п'ять, but without parallel forms. Observe the stress, including optional stress, in particular кільканáдцять 'eleven to nineteen' and кількадесят 'several tens'; 'thirty' or 'forty' (both colloquial) decline like дéсять (one may come across the form кількадесять), but note the stress:

N.	кільканáдцять	кількадесят	Н.
G.	кільканáдцяти ог кільканадцятьóх	кількадесяти ог десятьóх	Р.
D.	кільканáдцяти ог кільканадцятьóм	-десяти ог -десятьóм	Д.
A.	= nom. or gen.	= nom. or gen.	З
I.	кільканадцятьмá ог кільканадцятьомá	-десятьмá ог -десятьомá	О.
L.	кільканáдцяти ог кільканадцятьóх	-десяти ог -десятьóх	М.

One may also come across кількасóт 'several hundred' and стонáдцять 'over a hundred'. They decline as follows:

N.	кількасóт	стонáдцять	Н.
G.	кількасóт	стонадцяти ог стонадцятьóх	Р.
D.	кількастáм	стонадцяти ог стонадцятьóм	Д.
A.	= nom. or gen.	= nom. or gen.	З.
I.	кількастомá	стонадцятьмá ог стонадцятьомá	О.
L.	кількастáх	стонадцяти ог стонадцятьóх	М.

All the above behave in the same way. In the nominative and inanimate accusative they are constructed with the genitive plural (or genitive singular if appropriate for (не)багáто). In all the other cases they and the counted noun phrase go in the appropriate case, with the numeral as it were agreeing with the noun phrase.

Like **пів** 'half', and so on, **(не)ма́ло** 'little' and **чима́ло** 'rather a lot', 'a considerable amount' do not decline, but will tend only to be used with the genitive singular or plural, as appropriate, in the nominative and inanimate accusative. Where other cases are required, **(не)бага́то** may be used. Like **(не)бага́то** they may be used as adverbs, for example, **ма́ло працюва́ти** 'to work little'. One may note also the adverbs **тро́шки, тро́шечки** 'a little'.

'Majority', 'most' might be conveyed using the noun **бі́льшість**, gen. **бі́льшості**, with the genitive of the noun phrase. With a quantifier phrase including **бі́льшість** as subject, a verb will be singular and, if past or conditional, feminine:

Бі́льшість тури́стів була́ в готе́лі «Дніпро́».
Most of the tourists were in the hotel Dniepro.

Used similarly would be **со́тня** 'a hundred' (quite common in the plural), and **дві́йка** 'the number two', 'two points/marks', 'two people together' (**дві́йками** 'in twos'), **трі́йка** 'the number three', 'three points/marks', 'three people together' (**трі́йками** 'in threes', **утрі́йку** 'three together').

We might take this opportunity to mention numerical adverbs such as **раз, дві́чі, три́чі** 'once', 'twice', 'three times'; beyond this one can just use the cardinal plus **раз**, for example, **п'ять раз** 'five times'. 'Once' in the sense of 'formerly', 'once upon a time', would be **коли́сь**; 'not a single time' would be **ані́ ра́зу** (see **7.1.3** for numerical adverbs). One can also create verbs from numerals, for example **потро́їти**, imperf. **потро́ювати** 'to treble', 'triplicate'.

5.5 COMPOUNDS

Note the following examples of compounds involving numerals, paying particular attention to the ways in which the different numerals combine:

пі́вдень noon, south
пі́вніч midnight, north
піврі́чний semi-annual, half-yearly, six-months-old
півде́нний relating to half a day/noon, south(ern)
півні́чний relating to midnight, north(ern).

полу́кіпок heap of thirty sheaves (**копа́** three score, sixty)

напівживи́й half-alive

сорокарі́ччя forty-year period
п'ятдесят(и)рі́ччя fifty-year period (adj. **п'ятдесят(и)рі́чний** fifty-year-old, of fifty years)

двоособóвий for two persons

триповерхóвий three-storeyed

чотирикýтник quadrangle, square (adj. **чотирикýтний**), **шестикýтний** hexagonal

чвертьрíчний quarter (i.e. three months)

половúнчастий of two halves, with two sides (e.g. door(s))

6 THE VERB

6.0 GENERAL

The Ukrainian verbal system is, in general terms, very similar to that which is found in the other East Slavonic languages (Russian and Belarusian) as well as in West Slavonic (Polish, Czech, Slovak, and Upper and Lower Sorbian). This system is driven by the existence of 'aspectual' distinctions, which reflect the nature of the action expressed by the verb (see **6.1**); the tense system is loosely dependent on the aspect of the verb (**6.1**). Although this may at first seem to be complex, it does in fact mean that the number of tenses is strictly limited in comparison with such languages as French, Spanish, German, and even English. The verb is fully conjugated in the present tense ('non-past', see **6.1**, **6.3.1.1**, **6.3.1.2**), such that a complete paradigm exists expressing person ('I', 'you', and so on) and number ('singular', 'plural'); the past is comparatively minimalist, expressing only number and gender in the singular and number in the plural (**6.3.2**). Following a presentation of aspect (**6.2**) and the verbal paradigms (**6.3**), **6.4** examines the use of the verb (including aspect, verbs requiring particular cases, and such notions as the 'conditional' or 'mood', and so on); **6.5** describes the system of verbal derivation.

6.1 ASPECT AND TENSE

Practically every verb in Ukrainian exists as a member of an aspectual pair. There are two 'aspects' in the system, 'imperfective' and 'perfective'; readers who are familiar with languages such as French and Spanish are cautioned not to assume this can be equated with the respective tenses in those languages known as the 'imperfect' and 'perfect': although some parallels can be drawn between the use of Ukrainian aspects and Romance tenses, they are not equivalent. The two aspects, in very broad terms, express two different kinds of action. The imperfective expresses action of a general nature, ongoing, or repetitive; the perfective, on the other hand, expresses the fact that an action is one-time, completed ('completion' can also mean any one particular point during a larger action), or restricted in some way. Thus, for example:

Він чита́в кни́жку.	He was reading a/the book. *vs.*
Він прочита́в кни́жку.	He read (finished reading) the book.

These are basic rules of thumb, but there are many instances when it will appear that they are violated. The important point for English speakers is the fact that there are sometimes no clear or exact boundaries between the use of verbs of one or the other aspect; occasionally a verb of either aspect is acceptable in a given situation, and even a native speaker would say that he or she is unable to say which form is 'right' or 'wrong'. Far from being a negative point, this shows that there are often no absolutes, and the learner is encouraged to note particular usages, whether in speech or in writing, and follow them. We shall discuss aspect in more detail in the following sections, in connection with tense, conjugation, syntax, and word formation.

There are three tenses in Ukrainian: present, past, and future. Because of their very general nature, imperfective verbs have all three; as perfective verbs essentially express completed action, however, they can have no present tense – what is past is past, but what looks like a present tense form in a perfective verb therefore on the whole expresses future time. In this book we shall use the term 'non-past' in reference to the present tense forms of imperfective verbs and the future tense forms of perfectives, as they are exactly the same in form, differing with regard to tense only for aspectual reasons. Unlike many European languages, the standard Ukrainian language admits only one compound tense, that of one form of the imperfective future (much as in English: I will/shall read the book). In section **6.2** we describe the formal side of the aspectual system, by supplying aspectual pairs and outlining how the learner can come to recognize the aspect of a given verb. The various tense forms are examined in **6.3**, while the intersection of tense and aspect is described in **6.4**.

6.2   ASPECTUAL PAIRS

Both imperfective and perfective verbs can be the 'basic' form, from which corresponding perfective or imperfective verbs are generated. In essence, there are six types of imperfective-perfective pairs:

1 Pairs in which the imperfective (usually a simplex verb) is basic; the perfective member of the pair is generated by the addition of a prefix (X: prefix + X).

2 Pairs in which the sole difference between the two aspectual variants is the vowel preceding the infinitive marker -ти, generally imperf. -á-/-я́-, perf. -и- (X – áти/-я́ти : X-ити).

3 Pairs in which an expansion of the root or stem takes place in the formation of an imperfective based on a perfective, by means of:

   (a) the addition of an imperfectivizing suffix -ува-/-юва or -ава́- to a prefixed perfective (prefixed X: prefixed X + ува/ава́), as in: доноси́ти –

доно́шувати 'to wear out', **уста́ти –устава́ти** 'to stand up', 'rise' (this process as a whole is structurally close to Type 2);

(b) the expansion of the root of a prefixed perfective by the appearance of a vowel not present in the base form: thus imperf. **бра́ти** – perf. **ви́брати** > new imp. **вибира́ти**;

(c) the addition of the suffix -ай- to a number of simplex perfectives (usually consonant stems): **лягти́** (1*sg.* **ля́жу**) – **ляга́ти** (1*sg.* **ляга́ю**).

4 Pairs in which the perfective is marked by the presence of the suffix -ну-.

5 Pairs differentiated only by the place of stress.

6 Anomalous pairs in which the two members are not formally related ('suppletion', X:Y).

Type 6 involves only a few verbal pairs; in the following sections all six types are described in turn.

6.2.1 TYPE 1: PREFIXATION

Of the prefixes that are used in the formation of perfectives, з- (зі-), на-, про-, and especially по- are the ones that can occur solely as markers of the perfective aspect. Others (and indeed these four as well) impart additional lexical meaning to the verbs in question; a full treatment of the semantic component, and of all the prefixes, is provided in **6.5**, as the primary purpose of this section is to describe the nature of aspectual pairs.

ПО-

Imperfective	Perfective	Meaning
зва́ти	позва́ти	to call, name
дарува́ти	подарува́ти	to give (as a gift)
чу́ти	почу́ти	to feel
кли́кати	покли́кати	to call, name
нести́	понести́	to carry
проси́ти	попроси́ти	to request
дзвони́ти	подзвони́ти	to phone
обіця́ти	пообіця́ти	to promise
ми́ти	поми́ти	to wash
про́бувати	попро́бувати	to try, test
цілува́ти	поцілува́ти	to kiss

At times the new perfective has to be translated more precisely in order more satisfactorily to express its perfectiveness, for example, the onset of an action; compare the pair **люби́ти** 'to love' *vs.* **полюби́ти** 'to fall in love'.

Imperfective	Perfective	Meaning
НА-		
писа́ти	написа́ти	to write
ли́ти	нали́ти	to pour
малюва́ти	намалюва́ти	to paint, depict
ПРО-		
чита́ти	прочита́ти	to read
чи́стити	прочи́стити	to clean
З-		
ї́сти	з'ї́сти	to eat
ну́дити	зну́дити	to tire, bore

The intersection of prefixation, stress, and aspect is one of the more complex sides of Ukrainian grammar, as there are many instances in which a given form is either (a) not the aspect that one expects, or (b) not semantically compatible with a seemingly related form or partner. Thus, **зла́зити** 'to crawl', 'creep (down)' is not the perfective partner of *ла́зити, but the imperfective partner of **злі́зти**; compare the analogous **прола́зити-пролі́зти** 'to crawl through or over', and **намерза́ти – наме́рзнути** 'to freeze'. For a complete inventory of verbal prefixes and their meanings, see **6.5.1**.

6.2.2   TYPE 2: -ити: -ати

In the -ити: -а́ти (-ити: -я́ти) pairs it is the perfective that may be considered the basic form, but this is very often not obvious; as it is basic, however, we cite the perfective first. If the consonant preceding -ити can mutate (see **1.1.9**), it will do so in the generation of the imperfective (the fact that there is a mutation in the imperfective indicates that it is the perfective that is basic); here are some typical -ати: -ити pairs:

Perfective	Imperfective	Meaning
навчи́ти	навча́ти	to teach, instruct
кінчи́ти	кінча́ти	to finish
озари́ти	озаря́ти	to illuminate
доста́вити	доставля́ти	to provide
лиши́ти	лиша́ти	to abandon, leave
появи́тися	появля́тися	to appear
змісти́ти	зміща́ти	to contain, include
схили́ти	схиля́ти	to incline, bend down
утра́тити	утрача́ти	to lose
пригости́ти	пригоща́ти	to entertain, receive (a guest)

Note as a rule, those imperfective verbs which are derived from stem-stressed perfectives will be end-stressed, as they will be when derived from end-stressed perfectives.

6.2.3 TYPE 3: SUFFIXATION AND ROOT ENLARGEMENT

Enlarged forms, whether by suffixation or root expansion, are also generated from perfective base forms, as in Type 2. In contrast to that type, however, we find that forms based on end-stressed perfectives will tend to have stress retracted to the stem.

Perfective	Imperfective	Meaning
наламáти	налáмувати	to break many things
обговори́ти	обгово́рювати	to talk over, discuss
змішáти	змі́шувати	to mix, blend, to confuse
зміцни́ти	змі́цнювати	to strengthen, reinforce
повтори́ти	повто́рювати	to repeat (cf. **6.2.2**)
пригрі́ти	пригріва́ти	to warm up
ви́брати	вибирáти	to choose, elect
послáти	посилáти	to send
утопи́ти	утóплювати	to drown
відірвáти	відривáти	to pull/tear off
почáти	починáти	to begin
відпочи́ти	відпочивáти	to rest

Stress immediately precedes the suffix ⸗ува-/⸗юва-, otherwise it is on -á-. Note that not all -ува-/-юва verbs are new derived imperfectives, thus, працювáти 'to work', страйкувáти 'to strike' are basic or primary (non-derived) imperfectives. Derived forms are extremely numerous, as this process is productive: i.e. it is a living process used in the formation of new verbs. In a pair of the почáти – починáти type, the -н- of the imperfective does not represent an addition, but is present in the non-past paradigm of почáти (see **6.3.1.1.2**).

6.2.4 TYPE 4: PERFECTIVES IN -ну-

This suffix is frequently used to form perfectives indicating a short or momentary action; it is not limited to perfectives, although imperfectives with -ну- are relatively few in number (for example, сóхнути 'to grow dry').

Imperfective	Perfective	Meaning
зникáти	зни́кнути	to disappear
кліпати	клі́пнути	to blink, bat one's eyelids
достигáти	дости́гнути	to mature, ripen (also perf. inf. дости́гти)
мигáти	мигнýти	to wink, vacillate, glimpse

зника́ти	зни́кнути	to disappear, vanish
крича́ти	кри́кнути	to shout
відкида́ти	відки́нути	to reject, abandon
огляда́ти	огля́нути	to see, look around
змика́ти	зімкну́ти	to close, lock, cover

Note 1: The tendency is for stress to retract in the new perfectives if the base imperfective is end-stressed (for example, зника́ти > зни́кнути); but, as the pair мига́ти – мигну́ти illustrates, this is a tendency (albeit a strong one) and not a rule.

Note 2: A root consonant (especially the stops т and д) can be lost before -ну-, as in відкида́ти – відки́нути.

6.2.5   TYPE 5: PLACE OF STRESS

Imperfective	*Perfective*	*Meaning*
посипа́ти	поси́пати	to strew, sprinkle
склика́ти	скли́кати	to summon, convene
розкида́ти	розки́дати	to scatter about
виміря́ти	ви́міряти	to measure
відклика́ти	відкли́кати	to call back, revoke
покида́ти	поки́дати	to throw, cast away

For the last pair listed there is another perfective, *viz.* поки́нути (Type 4 above), which is more common than поки́дати. Great care must be taken not to assume that all pairs of this kind are aspectual pairs, as sometimes there can be a semantic difference (with or without aspectual differentiation), as in:

ви́никати (perf.) to search through
but
виника́ти (imperf.) to arise, proceed from

са́пати (imperf.) to breathe hard
but
сапа́ти (also imperf.) to weed with a hoe

доси́пати (perf.) to fill in (with grain), to add more (of a substance)
but
досипа́ти (imperf.) to sleep until a certain time, catch upon sleep

ко́пати, ко́пнути (imperf., perf.) to kick
but
копа́ти, копну́ти (imperf., perf.) to dig, scoop out

похо́дити (imperf.) to resemble, be like
but
походи́ти (perf.) to walk a little

Where they do form aspectual pairs, there may be a difference in their conjugation. Compare:

скли́кати: скли́чу, скли́чеш
but
склика́ти: склика́ю, склика́єш (compare **розки́дати – розкида́ти**, which have identical conjugations)

The system is characterized by a considerable amount of variation, thus there may be more than one permissible imperfective or perfective with or without a slight change in meaning. Thus:

ви́міряти (perf.), but also **ви́мірити** (perf.); **вимір́яти** (imperf.), but also the expanded form **вимі́рювати** (imperf.); cf. Type 3 above.

вино́сити (imperf.) 'to carry out/away', with its basic partner **ви́нести** (perf.), but cf. **ви́носити** (perf.) 'to carry out/away, one after another'; the last mentioned also has an expanded partner **вино́шувати** (imperf.).

Compare also the following pairs, in which there is variation in form: the perfectives **зустрі́ти – зустрі́нути** 'to meet' can be paired with either **зустріча́ти** or **зустріва́ти** (the latter is considered less common). In all such instances, whether there is variation in form or in stress, a good dictionary will provide the necessary information.

6.2.6 TYPE 6: SUPPLETION

The members of the following pairs are either unrelated to each other, or they merely look unrelated as a result of their historical development; either way, they may look as though they do not belong together.

Imperfective	*Perfective*	*Meaning*
бра́ти	узя́ти	to take
займа́тися*	зайня́тися*	to be occupied with
знахо́дити*	знайти́*	to find, come upon

*and all other prefixed pairs involving the roots **-йматися/-йнятися** and **-ходити/-йти**.

6.2.7 VERBS OF MOTION: DETERMINATE AND INDETERMINATE

One final set of verbs, the verbs of motion, require separate treatment with respect to aspect. These verbs have a further subdivision within the imperfective aspect, known as 'indeterminate' and 'determinate' (sometimes termed 'multidirectional' and 'unidirectional', respectively). The most common verbs belonging to this category are:

	Imperfective		Perfective	Meaning
	Indeterminate	*Determinate*		
	ходи́ти	іти́/йти́	піти́	to go (by foot)
	ї́здити	ї́хати	пої́хати	to go (by vehicle)
	носи́ти	нести́	понести́	to carry (by foot)
	вози́ти	везти́	повезти́	to convey (vehicle)
	води́ти	вести́	повести́	to lead (on foot)
	літа́ти	летіти	полеті́ти	to fly
	пла́вати	пливти́	попливти́	to swim
	бі́гати	бі́гти	побі́гти	to run

Note that it is from the determinates that perfectives are formed, without
exception by adding the prefix **по-**, and without a change in the basic meaning
of the verb (other than 'to set off'). Perfectives with the same prefix can also
be generated from the indeterminates (i.e. **походи́ти, поноси́ти, попла́вати**),
but these verbs express the notion of 'walking', 'carrying', 'swimming', and
so on, 'for a little while', rather than the purely perfective idea of the onset or
completion of an action. As with all other imperfective verbs, both sets of
imperfective verbs of motion have a present tense in addition to the past and
future, while the perfectives can express only past and future meaning. Note
that most of the determinates are consonant-stem verbs, while most of the
indeterminates are -**и**-type verbs (compare their conjugations in **6.3.1.1.2** and
6.3.1.2.1, respectively).

When other prefixes are used (those that alter the meaning of the basic
verb in addition to its aspect), a new imperfective-perfective pair is formed;
thus

Imperfective	*Perfective*	*Meaning*
прихо́дити	прийти́	to come, arrive
перехо́дити	перейти́	to cross (over), go across

Note that the place of stress shifts in the new imperfective: **ходи́ти** but
прихо́дити, перехо́дити, and so on. On the use of unprefixed and prefixed
verbs of motion see **6.4.3.4**, and compare also the inventory of prefixes in
6.5.1.

6.3 CONJUGATION

The sequence of topics discussed below will be (1) the infinitive, (2) the non-
past, (3) the past, (4) the future, (5) the imperative, and (6) participles and
gerunds.

6.3.0   THE INFINITIVE

The infinitive is that form which is typically listed first in dictionaries, that is, the 'citation' (or 'dictionary') form. It is the unchanging form of a verb that is expressed in English by means of 'to': 'to do', 'to read', 'to work', and so on. The Ukrainian infinitive marker is -ти in every verb, with no exception:

говори́ти to speak
ходи́ти to go, walk
чита́ти to read
везти́ to convey (by vehicle)

Verbs that are inherently reflexive and/or intransitive and require the presence of the marker -ся (= German *sich*, French *se*, Polish *się*, and so on) simply have this element added to the end of any form of the verb, including the infinitive: **уми́тися** 'to wash oneself', *vs.* **уми́ти** 'to wash something or someone'; the use of these verbs is described in detail in **6.4.2** and **6.4.4.3**.

6.3.1   THE NON-PAST

There are two conjugations in Ukrainian, sharing most endings but differentiated in many forms by the 'connector' vowel that appears between the stem of the verb and the ending itself (in Conjugation I this is -e-, in Conjugation II -и-). An analogy with English is impossible, as the conjugational system has become exceptionally streamlined over the centuries; thus, in 'he read-s', there is but a stem *read-* and an ending *-s*, whereas Ukrainian will generally have a connector vowel between them. Within the two major conjugations there are numerous stem types, and every stem type belongs to only one of the conjugations. A familiarity with stem types will allow the learner to recognize and acquire many new verbs as they are encountered, especially as the infinitive, or 'dictionary' form, often gives no hint as to how the verb is conjugated; it may look just like another verb, but then conjugate differently. Knowing to which type a verb belongs is exceptionally useful as all forms of the verb can be generated from the one stem alone, by applying a number of simple rules that will be given throughout this chapter. In the following description of forms, the person and number of the verb are expressed as:

1sg. = I (i.e. first-person singular)
2sg. = you (one person)
3sg. = he, she, it
1pl. = we (first-person plural)
2pl. = you (more than one person, or singular polite; cf. German *Sie*)
3pl. = they

Typically it is the infinitive of a verb that is the primary focus for learners, precisely because this is the form cited in dictionaries. One cannot always tell from the infinitive to which conjugation a given verb belongs, although the presence of a particular vowel (or consonant) preceding -ти will provide some clues. In the following table the relevant combinations are listed, according to conjugation and where they are described (note the few areas of overlap):

Conjugation I		*Conjugation II*	
-ати, -яти	(6.3.1.1.1; 6.3.1.1.3)	**-ити**	(6.3.1.2.1)
-іти	(6.3.1.1.1; 6.3.1.1.3)	**-жати, -чати, -шати**	(6.3.1.2.2)
-ити	(6.3.1.1.1)	**-іти**	(6.3.1.2.3)
-ути	(6.3.1.1.1)	**-ояти**	(6.3.1.2.4)
-авати, -явати	(6.3.1.1.1)	Consonant + -ти	(6.3.1.2.5)
-увати, -ювати	(6.3.1.1.1)	Irregulars	(6.3.1.2.6)
Consonant + -ти	(6.3.1.1.2)		
-нути	(6.3.1.1.4)		
Irregulars	(6.3.1.1.5)		
бу́ти	(6.3.1.1.6)		

6.3.1.1 Conjugation I

Verbs of Conjugation I have the following structure, in which -e- is the connector vowel; the sample verb is **нести́** 'to carry', **нести́ся** 'carry oneself', 'hurry', 'rush along'.

1*sg.*	stem + –	-у or -ю	нес-у́
2*sg.*	stem + e +	-ш	нес-е́-ш
3*sg.*	stem + e +	-∅	нес-е́
1*pl.*	stem + e +	-мо	нес-е-мо́
2*pl.*	stem + e +	-те	нес-е-те́
3*pl.*	stem + –	-уть or -ють	нес-у́ть

In verbs marked by the presence of -ся:

1*sg.*	stem + –	-у or -ю	+ -ся	нес-у́-ся
2*sg.*	stem + e +	-ш	+ -ся	нес-е́-ш-ся
3*sg.*	stem + e +	-ть	+ -ся	нес-е́-ть-ся
1*pl.*	stem + e +	-мо	+ -ся	нес-е-мо́-ся
2*pl.*	stem + e +	-те	+ -ся	нес-е-те́-ся
3*pl.*	stem + –	-уть or -ють	+ -ся	нес-у́ть-ся

Note first the lack of a person marker in the 3*sg.* except in the presence of a following -ся, and second the lack of a connector vowel in the 1*sg.* and 3*pl.*

The latter can be explained structurally as a result of truncation brought on by the following person markers, which are themselves vowels: in essence two vowels coming together cannot be sustained, and the second causes the first to be lost. In stems ending with the consonant 'j', the connector vowel will be realized as the Cyrillic letter є, which expresses the sound sequence [je]; we begin with verbs of this type, which include a large number of basic verbs.

6.3.1.1.1 Stems in vowel + j

INFINITIVES IN **-ати, -іти, -ити, -ути**: STRESS: STABLE THROUGHOUT

читáти 'to read'	розумíти 'to understand'	умúти 'to wash'
читáю	розумíю	умúю
читáєш	розумíєш	умúєш
читáє	розумíє	умúє
читáємо	розумíємо	умúємо
читáєте	розумíєте	умúєте
читáють	розумíють	умúють

чýти 'to hear'		умúтися 'to wash oneself'
чýю		умúюся
чýєш		умúєшся
чýє		умúється
чýємо		умúємося
чýєте		умúєтеся
чýють		умúються

Of these verbal types, the 'aj' (**читáти, читáє-**) type is the most common; note that the infinitive gives no hint as to the presence of 'j' in its stem. Verbs of the -іти and -ити types are fewer in number, but include such common verbs as:

болíти to be ill (**болíю**, and so on, not to be confused with the Conjugation II verb **болíти, болúть**: see **6.3.1.2.3**)
жалíти to pity
володíти to possess
крúти to cover, close
шúти to sew
рúти to dig

Verbs of the **чýти** type are even rarer in Ukrainian.

INFINITIVES IN **-авати, -увати (-ювати)**: STRESS: STABLE THROUGHOUT
Two stem types traditionally treated separately are marked by the presence of a suffix -ва-, preceded by a vowel, in the infinitive but not in the non-past; as their non-past structure is also vowel + j, however, they are treated here:

-ава́-	-ува́-	ʼ-ува-
устава́ти	працюва́ти	вирахо́вувати
'to stand up', 'rise'	'to work'	'to calculate precisely'
устаю́	працю́ю	вирахо́вую
устає́ш	працю́єш	вирахо́вуєш
устає́	працю́є	вирахо́вує
устаємо́	працю́ємо	вирахо́вуємо
устасте́	працю́сте	вирахо́вусте
устаю́ть	працю́ють	вирахо́вують

The only difference between the -(a)ва- and -(у)ва-/-(ю)ва- types is the place of stress: in the former stress is always on the absolute final vowel; in the latter stress is on stem-final -y- (or -ю-) if the infinitive is stressed as in працюва́ти, while it follows the place of stress of the infinitive if it occurs in any position further to the left, as in вирахо́вувати.

пи́ти, би́ти, ви́ти, ли́ти: STRESS: STABLE THROUGHOUT   These four common verbs also belong to the greater set of vowel + j stems, although they too are treated separately in most presentations of the Ukrainian verb. Here again 'j' is present at the end of the stem, but it is not overtly preceded by a vowel; in linguistic terms we would say that a 'zero' vowel is present, and the reasons for their inclusion here will become clear in the discussion of imperatives (**6.3.4**), as they follow the 'vowel + j' type even more closely in the imperative than they do in the non-past:

пи́ти 'to drink'	би́ти 'to hit', 'strike', 'beat'	ви́ти 'to twist', 'wind'
п'ю	б'ю	в'ю
п'сш	б'єш	в'єш
п'є	б'є	в'є
п'смо́	б'ємо́	в'смо́
п'єте́	б'єте́	в'єте́
п'ють	б'ють	в'ють

In verbs of this kind, as the consonant before 'j' is a labial, an apostrophe indicates that this consonant is in fact hard, or not palatalized (see **1.1.6**); prefixed forms of these verbs conjugate in the same fashion. In the one verb in which the consonant is not a labial, the effect of the 'j' is to lengthen that consonant and preserve the softness:

ли́ти 'to pour'
ллю
ллеш
лле
ллемо́
ллете́
ллють

The infinitives alone, as we have seen already, may not give you enough information; compare the stems **кри́ти**, **ми́ти**, **ши́ти**, **ри́ти**, of the vowel + j type, described above.

6.3.1.1.2 Consonant stems

A large number of common Conjugation I Ukrainian verbs are termed 'consonantal', as the stem ends in a consonant; this is clearest in the infinitive, as seen in the examples below. Others of this type have a consonant that disappears in the infinitive but reappears in the non-past; we shall examine both groups in turn.

INFINITIVES IN CONSONANT + **ТИ**: STRESS: STABLE THROUGHOUT

нести́ 'to carry'	могти́ 'to be able'	мести́ 'to sweep'	вести́ 'to lead'
несу́	мо́жу	мету́	веду́
несе́ш	мо́жеш	метеш	веде́ш
несе́	мо́же	мете́	веде́
несемо́	мо́жемо	метемо́	ведемо́
несете́	мо́жете	метете́	ведете́
несу́ть	мо́жуть	мету́ть	веду́ть

The infinitive of the verbs **мести́, вести́** lead one to expect the consonant -с- in the non-past (as in **нести́**), but historically there was stem-final -т- and -д-, and these became -с- before the -т- of the infinitive: **мет-ти – мес-ти, вед-ти – вес-ти**.

везти́ 'to transport'	пекти́ 'to bake'	текти́ 'to flow'	лі́зти 'to crawl'
везу́	печу́	течу́	лі́зу
везе́ш	пече́ш	тече́ш	лі́зеш
везе́	пече́	тече́	лі́зе
веземо́	печемо́	течемо́	лі́земо
везете́	печете́	течете́	лі́зете
везу́ть	печу́ть	течу́ть	лі́зуть

пли́сти ог пливти́ 'to swim'	сі́кти 'to cut', 'chop'	лягти́ 'to lie down'
пливу́	січу́	ля́жу
пливе́ш	січе́ш	ля́жеш
пливе́	січе́	ля́же
пливемо́	січемо́	ля́жемо
пливете́	січете́	ля́жете
пливу́ть	січу́ть	ля́жуть

берегти́ 'to look after', 'protect'	стри́гти 'to cut', 'shear'
бережу́	стрижу́
береже́ш	стриже́ш

бережé	стрижé
бережемó	стрижемó
бережетé	стрижетé
бережýть	стрижýть

Note that stress in the majority of these verbs is in absolute final position, and never mobile within the non-past. Note, however, that in **могти́** and **лягти́** stress is also on the final syllable in the infinitive, but uniformly on the initial syllable in the non-past; the pattern is reversed in **сі́кти** and **стри́гти**. The remaining roots of the **-гти** type are:

Root	Example	
-баг-	забагти́	wish, desire
-стерег-	стерегти́	watch, guard
-стиг-	достигти́	mature, ripen, reach, attain
-дяг-	одягти́	clothe, dress
-пряг-	запрягти́	harness (of horses)
-сяг-	досягти́	reach, procure
-тяг-	тягти́	draw, pull, drag

The last group to be treated here are those with an infinitive in **-рти**; these verbs are particularly worthy of note as the vowel preceding **-рти** disappears throughout the non-past paradigm:

мéрти 'to die'	опéрти 'to rest upon'	запéрти 'to lock'	тéрти 'to rub'
мру	опрý	запрý	тру
мреш	опрéш	запрéш	треш
мре	опрé	запрé	тре
мремó	опремó	запремó	тремó
мретé	опретé	запретé	третé
мруть	опрýть	запрýть	труть

INFINITIVES IN VOWEL + **ТИ**: STRESS: STABLE THROUGHOUT FOR THE MAJORITY OF VERBS The following are examples of verbs in which the consonant of the stem disappears in the infinitive; just as the coming together of two vowels (described above: -e- + -y-) causes the loss of the former, certain stem-final consonants are truncated in the presence of the -т- of the infinitive ending. This stem type as a whole is not productive, and is made up of only a few – but common – verbs. Thus:

стáти 'to become'	жи́ти 'to live'	іти́ 'to go'	ді́ти 'to put (away)'
стáну	живý	ідý	ді́ну
стáнеш	живéш	ідéш	ді́неш
стáне	живé	ідé	ді́не
стáнемо	живемó	ідемó	ді́немо
стáнете	живетé	ідетé	ді́нете
стáнуть	живýть	ідýть	ді́нуть

All prefixed verbs containing these stems conjugate in the same way (for example, **постáти**, **дістáти**, **устáти** and **ужúти**, **прожúти**, **пережúти**, and so on). The reader will note that the basic stems of all verbs of this type are short, *viz.* one syllable (**стан-**, **жив-**, **ід-**, **дін-**). Compare the following, in which the roots are also monosyllabic; note that the verbs 'to begin' occur only as prefixed verbs:

жáти 'to squeeze'	жáти 'to harvest'	почáти, зачáти 'to begin'	
жму	жну	почнý	зачнý
жмеш	жнеш	почнéш	зачнéш
жме	жне	почнé	зачнé
жмемó	жнемó	почнемó	зачнемó
жметé	жнетé	почнетé	зачнетé
жмуть	жнуть	почнýть	зачнýть

One set of verbs in this category has shifting stress; the first of these is the common verb 'to take', while the second and third examples (also expressing 'taking' in one sense or another) are representative of a small group of verbs remarkable for the shape of the infinitive (**-йняти**) in comparison with the non-past (in which **-н-** disappears and **-м-** appears):

узя́ти (взя́ти) 'to take'	зайня́ти 'to occupy'	прийня́ти 'to accept'
візьмý	займý	приймý
візьмеш	займеш	приймеш
візьме	займе	прийме
візьмемо	займемо	приймемо
візьмете	займете	приймете
візьмуть	займуть	приймуть

The last, common but very small, set of verbs that can be included in this category consists of those that have the structure consonant + consonant + **-ати** (referred to in the literature as 'non-syllabic'-a stems, as the root in the infinitive has no vowel). In one of these a vowel appears between the consonants in the non-past paradigm:

брáти 'to take'	звáти 'to call', 'name'	рвáти 'to pluck', 'pull', 'tear'
берý	зву	рву
берéш	звеш	рвеш
берé	зве	рве
беремó	звемó	рвемó
беретé	зветé	рветé
берýть	звуть	рвуть

6.3.1.1.3 Stems with consonant mutations: -ати (-іти)

A number of extremely common verbal stems appear at first glance to look
like vowel + j stems in the infinitive; thus, **писа́ти** 'to write' looks as though it
ought to conjugate in the same way as **чита́ти** 'to read', but in fact it does not.
The main feature of this type is the appearance throughout the non-past
paradigm of a stem-final consonant that is different from the consonant occur-
ing in the infinitive; this consonant is the product of a mutation of that base
consonant (cf. **1.1.9**). Note the following rules regarding the place of stress:

(i) if the stress falls after the root (infinitives in **-а́ти**), it will shift to the left
after the 1*sg.*;

(ii) if it is on the stem, then stress remains stable throughout (stress will
never shift to the right within the paradigm, from the stem to the ending). Thus:

писа́ти 'to write' (shifting stress)	каза́ти 'to say', 'tell' (shifting stress)	пла́кати 'to cry' (fixed stress)
пишу́	кажу́	пла́чу
пи́шеш	ка́жеш	пла́чеш
пи́ше	ка́же	пла́че
пи́шемо	ка́жемо	пла́чемо
пи́шете	ка́жете	пла́чете
пи́шуть	ка́жуть	пла́чуть

Other common verbs of this type include the following (the consonant
alternation is noted in brackets):

в'яза́ти (з – ж) to tie, bind
кли́кати (к – ч) to call or cry out
ма́зати (з – ж) to smear, grease
чеса́ти (с – ш) to comb (one's hair)
рі́зати (з – ж) to cut, slice
свиста́ти (ст – щ) to whistle
си́пати (п – пл: си́плю, си́плеш, си́плють) strew, pour
шепта́ти (т – ч) to whisper

One anomalous verb in **-іти** belongs to this general conjugational type;
note that the infinitive is end-stressed, while the non-past paradigm is stem-
stressed:

хотı́ти 'to want'

хо́чу
хо́чеш
хо́че
хо́чемо
хо́чете
хо́чуть

The reader is advised always to look up a given verb in a good dictionary (see the Bibliography) in cases of doubt, as the *1sg.* and *2sg.* or *3pl.* forms are generally provided, with the mutation and place of stress indicated. All prefixed variants of the stems presented here are identical to the non-prefixed forms of the non-past.

6.3.1.1.4   Stems with the suffix -ну-

A substantial number of Ukrainian verbs contain the suffix -ну-, one that frequently suggests a one-time or sudden action; accordingly, such verbs are often (but not always) perfective. Their conjugation is straightforward, involving the simple loss of -y- in the presence of the connector vowel and/or personal endings:

пірну́ти 'to dive'	кри́кнути 'to shout'	зни́кнути 'to disappear'
пірну́	кри́кну	зни́кну
пірне́ш	кри́кнеш	зни́кнеш
пірне́	кри́кне	зни́кне
пірнемо́	кри́кнемо	зни́кнемо
пірнете́	кри́кнете	зни́кнете
пірну́ть	кри́кнуть	зни́кнуть

The stress pattern of this type is stable, as the examples suggest; exceptions to the rule with shifting stress will occur, but only rarely.

6.3.1.1.5   Irregular conjugation I verbs

There are only two Conjugation I verbs that can be treated as irregular in one way or another: да́ти 'to give', with a truly anomalous conjugation (except for the *3pl.*, which is the Conjugation I form), and і́хати 'to go (by vehicle)', in which the infinitive does not correspond to the forms of the non-past paradigm. Thus:

да́ти	і́хати
дам	і́ду
даси́	і́деш
дасть	і́де
дамо́	і́демо
дасте́	і́дете
даду́ть	і́дуть

Two further irregular verbs of the да́ти type belong to Conjugation II, on the basis of the *3pl.* form (see **6.3.1.2** below).

6.3.1.1.6 'To be'

The verb **бу́ти** 'to be' is not conjugated in the present tense; where a copula is needed, the invariant form **є** may be used for all the forms. **Бу́ти** does have a (consonant stem) conjugation, but it has future meaning:

бу́ду I shall/will be . . .
бу́деш
бу́де
бу́демо
бу́дете
бу́дуть

6.3.1.1.7 'To have'

Unlike some European languages, Ukrainian has a fully conjugated verb 'to have', *viz.* **ма́ти**, a vowel + j verb of the **чита́ти** type:

ма́ю
ма́єш
ма́є
ма́ємо
ма́єте
ма́ють

See **6.4.1.3.1** on the use of this verb in expressions of obligation or necessity; see also **2.4.2.2.1** on the use of the preposition **у/в** + G. in expressions of 'having'.

6.3.1.2 Conjugation II

A large number of Ukrainian verbs belong to Conjugation II; verbs of this conjugation have a structure similar in nature to those of Conjugation I, but with the connector vowel **-и-** instead of **-е-**; the sample verb is **говори́ти** 'to speak' (stress is not marked here, in order to focus on the endings):

1*sg.*	stem + –	-у/-ю	(-ся)	говор-ю
2*sg.*	stem + и +	-ш	(-ся)	говор-и-ш
3*sg.*	stem + и +	-ть	(-ся)	говор-и-ть
1*pl.*	stem + и +	-мо	(-ся)	говор-и-мо
2*pl.*	stem + и +	-те	(-ся)	говор-и-те
3*pl.*	stem + –	-ять/-ать	(-ся)	говор-ять

Three features of Conjugation II ought to be noted: (1) in the 3*sg.* the ending -ть is always present; (2) the ending in the 3*pl.* contains the vowel -я- (-а- after hushings **ж, ч, ш, щ**) rather than **-у- (-ю-)**; (3) **-ся** verbs conjugate in the same way as non-**ся** verbs. See **6.3.1.2.1** on stress and consonant mutations.

·6.3.1.2.1 The -и- type – stress patterns and consonant mutations

In addition to the differences noted above, Conjugation II (especially those of the **-и-** type) differ from the vast majority of Conjugation I verbs in two ways:

STRESS Stress is generally not stable, but will shift in the non-past in most verbs when stress is on **-и́-ти**; stress is stable in the past.

MUTATIONS Consonant mutations are much more common within Conjugation II paradigms: if a consonant can mutate, it will in the 1*sg.* Labial stems are an exception in this regard, as the mutation takes place in the 1*sg.* and 3*pl.*

The following are all the mutations that take place in this conjugation, *viz.*:

Voiceless	*Voiced*	*Labials*
т – ч	з – ж	п, б, в, м –
с – ш	д – дж	пл, бл, вл, мл
ст – щ	зд – ждж	

-ТИТИ, -СИТИ, -СТИТИ

платити 'to pay'	просити 'to request'	носити 'to carry'
плачу́	прошу́	ношу́
пла́тиш	про́сиш	но́сиш
пла́тить	про́сить	но́сить
пла́тимо	про́симо	но́симо
пла́тите	про́сите	но́сите
пла́тять	про́сять	но́сять

-ЗИТИ, -ДИТИ, -ЗДИТИ

возити 'to convey'	ходити 'to walk'	їздити 'to go (vehicle)'
вожу́	ходжу́	їжджу
во́зиш	хо́диш	їздиш
во́зить	хо́дить	їздить
во́зимо	хо́димо	їздимо
во́зите	хо́дите	їздите
во́зять	хо́дять	їздять

LABIAL STEMS: **-БИТИ, -ПИТИ, -ВИТИ, -МИТИ** Note the mutation in the 1*sg.* and 3*pl.*

любити 'to love'	топити 'to sink'	ловити 'to catch'	утомити 'to tire'
люблю́	топлю́	ловлю́	утомлю́
лю́биш	то́пиш	ло́виш	уто́миш

любить	топить	ловить	утомить
любимо	топимо	ловимо	утомимо
любите	топите	ловите	утомите
люблять	топлять	ловлять	утомлять

NON-MUTATING STEMS   Stems in which there is no mutation are of two kinds: those with primary consonants (н, р, л) and those with consonants which are historically themselves the result of mutations (ж, ш, ч, щ).

-нити, -рити, -лити

дзвони́ти 'to phone'	говори́ти 'to speak'	пали́ти 'to burn'
дзвоню́	говорю́	палю́
дзво́ниш	гово́риш	па́лиш
дзво́нить	гово́рить	па́лить
дзво́нимо	гово́римо	па́лимо
дзво́ните	гово́рите	па́лите
дзво́нять	гово́рять	па́лять

Note that stress shifts in all of these examples; the pattern may be taken as generally valid for this set of verbs as a whole, but stable stress occurs as well (in the case of the third example, stable stress is expected as it is already on the root):

кори́ти 'to scold', 'blame'	весели́ти 'to cheer'	жа́рити 'to heat'
корю́	веселю́	жа́рю
кори́ш	весели́ш	жа́риш
кори́ть	весели́ть	жа́рить
коримо́	веселимо́	жа́римо
корите́	веселите́	жа́рите
коря́ть	веселя́ть	жа́рять

-жити, -шити, -чити (rarely -щити)

служи́ти	скінчи́ти	ви́рішити	ба́чити
'to serve'	'to finish'	'to decide'	'to see'
служу́	скінчу́	ви́рішу	ба́чу
слу́жиш	скінчи́ш	ви́рішиш	ба́чиш
слу́жить	скінчи́ть	ви́рішить	ба́чить
слу́жимо	скінчимо́	ви́рішимо	ба́чимо
слу́жите	скінчите́	ви́рішите	ба́чите
слу́жать	скінча́ть	ви́рішать	ба́чать

Neither stress pattern – shifting or non-shifting – predominates in this group of verbs, but stem-stress in the infinitive (as in **ба́чити**) will always indicate stable stress on the stem. Note particularly that perfectives with the prefix **ви-** are always stressed on the prefix.

6.3.1.2.2 A few stems in -жати (rarely -шати), -чати, -щати

STRESS: END STRESS STABLE THROUGHOUT

лежа́ти 'to lie (down)'	крича́ти 'to scream', 'shout'
лежу́	кричу́
лежи́ш	кричи́ш
лежи́ть	кричи́ть
лежимо́	кричимо́
лежите́	кричите́
лежа́ть	крича́ть

пища́ти 'to squeal'	звуча́ти 'to sound'
пищу́	звучу́
пищи́ш	звучи́ш
пищи́ть	звучи́ть
пищимо́	звучимо́
пищите́	звучите́
пища́ть	звуча́ть

6.3.1.2.3 Stems in -іти

Conjugation II verbs in -іти are not extremely numerous, and are characterized by a certain amount of variation; as such we might term this group
'unstable': one and the same verb can have two different stress patterns, or
indeed different conjugations in the non-past. Note that mutations will take
place (if possible) in the 1sg. as they do in -и- verbs. Thus:

свисті́ти 'to whistle'	болі́ти 'to hurt'	ви́сіти or	виси́ти 'to be hanging'
свищу́	(болю́)	ви́шу	вишу́
свисти́ш	(боли́ш)	ви́сиш	виси́ш
свисти́ть	боли́ть	ви́сить	виси́ть
свистимо́	(болимо́)	ви́симо	висимо́
свистите́	(болите́)	ви́сите	висите́
свистя́ть	боля́ть	ви́сять	вися́ть

The verb болі́ти commonly only occurs in the 3sg. and 3pl., in order to
express that something is causing one pain (Мені́/в ме́не боли́ть голова́ 'My
head hurts', for example). Note the two stress patterns in ви́сіти, which is also
found in те́рпі́ти, below; свисті́ти has an alternate conjugation, following the
Conjugation I type as exemplified by писа́ти (6.3.1.1.3), in which consonant
mutation takes place throughout the paradigm, with a stress shift after the
1sg.:

терпі́ти 'to endure'		свисті́ти 'to whistle'
терплю́	терплю́	свищу́
те́рпиш	терпи́ш	сви́щеш

те́рпить	терпи́ть	сви́ще
те́рпимо	терпимо́	сви́щемо
те́рпите	терпите́	сви́щете
те́рплять	терпля́ть	сви́щуть

6.3.1.2.4   Stems in -оя́ти

Two verbs conjugate according to the -и- type, but have infinitives in -оя́ти:

стоя́ти 'to stand'	боя́тися 'to be afraid of'
стою́	бою́ся
стої́ш	бої́шся
стої́ть	бої́ться
стоїмо́	боїмо́ся
стоїте́	боїте́ся
стоя́ть	боя́ться

6.3.1.2.5   Consonant + -ти

In contrast to Conjugation I, there is no class of verbs in Conjugation II that can specifically be classified as consisting of 'consonant' stems. There is, however, one verb that fits such a classification by virtue of its structure:

бі́гти 'to run'

біжу́
біжи́ш
біжи́ть
біжимо́
біжите́
біжа́ть

Note 1: It is stem-stressed in the infinitive, but end-stressed throughout the non-past paradigm.
Note 2: **г** mutates to **ж**, also in the entire paradigm. Compare the same pattern in **стри́гти**, **стрижу́ – стрижéш** in **6.3.1.1.2**.

6.3.1.2.6   Irregular conjugation II verbs

ї́сти 'to eat'	оповісти́ 'to tell', 'relate' (and відповісти́ 'to answer')
їм	оповім
їси́	оповіси́
їсть	оповість
їмо́	оповімо́
їсте́	оповісте́
їдя́ть	оповідя́ть

Compare these two with the forms of **да́ти** (**6.3.1.1.5**) above, identical but for the form of the *3pl*. Note that two stresses are possible in the infinitive of **оповісти́**, while only one pattern holds for the non-past paradigm.

6.3.2 THE PAST

6.3.2.1 *Infinitives in vowel + –ти*

In contrast with the non-past tense, the formation of the past is extremely straightforward: there are no consonant mutations or stress alternations, the place of stress in the past essentially follows that of the infinitive. For the vast majority of verbs of both conjugations with an infinitive ending in vowel + -ти, the infinitive marker -ти is dropped and replaced by the following:

-в	masculine singular (he)
-ла	feminine singular (she)
-ло	neuter singular (it)
-ли	plural, all genders (we, you, they)

Verbs marked by the presence of the particle -ся simply add this particle to the form of the past tense; thus:

чита́-ти –	**чита́в, чита́ла, чита́ло, чита́ли**
писа́-ти –	**писа́в, писа́ла, писа́ло, писа́ли**
пи́-ти –	**пив, пила́, пило́, пили́** (compare final stress in the non-past as well)
ли́-ти –	**лив, лила́, лило́, лили́**
дзвони́-ти –	**дзвони́в, дзвони́ла, дзвони́ло, дзвони́ли**
уми́-ти-ся –	**уми́вся, уми́лася, уми́лося, уми́лися**

The form of the verb is dependent on the gender and number of the subject of the sentence or clause:

Бори́с чита́в.	Borys read, was reading.
Вона́ уми́лася.	She washed (herself).
Ба́тько працюва́в.	Father was working.
Вони́ пили́ вино́.	They were drinking wine.
А́нна ста́ла медсестро́ю.	Anna became a nurse.
Де студе́нти жили́?	Where did the students live?
Я́блуко було́ на столі́.	The apple was on the table.

Although the formation of the past tense functions in this way for most Ukrainian verbs, an exception to the rule is found among a number of verbs in -нути. Some of them will drop the syllable -ну- in the past tense, but generally only if these verbs:

(1)   have a consonant preceding -ну- and

(2)   if stress falls to the left of -ну- in the infinitive (-ну-).

There are even exceptions to this pattern, however, and some verbs may have two acceptable past tense forms. Thus:

слáбнути to become weak:	слаб, слáбла
посóхнути to dry up:	посóх, посóхла, or посóхнув, посóхнула
зблíднути to grow pale:	зблíд, зблíдла

Compare:

| тягнýти to pull: | тягнýв, тягнýла, but also |
| крúкнути to shout: | крúкнув, крúкнула |

Even good dictionaries rarely provide such information; the guidelines given above ought therefore to be taken as rules, for which exceptions may exist. One feature which all of the verbs cited above share is that two of them have adjectival roots (слаб- слабúй 'sick', 'weak', блід- блідúй 'pale'); deadjectival verbs of this sort will tend to lose -ну- in the past tense.

6.3.2.2   Infinitives in consonant + -ти

The formation of the past tense of consonant stems is slightly more complex, for the simple reason that adding consonantal past tense markers (-в, and so on) to stem-final consonants can result in changes to the new form. This is especially true of the masculine, as no vowel is present in the ending. Thus:

(i)   These stems either retain or lose their stem-final consonant in the past tense; those that retain them lack the masculine past tense marker -в.

(ii)   Stem vowels -e- and -o- usually – i in the masculine (see 'vowel alternations' in 1.1.10); the alternations may not occur in every such verb, however (such verbs are marked by an asterisk*).

Here we present a list of the most commonly used verbs characterized by these features (all but one are Conjugation I verbs); only unprefixed variants are supplied, as the past tense of prefixed forms is identical to that of the base forms.

VERBS PRESERVING THE STEM-FINAL CONSONANT

нестú:	ніс, неслá, неслó, неслú
везтú:	віз, везлá, везлó, везлú
лíзти:	ліз, лíзла, лíзло, лíзли
могтú:	міг, моглá, моглó, моглú
пектú:	пік, пеклá, пеклó, пеклú
тектú:	тік, теклá, теклó, теклú
сíкти:	сік, сіклá, сіклó, сіклú

пливти́:	плив, пливла́, пливло́, пливли́ (compare the variant плисти́ in the next set below)
гребти́:	гріб, гребла́, гребло́, гребли́ (to dig, row)
*повзти́:	повз, повзла́, повзло́, повзли́ (to creep, crawl)
гри́зти:	гриз, гри́зла, гри́зло, гри́зли (to gnaw)
*ме́рти:	мер, ме́рла, ме́рло, ме́рли (to die)

VERBS IN WHICH THE STEM-FINAL CONSONANT IS LOST

вести́:	вів, вела́, вело́, вели́
мести́;	мів, мела́, мело́, мели́
плисти́:	плив, плила́, плило́, плили́

Note that the stem-final consonant is preserved if it is other than -т- or -д-. 'To swim' has two different past tenses depending on whether the infinitive is пливти́ or плисти́, although there is only one non-past paradigm (пливу́, пливе́ш, and so on); the past tense of плисти́ has clearly developed by analogy with such verbs as вести́, мести́. Note that stress in these verbs is uniformly on the final syllable, with the sole exceptions of гри́зти and ме́рти.

6.3.2.3 Irregular verbs

Irregular verbs of both conjugations are in fact regular in the past tense; note the place of stress, which follows the place of stress in the non-past in some, but not in others (where the two patterns diverge, the verbs are marked by an asterisk*):

да́ти	ї́хати	бу́ти*	ї́сти*	оповісти́ (give)
дав	ї́хав	був	їв	оповів (drive)
дала́	ї́хала	була́	ї́ла	оповіла́ (be)
дало́	ї́хало	було́	ї́ло	оповіло́ (eat)
дали́	ї́хали	були́	ї́ли	оповіли́ (answer)

One consonant stem verb has an anomalous past tense, *viz.* іти́ 'to go (on foot)':

ішо́в or йшо́в
ішла́ or йшла́
ішло́ or йшло́
ішли́ or йшли́

On the alternation i-й see **1.2.3**.

6.3.3 THE FUTURE

The forms of the future depend on the aspect of a given verb. In perfective verbs the future is simply the non-past paradigm, while in imperfective verbs two future formations exist.

6.3.3.1 Perfective future

Little needs to be said about the perfective future (the formation has been described in the context of the non-past, **6.3.1**), save that it expresses an action to be completed or carried out in its entirety:

Сього́дні напишу́ листа́.	Today I shall write the letter.
Вона́ прийде́ о четве́ртій.	She will arrive at 4 (o'clock).
Подзвоню́ до те́бе уве́чері.	I'll phone you this evening.
Відповіси́ на це?	Will you give an answer to this?
Коли́ прочита́єш статтю́?	When will you (finish) read(ing) the article?

6.3.3.2 Imperfective future: analytic and synthetic

The two imperfective future formations may be termed 'analytic' and 'synthetic'; the former means that it is formed by using discrete words (much as in English 'I shall + verb X'), while the latter refers to the expression of futurity by the means of an ending ('verb X-ending'). In terms of their formation, both variants of this tense as a whole are straightforward and regular.

THE ANALYTIC FUTURE   This formation consists of the non-past of **быть** 'to be', which has future meaning, together with the infinitive of the imperfective verb:

Бу́ду чита́ти.	I shall read.
Бу́деш працюва́ти.	You will work.
Бу́де писа́ти.	He/she will write.
Бу́демо пи́ти.	We will drink.
Бу́дете ходи́ти.	You will walk.
Бу́дуть телефонува́ти.	They will phone.

THE SYNTHETIC FUTURE   The synthetic future is constructed by means of the imperfective infinitive + personal endings; the endings are:

1*sg.*	-му
2*sg.*	-меш
3*sg.*	-ме
1*pl.*	-мемо
2*pl.*	-мете
3*pl.*	-муть

Thus the future forms, with **чита́ти** 'to read' and **диви́тися** 'to look at' as our sample verbs, are:

1*sg.*	чита́тиму	диви́тимуся
2*sg.*	чита́тимеш	диви́тимешся
3*sg.*	чита́тиме	диви́тиметься

1*pl.*	читáтимемо	диви́тимемося
2*pl.*	читáтимете	диви́тиметеся
3*pl.*	читáтимуть	диви́тимуться

There is no functional or semantic difference between the two future formations; the synthetic tends to be used less frequently than the analytic, especially in West Ukraine. Note particularly that the verb **бу́ти** does not have the -**му, -меш**, and so on, future.

6.3.4 THE IMPERATIVE

The imperative is the form of the verb used in giving commands ('Read this!', 'Go home!'); the formation of this category is directly tied to the non-past, in terms of the form as well as of the place of stress. Strictly speaking, truly 'imperative' forms exist only in the 2*sg.*, 2*pl.*, and 1*pl.*; the 1*pl.* (inclusive) corresponds to the English 'Let's (do something)', as it is of course impossible to give oneself a command. The use of the imperative, including 1*pl.* constructions involving **давáйте** 'Let's' and 3*sg.*/3*pl.* constructions with **хай/нехáй** 'Let', is described in **6.4.3.3**.

The formation of the imperative is dependent on (a) stem-type and (b) the stress pattern of the given verb; in essence, the imperative endings are attached directly to the stem itself, without the connector vowels that are present in the non-past (i.e. -**e**- or -**и**-). For some verbal types, as we have seen in the non-past, the identity of the stem cannot be deduced from the infinitive:

inf. **читáти**, but stem **читáй-**
inf. **працювáти**, but stem **працю́й-**

Although it is crucial to know the stem of a given verb, it is the place of stress within a paradigm that plays the deciding role in the choice of endings, regardless of the stem-type:

TYPE A: STEMS WITH FINAL STRESS IN THE 1 *SG.*

2*sg.*	-и́	Роби́! 'Do! Make!' (1*sg.* **роблю́**)
2*pl.*	-і́ть	роби́ть!
1*pl.*	-і́м(о)	роби́м! (роби́мо!)

TYPE B: STEMS WITH STEM STRESS

2*sg.*	-Ø	ви́бач! Excuse! Pardon. (1*sg.* **ви́бачу**)
2*pl.*	-те	ви́бачте!
1*pl.*	-мо	ви́бачмо!
2*sg.*	-Ø	читáй! Read! (1*sg.* **читáю**)
2*pl.*	-те	читáйте!
1*pl.*	-мо	читáймо!

TYPE C: STEMS WITH STEM STRESS, ENDING IN A CONSONANT CLUSTER

2sg.	-и	помо́вчи! Be silent! (1sg. помо́вчу)
2pl.	-іть	помо́вчіть!
1pl.	-ім(o)	помо́вчімо!

TYPE D: -aвa- VERBS

2sg.	-ава́й- –	дава́й! Give! Let's! (see Note 5 below)
2pl.	-ава́й-те	дава́йте!
1pl.	-ава́й-мо	дава́ймо!

Note 1: The endings in Type A will occur with all verbs with stress on the ending in the 1sg., regardless of whether or not stress shifts to the stem after the 1sg..

Note 2: If there is a consonant mutation in the non-past in the 1sg. only, then it is the unmutated consonant that appears in the imperative; if the mutation affects the entire non-past, then it is the mutated consonant that appears.

Note 3: The 1pl. ending -імо is frequently encountered (indeed preferred by some informants), and owes its final -o to the influence from the non-past; in verbs that are stem-stressed throughout, however, -o is obligatory: * виба́чм would be almost unpronounceable.

Note 4: The endings in Type C are identical to those in Type A, except that they are unstressed.

Note 5: Type D has the same endings as Type B and looks just like the чита́й- type; in this group of verbs, however, the suffix -ава́-, present in the infinitive and past tense but absent in the non-past, reappears in the imperative.

Here is a list of further examples, representative of the stem-types described in **6.3**:

A	нести́:	неси́, несі́ть, несі́м/несі́мо!
	вести́:	веди́
	пекти́:	печи́
	іти́:	іди́
	зача́ти:	зачни́
	зва́ти:	зви́
	узя́ти:	візьми́
	бра́ти:	бери́
	писа́ти:	пиши́
	плати́ти:	плати́
	носи́ти:	носи́
	ходи́ти:	ходи́
	говори́ти:	говори́
	лежа́ти:	лежи́
	терпі́ти:	терпи́
	бі́гти:	біжи́

B	уми́тися:	уми́йся, уми́йтеся, уми́ймося!
	пи́ти:	пий
	діста́ти:	діста́нь, діста́ньте, діста́ньмо
	ді́ти:	дінь
	бу́ти:	будь
	прихо́дити:	прихо́дь

Note that if the verbal stem ends in a consonant д, т, з, с, л, or н then a soft sign appears after that consonant, in all forms. Note also that the vowel и occurs in the imperative of the пйти type; in the non-past there is no vowel before the personal endings, but as the 1*sg.* imperative ending is zero a vowel is required in the stem.

C   крйкнути: крйкни, крйкніть, крйкнім!
    щéзнути: щéзни
    мйслити: мйсли (to consider, think)

D   уставáти: уставáй, уставáйте, уставáймо!
    продавáти: продавáй (to sell)
    узнавáти: узнавáй (to recognize, admit)

IRREGULAR VERBS

    дáти: дай, дáйте, дáймо!
    їсти: їж, їжте, їжмо!

Imperatives are not formed from the -повíсти stems; thus, for оповíсти 'to relate', відповíсти 'to answer', an imperative will be formed from the corresponding imperfective: оповідáй! відповідáй!

One final form requires a short note, *viz.* the imperatives of стоя́ти 'to stand' and боя́тися 'to fear': although they are end-stressed (стою́, стоя́ш, and so on), the stems are стой-, бой-; in the presence of a zero ending о becomes і, as seen in the masculine past tense of verbs such as могти́ – міг. Thus: стій, стíйте, стíймо! бійся, бíйтеся, бíймося!

6.3.5   PARTICIPLES AND GERUNDS

As a general principle, participles and gerunds are a feature of written (especially journalistic) Ukrainian rather than of the spoken language, and most need only be recognized; others are more frequently encountered, however, and require attention. Ukrainian participles are adjectival in form (i.e. used with adjectival endings, compare Chapter 3).

6.3.5.1   *Active participles (present and past)*

Of the four participles historically present in Ukrainian, the present active (PrAP.) and past active (PAP.) now exist as purely adjectival forms; this is true also of the present passive participle, but their number is now extremely small. The past passive (PPP.) is the the most widely occurring form; whereas the formation of the PrAP. and PAP. is no longer productive (i.e. since they are readily identified as adjectives and not every verb will have a PrAP. or PAP.), a given verb will readily form the PPP.

The PrAP. and PAP. essentially express 'who or which is/was X-ing', or 'X-ed', in which X is the base verb; as the PrAP. refers to the present tense, it can only be formed from an imperfective verb, while the PAP. can be either imperfective or perfective depending on the nature of the action.

PRESENT   The marker of the old PrAP. is the suffix -уч-(-юч-) or -ач-(-яч-), formed on the basis of the 3pl. non-past form, Conjugations I and II, respectively:

чита́ють	–	чита́ючий	. . . reading
працю́ють	–	працю́ючий	. . . working
реву́ть	–	реву́чий	. . . roaring
сидя́ть	–	сидя́чий	(who is) sitting
*терпля́ть	–	те́рплячий	. . . enduring
лежа́ть	–	лежа́чий	. . . lying

*Note the place of stress: the expected терпля́чий has now been reanalysed as an adjective meaning 'patient'.

PAST   The marker of the old PAP. is -л-, the same element present in the (non-masculine) forms of the past tense:

позелені́л-	–	позелені́лий	(which had become) green
зме́рзл-	–	зме́рзлий	(which had become) frozen, chilled
застарі́л-	–	застарі́лий	grown old, obsolete

Compare also the rare formation перемі́гший from перемогти́ 'to over-power', reflecting the old East Slavonic PAP. The definitions given above indicate to what extent the PAP. is now clearly adjectival; as neither it nor the PrAP. will be used as true participial forms, preference is given to the relative constructions using яки́й, хто, and the invariable що (see **4.3**; as their use is adjectival and not verbal, there is no need to describe the use of these particular participles; but compare **6.4.4** on the use of PPP.). Note particularly that participial forms with the suffixes -ущий, -ащий (PrAP.), -вший (PAP.) may be encountered now and again, but these forms have appeared under the influence of Russian and are unlikely to remain in the spoken language, although they may endure in the written media.

6.3.5.2   Passive participles

The only commonly used participial form – both in written and in spoken Ukrainian – is the past passive (expressing something/someone 'which was X-ed'); past passives can be formed from both imperfective and perfective (transitive) verbs, although perfective formations are more commonly found. There are two markers of the PPP., depending on which stem-type a given verb belongs to: -н- for the majority of verbs, -т- for those verbs belonging to a number of small sets of stems; where needed (i.e. where the structure of the stem requires it), the suffix -н- is expanded to -ен-, -єн-.

-н-: all infinitives in -ати

Note the place of stress in each instance, as it will generally retract by one syllable (including some but not all prefixes):

бажа́ти	–	ба́жаний	which/who was/has been desired
прочита́ти	–	прочи́таний	. . . read
написа́ти	–	напи́саний	. . . written
прода́ти	–	про́даний	. . . sold
коха́ти	–	ко́ханий	. . . loved
ви́грати	–	ви́граний	. . . won
обду́мати	–	обду́маний	. . . considered
забра́ти	–	за́браний	. . . taken away
рва́ти	–	рва́ний	. . . torn
да́ти	–	да́ний	. . . given
прозва́ти	–	про́званий	. . . called, named

Note the expected formation of -ува- verbs when stress is on the stem:

Infinitives in -ува́ти, -юва́ти > -у́ваний, -ю́ваний

переслі́дувати	–	переслі́дуваний	who/which was persecuted
повто́рювати	–	повто́рюваний	. . . repeated
очі́кувати	–	очі́куваний	. . . awaited
ви́працювати	–	ви́працюваний	. . . worked out, elaborated
обстрі́лювати	–	обстрі́люваний	. . . bombarded

But compare those verbs in which stress falls on the suffix in the infinitive:

Infinitives in -ува́ти, -юва́ти – -о́ваний, -ьо́ваний

нормалізува́ти	–	нормалізо́ваний	which/who was normalized
механізува́ти	–	механізо́ваний	. . . mechanized
стилізува́ти	–	стилізо́ваний	. . . stylized
ізолюва́ти	–	ізольо́ваний	. . . isolated
арештува́ти	–	арешто́ваний	. . . arrested

-ен-, -єн-: consonant stems, infinitives in -ити (rarely -їти, -їти)

нести́	–	не́сений	which/who was carried
привезти́	–	приве́зений	. . . brought (by vehicle)
привести́	–	приве́дений	. . . led (on foot)
пекти́	–	пе́чений	. . . baked
підстри́гти	–	підстри́жений	. . . given a little haircut
повідо́мити	–	повідо́млений	. . . notified
напоїти	–	напо́єний	. . . well-watered (of animals)
доно́сити	–	доно́шений	. . . worn out
попроси́ти	–	попро́шений	. . . requested
утоми́ти	–	уто́млений	. . . tired out

жа́рити	–	жа́рений	. . . heated
зни́зити	–	зни́жений	. . . lowered, abased
сікти́	–	сі́чений	. . . cut
очи́стити	–	очи́щений	. . . cleansed
дослідити́	–	дослі́джений	. . . investigated
скінчи́ти	–	скі́нчений	. . . finished

Note that stress retracts in many of these verbs as well; when there is a
consonant mutation in the non-past, that mutated consonant will appear in
the PPP., even if the mutation takes place in the 1*sg.* only (for example,
доно́сити, утоми́ти, and so on).

-т-: monosyllabic stems containing **-и- (-і-), -а- (-я-), -у-, -ер-** (and prefixed
derivatives thereof)

There are no consonant mutations or stress shifts in this group as a whole, as
the PPP. can be formed entirely on the basis of the infinitive:

ми́ти	–	ми́тий	who/which is washed
би́ти	–	би́тий	. . . beaten
ли́ти	–	ли́тий	. . . poured
ви́-пити	–	ви́питий	. . . drunk up
жа́ти	–	жа́тий	. . . reaped, harvested
грі́ти	–	грі́тий	. . . warmed
де́рти	–	де́ртий	. . . torn
за-бу́ти	–	забу́тий	. . . forgotten
на-ду́ти	–	наду́тий	. . . puffed up
від-кри́ти	–	відкри́тий	. . . opened
по-ча́ти	–	поча́тий	. . . begun
уз-я́ти	–	узя́тий	. . . taken
зай-ня́ти	–	за́йнятий	. . . occupied
на-ді́ти	–	надіті́й	. . . put on
за-пе́рти	–	запе́ртий	. . . closed, locked
про-жи́ти	–	прожи́тий	. . . lived through

VARIATION   As is the case in other verbal formations, there can be variation in
the PPP.; in other words, more than one acceptable form can occur, especially
among verbs with a root vowel -o- or the suffix -ну-:

коло́ти	–	ко́лотий – ко́лений	. . . stung, pricked
моло́ти	–	мо́лотий – ме́лений*	. . . ground, milled
поро́ти	–	по́ротий – по́рений	. . . unstitched, ripped up
одя́гнути	–	одя́гнутий – одя́гнений	. . . dressed, clothed
замкну́ти	–	замкну́тий – за́мкнений	. . . closed, shut up
згорну́ти	–	зго́рнутий – зго́рнений	. . . gathered, raked together

*Note PPP. мел- *vs.* моло́ти, мо́лотий.

6.3.5.3   *Present gerund (verbal adverb)*

The gerunds are also termed 'verbal adverbs' because they describe or modify action rather than things/people (on the adverbialization of such forms, compare **7.6**; on the use of the gerunds, see **6.4.5**). They are invariant, and refer to an action, subordinate to the main action, which takes place either before or at the same time as the main action. The 'present' gerund refers to the latter, and therefore can only be formed from an imperfective verb (it is therefore also termed the 'imperfective gerund'). It is formed as follows:

(1) *3pl.* non-past of an imperfective verb, minus **-ть + чи**:

      читáю-(ть) + чи – читáючи while reading

(2) If stress is on the ending in the *3pl.* non-past then **-чи́** is stressed:

      живу́-(ть) + чи – живучи́ while living

Note the place of stress: verbs stressed on the ending in the non-past will have end-stress in the gerund.

(3) In **-ся** verbs this particle is reduced to **-сь**:

      умíю-(ть) + чи + -сь – умíючись while washing oneself

Further examples:

уставáти	–	**устаючи́**	while standing up
працювáти	–	**працю́ючи**	. . . working
пи́ти	–	**п'ючи́**	. . . drinking
нести́	–	**несучи́**	. . . carrying
плисти́	–	**пливучи́**	. . . swimming
іти́	–	**ідучи́**	. . . going (on foot)
брáти	–	**беручи́**	. . . taking
писáти	–	**пи́шучи**	. . . writing
проси́ти	–	**прóсячи**	. . . requesting
носи́ти	–	**нóсячи**	. . . carrying
люби́ти	–	**лю́блячи**	. . . loving
говори́ти	–	**говóрячи**	. . . speaking
служи́ти	–	**слу́жачи**	. . . serving

IRREGULAR FORMS

стоя́ти, стоя́ть	but stress:	**стоячи́**
лежáти, лежáть	but	**лежачи́**
сидíти, сидя́ть	but	**сидячи́**

And note especially the verb **хотíти, хóчуть**; here the gerund **хотячи́** is not based on the expected *3pl.*

6.3.5.4 Past gerund (verbal adverb)

The past gerund expresses 'having done X', therefore it is formed more commonly from perfective verbs than from imperfective ones, although the latter formations do exist. Their formation is even more straightforward than that of the present gerund:

Masculine past tense + -ши (сь)

Examples

Masculine past		Past gerund	Meaning
написа́в	–	написа́вши	having written
нали́в	–	нали́вши	. . . poured
уми́вся	–	уми́вшись	. . . washed oneself
ви́пив	–	ви́пивши	. . . drunk (up)
прині́с	–	прині́сши	. . . brought
попли́в	–	попли́вши	. . . swum for a bit
прові́в	–	прові́вши	. . . spent (time)
прийшо́в	–	прийшо́вши	. . . arrived
зблі́д	–	зблі́дши	. . . turned pale (-ну- verb)
чита́в	–	чита́вши	while reading (in the past)
був	–	бу́вши	being (in the past)
ішо́в	–	ішо́вши	going (in the past)

6.4 THE USE OF THE VERB

6.4.0 AGREEMENT

The basic rules for the use of the verb are common to most inflecting languages: the verb must agree in form with the subject of its sentence or clause. For the non-past, this means agreement in person and number, while for the past this means agreement in number and gender:

О́льга чита́є кни́жку.	Ol'ha reads/is reading a/the book.
Я чита́ю кни́жку.	I am reading a/the book.
Ді́ти прочита́ють кни́жку.	The children will read the book.
Ми прочита́ємо кни́жку.	We will read the book.
О́льга чита́ла кни́жку.	Ol'ha was reading the book.
Вони́ прочита́ли кни́жку.	They read the book.

In the following sections we shall describe the grammatical categories relevant to the Ukrainian verb.

6.4.1   THE USE OF THE INFINITIVE

The infinitive in Ukrainian is used much as it is in many of the languages of the world, including English; in essence, it is the equivalent of the English 'to + verb' ('to read', 'to understand', and similar).

6.4.1.1   *The infinitive as subject of the sentence*

The most common occurrences of the Ukrainian infinitive in the role of the subject involve:

(1) constructions with це 'this is', 'that is' with or without following **значить** or **означáє** 'this means', expressing a juxtaposition of ideas (the focus of the following clause can be either a noun or another infinitive); and
(2) constructions with the instrumental case.

In both instances, equivalent English constructions most commonly involve the use of the gerund; the infinitive can stand alone, or it may have an object of its own – in which case the infinitival phrase as a whole acts as a subject. The infinitive does not have to occur at the beginning of the sentence. Thus:

Читáти– це рáдість.
Reading is pleasure.

Читáти укрáїнську літерату́ру – (це означáє) розумíти Украї́ну.
Reading Ukrainian literature means (equals) understanding Ukraine.

Найви́ще умíння – *почáти* спочáтку життя́, розумíння, доро́гу, себé.
The greatest capability is *beginning* (the ability to begin) life, understanding, (one's) path, for oneself. (Л. Костенко)

Пéршою ду́мкою в Степáна було́ *довíдатися*, де вони́.
Stepan's first thought was *to find out* where they were. (Коцюбинський)

Писáти листи́ дру́зям щомíсяця – її́ дáвня зви́чка.
Writing letters to her friends every month was her custom from long ago (it was long her custom to . . .).

Допомагáти дру́зям – це наш обо́в'язок.
It is our duty *to help* (our) friends. (Helping friends is . . .)

Зустрíти його́ було́ для мéне втíхою.
Meeting him was a pleasure for me.

6.4.1.2   *The infinitive in the predicate*

The infinitive can have a variety of functions in the predicate. As a direct object, as in the case of subjectival constructions, the verb is in a sense nominalized ('the act of X'), appearing in place of a noun:

| Ба́тько лю́бить *чита́ти* (газе́ту). | Father loves *reading* (to read) (the newspaper). |

The infinitive often occurs in impersonal constructions, in which the sense expressed varies according to the presence or absence of other elements. The presence of an element in the dative case clearly emphasizes the person at whom the verbal action is directed:

Тут *нам* жи́ти ле́гко.	It is easy for us to live here.
Куди́ (мені́) йти́?	Where can (I) go? (lit. Where is there for me/one to go?)
Що (мені́) роби́ти?	What can one (I) do?

Whereas the absence of the dative allows the infinitive to be interpreted as a subjectival element, even if the speaker/writer intended it to be seen as an impersonal statement:

| Тут жи́ти ле́гко. | Living here is easy. |
| Де схова́тися від во́рога? | Where can one hide from the enemy? |

In the second example the absence of the dative does not affect the status of the construction, as the interrogative element де? causes it to retain its 'impersonal' focus. A statement beginning with схова́тися від во́рога ... would on the other hand clearly be subjectival: 'hiding from the wind ...'.

The inclusion of the element було́ (neuter past of бу́ти 'to be') injects a modal sense, with or without an accompanying form in the dative case; in such instances there is an understood тре́ба 'must', мо́жна 'could', 'might', and such. Note the possible difference between sentences with and without не, expressing 'should/would' and 'could', respectively:

Не говори́ти було́ з не́ю ...	It *would* have been better not to speak with her ...
Було́ вам прочита́ти ...	You *could* have read ...
Не було́ вам прочита́ти ...	You *should not* have read ...

As against, again, a purely neutral sense:

| Не пізна́ти (було́) чому́ ... | One can (could) not tell why ... |

An understood or implied modal is also present in constructions consisting of the conjunction якщо́ 'if' (cf. **8.1.3.3**) + infinitive:

Якщо́ вибира́ти між красо́ю і пра́вдою, я вибира́ю красу́.
If (I had/have to) choose between beauty and truth, I choose beauty.
(О. Довженко)

One further use of the infinitive in the predicate expresses the idea of a 'goal', 'desire', or 'in order to':

| Подорожува́ти! Поба́чити світ! | (Oh, if one could) travel! See the world! |
| Ми пішли́ (щоб) поба́чити за́хід со́нця. | We went to see the sunset. |

The second example is typical of sentences with verbs of motion, in which the goal of the action (a second verb in the infinitive) may be expressed with or without щоб 'in order to'. Note: the use of the conjunction щоб with and without infinitives is described in Chapter 8.

6.4.1.3 Verbs requiring the use of an infinitive

There are a number of Ukrainian verbs that cannot take a direct object (i.e. a nominal form in the accusative case), requiring instead a second verb in the infinitive. Such verbal juxtapositions are common in English as well, for example, 'to be able to + X' ('He *cannot read*', 'He *is unable to read*'), 'to begin to + X', 'to begin X-ing' ('She *began to sing*', '*began singing*'), and likewise. The most common of these are the following:

переставати/перестати	'stop (doing X)' + imperfective
Ольга перестала говорити.	Ol'ha stopped talking.
могти/змогти	'be able to'
Не мо́жемо чека́ти.	We cannot wait.

Other verbs can be used either with verbal complements (again with infinitives) or with other complements, nominal or adverbial:

продо́вжувати/продо́вжити	'continue' + imperfective
Вони́ продо́вжили сперечатися.	They continued arguing.
Вони́ продо́вжили супере́чку.	They continued the argument.
умі́ти	'know how to' + imperfective
Умі́сте пла́вати?	Do you know how to swim?
устига́ти/усти́гнути (усти́гти)	'manage to' + perfective
Оле́кса не встиг дописа́ти листа́.	Oleksa didn't manage to finish writing the letter.
Вона́ не всти́гла на сніда́нок.	She didn't make it to breakfast.

(Note the need for a preposition here, showing that the verb does not occur with a true direct object.)

ста́ти	'begin', 'become' + imperfective
Ми ста́ли чита́ти.	We began reading.
Ста́ло теплі́ше.	It became warmer.
почина́ти/поча́ти	'begin' + imperfective
Виклада́ч поча́в говори́ти.	The lecturer began speaking.
Виклада́ч поча́в ле́кцію.	The lecturer began the lecture.

кінча́ти/скінчи́ти	'finish' + imperfective
Бори́с скінчи́в писа́ти.	Borys finished writing.
Бори́с скінчи́в лист.	Borys finished the letter.

6.4.1.3.1   Verbs of obligation or necessity + infinitive

As a particular subset of **6.4.1.3**, verbs of obligation/necessity need to be noted; these also require an infinitive:

му́сити (or **му́сіти**)	'be obliged to', 'must'
Му́шу дзвони́ти до ньо́го.	I must phone him.
Note: **му́сить бу́ти.**	'apparently', 'probably'
ма́ти	'have to', 'be supposed to' (cf. primary meaning 'to have')
Що ма́єш роби́ти?	What are you supposed to do? What do you have to do?
Це ма́є бу́ти зро́блено нега́йно.	This must be done immediately.
дово́дитися (impersonal)	'an obligation to do X'
Мені́ дово́диться плати́ти їй . . .	I must pay her, I feel I must . . .

6.4.1.4   The infinitive in place of the imperative

The infinitive can be used in place of the imperative in limited contexts (see **6.4.3.3**): this use of the infinitive expresses the highest or most urgent level of commands, to be expected not in ordinary speech, but typically in situations involving the military or law enforcement. Thus:

Мовча́ти!	Silence!
Не говори́ти!	No talking! (= silence!!)

6.4.2   INTRANSITIVE *VS.* TRANSITIVE: -ся VERBS

The majority of Ukrainian verbs are inherently transitive or intransitive. Transitive verbs occur in conjunction with a direct object, which in Ukrainian is a noun or noun phrase in the accusative case; the genitive can also occur in this function (see **2.4.1.2** on the genitive-accusative for animate masculine nouns, and **2.4.1.3** on the partitive genitive). Intransitive verbs stand alone without a direct object (as can transitives), while -ся verbs are either (a) intransitive, (b) reflexive/reciprocal, or (c) passive (see **6.4.4** on the passive uses of -ся).

6.4.2.1 *Transitive verbs with an accusative direct object*

Сього́дні він знайшо́в готе́ль.	Today he found a hotel (acc.).
Чи зна́єш цю студе́нтку?	Do you know this/that (female) student?
Ти поба́чила А́нну?	Did you see Anna?
А́нна поба́чила Іва́на.	Anna saw Ivan.
Оле́ксо, ви́пий молоко́!	Oleksa, drink (up) the milk!
Ба́тько купи́в хлі́ба.	Father bought (some) bread.
. . . похова́йте мене́ на моги́лі . . .	. . . bury me in a grave . . . (Shevch.)
Люди́на створи́ла культу́ру, а культу́ра – люди́ну.	Man created culture, and culture (created) man. (KUM)

Note the use of transitive verbs without an object, when reference is to a given action in general:

Люблю́ чита́ти.	I like to read.
Тре́ба ї́сти та пи́ти.	One has to drink and eat.

6.4.2.2 *Intransitive verbs without -ся*

Тре́ба працюва́ти.	One must work.
Ді́ти лю́блять гра́ти в па́рку.	Children like to play in the park.
Чи мо́жна сиді́ти тут?	May I/can one sit here?
Будь ла́ска, говорі́ть пові́льно!	Please speak slowly!
Ці́лий день ми стоя́ли в черзі́.	We stood in a queue all day.
Ма́ма спить.	Mum is sleeping.
Чого́ ти так гово́риш?	Why are you speaking in such a way?
Лі́кар мовча́в.	The doctor was silent (did not speak).

6.4.2.3 *Intransitive verbs with -ся*

At times the dividing line between 'intransitive' and 'reflexive' -ся verbs (compare **6.4.2.4**) can be a fine one. The former essentially expresses 'doing X oneself', while the latter is more akin to 'doing X *to* oneself'; very often an intransitive verb has a transitive partner (without -ся) that expresses 'doing X to another'. This is the case in the following:

Вчи́тель зно́ву розсе́рдився.	Once again the teacher became angry.
vs. Вчи́тель розсе́рдив ба́тька.	The teacher made father angry.
Вони́ одружи́лися.	They got married.
vs. Бори́с ви́рішив одружи́ти си́на.	Borys decided to marry (off) his son.

Ми залишúлися позáду.	We lagged (stayed) behind.
vs. **Я залишúв листá на столí.**	I left the letter (caused it to stay) on the table.
Стілéць зламáвся.	The stool/seat broke.
vs. **Хлóпець зламáв стілéць.**	The boy broke the stool/seat.

Similarly:

різнúтися – різнúти	to be different – to make different
переселúтися – переселúти	to move to another place – to remove, make settle in another place
повернýтися – повернýти	to return, go back – to return (something)
сушúтися – сушúти	to get dry – to dry (something)
скінчúтися – скінчúти	to come to an end – to finish, end
початúся – початú	to begin – to begin (something)

Many other **-ся** verbs may be treated as simple intransitives, as they will not have semantically satisfactory partners without **-ся** (in other words, corresponding verbs without this particle do not simply mean 'doing X to another'). Thus:

Ми дізнáлися, як тудú добрáтися.	We found out how to get there.
But: **дізнáти**	to investigate, explore
добрáти	to make up for, supplement

Compare also:

наїдáтися	to eat one's fill, too much
but	
наїдáти	to eat a certain quantity
договорúтися	to come to an agreement
but	
договорúти	to finish speaking
простудúтися	to catch a cold, to be cooled/frozen through
but	
простудúти	to cool, make cold (*not* *to give someone a cold!)
удавáтися	to succeed in
but	
удавáти	to pretend, feign, simulate
проспáтися	to wake up, to have a good sleep
but	
проспáти	to miss by oversleeping, to sleep for some time

We also find -ся verbs without corresponding base verbs:

посмі́ятися   to laugh (a little)
but: no form without -ся
розплати́тися   to settle (financial) accounts
but: no form without -ся
прислу́хатися   to give an ear to, listen
but: no form without -ся in the literary language (although one does occur in dialects)

Some of the apparent incongruities are due to the particular prefix in question, as a number of combinations of prefix + ся express very specific notions: for example, на + verb + ся generally expresses 'to do something to excess'; these constructions are described in **6.5.1.2**.

When the reader comes across a new -ся verb that is not obviously reflexive (as in the next group to be discussed), a dictionary will explain whether that verb is a simple intransitive or one that has a suitable transitive partner. Note particularly that the occasional -ся verb may appear to have transitive meaning, for example, **диви́тися** 'to look at', 'to watch', but where an object is used a preposition will be required, as a -ся verb will generally not occur alone with an accusative object: **диви́тися** *на* **телеба́чення**, *на* **програ́му** 'to watch television, a programme', **не ди́влячись на це** 'notwithstanding', 'nevertheless'. But **диви́тися телеві́зор** is possible.

6.4.2.4   *Reflexive or reciprocal verbs with -ся*

уми́ти – уми́тися	to wash – to wash oneself (refl.)
уби́ти – уби́тися	to kill – to kill oneself (refl.)
показа́ти – показа́тися	to show – to show oneself (as . . .) (refl.)
томи́ти – томи́тися	to tire (out) – to tire oneself (out) (refl.)
одяга́ти – одяга́тися	to clothe, dress – to dress oneself (refl.)
уплести́ – уплести́ся	to braid – to braid one's own hair (refl.)
відкида́ти – відкида́тися	to throw back – to throw oneself back(wards) (refl.)
ба́чити – ба́читися	to see – to see each other, meet (recip.)
перепроси́ти – перепроси́тися	to apologize – to apologize to each other (to make up) (recip.)
руба́ти – руба́тися	to cut, hew – to slash each other (recip.)
гри́зти – гри́зтися	to gnaw, bite – to quarrel, bicker (lit. 'gnaw at each other'!) (recip.)
мири́ти – мири́тися	to reconcile, mediate – to make peace (with each other) (recip.)

It is also possible for a reciprocal -ся verb not to have a corresponding base verb without the particle:

листува́тися   to correspond (with each other)
but
not *листува́ти

6.4.3 ASPECT

As the use of the Ukrainian verb is to such an extent a function of its aspect, we present here the notions of tense, sequence of actions, and the imperative under the global umbrella of 'aspect'.

6.4.3.1 *Tense*

The basic distribution of tenses *vis-à-vis* aspect was described in **6.1**: the imperfective verb has all three basic tenses (past, present, and future) while the perfective verb is limited to two (past and future) by virtue of the notion of 'completed' action:

Imperfective:

Ко́жного дня Ма́ша хо́дить до шко́ли.	Every day Masha goes to school.
Іва́н Франко́ був письме́нником.	Ivan Franko was a writer.
Ба́тько працюва́в на заво́ді.	Father worked in a factory.
Ми ду́же лю́бимо танцюва́ти.	We really like to dance.
Чи бу́деш відпочива́ти лі́том?	Will you rest (this) summer?
У шко́лі ді́ти чита́тимуть (бу́дуть чита́ти) украї́нську літерату́ру.	In school the children will be reading Ukrainian literature.

Perfective:

Його́ ви́ключили з па́ртії.	He was expelled from the party.
Наре́шті Ле́ся дописа́ла кни́жку ві́ршів.	Lesja finally finished writing the book of verse.
Зайде́ш до ме́не уве́чері?	Will you visit me (come by) this evening?
Запишу́ тобі́ свою́ адре́су.	I'll write down my address for you.

6.4.3.2 *Sequence of actions*

Actions that are taking place concurrently (in any of the three tenses) must by their very nature be imperfective:

Та́то сиді́в за столо́м, пив ка́ву, та чита́в газе́ту.

Dad was sitting at the table, drinking (some) coffee and reading the newspaper.

Graphically we can describe these actions as follows:

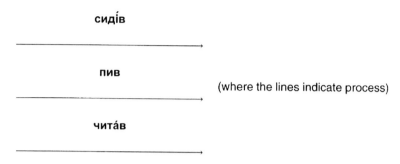

сиді́в

пив

(where the lines indicate process)

чита́в

If **сиді́ти** sets the stage – or is the background action – other completed, perfective, actions can take place during the larger process:

Коли́ він сиді́в за столо́м, він ви́пив ка́ви та прочита́в три листи́.
When he was sitting at the table, he drank (some) coffee and (then) read three letters.

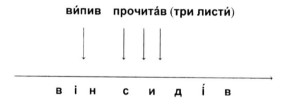

ви́пив   прочита́в (три листи́)

в і н   с и д і в

A sequence of completed actions can be expressed without a background action, and these actions will naturally be perfective:

Ко́ля прийшо́в додо́му, розідя́гся та ви́пив ча́шку ка́ви.
Kolja came home, (then) took off his coat, and (then) drank (up) a cup of coffee.

These are completed, temporally unconnected (sequential) actions:

прийшо́в   розідя́гся   ви́пив (ча́шку ка́ви)

X   X   X

6.4.3.3 *The use of imperatives*

As described in the section on the formation of the imperative, there are distinct imperative forms for the *2sg.*, *2pl.*, and *1pl.* The **ти** form is used with individual friends, students, and family members, while the **Ви** form is used with individuals as a mark of respect (i.e. with people one either does not know or whose position requires respect) or in reference to more than one person.

6.4.3.3.1 Positive commands: ти and Ви

The aspect of an imperative is crucial to the correct delivery of an intended message. Commands of a general nature – in the form of suggestions, guidelines as to manner of action, and likewise – will require the imperfective aspect, while a specific command (pertaining to most situations) will usually be formed from perfective verbs. Compare the following two groups of examples, the first of which can be described as 'general', the second as 'specific':

1 **Говорі́ть пові́льно, будь ла́ска.** Speak slowly, please.
Говори́ украї́нською (мо́вою), О́льго. Speak in Ukrainian, Ol'ha.
Пиші́ть я́сно, будь ла́ска. Please write clearly.
Відповіда́йте, коли́ зна́єте відповідь. Answer when you know the answer.

2 **Скажі́ть, будь ла́ска, де Іва́н.** Please tell (me) where Ivan is.
Запиши́ свою́ відповідь. Write down your answer.
Прочита́йте во́сьму ле́кцію. Read lesson eight.
Візьми́ кни́жку – вона́ ду́же ціка́ва. Take the book – it's very interesting.

Ви́бачте! Sorry! (Excuse me!)

The imperfective may be used for specific commands if there is some urgency to the request; thus (i) if the action is required immediately or (ii) if the request had been made once (using the normal perfective) but had not been acted upon and needed repeating. Note the following examples:

Іва́не, відчиня́й вікно́! Ivan, open the window!
Прочита́йте пе́ршу сторі́нку. Ну, чита́йте! Read the first page. Well, read!
Стій! Stop! (lit. 'Stand!' cf. **6.4.1.4**)

6.4.3.3.2 Negative commands: ти and Ви

The rule of thumb for negative commands is: (a) imperfective for neutral statements and (b) perfective when a sense of warning is implied; the latter might express 'be careful', 'not to', 'lest . . .'. Compare:

Не говори́ мені́ про це – це неціка́во. Don't tell me about this – it's uninteresting
Не скажи́ йому́: це таємни́ця. Don't tell him: it's a secret.
Не чита́й цей ро́зділ. Don't read this chapter.
Іде́ дощ; не забу́дь парасо́льку. It's raining; don't forget the umbrella.

6.4.3.3.3   Inclusive ('Let's') commands

The 1*pl.* imperative, or inclusive, is the form used when asking one or more individuals to do something together, as a group. For imperfective verbs the forms **Давайте/Даваймо** 'Let's' may be used in conjunction with the infinitive:

Давайте (-мо) грати в карти!   Let's play cards!
Давайте (-мо) йти до театру!   Let's go to the theatre!

But for both imperfective and perfective verbs the 1*pl.* imperative form may be used alone, although this is more common for perfective verbs than for imperfectives:

Прочитаймо газету   Let's read the newspaper!
Забудьмо цю дурість   Let's forget this silliness!
(С)питаймо його!   Let's ask him!

The use of **давайте** with perfectives is found, but less frequently; note the following example:

Давайте, хлопці, провчімо вражого пана . . .
Come on, boys, let's teach the hostile/inimical lord . . . (Н-Л)

Here **давайте** functions not, strictly speaking, as part of the compound 1*pl.* imperative, but as a general exhortation.

The corresponding negative consists of **не будьмо** + imperfective verb or **не** + 1*pl.* perfective imperative:

Не будьмо сперечатися!   Let's not quarrel!
Не забудьмо послати листа!   Let's not forget to post the letter!

6.4.3.3.4   Third-person commands

A third person (he, she, they) may be asked to do something *via* someone else; i.e. 'Have' or 'Let him do this'. The key element is **Нехай** or **Хай** 'Have'/'let', commonly in conjunction with the 3*sg.* or 3*pl.* perfective verb, as the action has not begun yet and future time is implied; if the action is clearly of a general nature (for example, with no direct object), the imperfective will be used:

Нехай Олекса прочитає відповідь.   Have Oleksa read the answer.
Нехай Олекса читає.   Let Oleksa read.

A corresponding negative 'Do not have/let X do Y' does not involve **хай/нехай**; instead we would find a circumlocution of the kind 'Do not let/allow X to do Y':

не дозволяй йому це (з)робити.   Don't allow him to do this.

6.4.3.4　Use of the verbs of motion

The verbs of motion were listed in **6.2.7**. The most important factor to bear in mind is that both indeterminate and determinate verbs of motion are imperfective: i.e. they can express action in all three tenses. The perfectives act as pure perfectives, with two overt tenses, past and future. A small portion of the table given earlier bears repeating:

Imperfective		Perfective	Meaning
Indeterminate	*Determinate*		
ходи́ти	іти́	піти́	to go (by foot)
ї́здити	ї́хати	поїхати	to go (by vehicle)
носи́ти	нести́	понести́	to carry (by foot)
літа́ти	летіти	полетіти	to fly

6.4.3.4.1　Indeterminates

Indeterminate verbs of motion indicate: (1) habitual action, (2) round trip (return) action, (3) the action in general, and (4) the natural ability to carry out the action:

(1)　**Він ко́жного дня хо́дить до шко́ли.**
　　　Every day he goes (walks) to school.

　　　Ко́жної о́сені птахи́ літа́ють на пі́вдень.
　　　Every autumn birds fly (to the) south.

(2)　**Учо́ра вра́нці Петро́ ї́здив до Ки́єва.**
　　　Yesterday morning Petro went (by vehicle) to Kyiv (and returned: he's back).

　　　Учо́ра вве́чері я ходи́ла до теа́тру.
　　　Last night I went to the theatre (and returned: I'm telling you about it now).

(3)　**Наста́ла весна́. Подиви́ся: птахи́ співа́ють, ри́би пла́вають в о́зері.**
　　　Spring has come. Look: the birds are singing, the fish are swimming in the lake.

(4)　**Йому́ тільки оди́н рік, а він вже хо́дить.**
　　　He's only one year old, and he's already walking.

Note that the strict division between motion 'on foot' and 'by vehicle' is lost in some contexts, particularly when speaking of going to the theatre, cinema, or the like; although one probably used some mode of transport to get to one's destination, the verb **ходи́ти** is preferred.

6.4.3.4.2　Determinates

Determinate verbs indicate that an action was, is, or will be in progress, implying that another action takes place at some point during the motion; in other words, the verb of motion sets the stage for another (usually perfective) action. If more than one verb of motion is present in the sentence, they will be of the same type:

Коли вона йшла додому, побачила свого вчителя.
When she was walking home, she caught sight of her teacher.

Коли ми їхали в гори, ми помітили, що скоро буде гроза.
As we drove (were driving) into the mountains, we noticed that there would soon be a thunderstorm.

Наш професор ішов по вулиці до університету; я хотів йому допомогти тому, що він ніс декілька тяжких книжок.
Our professor was walking along the street to the university; I wanted to help him because he was carrying several heavy books.

Note that such verbs will often be translated into English by means of the progressive present, *viz.* verbs marked by '-ing'. The determinates can also be used to designate a future (especially an immediate future), much as the English 'Tonight *I'm going*' is present in form, but future in meaning:

Сьогодні ввечері ми йдемо до театру.
This evening we're going to the theatre.

6.4.3.4.3 Perfectives

Perfective verbs of motion express the beginning of the action in question; whether the particular verb means 'enter', 'exit', 'go', and so on, the final result is not known unless context provides that information. A series of consecutive actions will all be perfective, and only in such an instance ('He went here, then went there, and likewise') will the successful outcome of the actions be clear:

Де дочка? – Вона пішла в магазин/до магазину.
Where's (my) daughter? – She's gone (left for) the shop. (We do not know whether she has reached the store or not, we only know she isn't here now.)

Батько поніс подарунок до дідуся.
Father has (gone and) taken a present to Granddad. (He has left; we do not know if he has reached his destination yet.)

Маша пішла додому, подзвонила до подруги і вийшла в магазин/до магазину.
Masha went home, phoned her (girl-) friend, and went out to the shop. (The successful completion of the first two verbs is clear, but all we know of the last is that she left.)

6.4.3.5 Results of an action: in force or annulled

The use of a verb in the past tense, unless accompanied by specific contextual information, can imply – merely by virtue of its aspect – whether or not the results of an action are still in force or have been annulled. The perfective past implies that the results are still in force, while the imperfective indicates that something happened to annul them; this is true of verbs of motion as well as other verbs. Thus:

Окса́на відчини́ла вікно́; тепе́р хо́лодно.
Oksana opened the window; now it's cold. (The window is still open.)

Сього́дні вра́нці Катери́на відчиня́ла вікно́. (Хто його́ зачини́в?)
This morning Kateryna opened the window. (Who closed it?)

Марко́ прийшо́в о шо́стій (і Вас чека́є).
Marko arrived at 6 (and he's waiting for you).

Де О́ля! – Вона́ прихо́дила о деся́тій, але́ тре́ба було́ поверну́тися додо́му.
Where's Olya? – She came at 10, but had to return home.

6.4.4 THE PASSIVE

In many languages actions may be described as 'active' as opposed to 'passive': in the former 'X does Y', while in the latter 'Y is done by X' ('John reads the book' *vs.* 'The book is read by John'). There are three ways of expressing passive actions in Ukrainian: (1) by means of the past passive participle, (2) the particle **-ся**, and (3) the 3*pl.* form of the verb.

6.4.4.1 Use of the past passive participle (PPP.): attributive

The past passive participle is the only form that unambiguously expresses the notion 'passive' in the Ukrainian language; as we noted earlier, the present passive is no longer used in Ukrainian (apart from forms frozen as adjectives). The PPP. is only formed from transitive verbs (see **6.3.5.2**), since the object of the action functions as the subject of the passive sentence. In contrast to other Slavonic languages, the PPP. can be either perfective or imperfective, although perfective formations are in practice far more common (compare Russian, in which it is perfective in almost all instances). A perfective refers to an action that has been completed, while an imperfective form refers to an ongoing or lasting act in the past. Note that the form of the PPP. is that of an adjective, and, as such, when modifying a noun it must agree with it in case, gender, and number. Examples (with literal translations):

збудо́ваний теа́тр	a built theatre (a theatre that was built)
прочи́тана кни́жка	a read book (a book that was read)
відчи́нене вікно́	an open(ed) window
при́слані листи́	posted letters (letters that were posted)
Він ба́тько вби́того солда́та.	He's the father of the soldier who was killed.
недопи́тий чай	the unfinished tea (lit. 'not drunk up')
недосо́лена ри́ба	fish that hasn't been quite salted (enough)
дова́рений суп	soup that has been cooked (enough)
позна́чення подо́вженої вимо́ви приголо́сних	the marking of lengthened pronunciation of consonants (re transcriptions in the dictionary)

The imperfective PPP., in addition to referring to an action that was taking place in the past, can express results that continue to be in effect in the present; Dudyk (1988: 320–1) makes the point that some of these participial forms could therefore easily be replaced by present tense active forms. Thus:

ба́жаний результа́т	the desired effect (not necessarily just in the past)
сі́чене сі́но	the cut hay (hay that has been, was being cut)

And citing the writer Ivan Franko (Dudyk, ibid.):

I почува́є він себе́ таки́м сла́бким, безси́льним і безві́льним, мов пили́на, ві́трами гна́на.

And he feels so weak, powerless and 'unfree', like a speck of dust driven by the winds. (Implied: that is being driven by the winds.)

When the agent (the one who carried out the action) is mentioned, it appears in the instrumental case:

Ти чита́ла кни́жку, напи́сану мно́ю?	Have you read the book (that was) written by me?
Ось стаття́, перекла́дена ним.	Here is the article translated by him.
У тому буди́нку, збудо́ваному робітника́ми ...	In this building built by the workers ...
До краї́ни, відкри́тої на́ми ...	To the country discovered by us ...

6.4.4.2   Use of the PPP.: predicative

In the predicate the PPP. is used in constructions which involve the copula 'to be' in English: 'The stadium was built', 'the book was written', and so on. The standard formulation is as follows: an impersonal form of the PPP. in -но, -то is used, and – against expectation – the object will appear in the accusative; this shows an incomplete separation of the passive from the active, as the object would occur in the accusative in active constructions. The ending of the PPP. is not neuter (the neuter ending being -e), but strictly a marker of the impersonal quality of the formulation:

Цю кни́жку було́ напи́сано мно́ю.
This book was written by me.

На одні́й стіні́ зобра́жено си́на Іва́на.
On one wall is depicted the son of Ivan.

Собо́р збудо́вано в 1422 ро́ці.
The Cathedral was built in the year 1422.

Статтю́ напи́сано в Англі́ї.
The article was written in England.

Його́ перемі́щено на ка́федру росі́йської мо́ви.
He was/has been transferred to the department of Russian language.

У цьо́му тво́рі відобра́жено життя́ украї́нського наро́ду.
In this work is/was reflected the life of the Ukrainian people.

Note that a form of **бу́ти** is not necessary here, as it is felt to be superfluous: the PPP. expresses past tense in and of itself. If a form of **бу́ти** is used, it will be **було́**, agreeing with the impersonal form in -**но**, -**то**; in such a case, this form may reflect a pluperfect sense '*had* been done':

При Софі́йському собо́рі було́ засно́вано шко́лу . . .
At St Sophia Cathedral a school was/had been founded . . . (Жлуктенко *et al.*, 1978)

6.4.4.3   *Passive constructions with* **-ся** *verbs*

In addition to the uses of **-ся** verbs noted above, they can also be used in a passive sense:

Як пи́шеться це сло́во?	How is that word written (spelt)?
Ці слова́ не вжива́ються.	These words are not used.
Як ро́биться ка́ша?	How is gruel/are grits made?

Note that some of these constructions could be interpreted either as passives or as neutral intransitives:

Вікно́ відчини́лося.	The window was opened *or*
	The window opened (by itself)

In practice, making such fine distinctions is not necessary; if the question 'by whom/what' cannot be answered in relation to a given sentence, it may be treated as a simple intransitive construction rather than as a passive.

6.4.4.4   *Passive constructions with the 3pl. form of the verb*

Although not a true passive formation, the *3pl.* of the verb is used very frequently to express that something 'was/is done'; these constructions should therefore be translated as such, and not literally as *3pl.* verbs:

По ра́діо передали́, що . . .	(The message that . . .) was broadcast by radio
У газе́тах пи́шуть, що . . .	It is written in the papers that . . .
Гово́рять, що . . .	It is said that . . .

6.4.5 THE USE OF THE GERUND

The use of the gerund is strictly dependent on whether two (or more) actions are concurrent, or sequential:

(i)   If the action expressed by the gerund is taking place at the same time as another, then the gerund will be imperfective: 'While/when X-ing, Y (and Z) took place.' This gerund is sometimes referred to as the 'imperfective' gerund, but the designation 'present' is acceptable: no matter what tense the gerund is associated with, its action is taking place at the same time.

(ii) If an action was completed before the action of the second verb, the gerund will generally be perfective: 'Having X-ed, Y took place.' This form can express both 'When/after X had taken place' and 'When/after X will have taken place', thus it is often termed the 'perfective' gerund rather than the 'past' gerund; as imperfective past gerunds do occur (however rarely), we shall use 'past' here.

PRESENT

Ідучи́ до шко́ли, Ва́ня поба́чив свого́ вчи́теля.	While walking to school, Vanya saw his teacher.
Сидячи́ в крі́слі, ба́тько чита́в газе́ту.	While sitting in the armchair, father read the newspaper.
Вона́ йшла в магази́н несучи́ мішо́к.	She was walking to the store carrying a bag.
Па́сучи че́реду корі́в, Оле́кса побі́г напи́тися води́.	While pasturing a herd of cows Oleksa ran to drink his fill of water.
Лежачи́ в лі́жку, А́нна чита́тиме кни́жку.	Anna will be reading a book while lying in bed.
Стоячи́ в че́рзі, ми розмовля́ємо, жарту́ємо . . .	While standing in the queue, we converse, joke . . .

Note that all of these gerunds can be replaced by коли́ + verb phrase, as in коли́ Ва́ня йшо́в . . ., коли́ Ба́тько сиді́в . . ., коли́ А́нна лежа́ла . . ., and so on.

PAST

| Написа́вши до́вгого листа́, я пішо́в на по́шту. | Having written the long letter, I set off for the post office. |

Умившись та одягнувшись, дочка поснідала.	Having washed and dressed herself, (my, the) daughter had breakfast.
Провівши два роки в Росії, він тепер дуже добре говорить російською.	Having spent two years in Russia, he now speaks Russian very well.
Діждавшись слушного часу, він зробив так, як порадив батько.	Having waited for the right time, he did as his father advised.
Ішовши до театру, ми зустріли друзів.	While walking to the theatre, we met friends.

Note that the last example is an imperfective, which could easily be replaced by the corresponding present gerund; as in the case of present gerunds, the past forms can be replaced by the **коли** construction, or by **після того, як** + verb phrase. Gerunds can assume properties typical of an adverb (hence the alternate designation 'verbal adverbs'); adverbialized gerunds are examined in **7.6**.

6.4.5.1 *не* + *gerunds*

A negated gerund is not difficult to understand, but is translated into English using the word 'without'; conversely, rendering an English gerundial construction into Ukrainian must not be done literally (i.e. using **без** 'without'):

| не зважаючи на те, що . . . | *without* paying attention to the fact, that . . . |
| не діждавшись відповіді . . . | *without* having waited for the answer . . . |

6.4.6 THE CONDITIONAL

'Conditional' constructions may be termed either 'real' or 'unreal'. 'Real' conditions involve 'if–then' propositions, where one situation follows from the first. Thus:

| Якщо піде, (то) не підемо на пікнік. | If it rains, (then) we won't go to the picnic. |

'Unreal' conditions will involve the 'conditional' mood (subjunctive in many languages), in which the propositions are hypothetical or express a desire or wish – which may or may not be fulfilled. The Ukrainian construction is very simple, involving the particle **би**, **б** + past tense form of the verb; it is important to note here that the verb itself is not necessarily expressing true past tense: the form is simply required (for historical reasons) with the particle. As a rule, **би** will follow a word ending in a consonant, while **б** follows a vowel:

| Я хотів би піти додому. | I would like to go home. |
| Я хотіла б піти додому. | (masc. and fem., respectively) |

As many conditional constructions begin with 'if', it is important to note that it is not **якщо́** that is used, but the clearly conditional **якби́, коли́ б**; the first clause will begin with **якби́**, but the following clause must contain **би/б** as well, as if to emphasize the conditional nature of the whole (paralleling English 'could/would' in the first example):

Якби́ він міг, то прийшо́в би.	If he could, (then) he would come.
Якби́ пішо́в дощ, то ми могли́ б залиши́тися вдо́ма.	If it were to rain (start raining), (then) we could stay at home.
Якби́ не було́ війни́, усі́ ще жили́ б у своі́х стари́х місте́чках.	If there hadn't been a war, (then) everyone would still be living in their old little towns.
Якби́ ти не знайшо́в цю кни́жку, то не міг би готува́тися до уро́ку.	If you hadn't found this book, you couldn't have prepared for the lesson.

See Chapter 8 on the general use of such conjunctions as **що, щоб, якби́**, and others.

6.4.7 VERBS REQUIRING CASES OTHER THAN THE ACCUSATIVE

In addition to the vast numbers of Ukrainian verbs – strictly transitive – governing the accusative case, and the large numbers of intransitive verbs (with or without **-ся**), a number of common verbs require the use of other cases: genitive, dative, and instrumental. The locative case occurs only with prepositions, and verbs requiring the use of prepositions are detailed in **6.4.8**. Here we consider the accusative of animate beings (genitive for masculines in the singular, for all living beings in the plural) to be a subset of the accusative, and such constructions as **ба́чу Іва́на** are not included among verbs governing the genitive. Other verbs may govern both the accusative and the genitive, and these are described in **6.4.7.1.1**.

6.4.7.1 *Verbs governing the genitive*

бажа́ти	'wish' (+ dative of person)
Бажа́ємо тобі́ усьо́го до́брого.	We wish you all the best.
боя́тися	'fear'
Бої́шся соба́к?	Are you afraid of dogs?
вчи́тися	'study'
Вчу́ся украї́нської мо́ви.	I'm studying the Ukrainian language.
навча́ти, навчи́ти	'teach' (+ accusative of person)
Навчу́ вас цього́ уро́ку.	I will teach you this lesson.
шкодува́ти	'begrudge' (+ dative of person)
Не шкоду́й мені́ грошє́й.	Don't begrudge me money.

(за)бракувáти	'be lacking', 'not have enough of' (+ dative of person)
Менí нічóго не бракýє.	I lack nothing.

6.4.7.1.1   Verbs governing both the accusative and the genitive

The use of the genitive case with a 'partitive' meaning (= 'some of' an object) was described in Chapter 2, but it is worth seeing again in the present context:

Шукáю папéру.	I'm looking for (some) paper.
Хóчеш кáви?	Do you want (some) coffee?
Тобí захотíлося кáви?	Would you like (some) coffee?

Whereas a plural form tends to be in the accusative, as in:

Ми варúли варéники.	We cooked/made some *varenyky*.

But occasionally one will encounter a genitive object where it has no partitive meaning, and such cases must simply be noted as they are found:

Він написáв листá.	He wrote the letter.

Here **Він написáв лист** would not be impossible, but the genitive is preferred. With a few verbs, the use of the genitive is preferred when the object refers to an abstract noun, a concept, or if it is non-specific or unknown:

Ми чекáли автóбуса	We were waiting for a bus, but:
Ми чекáли п'я́тий автóбус.	We were waiting for bus no. 5.
Вáня шýкає вчúтеля	Vanya is looking for a teacher, but:
Шýкає свогó вчúтеля.	He's looking for his teacher.
Хóчемо спокóю (мúру).	We want peace.

As a general rule of thumb, this will be the case for verbs of wanting, desiring, demanding, and wishing.

6.4.7.2   *Verbs governing the dative*

допомагáти, допомогтú	'help'
Допомóжеш менí?	Will you help me?
(по)вíрити	'believe'
Йомý не мóжна вíрити.	One cannot believe him.
(по)обіця́ти	'promise'
Син пообіця́в повернýтися додóму скóро.	(The) son promised to return home soon.
(с)подóбатися	'be pleasing', 'like'
Вам подóбається Украї́на?	Do you like Ukraine?
розповідáти, розповістú	'relate', 'tell a story'

Дідусь розповідав нам про старі часи.	Grandfather told us about the old days.
відповідати, відповісти	'answer'
Кожному учню треба відповідати вчителеві.	Every pupil must answer the teacher.
зава(д)жати, завадити	'pester', 'prevent', 'hinder'
Чому ти мені заважаєш?	Why are you bothering me?

6.4.7.3   Verbs governing the instrumental

(с)користуватися	'make use of', 'enjoy'
Користуємося усякими кпижками.	We use all sorts of books.
Ми користуємося життям.	We enjoy life.
займатися (imperfective in this meaning)	'be occupied with', 'engaged in'
Здорові діти займаються спортом.	Healthy children do sports.
виглядати (+ adjective)	'have the appearance of'
Він виглядає щасливим.	He looks happy.
(за)цікавитися	'be interested in'
Чи твоя дочка цікавиться музикою?	Is your daughter interested in music?

6.4.8   VERBS USED IN CONJUNCTION WITH PREPOSITIONS

Some verbs will occur only with prepositions at all times, while others can stand alone without an object (for example, **познайомитися** 'become acquainted', below, or **чекати** 'wait'). Still others can occur with an object with or without a preposition, involving a subtle change in meaning (compare the dative verb **вірити** above, but **вірити у** + A. below). The following list is far from complete, and is meant to supply examples only; a complete list would be many pages long; for example, one could theoretically include all verbs of motion ('going to' a place/person), which require the preposition pertaining to the object of the motion: i.e. **їхати до Києва, на станцію, до лісу**, and likewise. But the use of the preposition in these examples will always be a function of the noun and not the verb. Compare:

дивитися на + acc.	'look at', 'watch'
Дивись на неї!	Look at her!
чекати на + acc.	'wait for' (also possible without **на**)
На кого чекаєш?	For whom are you waiting?
листуватися з + instr.	'correspond with'
Петро листується з однією англійською дівчиною.	Petro is corresponding with a certain English girl.
натрапити на + acc.	'come upon' (by chance)

Детекти́в натра́пив на злочи́нця на ву́лиці.	The detective happened upon the criminal on the street.
обвинува́чувати кого́ у/в + loc.	'accuse someone of something'
Його́ обвинува́чували в цьо́му злочи́ні.	He was accused of this crime.
попроща́тися з + instr.	'say goodbye to'
Ми попроща́лися з на́шими нови́ми дру́зями.	We said goodbye to our new friends.
познайо́митися з + instr.	'become acquainted with'
В Ки́єві ми познайо́милися з украї́нськими журналі́стами.	In Kyiv we became acquainted with Ukrainian journalists.
телефонува́ти, дзвони́ти до + gen.	'phone', 'call'
Ти дзвони́ла до ба́тька?	Did you phone father?
вигляда́ти на + acc.	'look like' (+ noun)
Та ді́вчина вигляда́є на 25 ро́ків.	That girl looks like (she's) twenty-five.
залє́жати від + gen.	'depend on'
Економі́чний ро́звиток залє́жить від багатьо́х фа́кторів.	Economic growth depends on many factors.
(по)вози́тися з + instr.	'pay too much attention to'
Не ва́рто з ним вози́тися.	It's not worth making too much of him.
(по)ві́рити у + acc.	'believe in'
Хто з вас ві́рить у Бога?	Who of you believes in God?
(з)роби́тися з + instr.	'happen to (a person)'
Що з ним зроби́лося?	What happened to him?

6.5   VERBAL WORD FORMATION

In contrast to substantival word formation, verbal word formation is primarily prefixal in nature; suffixation is limited to the derivation of new imperfectives – and the number of suffixes is also limited. This is in stark contrast to substantival suffixation, which is extremely rich in its suffixal inventory. In the following sections we examine various prefixal formations (suffixation is treated in **6.2.3** as a function of the construction of new aspectual pairs, i.e. of imperfective derivation), as well as other word-formational phenomena.

6.5.1   PREFIXATION

The following is a complete list of Ukrainian verbal prefixes, together with their general meanings and examples; as in the description of substantival word formation, obviously foreign (such as Latin) prefixes are omitted. In many cases (especially shorter verbs) what was historically a prefix is no longer separable or perceived as a prefix; thus, verbs like **спасти́** 'save', 'preserve' will not be cited here. Where a given prefix will tend to require the presence of a particular preposition, the preposition will be provided. The reader will note that many prefixes can express the same basic meaning; the use of one prefix over another (for example, for the expression of 'inception of an action') will therefore often be a function of the verb with which it occurs. In the examples which follow, only one member of the aspectual pair is given; a prefixed verb can be either imperfective or perfective, but the imperfective member will usually be a derived (i.e. suffixed) form, as described in **6.2.3**. Many verbs can occur with a number of different prefixes, with no change in meaning; this feature – like multiple prefixation (**6.5.1.1**) – is characteristic of the richness of the language.

Prefix	Meaning	Examples	Meaning
в-/у- (+ в/у) see **у-** below	in, into	вбíгти	run into
		вхóдити	enter, walk into
ви- (+ з)	(motion) out of	вихóдити	go out, exit
		вúнести	carry out
		вúбити	beat, knock out
		вибирáти	select
	completion of an action	вúбілити	have made white
		вúголосити	have declared
від-, віді-, відо-	motion away from	відійтú	go away from
		віддалúти	remove, dismiss
		відколóти	cleave, chop off
		відірвáти	tear off
	completion, ending of an action (sometimes negative)	відгуляти	finish dancing
		відцвістú	finish blooming, wither
		відсидіти	sit out, for a certain time (e.g. **кáру** sentence)
	complete an action	віддавáти	give back
	in response, a reverse action	віддячити	be thankful, repay with gratitude
		відімстúти	avenge (oneself on)
	or: відомстúти		
до-, ді- (+ до)	reach, attain, get to	дійтú	reach (on foot)
		доїхати	reach (vehicle)
	bring an action to its end	дописáти	finish writing
		доварúти	cook sufficiently
	do more than required	доплатúти	pay extra
		докупúти	buy more (also: finish buying)

з-, зі-, із-, с-	completely use up	змилити	use up soap, soap up
(note variants			
as they are		зносити	wear out
encountered)	bring an action to	змерзнути	be chilled, frozen
	completion	зігріти	heat up
	motion from many	скликати	convoke, summon
	places to one,	звести	bring together
	join together	сходитися	come together
	motion downwards	зійти	descend
		скинути	throw down
	remove an object,	збрити	shave off
	cause to move	зрізати	cut off
	away		
за-	inception of an	засміятися	begin, burst out
	action		laughing
		замовкати	cease speaking (fall silent)
		заплакати	begin crying
	attain a result	заслужити	deserve
		заробити	gain, earn, merit
	cover an object	запудрити	powder
	with a material	забризкати	bespatter
(+ за)	movement in a	зайти	drop in (visit)
	particular	зайти за	go behind
	direction	завезти	take something to, drop off
	carry an action too	заговорити	tire out by talking
	far, overdo		(also: begin talking)
		заїздити	override (a horse)
на- (+ на)	motion onto	наскочити	jump upon
		наклеїти	paste onto
		нашити	sew on
	action indicating	набрати	gather in quantity
	quantity	наростити	grow in quantity
		намити	wash many things
	carry out an action	награвати	play casually
	to a minor extent	наспівувати	sing a bit, hum (or: sing much)
над-, наді-	addition of one	надбудувати	build onto, add
	element to another		
	action affecting an	надгризти	bite off (a bit)
	object only	над'їсти	eat a bit of
	partially		

	action incompletely developed	надхо́дити	draw near
	unexpected action	надісла́ти	send suddenly
		над'їхати	arrive suddenly
не- (rare)	negative	нездужа́ти	feel weak
недо-, неді-	incomplete action, not enough	недоспа́ти	not to sleep enough
		недоли́ти	not to pour enough
		недосоли́ти	not to salt enough
о-, об-, обі-	motion around	обхо́дити	go around
		обсіка́ти	cut around
		оббі́гати	run around
	direction past an object	обхо́дити	avoid, go past
		обмину́ти	pass by
	take an action to its end or completion, sometimes to excess	об'їсти	eat up
		обпоїти	make one drunk
	thoroughness of action indicated	обду́мати	deliberate
		обговори́ти	discuss (thoroughly)
пере-	motion across	перебі́гти	run across
		пересі́сти	change seats
	do an action again or differently	перероби́ти	do again
		переписа́ти	rewrite
	do to an excessive degree (undesired)	перегрі́ти	overheat
		пересоли́ти	oversalt
	division of an object into parts (two)	переколо́ти	split
		переруба́ти	cut through (in two)
	focus on length of time of an action	перезимува́ти	spend the winter
		перечека́ти	outwait, stay a while
		переси́діти	be sitting (too long)
	action encompassing all or a number of objects	переба́чити	see much
		перепро́бувати	taste everything
по-	beginning of an action	побі́гти	set off (running)
		поду́ти	give a puff
		піти́	set off
	completion of an action	поголи́ти	to have shaved
		подя́кувати	to thank (someone)

This prefix can also impart the meaning of 'for a little while', especially with verbs denoting a process of some kind. This use of **по-** is very common in Ukrainian; note the first example given, as **по-** can express both 'simple perfective action', as in the list above, and 'for a little while' (the meanings given refer here only to the perfective):

дзвони́ти	подзвони́ти	to ring a bell for a while
сиді́ти	посиді́ти	to sit for a while
стоя́ти	постоя́ти	to stand for a while
говори́ти	поговори́ти	to have a chat
ми́гати	поми́гати	to twinkle for a while

Note that a stress shift to the left is possible in some verbs when **по-** is affixed to them; such forms should be noted as they are encountered.

під-, піді-, підо-	motion under or from under	підста́вити	place under
		підки́нути	throw under
		підня́ти	lift, pick up
	motion towards	підійти́	approach
		підплисти́	swim up to
	extra, additional action	підли́ти	pour a little more
		підмалюва́ти	touch up, colour more
	action in small amounts	підсо́хнути	dry up a little
		підхвали́ти	flatter a little
	surreptitious or secretive action	підмо́вити	incite, instigate
		підслу́хати	eavesdrop
пред- (rare)	various, generally = Eng. pre-	представити	present
при-	motion expressing arrival at a place	прийти́	arrive (on foot)
		принести́	bring (on foot)
		привезти́	bring (by vehicle)
	join things together or bring them near	прибудува́ти	build on, annex
		прив'яза́ти	bind together
	action expressing pressure on an object, downwards	придуши́ти	smother, press down
		причави́ти	squeeze down on
	direct an action towards oneself	призва́ти	summon, call to one
		примани́ти	allure, entice
	action partially completed	пригаси́ти	extinguish (partially)
		приглуши́ти	deaden noise (a little)

	additional or supplementary action	прива́ри́ти	cook a little more
		прикупи́ти	buy more (enough)
		приплати́ти	pay a little more
		приказа́ти	say a little more
	completion of an action	пригото́вити	make ready
		привчи́ти	train, accustom
		приду́мати	think up, invent
	action accompanying or adding to another	примовля́ти	repeat, add a word
		приспіва́ти	accompany with singing
про-, + через	action through	проби́ти	pierce
		проїхати	drive through
no preposition	action past	проїхати	go past, miss
		пробі́гти	run past
	action, duration or distance of which is specified	пройти́ сто ме́трів	go 100 metres
		прочека́ти рік	wait for a year
		просиді́ти годи́ну	be sitting for an hour
	completed action, covering its object in its entirety	прогрі́ти	heat thoroughly
		промасли́ти	cover with butter
		просоли́ти	salt thoroughly
роз-, розі-	action directed in a variety of directions	розда́ти	distribute
		розійти́ся	be dispersed, go different ways
		розподіли́ти	distribute, deal out
	separate or break apart an object	розби́ти	break, smash
		розрі́зати	cut into pieces
	annul a previous action	розв'яза́ти	unbind, untie
		розморо́зити	unfreeze, thaw
	take an action to its conclusion, do completely	розбуди́ти	awaken, rouse
		розквітнути	be in full bloom
		роз'ясни́ти	explain (fully)
		розрахува́ти	calculate thoroughly
	action carried out intensively, too much (rarer)	розхвали́ти	praise (too) much
с: see з above			
спів- (rare)	co-	співчува́ти	commiserate, sympathize

у- (see в- above), уві-	motion away from (rare)	утекти́	flee, run away
		усу́нути	push away, remove
	action encompassing an object in total	укута́ти	wrap up
		устели́ти	cover, spread with
	achieve a result	умо́вити	persuade, convince
		утихнути	become silent
	reduce or lessen by action or motion into an object	увари́ти	boil or stew down
		утягти́	pull or draw in
		увіхо́дити	enter

6.5.1.1 Multiple prefixation

Ukrainian differs to a certain extent from a cognate language such as Russian in the productivity of multiple prefixation, particularly involving the prefix по-. Here we shall focus on the formations попо- and по- + other prefixes: the former can express either greater or lesser intensity of an action (or 'enough' of), while the latter generally express a greater intensity of an action (or numbers of persons or things involved), no matter what the second prefix is. All of these formations are perfective.

It is interesting to note that по-, when added to another по-, annuls the sense of 'a little bit', 'for a little while' that по- on its own can impart; other prefixes generally retain their original meaning, especially when they express spatial motion or position.

попо-

попоби́ти	beat a great deal
попоноси́ти	carry around for a long time, carry many things
попої́сти	eat a lot, have a large meal
попоговори́ти	converse for a long time
попому́чити	torment much
попослужи́ти	serve a long time
попоси́діти	sit for a long time (compare поси́діти above)
попостоя́ти	stand around for a long time (compare постоя́ти above)
попопроси́ти	beg or ask much

пов-

повмуро́вувати	wall up in many places
повстава́ти	Many people stand up.
повто́млюватися	Many become tired out.
повхо́дити	Many enter, one after another.
повтиха́ти	Many fall silent.

пови-

повибіга́ти	many come running out
повиверта́ти	overturn one thing after another
повиві́трювати	air out many places
повиміта́ти	sweep out everything
повислу́хувати	listen to many people, one after another

повід-

повідлуча́ти	separate things one after another
повідпливати	many sail away
повідпи́сувати	answer many people in writing
повідліта́ти	many fly away, one after another
повідбіга́ти	many run away one after another

подо-

подомі́рювати	finish measuring many things
подоно́сити	carry many things to a certain place
подопіка́ти	finish baking many things
подосіва́ти	sow everything, finish sowing
подокупля́ти	buy things one after another, finish buying

поз-

позлива́ти	pour together from many containers
поздава́ти	give back many things, in turn
поз'їжджа́тися	arrive in vehicles from all directions
позніма́ти	take down many things one after another
позрі́зувати	cut off many things

поза-

позалива́ти	submerge, inundate many things
позаклика́ти	call in everyone one after another
позано́сити	carry everything to a certain place in turn
позара́жувати	infect many with an infectious disease
позасила́ти	send away or exile many

пона-

понабіга́ти	come running together in crowds
понабува́ти	acquire many things, provide shoes for many
понаво́дити	bring many people to a place
понагото́влювати	cook many dishes, cook much
понаклада́ти	lay much upon, impose heavily
поналіта́ти	come flying together in great numbers
понано́сити	bring many things, pile up
понаріка́ти	complain for a long time
понахо́дити	find, recover many things, come in large numbers

поо-, пооб-

пообставля́ти	place many things all around
поопуска́ти	let down, abandon many one after another
поосмі́ювати	scorn many
поосві́тлювати	light up, illuminate all over
поочища́ти	clean many things, purge many

попере-

поперев'я́зувати	bind, tie around many things
попередава́ти	hand over, transmit many things
попереказувати	retell to many
поперепи́сувати	rewrite many things or much material
поперехо́дити	many walk across, go over

попід-

попідпира́ти	support, prop up many things
попідсіка́ти	hew or cut under many things (e.g. trees)
попідслу́хувати	overhear, eavesdrop on many
попідстила́ти	spread (e.g. a bedspread), strew many things
попідмовля́ти	incite, encourage, persuade many people

попри-

поприбіга́ти	many come running
поприганя́ти	drive, chase in one after another
поприліта́ти	many come/arrive by flying
поприпада́ти	many fall down (upon)
поприхо́дити	many arrive from several directions

попро-

попрочища́ти	clean many things thoroughly
попрої́дати	eat through many things
попрокида́тися	wake up one after another

пороз-

порозво́дити	lead to various places
порозбіга́тися	run off in different directions
пороздво́юватися	divide many things in two

6.5.1.2 Prefixed verbs + -ся

Most prefixed verbs with the suffix -ся are the intransitive or reflexive/ reciprocal partners of the same verbs without -ся, as in накри́ти 'cover' – накрива́тися 'be covered'. However, constructions involving a specific set of prefixes + -ся can impart additional semantic nuances; in particular, this primarily involves the prefixes на-, до-, and за-. Note that not all of the resulting verbs are strictly intransitive, even though they are marked by the presence of -ся (for example, добудитися below); these verbs can be of either aspect, but only one member of each aspectual pair is given below as an example.

на-ся action to the point of saturation

нагулятися	have a long walk (sometimes too long)
наїжджатися	have enough of driving/riding
наїдатися	eat one's fill
напитися	drink one's fill, drink too much
наговоритися	talk to satiety, be talked out
намахатися	do much hard work, shake (something) to the point of weariness
набігатися	tire oneself out by running

до-ся action achieved requiring great effort; action carried out until a result is achieved (where not strictly transitive, with the preposition до)

додзвонитися	ring the bell until one answers, (negative) ring in vain
дограватися	playing until . . ., with emphasis on the process
дозватися	call until one is answered (perseverance of the action is emphasized here)
добудитися	succeed in waking one up
докупитися	(neg.) 'No matter how hard one tries, it is impossible to buy X' (i.e. cannot afford to buy X).
допитатися	enquire after, succeed in finding after enquiries
дослужуватися	serve until . . ., achieve promotion by serving one's time

за-ся complete involvement in an action

задуматися	be lost, absorbed in thought
заграватися	be thoroughly engaged in playing, play too long
заговоритися	talk so long that one loses track (e.g. of the subject)
зачитатися	be thoroughly engrossed in reading
заслухатися	listen attentively, with pleasure
запитися	be given to drinking, drinking to excess
заповзятися (+ за)	undertake a task seriously
запрацюватися	work oneself to death

6.5.2 VERB FORMATION FROM OTHER PARTS OF SPEECH

Verbs can be formed from substantival and adjectival roots; the majority of such new verbs have been present in the language for a very long time, therefore the processes at work cannot be seen as active or productive. In the generation of verbs from substantival bases the essential suffix used is:

-увати/-ювати

It is clearly productive, and (as seen earlier) it is prominent in the formation of derived imperfectives as well; an apparent extended suffix **-изувати/-ізувати** is not a productive formant on its own, but reflects a stem in **-из-/-із-** present in borrowings from other languages – and these will be verbs in the source languages. Compare the following (note the stress pattern, which is regularly at the end of the suffix):

перефразува́ти
характеризува́ти
поляризува́ти
конкретизува́ти
ідеалізува́ти
аналізува́ти
канонізува́ти

The sources of these are obviously Western: compare 'characterize', 'polarize', 'analyse', 'canonize', and similar. The suffix **-увати** is of course not limited to borrowings, as the following verbs, based on native Ukrainian/Slavonic roots, show:

панува́ти	reign, govern	«	**пан** sir, lord (desubst.)
спрямува́ти	direct, show the way	«	**прям-** direct, straight (deadj.)
членува́ти	dissect, analyse	«	**член** limb, member (desubst.)
районува́ти	divide into districts	«	**райо́н** district (desubst.)
марнува́ти	waste, dissipate	«	**марн-** useless, empty (deadj.)
чарува́ти	bewitch, enchant	«	**чар** charm, spell (desubst.)
столярува́ти	be a joiner, carpenter	«	**сто́ляр** carpenter (desubst.)
голосува́ти	vote	«	**го́лос** voice (desubst.)

For substantival roots, then, it is **-увати/-ювати** that is used in the formation of new verbs; for adjectives (alongside the occasional form with **-увати**) a variety of other suffixes can occur, including **-і-ти, -и-ти, -ну-ти, -а-ти**. Of these, **-і-ти** and **-и-ти** are the most productive suffixes and they have very specific functions: the former expresses intransitivity, while the latter expresses the corresponding transitive notion; both can occur with the same base form, as seen in the second group of examples below. The suffix **-ати** is semantically neutral, while **-нути** (also intransitive) may express some limitation in time, analogous to the 'one-time' notion found in perfective **-ну-** verbs; in deadjectival formations the suffix can occur in imperfective verbs as well. Note that **-іти**-verbs are Conjugation I (**-ію, ієш,** and similar) and **-ити**-verbs are Conjugation II (**-ю, -иш,** and so on); both suffixes are almost always stressed. Compare:

хворі́ти	be ill		
блі́днути	turn pale		
дешеві́ти	fall in price, become cheap(er)		
старі́ти	grow old (less commonly, but also **старі́тися**)		

зелені́ти	look green, turn green	– зелени́ти	make, paint green
білі́ти	become white, turn pale	– біли́ти	whiten, bleach
червоні́ти	grow red, blush	– червони́ти	make red, dye red
збідні́ти	become impoverished	– збідни́ти	make poor, impoverished
холоді́ти	grow cold, freeze	– холоди́ти	cool, freeze, make cold
тверді́ти (= тве́рднути)	become hard, solid	– тверди́ти	harden, temper iron
		тве́рдити	affirm, assert
зазолоті́ти (по-)	be, become gilded, golden in colour	– зазолоти́ти	gild, make golden in colour

(Note: **зазолоти́тися = зазолоті́ти**)

As the last example shows, the suffix **-іти** is close in function and meaning to the element **-ся**; but the deadjectival **-іти/-ити** correlation is more common than the **-ити/-итися** type.

Such processes as compounding, compounding incorporating abbreviations, and the like, are not a factor in verbal word formation; compounds can be the basis of new verbs, but these will involve processes already noted above.

7 THE ADVERB AND ADVERBIAL CONSTRUCTIONS

7.0 GENERAL

The term 'adverb' encompasses many lexical items and constructions that may not immediately be identified as an adverb by the student of any given language. The term is first and foremost applied to words (adjectival in origin) that modify verbs (and adjectives), as opposed to adjectives, which modify nouns: 'He spoke *quietly*', 'We wrote *clearly*'. An entire range of forms is added to this basic adverbial group, forms which in some way or other describe or set the stage for an action; this includes expressions of time (when?), place (where?), manner (how?), and the like. Each of these sets of forms is listed in the following sections. The use of the adverb is described in brief (with examples) where this is not immediately clear; two particular sets of forms that receive more in-depth treatment are those of (i) time expressions (excluding formations involving numerals such as dates and years, which are treated in Chapter 5), and (ii) modal and impersonal expressions; the latter are described here because many of them are centred upon adverbs or adverb-like elements.

7.1 DEADJECTIVAL ADVERBS: FORMATION

Adverbs formed from hard-stem adjectives end primarily in -o, although a small group is characterized by the ending -e (identical in form to the neuter N.*sg.* adjectival ending):

добре	well
задобре	too well
зле	badly
дешево	cheaply
швидко	quickly
високо	highly, greatly
широко	widely
весело	happily
виразно	clearly, distinctly
чисто	cleanly
глухо	dully
вузько	narrowly

The majority of adjectives in -ний will occur with the marker -o, although a few may be found with both -o and -e, with no change in meaning:

дрíбно	minutely, in detail
пéвно	certainly, surely, probably
рíвно	straight, evenly, equally
склáдно	with difficulty
очевúдно	evidently
вирáзно	distinctly
дарéмно	in vain, vainly
таємно	secretly, mysteriously
щодéнно	daily
неодмíнно	without fail
закóнно	legally, according to the law
неймовíрно	improbably
умúсно	intentionally
елегáнтно	elegantly
смíшно	comically

but also:

пéвне
дарéмне
умúсне
конéчне

Adverbs formed from the few soft-stem adjectives also occur with -o, with the softness of the preceding consonant expressed in writing by means of the soft sign:

достáтній – достáтньо	abundantly, plentifully
серéдньо	pertaining to the middle
самобýтньо	originally
худóжньо	artistically
могýтньо	mightily

7.1.1   USE OF THE DEADJECTIVAL ADVERB

As a rule, the adverb in -o or -e occurs before the verb which it is modifying unless special emphasis is required (for example, with imperatives or in questions), in which case it may occur as the last element of a statement:

Він *погáно* грáє на скрúпці.
He plays the violin badly.

Бáтько *дóбре* говóрить пóльскою (мóвою).
Father speaks Polish well.

But:

Будь ла́ска, говорі́ть *повільно*!
Please speak slowly!

Чи діду́сь поверне́ додо́му *пі́зно*?
Is grandfather returning home late?

7.1.2 'IT' IS . . . – IMPERSONAL CONSTRUCTIONS

The adverb by itself (that is, when not modifying a verb) can express a state or condition that is expressed in English by means of the pleonastic 'it':

Тут тепло́.	It's warm here.
Сього́дні хо́лодно.	It's cold today.
Вже пі́зно – поспіша́й!	It's already late – hurry!
Ва́рто пам'ята́ти, що . . .	It's worth remembering that . . .
До́бре, що ти прийшо́в.	It's good that you came.
ду́же приє́мно!	very pleased (to meet you)! (lit. 'It is very pleasing . . .')

This use of the adverb may be termed 'impersonal', as there is no subject involved; when a person is indicated, however, the one to whom reference is made will occur in the dative case:

Мені́ хо́лодно.	I'm cold (lit. 'It is cold to me').
Йому́ (ба́тькові) жа́рко.	He's (father's) hot.
Нам усі́м ду́же приє́мно . . .	We are all very pleased . . .
Ва́лі тя́жко на се́рці.	Valya's heart is heavy.
Мені́ ціка́во.	I am interested, curious.

7.1.3 NUMERICAL ADVERBS

Adverbs can be formed from numerals as well, in particular from the ordinal numerals, which are adjectival in form. Note that these consist of the numeral + the formant -е; the basic adverb will have a hyphenated prefix по- ('-ly'), while the prefix у- imparts the sense 'for the Xth time':

по-пе́рше	firstly, in the first place
упе́рше	for the first time, firstly
по-дру́ге	in the second place, secondly, after all
удру́ге	for the second time
по-тре́тє	thirdly, in the third place
утре́тє	for the third time
по-четве́рте	fourthly, in the fourth place
учетве́рте	for the fourth time
по-п'я́те	fifthly, in the fifth place
уп'я́те	for the fifth time

Adverbs can also be formed from the collective numerals by means of prefixation alone; in other words, their final vowel is not an adverbial marker, but merely the same vowel that occurs at the end of the original collective form. Note that after 'four', it is only the prefix **y-** that will occur in the standard language.

вдво́є (у-)	twice more, double, twofold
на́двоє	in two
втро́є (у-)	three times as much, triply/trebly
на́тро́є	in three ways, in three parts
вче́тверо (у-)	fourfold, four times as much
нача́тверо	in four parts, in four ways
вп'я́теро (у-)	fivefold, five times as much
вше́стеро (у-)	sixfold, six times as much

7.2 ADVERBS OF LOCATION

Adverbs of location indicate 'where?', 'place in, to' , and 'from'; this category, as is also the case with adverbs of time (**7.3**), includes primary (non-derived) adverbs and a large number of derived, or secondary, formations. Such derived forms are by and large composed of prefixal elements + base nouns; as the prefixes were originally prepositions, these adverbs are often marked by the presence of a case ending corresponding to the original preposition (commonly the genitive or locative, but where 'motion to' is indicated, the accusative). Among other formations we find an original noun in the instrumental case; whatever the original case form, the new construction is fossilized as an adverb and as such is invariable; compare the same phenomenon among conjunctions (**8.0**).

7.2.1 INTERROGATIVES

де?	where?
куди́?	to where (whither)?
зві́дки, зві́дкіль, відкіля́, звідкіля́?	from where (whence)?

7.2.2 STATEMENTS OF LOCATION

там	there
та́мки, та́мечки, та́меньки	there (dim. of **там**, coll.)
ота́м	there, down there
тут, ту́та	here
ту́тенька, ту́течка, ту́теньки, ту́течки	= **тут** (dim.)
ту́тка, ту́тки	= **тут** (dial.)

о́тут (отту́т)	right here
оту́течки	right here (dim. о́тут)
ось, ось тут	over here, here is/are
он, он там	over there, there is/are
о́нде, о́ндечки,	there, over there
туди́	to there (thither)
сюди́	to here (hither)
куди́	to where (whither)
скрізь	everywhere
усю́ди	everywhere
і́нде	elsewhere
ві́дси, відсі́ль, відсіля́, зві́дси	from here
ві́дти, відті́ль, відтіля́, зві́дти, звідта́м, звідті́ль, звідтіля́	from there
ві́дки, відкі́ль, відкіля́, зві́дки, звідкі́лъ, звідкіля́	from where
вгорі́	above, on top
вго́ру	upwards
згори́	from above
догори́	up there, upwards
внизу́	at the bottom, downstairs
вниз	downwards
зни́зу	from below
дони́зу	down, down below
здо́лу (rare)	= зни́зу
зве́рху	from above
дове́рху	up, up above
зза́ду	from behind, behind
з-поза́ду	from behind
зви́сока	from up high
спе́реду	before, in front
спере́д	out of, from, from under
удо́ма, до́ма*	at home
додо́му	homewards, to home

*до́ма is seen by some informants as a Russianism, but it is present in the 1997 orthographic dictionary.

влі́во	to, on the left
впра́во	to, on the right
право́руч	to, on the right (side)
ліво́руч	to, on the left (side)
навко́ло	round, around, all around
по всіх усю́дах	all over
з усіх усю́д (усю́дів)	from everywhere

7.2.3   INDEFINITES

Forms containing the elements **-сь**, **-будь-**, **-небудь** are structurally and semantically the same as the corresponding indefinite pronouns, in which these elements express 'some-' and 'any-' (compare the indefinite pronouns in **4.5.2**).

десь	somewhere (secondary meaning: probably, likely)
десь інде	somewhere else
десь-не-десь	somewhere or other
де-небудь	anywhere, somewhere
будь-де	everywhere, wherever . . .
де-не-де, де-де	here and there
кудись	to somewhere
куди-небудь	to anywhere
подекуди	here and there, somewhere (secondary meaning: partly, somewhat)

7.2.4   NEGATIVES

Negative adverbs are marked by the addition of the prefix **ні-** to the positive adverb; note the retraction of stress in the second example, *viz.* **куди – нікуди**.

ніде	nowhere
нікуди	(motion) to nowhere, to no place
нізвідки, нізвідкіль, нізвідкіля, нівідкіль	from nowhere
Ніде	There is nowhere (to do X).
Нікуди	There is nowhere to go.
нівідкіль	there is no place from which . . .

The place of stress is crucial in these forms, as initial stress upon the negative prefix adds the notion of a 'lack' of something to the base adverb (compare also **7.3.4**).

7.3   ADVERBS OF TIME AND TIME EXPRESSIONS

Adverbs and adverbial constructions indicating the time frame in which an action takes place are termed 'adverbs of time'. Note below the large number of derived formations (both compounds and diminutive, expressive forms), as is the case with adverbs of location.

7.3.1 INTERROGATIVES OF TIME

коли́?	when?
до́ки?	until when?
відко́ли?	how long since?
звідко́ли?	since when?

Entire phrases may function adverbially in the same way, thus we can include the following (compare the same phenomenon among statements of time, **7.3.2**):

з яко́го ча́су?	since when?
по яки́й час?	until which time?

7.3.2 STATEMENTS OF TIME

7.3.2.1 General

тепе́р, тепе́ра	now
отепе́р, отепе́рки	at present
тепе́рка, -ки, -енька, -ечка, -еньки, -ечки, -ісінько, -ісічко	just now (coll., dim. of тепе́р)
за́раз	now, at the moment, at once
ни́ні	today, this day
тоді́, отоді́	then
давно́	long ago
і́ноді, і́нколи	sometimes
нега́йно	immediately
за́вжди́	always
наза́вжди	for ever
все	always, all the time, ever
ча́сто	often
рі́дко, ма́ло коли́, не ча́сто	seldom
по́тім	then, afterwards
скрізь	continually, always
незаба́ром	soon
вча́сно	on time, in time
вре́шті, наре́шті	at last
щойно, допі́ру, ті́льки що, ті́льки-но	just now (as in: 'X just happened')
ще ні	not yet
все ще	still
ось-ось	at any moment, imminently

7.3.2.2   The day

вдень	by day, during the day
вночі	at night
вранці	in the morning
ввечері, звечора	in the evening
день поза день	day after day, one day after another
що другий день	every other day
щодня, кожного дня, щоденно, щодень	every day, daily
що два дні, кожні два дні	every two days
щоранку, кожного ранку	every morning
щоніч	every night, nightly
щовечір, щовечора	every evening
за дня	by daylight
з дня на день	from day to day
цими днями	these days, some of these days
одного дня	once, one day
цілими днями	day in and day out
сьогодні	today
вчора	yesterday
завтра	tomorrow
позавчора	the day before yesterday
позавтра, післязавтра	the day after tomorrow
удосвіта	before, at dawn
надвечір	towards evening

7.3.2.3   The seasons, year ('this', 'last', 'next')

улітку, уліті	in the summer
взимку	in the winter
восени, увосени (coll.)	in the autumn
на весні	in the spring
торік	last year
щорік, кожного року	every year, yearly, annually
щомісяця, кожного місяця, тижня	every month/week, monthly/weekly
цього року, місяця, тижня	this year, month, week
наступного року, місяця, тижня	next year, month, week
минулого року, місяця, тижня	last year, month, week
за/через день, місяць, рік	in (after) a day, month, year

Note, as seen in **5.2**, that the expression of 'the/in the year X' is simply the ordinal numeral in the nominative or locative, respectively.

7.3.2.4 Days of the week, months of the year

The days of the week and names of the months are, strictly speaking, nouns (with the exception of one month, which is adjectival); however, when saying that X happened 'on day Y' or 'in month Z', such phrases belong in the same category as the adverbs of time, as they answer the question 'when?' For days of the week the preposition **у** is used with the accusative case, while for months it is **у** with the locative; note that **лютий** 'February' is the lone adjectival form in this set of words:

Days of the Week			Months of the Year		
Time	*Time When*		*Time*	*Time When*	
понеділок	у понеділок	(Mon.)	січень	у січні	(Jan.)
вівторок	у вівторок	(Tue.)	лютий	у лютому	(Feb.)
середа	у середу	(Wed.)	березень	у березні	(March)
четвер	у четвер	(Thur.)	квітень	у квітні	(April)
п'ятниця	у п'ятницю	(Fri.)	травень	у травні	(May)
субота	у суботу	(Sat.)	червень	у червні	(June)
неділя	у неділю	(Sun.)	липень	у липні	(July)
			серпень	у серпні	(Aug.)
			вересень	у вересні	(Sep.)
			жовтень	у жовтні	(Oct.)
			листопад	у листопаді	(Nov.)
			грудень	у грудні	(Dec.)

7.3.2.5 Miscellaneous

часом, часами	sometimes, by chance
давніми часами	in olden times, in times past
одного часу	once, once upon a time
тим часом	in the meantime, meanwhile
згодом	later
здавна	long ago, formerly
здавен-давна	from distant times
віддавна	for a long time (already)
донині	until now
зроду, зроду-віку	ever, in all one's life
миттю	instantly
надалі	henceforward
поки що	for the time being
спочатку	at first, in the beginning
поранéньку	very early in the morning
заздалегідь	in good time, beforehand
опісля	afterwards, hereafter, then

See **2.4.2.2.4** for other time expressions using the prepositions **в/у** and **на**.

7.3.3   INDEFINITES

Compare **7.2.3** above on the elements **-сь**, **-будь-**, and **-небудь** with adverbs of location.

коли-небудь	at any time, ever
коли́сь	some day or other, formerly, once
коли-бу́дь	whenever, at any time
коли́-не-коли́	at times, from time to time, seldom
бу́дь-коли	at any time
де-не-де́	now and then
де-не-коли́сь	only now and then
я́ко́сь	once (not long ago), the other day
поде́коли, де́коли	now and then, sometimes, at times

7.3.4   NEGATIVES

ніко́ли	never
Ні́коли	There is no time (to do X).

7.4   QUANTITATIVE ADVERBS (ADVERBS OF DEGREE)

Adverbs that are described as 'quantitative', or adverbs of degree, relate to the questions 'how much? how strongly?'; clearly the formations based on collective numerals (**втро́є**, and similar) could be included here, but they are not, as numerical adverbs deserve separate treatment.

скі́льки?	how much? (cf. **4.3.4** on the pronominal use of this form)
бага́то	much (of + gen.)
ма́ло	little (of + gen.)
чима́ло	a great deal (of + gen.)
бі́льш	more
ве́льми	very
деда́лі	ever more . . . (+ comparative)
до́сить	enough, sufficiently
ду́же	very, strongly
ду́жче	more strongly (comparative of ду́же)
здебі́льшого	mostly
зо́всім	quite
ле́две	hardly
ма́йже	almost
ма́ло не, ма́ло що не	almost, nearly
менш	less

на́дто	too much
сті́льки	so much, as much, so many
сті́льки … скі́льки …	so … as …, as … as …
ті́льки	only
тро́хи	a little, little
тро́шки	very little (diminutive of **тро́хи**)
тро́шечки	very little (diminutive of **тро́шки**)
чима́ло	quite a lot, considerably
чимра́з	ever more (+ comparative)
чим (бі́льше) тим (лі́пше)	the (more) the (better)

7.5   ADVERBS OF MANNER

Adverbs of 'manner' in part answer the question 'In what way is an action carried out?'; in this sense, they parallel the function of the deadjectival adverbs described in **7.1**. The two sets of forms differ in that (i) adverbs of manner consist of a small set of forms (whereas deadjectival adverbs can theoretically be formed from every adjective) and (ii) they are not generally deadjectival.

як? яки́м спо́собом? яки́м чи́ном?	how? in what manner?
так	thus
байду́же, байду́жно	indifferently
абия́к	somehow
ра́птом	suddenly
мо́вчки	silently
навми́сне	on purpose
дарма́, даре́мно, ма́рно	in vain, vainly
надаре́мно, надаре́мне	to no purpose
неда́рма, неда́ром	not in vain
да́ром, дарма́	gratis, free of charge
і́накше, іна́к	in a different way
ни́шком	quietly
гара́зд	skilfully, well
мимохі́ть	involuntarily
крадькома́	stealthily
босо́ніж	barefoot
спросо́ння	while asleep, in one's sleep
гурто́м	together, in common
по-ба́тьківськи, по-ба́тьківському	paternally, in a fatherly manner
по-на́шому, (по-ва́шому, and so on)	in our (your, and so on) manner, as we (you, likewise) do things
по-украї́нському, по-украї́нськи	in the Ukrainian manner (cf. **7.5.1**)

біго́м	running, at a run
заразо́м	simultaneously, all at once
тайко́м	secretly
цілко́м, цілкови́то	wholly, thoroughly, entirely
жартома́	in jest, in a joking manner
ве́рхи	on horseback

Ukrainian is particularly rich in adverbs of manner; it is not possible to list every form of this kind in the language, but the list above may be taken as more than representative.

7.5.1 'IN LANGUAGE X'

There are a number of ways of saying 'in Ukrainian', 'in English', and so on. Two of these are identical to the expressions 'in the Ukrainian manner' (p. 280):

по-украї́нському	in Ukrainian
по-украї́нськи	
по-англі́йському	in English
по-англі́йськи	

The two formations are described in some dictionaries and grammars as being interchangeable, although по-украї́нськи, and so on is especially common in areas with a strong Russian presence (as it is all but identical to the corresponding Russian expression). A more common alternative, currently growing in popularity (especially in new publications) is the feminine instrumental singular:

украї́нською	(where мо́вою 'language' is understood but not always
англі́йською	expressed)

7.5.2 INDEFINITES

A few indefinite adverbs of manner are found as well:

я́кось	somehow, in a manner unknown to the speaker
як-не́будь	in any manner, indifferently, carelessly
як-бу́дь	in any manner
будь-я́к	in any manner

7.6 ADVERBIALIZED GERUNDS AND PARTICIPLES

Present – or imperfective – gerunds, as described in Chapter 6, describe an action that is the setting for another action: 'While X was taking place, Y (and

Z) happened'. A few of these gerunds have been reanalysed as adverbs focusing not on the action, but on the position of the actor during another action. The three adverbs of this kind most commonly encountered are forms of сидíти 'sit', стоя́ти 'stand', and лежа́ти 'lie'; their identity as adverbs is a function (i) of stress, which is different from the place of stress in the gerund, and (ii) of their position in a sentence.

Gerund	Adverb
сидячи́	си́дячи
стоячи́	сто́ячи
лежачи́	лéжачи

Compare the following examples, in which the gerund occurs with a verbal adjunct, the adverb on its own; note that punctuation can reveal the difference as well – particularly when a sentence begins with the gerund clause.

Gerund: **Сидячи́ в крíслі, він читáв газéту.**
(While) sitting in an armchair, he read the newspaper.

Adverb: **Він читáв си́дячи.**
He read in a sitting position (seated).

Gerund: **Стоячи́ в чéрзі, вони́ розмовля́ли.**
(While) standing in a queue, they had a conversation.

Adverb: **Бáтько ви́пив кáву сто́ячи.**
Father drank up (his) coffee standing up (in a standing position).

Gerund: **Óльга слýхала рáдіо лежачи́ на дивáні.**
Ol'ha listened to the radio (while) lying on the sofa.

Adverb: **Не їж лéжачи!**
Don't eat in a lying position/lying down!

A very few present active participles have also been adverbialized by affixing the grammatical marker -e; thus:

рішýче	decisively, decidedly
бóлячé	painfully, aching
терпля́че	patiently, with patience
нетерпля́че	impatiently

7.7 ADVERBIAL COMPARATIVES AND SUPERLATIVES

Comparative and superlative forms of adjectives can be used adverbially in the form of the nominative singular neuter (compare **3.2.1** and **3.2.2**); they are used as one would use any other deadjectival adverb:

кра́ще	better
найкра́ще	best
ра́ніше	earlier, former
скорі́ше	more quickly
найскорі́ше	most quickly
гірше, згі́рше	worse
бі́льше-ме́нше	more or less
найда́льше	farthest
наймерзенні́ше	most despicably
холодні́ше	colder, more coldly
ясні́ше	more clearly
мі́цніше	more strongly, more firmly
щонайсильні́ше	in the strongest way possible
якнайшви́дше	with the greatest speed possible
якнайкра́ще	in the best way possible

Forms based on comparatives or superlatives with the formant **-іше** can occur without final **-e**, although the full form is preferred with most adjectives; compare:

частí́ш	more often
згі́рш	worse
скорí́ш	more quickly
ранí́ш	earlier, former
бі́льш-менш	more or less

7.8 ADVERBIAL MODAL CONSTRUCTIONS (NECESSITY, OBLIGATION, POSSIBILITY)

A number of crucial forms that can be described as adverbial in nature have to do with expressing the need, obligation, or possibility of carrying out an action. These forms (few in number but central to the language) are used in impersonal constructions, as described in **7.1**; in other words, they are used without a subject, but when the person involved is present in the sentence, that form will occur in the dative case. The words are:

Тре́ба.	One must; it is necessary.
Потрі́бно.	It is necessary.
Слід.	One must, ought; it is necessary, worth . . .
Необхі́дно.	It is absolutely necessary.
Мо́жна.	One can, may.
Не мо́жна.	One cannot, may not.
Можли́во.	It is possible (physically); (secondary meaning: perhaps, possibly).
Неможли́во.	It is impossible (physically).

Examples:

Нам тре́ба (потрі́бно) нега́йно відпові́сти на його́ запита́ння.
We must answer his question immediately.

Студе́нтам слід запи́сувати все, що говори́ть виклада́ч.
Students are supposed to (must) write down everything the lecturer says.

Слу́хай, необхі́дно (тобі́) повідо́мити поліце́йського про цей ви́падок.
Listen, it is absolutely necessary (for you) to inform the policeman about this accident.

Ви́бачте, чи мо́жна тут кури́ти? На жа́ль, не мо́жна.
Excuse me, is one allowed to smoke here? Unfortunately it's not allowed.

Чи мо́жна мені́ піти́ додо́му до кінця́ ле́кції?
May I go home before the end of the lecture?

Можли́во, (що) піде́ дощ.
It is possible that it will rain (perhaps it will rain).

Неможли́во відчини́ти две́рі.
It is impossible to open the door (it's stuck, locked, . . .).

To express obligation it is also possible to use the adjectival form **пови́нен** (masc.), **пови́нна** (fem.), **пови́нні** (*pl.*) with the person in the nominative:

Я пови́нен (був), вона́ пови́нна (була́), вони́ пови́нні (були́) це зроби́ти.
I, she, they ought to do (to have done) this.

See also **6.4.1.3.1** on expressions of this kind involving verbs (especially in conjunction with the infinitive).

7.9 OTHER INTERROGATIVE ADVERBS; 'YES', 'NO', 'NOT'

A few remaining interrogative adverbs do not fit easily into the categories described above; they are:

чому́, чого́, по́що?	why?
наві́що?	what for?
Хіба́?	. . . really? Is it the case that . . .? (not in questions: unless, except)
Невже́?	Is it possible that . . .? indeed?
чи?	interrogative particle: whether

The last three listed might also be described as interrogative particles rather than as adverbs; compare Chapter 8 on the use of some of these forms as conjunctions.

Note particularly that **чи** has two functions: as a conjunction it can express 'or'; as an adverbial form it introduces a question, as in **Чи мо́жна мені́ піти́** ... in **7.8**. In one and the same sentence, unless it is a clear case of 'either ... or ...', the first **чи** introduces a question while the second is the conjunction *or* in tag questions:

Не зна́ю, чи він бу́де вдо́ма/до́ма сього́дні.
I don't know if (whether or not) he will be home today.

Чи бу́деш працюва́ти за́втра, чи ні?
Are you going to work tomorrow, or not (lit, 'no')?

'YES', 'NO', 'NOT'

так	yes
ні	no
не	not

Note particularly that the adverbial **ні** 'no' should not be confused with the conjunction meaning 'neither ... nor' (compare Chapter 8). As the last example cited above shows, care must be taken when translating **ні**, as it is better translated as 'not' in some contexts.

8 THE CONJUNCTION

8.0 GENERAL

Conjunctions may be defined as: forming a '[c]losed lexical category, or a lexical item belonging to this category, whose members serve to construct coordinate structures, such as "and", "or" and "but" in English' (Trask 1993: 56). In this grammar, however, we retain the traditional approach, including conjunctions, or 'subordinators', which introduce subordinate clauses. Conjunctions thus cover a rather diffuse area, from linking elements of simple sentences to linking the clauses of composite sentences.

In other words, they are used to convey the coordination of parts of the clause and of separate clauses, and to convey the subordination of one clause to another. They may be:

(i) simple, for example,

і (й) and	**а** and, but
бо because, for	**що** that
та and	**(а)ні́** neither/nor, and not
чи or (also question particle)	**як** how, that

(ii) compound, for example,

щоб so that	**проте́** therefore, from (what) reason, but, besides
якщо́ if	**ні́би** as if
або́ or	**зате** instead, moreover, however

(iii) composite, for example,

че́рез те́ що since, because	**незважа́ючи на те́ що** in spite of the fact that
для то́го щоб in order to/that	**подібно до то́го як** like
тому́ що because	

COORDINATING CONJUNCTIONS EITHER

(i) correlate, for example,

і (й) and	**та** and
тако́ж also, too	**як . . . так і . . .** both . . ., and . . .
(а)ні́ . . . (а)ні́ . . . neither . . ., nor . . .	**не ті́льки . . . а й . . .** not only . . ., but also . . .

же and, but

(also emphatic, enclitic (after first accent-bearing element), many interpretations and in combination with various other particles)

(ii) contrast, for example,

а but	**алé** but
та but	**проте́** but
зате́ but	**одна́к** but, still, however, or

(iii) separate, for example,

або́ or	**чи** or
або́ . . . або́ . . . either . . ., or . . .	**чи . . . чи . . .** either . . ., or . . .

SUBORDINATING CONJUNCTIONS MAY BE

(i) causal, for example,

тому́ що because	**тим що** because, since
че́рез те́ що because, since	**бо** for
оскі́льки (in)sofar as	**у зв'язку́ з тим що** since, in connection with . . .

(ii) temporal, for example,

як and	**в мíру то́го як** as, in proportion as
як тíльки as soon as	**як лиш** as soon as
що́йно as soon as, hardly	**тíльки но** hardly, just, no sooner . . .
ско́ро when, if, as soon as	**коли́** when
відкóли since	**до́ки . . . не** until
по́ки while, as long as	**по́ки . . . не** until
перед ти́м як before	**пiсля́ то́го як** after
з то́го ча́су як since	

(iii) spatial, for example,

де where	**куди́** (to) where, whither
звíдки from where, whence	

(iv) conditional, for example,

як if	**якщо́** if
коли́ if	**коли́ б** if only
якби́ if, if only	**раз** if

(v) purposive (= aim), for example,

шо́б(и) so that	**для то́го щоб** in order that
з тим щоб so that	**зати́м щоб** so that
аби́ in order that, so that	

(vi) comparative, for example,

як as, since	що as
(не)мо́в as if, as it were	немо́вби as if, as it were
на́че(бто) as if, as it were	ні́би as if
нена́че as if, as though	бу́цім би/бу́цім то/бу́цім би то as if

(vii) consequential, for example,

так що so that

(viii) concessive, for example,

хоч/хоча́ although	хай let
неха́й let	дарма́ що although
незважа́ючи на те́ що despite, in spite of the fact that	

(ix) explanatory, for example,

то́бто that is	се́бто that is
а са́ме that is, in other words	

to which we may add the general subordinator що 'that' and the relatives який and що.

We may also add the markers of indirect speech, namely що 'that', чи 'yes/no' interrogative particle, and all the various question words, some of them already listed above and elsewhere, for example,

хто who	що́ what
чий whose	чому́/навіщо/по́що why
коли́ when	де where
куди́ where (to)	зві́дки where from (and many other variants)

Subordinating conjunctions may also occur in pairs (like coordinating conjunctions), for them one in the main clause and the other in the subordinate clause, for example,

чим + comparative . . ., тим + comparative . . . the x-er . . ., the x-er . . .
дарма́ що/хоч . . ., а(ле́) . . . although . . ., . . .
ті́льки . . ., як . . . hardly . . ., than . . .
який . . ., такий . . . like . . ., like . . .
як . . ., так . . . since/as . . ., (thus) . . .
коли́ . . ., тоді́ . . . when . . ., (then) . . .
де . . ., там . . . where . . ., (there)
відкіля́ . . ., відтіля́ . . . from where, (from there) . . .
не ті́льки . . ., але́ й/а й/а тако́ж/а на́віть . . . not only . . ., but also/even . . .
(о)скі́льки . . ., (о)сті́льки . . . insofar as . . .
якщо́ . . ., то . . . if . . ., (then) . . .

The pairs may be repetitions, for example,

і . . ., і . . . both . . ., and . . .	то . . ., то . . . now . . ., now . . .
або . . ., або . . . either . . ., or . . .	чи . . ., чи . . . either . . ., or . . .

8.1   USING CONJUNCTIONS

Essentially, the elements are simply linked, though we have the opportunity to see something more interesting in the relative clause.[12]

From the point of view of the written language, a major consideration can be punctuation. In publications there will be varied practices. In the simple sentence one uses the comma to link more than two elements and to link elements connected by repeated or paired conjunctions. In the composite sentence, a comma is the strict rule. An acceptable single rule is that, if the subordinate clause comes after the main clause, then the comma comes before the subordinating conjunction (including when it is composite); alternatively, where the subordinator is composite, the comma may precede the final component, namely що, щоб(и), як. If the composited conjunction is particularly 'large', it may even be recommended to precede both the final component and the entire conjunction by commas, as in:

Він ма́є ра́цію, *незважа́ючи на те́,* **що вона́ не зго́дна з ним.**
He's right, in spite of the fact that she doesn't agree with him.

Our main aim here is to give a few examples. We also occasionally give quite long sentences, simply to provide more data, even if we do not actually comment on it.

8.1.1   CONCATENATION

Coordination and subordination may be achieved simply by concatenating phrases and clauses, usually with the meaning, context, and intonation indicating the relations. A subordinate clause may have a gerund as verbal core. Here are a few examples:

Там сиді́ли ма́ма, ба́тько, ді́ти.
Mother, father, (and) the children were sitting there.

Вона́ підійшла́ до ме́не, вона́ хоті́ла порозмовля́ти зі мно́ю.
She came up to me, (because?) she wanted to have a chat with me.

Я взяв підру́чник, ви́йшов з поме́шкання, пішо́в до університе́ту.
I took my textbook, went out of the flat, (and?) set off to the university.

Вони́ залюбки́ пої́хали до Льво́ва, проведу́ть там усього́ п'ять днів.
They eagerly set off to L'viv, (but?) will spend only five days there.

Знайшо́вши бра́та, Іва́н поверну́вся з ним додо́му.

Having found (= when/since/because he had found) his brother, Ivan returned home.

Зга́дуючи часи́ ві́льної Украї́ни, я роблю́ся тако́ю су́мною.

Recalling (= as/when I recall) the days of a free Ukraine, I become so sad.

Не переодягну́вшись, він сів пообі́дати.

He sat down to dinner without getting changed.

Не бажа́я працюва́ти в магази́ні в Ки́єві, вона́ поі́хала за кордо́н, ніко́му не сказа́вши ані́ сло́ва.

Not wishing (= because she didn't wish) to work in a shop in Kyiv, she set off abroad without a word to anyone.

(Note the obligatory genitive after the single, emphatic, **(а)ні** 'not a'.)

Маши́на не заво́дилась: бачо́к був поро́жнім.

The car wouldn't start – the tank was empty. (Shevchenko: 207)

8.1.2 COORDINATION WITH CONJUNCTIONS

8.1.2.1 *Within a single clause*

Here we use the coordinating conjunctions.

8.1.2.1.1 Correlation: і (й), та, (а)ні́, and so on

Ма́ма й та́то, брат і сестра́.

Mum and dad, brother and sister.

Пта́шка летіла поля́ми та лі́сами.[13]

The bird flew over fields and forests.

У дити́нстві Оле́кса ме́шкав як у Берлі́ні, так і в Амстерда́мі.

In his childhood Oleksa lived both in Berlin and in Amsterdam.

Я не зна́ю ані́ Ната́лки, ані́ Ле́сі.

I know neither Natalka nor Lesja.

(Note that a genitive direct object is not required here, as distinct from when **(а)ні́** is used on its own.)

Ми не зна́ємо, де дру́зі. Вони́ тако́ж.

We don't know where our friends are. They don't either.

The conjunction **і** may also have a sense of 'also', 'too' when its position or the context indicates that. We may also find it, for example, after **як**, in the sense 'like . . . too', as in,

Марíя, як і брат її, вчи́ться в університе́ті.
Marija, like her brother (too), is studying at university

Note above certain recommended punctuation patterns. A simple correlation of two elements with one conjunction normally does not require a comma, but more than one element, or one conjunction, will normally have the elements separated by commas, with the comma coming before the conjunction:

І батьки́, і ді́ти чека́ли на авто́бус.
Both the parents and the children were waiting for the bus.

Сестра́ й до́нька, син і ма́ма стоя́ли та розмовля́ли.
Sister and daughter, son and mother were standing around chatting.

8.1.2.1.2   Contrast

This is better illustrated from the composite sentence.

8.1.2.1.3   Separation: або/чи

Оле́кса або/чи Богда́н бу́дуть у нас за́втра.
Oleksa or Bohdan will be with us tomorrow.[14]

Або/Чи Оле́кса, або/чи Богда́н бу́дуть у нас за́втра.
Either Oleksa or Bohdan will be with us tomorrow.

8.1.2.2   Within the composite sentence

8.1.2.2.1   Coordination: та, і (й), не ті́льки . . . але́ . . .

Він іде́ та слу́хає.
He walks along listening.

Вона́ взяла́ ру́чку й замо́вкла.
She took the pen and (then) fell silent.

Євге́н як співа́є, так і гра́є на скри́пку ду́же до́бре.
Jevhen both sings and plays the violin really well.

Тара́с не ті́льки бу́де в Жито́мирі у вівто́рок, але́ на́віть зали́шиться там до кінця́ мі́сяця.
Taras will not only be in Zhytomyr on Tuesday, but will even stay there till the end of the month.

8.1.2.2.2   Contrast: а, але́, та, проте́, зате́, одна́к

Ма́ма чита́є, а син пи́ше.
Mother is reading, but/while her son is writing.

Ігор пи́ше, але́ й ду́має про сього́днішні зу́стрічі.
Igor writes, but (also) thinks about today's meetings.

Я полеті́в би до те́бе, та гро́шей не ма́ю.
I'd fly off to see you, but I don't have any money.

Проте́ в констру́кціях таки́х із родо́вим відмі́нком, . . .
But in such constructions with the genitive case . . .

Моро́з припіка́є, зате́ комарі́в нема́є.
The frost is biting, but (at least) there are no mosquitoes.

Зате́ ж на де́яких, навпаки́, доведе́ться зупини́тися до́вше з о́гляду на
їх велику вагу́ в синта́ксисі та на те, що за ни́х упе́рше гово́риться.
But we shall, on the contrary, have to pause longer on certain of them on
account of their great importance in syntax and because we are discussing them for the first time. (Syn: 326, adapted)

Одна́к, він не зна́є, чому́ вони́ ви́рішили залиши́тися вдо́ма.
However, he doesn't know why they decided to stay at home.

8.1.2.2.3 Separation: **або́, чи . . . чи . . .**

Вона́ кана́дка або́ америка́нка – я то́чно не зна́ю.
She's Canadian or American – I don't actually know.

Чи вони́ всі зустрі́нуться на вокза́лі, чи ко́жен пі́де сам до кафе́.
Either they'll meet at the station, or each one will go alone to the café.

Чи вона́ вчо́ра написа́ла мені́ листа́, чи вона́ сама́ прийде за ти́ждень.
Either she wrote me a letter yesterday, or she'll be here herself in a week's
time.

8.1.3 SUBORDINATION WITH CONJUNCTIONS

Regarding punctuation, note that, within a sentence, the conjunction is
as a rule either preceded by a comma or, if it is a compound conjunction,
either entirely preceded by a comma or split by a comma, the comma coming
before the core conjunction if there is one, i.e. **що, щоб, як**. When the
conjunction is split by a comma, one might imagine a slight increase of
emphasis on the lexical meaning of the conjunction. If the conjunction
comes first in a sentence, then a comma precedes the main clause. Conjunctions are followed by finite forms of verbs unless the subject of the main and
adverbial clause are identical, in which case an infinitive is preferred, for
example,

Після́ то́го як увійти́ до ха́ти, я розпла́кався.
After entering the house, I burst into tears.

8.1.3.1 Noun or final clauses, and indirect speech

The most general link is **що** 'that', as in:

Ми до́бре зна́ємо, що вона́ бу́де тут за́втра.
We know perfectly well that she will be here tomorrow.

Учи́тель поя́снює у́чням, що англі́йська мо́ва ле́гша, ніж украї́нська.
The teacher explains to the pupils that English is easier than Ukrainian.

We can call these 'noun clauses' because the whole subordinate clause is akin to a noun or noun phrase, as if the first might be 'We well know her coming tomorrow'. One sometimes encounters the conjunction **як**, the second most general Ukrainian conjunction, in similar sentences, but note the difference, though the second remains interpretable nominally:

Я ба́чу, що він шука́є ножа́.
I can see [that] he's looking for the knife.

Я ба́чу, як він шука́є ножа́.
I can see him looking for the knife.

Similar is the construction to convey indirect or reported speech. We simply have to note that here Ukrainian on the whole retains the tense of the assumed original statement.[15]

Вона́ ка́же, що гото́ва пої́хати до Ха́ркова.
She says she's ready to set off for Kharkiv.

Вона́ ка́же, що споді́валася провести́ кі́лька днів на пля́жі.
She says she was hoping to spend several days on the beach.

Вона́ ка́же, що чита́тиме ві́рші сього́дні вве́чері.
She says she'll be reading the verses this evening.

Вона́ сказа́ла, що гото́ва пої́хати до Ха́ркова.
She said she *was* ready to set off for Kharkiv.

Вона́ сказа́ла, що споді́валася провести́ кі́лька днів на пля́жі.
She said she *had been* hoping to spend several days on the beach.

Вона́ сказа́ла, що чита́тиме ві́рші сього́дні вве́чері.
She said she *would be* reading the verses this evening.

Thus, if the verb of the main clause is in the non-past, there is no difference between Ukrainian and English, but if the verb of the main clause is in the past, then there may be a difference, with Ukrainian having one set of subordinate clauses as against the two of English. Do note that, where both verbs are in the past, both may be translated as past: 'She said she *was* hoping to spend several days on the beach'. Here verbal aspect plays a part, since a perfective past in the reported speech will certainly convey 'had done', for example:

Вона́ мені́ сказа́ла, що ви́рішила провести́ ці́лу ніч на пля́жі.
She told me she *had* decided to spend the whole night on the beach.

8.1.3.1.1   The indirect y/n question

Let us now illustrate this for an indirect yes/no question:[16]

Він пита́є, чи ми бу́демо вдо́ма сього́дні.
He asks if/whether we will be at home today.

Він спита́в, чи ми бу́демо вдо́ма сього́дні.
He asked if/whether we *would be* at home today.

Він пита́є, чи ми були́ вдо́ма вчо́ра.
He asks if/whether we were at home yesterday.

Він спита́в, чи ми були́ вдо́ма вчо́ра.
He asked if/whether we *had been* at home yesterday.

The indirect question, consequently, includes the characteristic interrogative particle of the direct y/n question, namely **чи** placed at the very beginning of the sentence. An 'optative, wondering, what-if' sense can be conveyed using the infinitive, for example,

Чи не поїхати б нам туди́ чо́вно́м?
What if we were to go there by boat?

This (the negation and modal particle **б** increase the speculation) could be incorporated as expected into an indirect structure, i.e.

Він спита́в, чи не поїхати б вам туди́ чо́вно́м?
He asked, what if you were to go there by boat?

Note how the subject of the infinitive is conveyed by the dative case.

8.1.3.1.2   Other indirect questions

The same will go for all other indirect questions. Here are a few examples of such sentences:

Я спита́в їх, з кі́м вона́ вчи́лася.
I asked them whom she studied with. (lit. 'with whom')

Чи вона́ тобі́ сказа́ла, що́ ста́неться?
Did she tell you what would happen?

Чи ти зна́єш ту люди́ну, чиє́ю ру́чкою я пишу́?
Do you know the person whose pen I am writing with?
(or better, in a relative clause, as here: **яко́ї ру́чкою** lit. 'with the pen of whom' for **чиє́ю ру́чкою**)

Вона́ поясни́ла мені́, чому́ вона́ хоті́ла відпочи́ти в Криму́.
She told me why she wanted to take a break in the Crimea.

Я не мо́жу не пита́ти, де Ви живете́.
I can't help asking where you live.

Я не міг не пита́ти, де вона́ рані́ше жила́.
I couldn't help asking where she used to live.

Не мо́жна не пита́ти, зві́дки вони́ сього́дні приї́хали.
One can't but ask where they travelled from today.

Я хоті́ла пита́ти, як до́вго Ти бу́деш у нас.
I wanted to ask how long you would be with us.

Скажі́ть, скі́льки ча́су бу́дете в крамни́ці.
Tell me how long you'll be at the store.

and so on, or **то́що** as one so often sees after a list in Ukrainian.

8.1.3.2 *Adjectival or relative clauses:* **яки́й, що**

First, the relative **яки́й** declines as an adjective and agrees in gender and number with the noun phrase to which it refers and takes the case required by the syntax of its own, relative, clause:

Чи Ви зна́єте ді́вчину, з яко́ю вони́ розмовля́ли.
Do you know the girl they were talking with?
(**Яко́ю** is feminine and singular because it refers to the feminine singular noun **ді́вчину**, but is instrumental rather than the accusative **ді́вчину** because it is governed by the preposition **з** 'with', which requires the instrumental.)

Чи ти ба́чиш того́ хло́пця, яки́й дві годи́ни тому́ стоя́в бі́ля це́ркви?
Can you see that boy, who a couple of hours ago was standing near the church?
(**Яки́й** is masculine and singular, because of **хло́пця**, but nominative because it is the subject of **стоя́в**.)

Ось там той літні́й чоловік, яко́го дружи́на неда́вно відійшла́.
There's that elderly man whose wife passed away recently.
(Here **яки́й** goes into the genitive to convey 'whose', and is masculine and singular because it refers to **літні́й чоловік**.)

Now for some examples of **що**, which itself never changes:

Ідемо́ гірськи́м хребто́м, що зве́ться Чорногора́, а що його́ найви́щою горо́ю є Говерля.

We walk along a mountain ridge which is called Chornohora and whose highest point is Hoverlja. (MT: 52)

This sentence illustrates the two cardinal uses of relative **що**, first, that it can be used to translate 'who', 'which' as subject – nominative case, any gender, either number – of the relative clause (as in **що зве́ться**), and, second, that it takes the appropriate form of the third-person pronoun after it to convey whatever other form – case, number, gender – might be needed; in other words, we could have **якого** here as the alternative to **що його́**.

Some more examples:

Рі́чка По́лтва, що виплива́є з ліску́ (. . .) на межі́ Льво́ва, перепливає́ че́рез ці́ле мі́сто, але́ зве́рху вона́ замуро́вана.

The river Poltva, which flows out from a little wood on the edge of L'viv, flows through the whole city, but is built over. (MT: 58)

(Here **що** is used for a nominative singular feminine.)

Зра́зу же ї́демо на так зва́ний Висо́кий За́мок, – це гора́, що на ні́й стоя́в коли́сь кня́жий за́мок.

And first we drive to what is known as the 'High Castle' – the hill on which the royal castle once stood. (MT: 58).

(**На ні́й** reflects the gender of the referent, **гора́**, and the prepositional phrase required in the relative clause.)

Third, one may refer to **котри́й**, which declines exactly as **яки́й**, i.e. as an adjective, but which is rarely encountered these days in relative clauses. One might just be tempted to use it where the emphasis is on identifying a particular entity (rather than a more general or qualitative identification), or in a Ukrainian heavily influenced by Russian. Thus, to illustrate the former:

З усі́х, що там були́, ось той, котри́й мені́ бі́льше подо́бається.
Of all who were there, there's the one whom I most like.

Це тре́тій, котро́го я б ви́брав.
It's the third one whom I would choose.

And even there **яки́й** might seem better, particularly in the first. Perhaps one might hypothesize that **котри́й** would be used as a relative in environments where one would expect it as an interrogative, as in **Вже та годи́на, о котрі́й батьки́ ма́ють приї́хати** 'It's already the hour at which my parents are due to arrive' (= **Котра́ годи́на?** 'What's the time?', **О котрі́й?** 'At what time?'), and linking to the last example above, **Котри́й з ни́х?** 'Which of them?'

8.1.3.3 Adverbial or oblique clauses

In what follows we provide a few examples. It has to be noted that the numbers of such conjunctions can be multiplied, given the use of the pattern те, що or те, як after prepositions or prepositional phrases to create them. Thus: з о́гляду + gen. means 'on account of', so з о́гляду на те́, що can quite easily be an extra adverbial conjunction of cause, namely 'on account of the fact that, because, since', and similar. Many of these elements are also adverbial in nature; for lists of those that also function adverbially (especially adverbs of time and location) see **7.2** and **7.3**.

(i) causal, for example,

тому́ що 'because'

> Я сиді́в удо́ма, тому́ що не ма́в гро́шей.
>
> I stayed at home because I didn't have any money.

зати́м що

> Коро́ви реву́ть, зати́м що хазя́йка не йде їх дої́ти.
>
> The cows are lowing because the farmer's wife isn't going to milk them.

че́рез те́ що 'because', 'since'

> Помилко́ві вони́ че́рез те́, що дієприслі́вники змі́стом свої́м не в'я́жуться з іме́нниками того́ ре́чення, де вони́ вжи́ті, а в'я́жуться з ти́ми, що їх у ре́ченні зо́всім нема́, (. . .).
>
> They are erroneous because the gerunds are not linked to the nouns in the sentence where they are used, but to nouns which are just not there in the sentence.
>
> (Syn: 300; Synjavs'kyj is referring to some examples of bad Ukrainian, where gerunds, or verbal adverbs, have an implicit subject who /which is different from the subject of the main clause.)

бо 'for'

> Ми пови́нні написа́ти *вранці́* (. . .), бо від іме́нника *ра́нок* місце́вий відмі́нок одни́ни́ звича́йно не бува́є на *і*.
>
> We must write **вранці́** because the locative singular of the noun **ра́нок** is not usually in **і**.

оскі́льки '(in)sofar as'

> Щодо вигуко́вих слів, то оскі́льки вони́ стоя́ть зо́всім по́за ре́ченням, і розділо́вими зна́ками їх тре́ба виділя́ти, найчасті́ше ко́мами.
>
> As for interjections, [then] insofar as they stand completely outside the sentence, they have to be set apart in addition by punctuation marks, most often commas.

у зв'язку з тим що 'since', 'in connection with the fact that'

Я повинна шукати праці в Києві, у зв'язку з тим що скоро будемо жити там.
I must look for work in Kyiv, since we will soon be living there.

(ii) temporal, for example,

як 'as'

Темніло, як ми йшли по дорозі.
It was growing dark as we walked along the road.

в міру того як 'as', 'in proportion as'

Тепліло в міру того, як сходило сонце.
It got warmer as the sun rose.

як тільки 'as soon as'

Як тільки він увійшов до спальні, він ліг і заснув.
As soon as he entered the bedroom, he lay down and fell asleep.

як лиш is synonymous with **як тільки**. **Щойно** and **тільки но** 'as soon as', 'hardly', 'just now' may be used as synonyms of **як тільки**, but they may also be used with, say, a past tense, in the sense of 'have just', as in **Вона щойно приїхала** 'She's just arrived'.

скоро 'when', 'if', 'as soon as'

Скоро ти будеш тут, ми порозмовляємо.
Once you're here, we'll have a chat.

коли 'when'

Щоранку він прокидається, коли син повертає з ресторану.
Every morning he wakes up when his son returns from the restaurant.

відколи 'since'

Відколи світ, такого не чувано.
Nothing of the kind has ever been heard. (lit. 'Since the world, such has not been heard.')

поки 'while', 'as long as'

Поки вони працювали в офісі, Олекса сидів у кафе.
While they were working in the office, Oleksa was sitting in the café.

поки . . . не, доки . . . не 'until'

Я буду стояти тут, поки Ви не вирішите.
I'll stand here till you decide.
(Note the non-past perfective, usual with **поки . . . не**.)

перед тим як 'before'

Пе́ред тим як поі́хати до теа́тру, він порозмовля́в із си́ном.
Before going to the theatre, he had a chat with his son.

Пе́ред тим як він поі́хав до теа́тру, жі́нка порозмовля́ла з ни́м.
Before he set off to the theatre, his wife had a chat with him.
(Note the different constructions, linked with identity or non-identity of
the subjects.)

після́ то́го як 'after'

Йому́ ста́ло хо́лодно пі́сля то́го, як зайшло́ со́нце.
He became cold after the sun set.

з то́го ча́су як 'since'

З то́го ча́су як вони́ ви́рушили в мандрі́вку, тут усі́ заспоко́їлися.
Since they set off on their journey, here everyone has calmed down.

(iii) spatial, for example,

де 'where'

Ось там, на ма́пі те мі́сто, де вони́ ра́ніше ме́шкали.
There on the map is that place where they used to live.

куди́ '(to) where', 'whither'

**Москва́, куди́ вона́ посла́ла до́ньку, знахо́диться на півні́чний схід
зві́дси.**
Moscow, where she sent her daughter, is north-east of here.

зві́дки 'from where', 'whence'

Львів, зві́дки вона́ приі́хала, знахо́диться на за́хід зві́дси.
L'viv, where she came from, is west of here.

(iv) conditional, for example,

як 'if'

**А як за де́які сполу́чники говори́лося й у попере́дніх ро́зділах, то
дово́диться і́ноді попро́сту посила́тися на ті місця́, додаю́чи лише́ те́,
що тре́ба дода́ти.** (Syn: 326)
And if certain conjunctions were already discussed also in earlier sections,
then we must sometimes simply refer to those places, just adding what
has to be added.

Як прийде́ котри́й хло́пець, ...
If any boy comes, ...
(Note the indefinite sense of **котри́й** in this indefinite, conditional
clause.)

якщо́ 'if'

Якщо́ він бу́де вдо́ма сього́дні вве́чері, я неодмі́нно зайду́ до ньо́го.

If he's at home this evening, I'll call on him without fail.

(Note the future tenses in both halves of the conditional sentence, since reference is to the future.)

Якщо́ б ми злеті́ли літако́м так висо́ко, що могли́ б охопи́ти ці́лу украї́нську зе́млю, то як вона́ вигляда́ла б?

If we were to fly in a plane so high what we would be able to take in the whole Ukrainian land, then what would it look like? (MT: 65)

(Note the conditionals in both halves (the middle section is a consequence clause), because the condition is remote or unreal. It would be more likely to find **якби́** or **коли́ б** in such instances. See below.)

коли́ 'if'

Коли́ поста́вити підкре́сленого прислі́вника пе́ред дієприкме́тником зро́блені, ми за́раз поміня́ємо зміст ре́чення.

If we place the underlined adverb in front of the participle **зро́блені**, we immediately change the content of the sentence. (Syn: 281, adapted)

(Note the use of the infinitive here to convey subject identity, though sometimes one might use it simply as an impersonal; also note the future **поміня́ємо** (recommended by an anonymous reader), supposing future reference. Synjavs'kyj had imperfective **зміня́ємо**.)

якби́, коли́ б 'if', 'if only'

Алé порá сходи́ти з Говерлі; було́ б недо́бре, якби́ нас тут захопи́ла ніч, бо ча́сом і влі́ті зі́рветься тут сніговія́.

But it's time to go down Hoverlja; it wouldn't be good if night caught us here, since sometimes even in summer a snowstorm breaks out. (MT: 53)

(Note the perfective non-past in **зі́рветься**, adding to the suddenness but suggesting too that it is quite frequent.)

(v) purposive (= 'aim'), for example,

щоб(и) 'so that'

Черемо́ш ду́же швидки́й, його́ рі́чище та береги́ камени́сті, то тре́ба до́брого керма́нича, щоб не розби́ти дара́би та й само́му не пропа́сти.

The Cheremosh is very fast-flowing, its bed and banks are rocky, so one needs a good helmsman so as not to break the raft and even come to grief oneself. (MT: 53)

Найду́жче ти боя́вся, щоб мене́ не розхвилюва́ти.

You were most apprehensive of worrying me.

(Note the pleonastic **не**.)

It is worth interjecting here that **щоб** on its own is an extremely widely used conjunction and does not have to be purposive. We note, for example:

Дівча́та співа́ли так, щоб було́ чу́ти на протиле́жному бе́резі рі́чки.
'The girls were singing in such a way that they could be heard on the other side of the river' (= manner) (Dudyk and Horpynyč 1988 (2): 145)

Я бажа́ю, щоб ти провела́ лі́то в Ха́ркові.
I want you to spend the summer in Kharkiv.

The last example corresponds neatly to constructs where a subjunctive would be used in some other European languages, i.e. after main verbs of 'wishing', 'asking', 'advising', 'permitting', 'allowing', 'fearing', where the subjects are different (note that the verb in the subordinate clause must be in the past tense), for example:

Я хо́чу/прошу́/ра́джу/нака́зую/кажу́/дозволя́ю, щоб ти прийшо́в.
I want/request/advise/order/tell/permit you to come.

Він бої́ться, щоб вона́ не прийшла́.
He is afraid she might come. (pleonastic negative)

For the last one may also have **якби́** here instead of **щоб**. Note the less strong, and slightly different **Він бої́ться, що вона́ не при́йде** 'He's afraid she won't come', and **Він бої́ться, що вона́ при́йде** 'He's afraid she'll come.'

для то́го щоб 'in order that'

Ната́лка посла́ла си́на до Полта́ви для то́го, щоб він прові́в ти́ждень у ді́да.
Natalka sent her son to Poltava so that he might spend a week with his grandfather.

Ната́лка посла́ла си́на до Полта́ви для то́го, щоб провести́ ти́ждень сама́ вдо́ма.
Natalka sent her son to Poltava so she could spend a week at home on her own.

аби́ 'in order that', 'so that'

Я б одда́в полови́ну життя́ свого́, аби́ ти була́ щасли́ва.
I would give up half of my life so that you might be happy. (P. Myrnyj, quoted in Syn: 327, note that **одда́в** would now normally be **відда́в**.)

One may, of course, adapt the above sentence by having identical subjects:[17]

Я б відда́в полови́ну життя́ свого́, аби́ бу́ти щасли́вим.
I would give up half of my life so as to be happy.

(vi) comparative, for example,

як 'as', 'like', 'as if'

Головни́й хребе́т Карпа́т спиня́є півні́чні холо́дні вітри́, як теж і хма́ри.
The main Carpathian range stops the cold northern winds, just as (it stops) the clouds as well. (MT: 53)

More or less synonymous with **як** in the above sense are **(не)мо́в, немо́вби, на́че(бто), ні, нена́че,** and **бу́цім (би), бу́цім то, бу́цім би то:**

А там да́лі, немо́в морські́ скам'яні́лі хви́лі, тя́гнуться гі́рські́ хребти́, оди́н по́біч о́дного, зі за́ходу на півде́нний схід.
And there further off, like petrified waves in the sea, stretch out the mountain ridges, one side-by-side with another, from the west to the south-east. (MT: 52)

І блідий мі́сяць (. . .) з-за хма́ри де́-де вигляда́в, нена́че чо́вен в си́нім мо́рі то вирина́в, то потопа́в.
And the wan moon would here and there peep out from behind a cloud, just as a boat in the blue sea would now emerge, now sink down. (Shevchenko, cited in Syn: 331)

Засі́в, бу́цім у боло́ті чорт.
He settled down (as if in ambush), like the devil in a swamp. (M. Kotljarevs'kyj, cited in Syn: 329)

(vii) consequential, for example,

так що 'so that'

На Закарпа́тті ме́нше дощі́в, зате́ бага́то теплі́ше, так що на дола́х бу́йно росте́ виногра́д, а ліси́ в го́рах перева́жно ли́стяні.
In Carpathian Ukraine there is less rain, and moreover it is much warmer, so that in the valleys grape vines grow vigorously, and the forests in the mountains are for the most part broad-leaved. (MT: 53)

Береги́ річо́к низькі́, тож навесні́ во́ди залива́ють про́стори, так що ті́льки човно́м мо́жна діста́тися з одно́ї осе́лі до дру́гої.
The river banks are low, and/so in spring the waters flood the open spaces, so that one can only get from one settlement to another by boat. (MT: 64)

(viii) concessive, for example,

хоч/хоча́ 'although'

Хоч пі́дмет та при́судок (головна́ па́ра) і найважні́ше словосполу́чення в ре́ченні, та все ж дале́ко не вся на́ша мо́ва вилива́ється в такі́ словосполу́чення (. . .).

Although the subject and predicate (the 'principal parts') are also the most important word-combination in the sentence, nevertheless far from all our language is encapsulated into such word-combinations (...). (Syn: 198)

(Note the balancing of the two clauses by conjunctions in both.)

Хоч такі конструкції звичайно й не рекомендовані граматиками, але ж вони трапляються.

Although such constructions are, of course, not recommended by grammarians/grammars, they do indeed occur. (Syn: 227)

дармá що 'although', 'for all that' (never **дармá, що**)

Дармá що вонá минýлого рóку жилá в Житóмирі й там булá нещаслúва, та хóче там жúти й цьогó рóку.

Although she lived in Zhytomyr last year and wasn't happy, she still wants to live there this year.

незважáючи на тé що 'despite', 'in spite of the fact that'

Незважáючи на тé, що я не згíдна з тобóю, менí здáється, що ти мáєш рáцію.

In spite of the fact that I don't agree with you, it seems to me that you are right.

(ix) explanatory, for example,

тóбто 'that is'

(...) в мóві натрапляємо на числéнні синтаксúчні паралелíзми, тóбто бíльш чи мéнш вúправдані вживáння рівнобíжних конструкцíй.

(...) in the language we come across numerous syntactic parallelisms, that is, more or less justified uses of equivalent constructions. (Syn: 234, adapted)

сéбто 'that is'

Це ускладнюється ще й тúм, що в мóві чималó імéнників *недостáтніх*, сéбто з непóвними фóрмами.

This is complicated also by the fact that in the language there are not a few *deficient* nouns, that is nouns with an incomplete set of forms. (Syn: 39, adapted)

And the following very dense sentence:

Нарéшті слід сказáти, що наперекíр основнóму прáвилу про тé, нíбито приймéнники бувáють тíльки в пáрах з додаткóвими імéнниками, сéбто, як кáжуть, вимагáють пíсля сéбе тíльки непрямúх відмíнків, приймéнник *за* мóже бýти й пéред називнúм відмíнком імéнника.

Finally it must be said that in defiance of the basic rule that, as it were, prepositions can only be paired with complementary nouns, in other words, as it is put, require after them only the indirect cases, the preposition **за** can occur also before the nominative case of a noun. (Syn: 265)

а са́ме 'that is', 'in other words'

> **Ті́льки зрі́дка, а са́ме звича́йно, коли́ ре́чення почина́ється з дієприслі́вника, між цим оста́ннім і його́ додатко́вими слова́ми кладе́ться підме́т.**
>
> Only occasionally, that is usually when the sentence begins with a gerund, is the subject placed between the latter and its complementary words. (Syn: 302)

8.1.3.4   Paired and repeated conjunctions

Subordinating conjunctions may also occur in pairs (like coordinating conjunctions), in their case one in the main clause and the other in the subordinate clause, for example,

чим + comparative . . ., **тим** + comparative . . .   the x-er . . ., the x-er . . .

> **Чим да́лі на схід, тим приступні́ші стаю́ть го́ри.**
>
> The further [one goes] to the east, the more accessible the mountains become. (adapted from MT: 55, where the second clause is simply «**, го́ри стаю́ть приступні́ші**»)

We have already met a good number in the examples above:

дарма́ що/хоч . . ., а(ле́) . . . although . . ., . . .
ті́льки . . ., як . . . hardly . . ., than . . .
яки́й . . ., таки́й . . . such a . . ., such a . . .
як . . ., так . . . since/as . . ., (thus) . . .
коли́ . . ., тоді́ . . . when . . ., (then) . . .
де . . ., там . . . where . . ., (there)
відкіля́ . . ., відтіля́ . . . from where, (from there) . . .
не ті́льки . . ., але́ й/а й/а тако́ж/а наві́ть . . . not only . . ., but also/even . . .
(о)скі́льки . . ., (о)сті́льки . . . insofar as . . .
якщо́ . . ., то . . . if . . ., (then) . . .

A few examples:

> **Він ті́льки прийшо́в, як поме́рла ма́ма.**
> Scarcely had he come than his mother died.

> **Де вони́ ме́шкали, там і працюва́ли.**
> Where they lived, (there) they worked too.

Яки́й пан, таки́й крам.
As is the master, so are his wares.

The pairs may be repetitions, such as **i . . ., i . . .** 'both . . ., and . . .', **то . . ., то . . .** 'now . . ., now . . .', **або́ . . ., або́ . . .** 'either . . ., or . . .', **чи . . ., чи . . .** 'either . . ., or . . .'. An extra example:

Вона́ й ме́шкає, і працю́є у Ві́дні.
She both lives and works in Vienna.

NOTES

1 References are to British English except where mentioned otherwise. We do not present a guide to handwriting in this work, but would refer readers to textbooks and teaching grammars.

2 Shev. (1993: 52–3) conveys this most succinctly.

3 Some examples from Shev. (1993: 56).

4 See Chapters 2 and 6.

5 Note in these two examples that there is an alternation between zero and a vowel. Basically, an **e** or **o** between consonants may be present before a zero ending or a consonant group and disappear before an actual ending. Most often, but not always, one has **o** when one of the surrounding consonants is a velar. Both may also be inserted (the other instances have a historical explanation, which can be disturbed by analogy), in order to reduce a syllabic sonorant (**р, л, м, н, й**), and in preverbs one will have an inserted **i** before a consonant group. Here are a few examples (nominative plus genitive singular unless mentioned otherwise): **лíкоть – лíктя** 'elbow', **орéл – орлá** 'eagle', **хлóпець – хлóпця** 'boy', **вогóнь – вогню́** 'fire', **день – дня** 'day', **сестрá – сестéр** 'sister' (N.*sg.* + G.*pl.*), **пíсня – пíсень** 'song'. (N.*sg.* + G.*pl.*). When we learn the language, we tend to take this for granted, particularly in such instances as **увéсь – уся́** 'all' (N.*sg.* m. + N.*sg.* f.), **тéмний – тьма** 'dark – darkness' (adj. + N.*sg.* f. noun). For the syllabic sonorants we can note **вíхор/ви́хор – вíхру/ви́хру** 'whirlwind', **крáпля – крáпель** 'drop' (N.*sg.* + G.*pl.*). We note the inserted **i** in verbs in, for example, **схóдити – зійти́** 'to come down', **зірвáти** (perf.) – **зрива́ти** (imperf.) 'to pluck', with the preverb **з-**.

6 In these three instances the source of [i] is the vowel *jat'* (*ě*), which might be seen as a long [e]. In this case, we have an earlier quantitative alternation, as in **летíти – літáти** 'to fly' (determinate and indeterminate respectively), **замéсти́ – заміта́ти** 'to sweep', 'cover up' (perfective and imperfective respectively), **розплéсти́ – розпліта́ти** 'to unbraid' (perfective and imperfective respectively).

7 Synjavs'kyj (1941: 60) considers that, in a pure pronunciation, soft adjectives are identical to hard adjectives even where the ending begins with **i** and **ï**, in that the former is pronounced as a soft consonant followed by [ɪ], and the latter as [j] followed by [ɪ], thus **си́ній** 'blue' and **безкра́їй** 'boundless' are pronounced as if written **синьый, безкрайий** respectively. This may probably be considered as non-standard in the modern language.

8 This suffix is very often, but not always, stressed. Unstressed examples would be **хоро́брий** 'brave', **хоро́бріший**, **обере́жний** 'prudent', 'cautious', **обере́жніший**. Sometimes two stresses are possible. The stress tends to stay on the basic stem in adjectives with suffixes such as -**ат-**, -**аст-**, -**ист-**, -**ічн-/-ичн-**, -**овит-**.

9 There is retraction of stress in the accusative-genitive of **я**, **ти**, **він**, **себе́**, **весь**, **хто**, **що**, **той**, **цей (сей)**, and the locative of **весь**, **хто**, **що**, **той**, **цей (сей)**, after prepositions.

10 **Нема́є** (**нема́є** is often recommended rather than **нема́**) is also the general expression for 'There isn't/aren't', and as such is constructed with the genitive case of what is absent/missing, for example, **Удо́ма нема́є хлі́ба** 'There's no bread at home'. The positive form is **є**, constructed usually with the nominative, though one may find the partitive genitive. In the past one has **не було́** + G. in the negative and in the positive the appropriate form of **був** (neuter for partitives). In the future one has **не бу́де** + G. for the negative and in the positive the appropriate form of the future paradigm.

11 = two females; if two males, then **оди́н о́дного**, if mixed then **одне́ о́дного**; note that the first component does not change, while the second goes into the case appropriate to the governing verb or is preceded by a preposition, for example, **Вони́ розмовля́ли оди́н з о́дним** — note the initial stress of the second component. See also Chapter 4, **4.1**. This unexpected stress is to be found in several similar expressions: **всі́ до о́дного** 'every single one', **ні о́дного** 'not one' (case as required). If one considers all these as instances where we have a compound construction, then, somewhat as with prepositions plus certain pronouns, we have a small generalization about stress retraction.

12 Needless to say, the subordinate clause is susceptible to profound investigation and analysis; however, for the purposes of this grammar, where general accessibility is paramount, this is minimized.

13 It is difficult to differentiate **і/й** and **та**. Synjavs'kyj (1941: 333–7) goes into considerable detail, concluding that **та** in general is more likely to coordinate grammatically and semantically like elements (usually also rather simple); he sees the difference as emerging particularly in compound sentences, where **та** is more likely to coordinate simultaneous events, such as **іде́ та кричи́ть** 'is walking and shouting', but **став і кричи́ть** 'got up/stopped and shouts'.

14 An anonymous reader has assured us that, even with two singular 'separated' subjects, the main verb in these two sentences will be plural. This requires more investigation, including, of course, where one of the subjects is first or second person.

15 In reading Ukrainian you will constantly note flexibility in the use of tenses, with the non-past very often selected in order to make the message more vivid. Do note too that the word 'speech' in the term

'indirect/reported speech' has to be taken in a broad sense. The phenomenon basically goes with all verbs of communication.

16 Note that we can identify an indirect question in English by the fact that 'whether' will be an acceptable alternative to 'if'. If this is not the case, then a conditional sentence, with **як, якщо, коли,** or **якби, коли б** must be used. See the following section.

17 The selection of the case of the predicate in copular sentences is quite a complex matter. If the copula is the present tense of the verb **бути,** unexpressed, then we have the nominative: **Він професор** 'He's a professor'. If expressed, then we may have the instrumental, say if the predicate comes first. In addition to **бути,** there are pseudo-copulae, for example, **ставати/стати, (з)робитися** 'to become', **зватися, називатися** 'to be called', **здаватися/здатися** 'to seem'. With the pseudo-copulae the instrumental is more common, though the nominative is possible. With **бути,** outside the present tense, either the nominative or the instrumental is acceptable, though the latter is more common. However, if the predicate is an adjective, the nominative is more common (hence the difference in the examples in the main text) and is indeed obligatory where the copula is zero. With pseudo-copulae like **здаватися** 'to seem', **уявлятися** 'to appear', **вважатися** 'to be considered', the adjective is likely to be in the instrumental. There is also the construction **бути за** + A.; this actually means 'to be like': **Він мені був за брата** 'He was a brother to me' (Shev.: 979–80).

SELECTED BIBLIOGRAPHY AND REFERENCES

Use has been made of many of the following works in composing this book. We have followed current practice in not always giving references within the text.

Andrusyshen, C.H. and Krett, J.N. (assisted by H.V. Andrusyshen) (1955) *Ukrainian-English Dictionary*, University of Saskatchewan: University of Toronto Press. (Reprinted 1981, 1985 with the assistance of the Canadian Institute of Ukrainian Studies.)

Bezpojasko, O.K., Horodens'ka, G.H. and Rusanivs'kyj, V.M. (1993) *Граматика української мови, Морфологія: Підручник*, Kyiv: Lybid'.

Cyganenko, G.P. (1982) *Словарь служебных морфем русского языка*, Kyiv: Radjans'ka škola.

Dingley, J., and Bekh, O. (1996) *Ukrainian Phrasebook*, London: Lonely Planet Publications.

——(1997) *Teach Yourself Ukrainian: a complete course for beginners*, London: Hodder & Stoughton.

Ditel', O.A. (ed.) (1993) *Український правопис*, 4th edn corrected and supplemented, Kyiv: Naukova dumka.

Dončenko, O. (1990) 'Пісовою стежкою', in N.F. Skrypčenko and O.Ja. Savčenko (eds), *Читанка*, Kyiv: Radjans'ka škola, 26–7.

——(1990) 'Маий помічник', in N.F. Skrypčenko and O.Ja. Savčenko (eds), *Читанка*, Kyiv: Radjans'ka škola, 146–50.

Dudyk, P.S. (ed. Part 1), Horpynyč, V.O., *et al.* (eds Part 2) (1988) *Українська мова I-II*, Kyiv: Vyšča škola.

Humesky, A. (1988) *Modern Ukrainian*, Edmonton–Toronto: Canadian Institute of Ukrainian Studies.

Isičenko, J.A., Kalašnik, V.S. and Svašenko, A.A. (1990) *Самоучитель украинского языка*, Kyiv: Vyšča škola.

Ivakin, O.P. (ed.) (1997) *Новий орфографічний словник української мови*, Kyiv: Akonit.

Jefimov, D. (1990) 'Орден Перемоги', in N.F. Skrypčenko and O.Ja. Savčenko (eds), *Читанка*, Kyiv: Radjans'ka škola, 273–5.

Koval', S.A. *et al.* (1997) *Словник: Англійсько-український. Українсько-англійский: Посібник для загальноосвіт. Шкіл та вищ. навч. закладів*, Kyiv, Irpin': Perun.

Krouglov, A., Kurylko, K. and Kostenko, D. (1997) *English-Ukrainian Dictionary of Business*, Jefferson, NC, and London: McFarland & Company, Inc.

Loboda, V.V. and Skurativs'kyj, L.V. (1993) *Українська мова в таблицях*, Kyiv: Vyšča škola.

Nosov, M. (1990) 'Огірки', in N.F. Skrypčenko and O.Ja. Savčenko (eds), *Читанка*, Kyiv: Radjans'ka škola, 86–7.

Olijnyk, S. (1990) 'Наші мами', in N.F. Skrypčenko and O.Ja. Savčenko (eds), *Читанка*, Kyiv: Radjans'ka škola, 217–18.

Palamar, L.M. and Bex, O.A. (1993) *Практичний курс української мови*, Kyiv: Lybid'.

Pickurel, J. (1999) 'The Position of Ukrainian Language in Ukraine', unpublished PhD dissertation, SSEES, University of London.

Podvez'ko, M.L. and Balla, M.I. (1988) *Англо-український словник/English-Ukrainian Dictionary*, Edmonton: Canadian Institute of Ukrainian Studies, University of Alberta (first published by Radjans'ka škola, Kyiv, 1974).

Ponomariv, O.D., *et al.* (1991) *Suchasna ukrayins'ka mova*, Kyiv: Lybid'.

Press, I. and Pugh, S. (1994) *Colloquial Ukrainian*, London and New York: Routledge (reprinted 1995).

Rusanivs'kyj, V.M., Žovtobrjux, M.A., Gorodenskaja, E.G., Griščenko, A.A. (1986) *Украинская Грамматика*, Kyiv: Radjans'ka škola.

Rusanivs'kyj, V.M., Pylyns'kyj, M.M. and Jermolenko, S.Ja. (1991) *Українська мова*, Kyiv: Radjans'ka škola.

Rusanivs'kyj, V.M. (ed.) (1990) *Культура української мови. Довідник*, Kyiv: Lybid'.

Ševčenko, L.Ju., Rizun, V.V. and Lysenko, Ju.V. (1993) *Сучасна українська мова. довідник*, Kyiv: Lybid'.

Shevelov, G. Y. (1980) 'Ukrainian', in A.M. Schenker and E. Stankiewicz (eds), *The Slavic Literary Languages: Formation and Development*, New Haven: Yale Concilium on International and Area Studies.

—— (1993) 'Ukrainian', in B. Comrie and G.G. Corbett (eds), *The Slavonic Languages*, London and New York: Routledge, 947–98.

Skrypčenko, N.F. and Savčenko, O.Ja. (1990) *Читанка. Підручник для 3 класу чотирирічної початкової школи*, Kyiv: Radjans'ka škola.

Sosnin, V.H.F. (1990) 'Поліська ластівка', in N.F. Skrypčenko and O.Ja. Savčenko (eds), *Читанка*, Kyiv: Radjans'ka škola, 190–3.

Словник української мови, Kyiv: Naukova Dumka, vols 1–11, 1970–80.

Stechishin, J.N. (1966) *Ukrainian Grammar*, Winnipeg: Trident Press.

Synjavs'kyj, O. (1941) *Норми української літературної мови*, L'viv: Ukrajins'ke vydavnyctvo.

Terlak, Z.M. and Serbens'ka, O.A. (1992) *Украинский язык для начинающих*, L'viv: Svit.

Terlec'kyj, M. (1971) *Мандрівка по Україні. Посібник для шкіл українознавства*, London: Vydavnyctvo Sojuzu Ukrajinciv u Velykij Brytaniji.

Tkač, D. (1990) 'Вчителька', in N.F. Skrypčenko and O.Ja. Savčenko (eds), *Читанка*, Kyiv: Radjans'ka škola, 211–12.

Trask, R.L. (1993) *A Dictionary of Grammatical Terms in Linguistics*, London and New York: Routledge.

Zazeka, Ja. (1990) in N.F. Skrypčenko and O.Ja. Savčenko (eds), Kgiv: Radjans'ka Škola.

Zilyns'kyj, I. (1979) *A Phonetic Description of the Ukrainian Language*, translated and revised according to the author's emendations by Wolodymyr T. Zyla and Wendell M. Aycock, Cambridge, MA: Harvard University Press/Harvard Ukrainian Research Institute.

Žluktenko, Ju.O, Totska, N.I. and Molodid, T.K. (1978) *Ukrainian. A Textbook for Beginners*, Kyiv: Vyšča škola. (Also consulted was an updated edition, as yet unpublished, by Lesja Palka.)

Žovtobrjux, M.A. (1984) *Українська літературна мова*, Kyiv: Naukova Dumka.
Žovtobrjux, M.A. (ed.) (1973) *Українська літературна вимова і наголос. Словник-довідник*, Kyiv: Naukova Dumka.
Žovtobrjux, M.A. and Kulyk, B.M. (1972) *Курс сучасної української літературної мови. Частина I*, 4th edn, Kyiv: Vyšča škola.

ABBREVIATIONS USED

HUM	See Bezpojasko *et al.* (1993).
KUM	See Rusanivs'kyj (1990).
MT	Terlec'kyj (1971).
Shev.	L.Ju. Shevchenko (1993).
Shevch.	Taras Shevchenko (literary works).
SUM	See *Словник* above.
Syn	Synjavs'kyj (1941).
UAS	See Andrusyshen (1955).
ULVN	See Žovtobrjux (1973).
Л.У.	Lesja Ukrajinka (literary works).
М.В.	Marko Vovchok (literary works).
Н.-Л.	Nečuj-Levyc'kyj (literary works).

INDEX

All numbers following each entry refer to the chapter and section in which it is to be found.

Printed in the United Kingdom by
Lightning Source UK Ltd., Milton Keynes
140104UK00001B/79/A